P9-DGQ-499

Employment, Race, and Poverty

Harcourt, Brace & World, Inc., New York

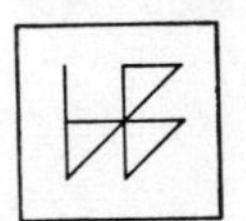

Employment, Race, and Poverty

Edited by Arthur M. Ross

and Herbert Hill

B.1.68

Library of Congress Catalog Card Number: 65-23537

Printed in the United States of America

Foreword

In 1962 a four-year program of research and conferences on the general subject of Unemployment and the American Economy was initiated on the Berkeley campus of the University of California. This program is based on the premise that persistent unemployment is the most serious and pressing domestic problem of the 1960's. The Ford Foundation made a generous contribution, which has been administered by the Institute of Industrial Relations, to support this undertaking, and the undersigned have had the privilege of serving as co-directors of the program from its outset. The books emerging from the program have been edited by us separately—the present book by Professor Ross and Herbert Hill.

Our research projects and conferences begin with the assumption that persistent unemployment calls for new policies, both public and private, with which we have had little experience in the United States. For this reason we are conducting a coordinated group of studies designed to furnish better guidelines for policies, and to provide critical evaluation of these policies as they are established and implemented. The program also includes closely related studies on employment goals, which will facilitate more accurate prediction of labor market trends in the next decade. We have held three annual conferences on unemployment, which have brought together key people involved in research, policy formulation, and administration. Research volumes based on the first two of the conferences have already been published. These are *Unemployment and the American Economy* (John Wiley, 1963) and *Employment and Labor Market Policy* (University of California Press, 1964).

Certainly there is no need to explain why we decided that our research program should include a volume dealing with the economic disabilities of Negro workers and the stakes and possibilities involved in economic integration.

We desire to acknowledge Mr. Herbert Hill's indispensable contribution to this volume. Mr. Hill participated in the original formulation of the project, and as co-editor he rendered valuable help in proposing subjects that ought to be covered, recruiting authors to deal with these subjects, and reviewing many of the manuscripts. His own chapter on the racial practices of organized labor represents an important contribution to the understanding of this topic in historical depth.

We also wish to acknowledge our indebtedness to Mrs. Marcia Schramm, who has served as secretary of the Research Program on Unemployment and the American Economy since its outset. In addition to arranging a conference of the authors in Washington during the spring of 1964, Mrs. Schramm has carried on much of the correspondence with them during the intervening months and has rendered important editorial assistance.

Arthur M. Ross
R. A. Gordon

Co-Directors, Research Program on Unemployment and the American Economy

University of California
Berkeley, California

Contents

VI. Discrimination and the Law

VII. Conclusions

I

The Negro's Position in the Labor Market

1 / The Negro in the American Economy

Arthur M. Ross

☐ Slave Origins and Subsequent Diffusion

Jobs and poverty are at the center of the racial crisis. But to understand the Negroes' economic situation today, it is necessary to begin with their place in the slave economy and to examine their experiences in the century since Emancipation, when they gradually moved out of principal slave occupations into other sectors of the economy.

During slavery, practically all Negroes were engaged in Southern agriculture or were household servants. This was still true of 87 percent in 1900 and 80 percent in 1910. But in 1960 less than 10 percent were in agriculture and 15 percent in domestic service. Approximately 10 percent were in the professional and semiprofessional occupations, 12 percent in wholesale and retail trade, 8 percent in clerical work, 20 percent in manufacturing, and 5 percent in construction. The Negroes' participation in these other sectors of the labor force was still far less than proportional, but considerable diffusion

TABLE 1

Gainfully Employed Negroes by Vocation, 1890–1960 (in thousands)

	1890	1900	1910	1920	1930
Agriculture	1984	2143	2893	2179	2019
Professional and semiprofessional	34	47	67	80	136
Domestic and personal service	957	1317	1122	1065	1576
Trade and transportation	146	209	375	452	581
Trade			256	312	398
Transportation			119	140	184
Manufacturing and mechanical	208	275	693	960	1100
Mining			61	73	75
			632	887	1025
Public service, n.e.c.			22	51	50
Clerical			19	37	41
TOTAL	3329	3992	5152	4824	5504

	1940	1950	1960
Agriculture	1485	1035	554
Professional and semiprofessional	177	356	670
	1374	1331	1469
Business and repair	49	72	103
Amusement, recreation, and related	32	35	47
Personal service	1293	1224	1318
	589	1029	1171
Wholesale and retail	288	617	748
Transportation, communication, public utilities	197	329	326
Finance, insurance, and real estate	105	84	97
	738	1336	1498
Mining	56	43	19
Manufacturing	479	998	1151
Construction	203	294	327
	56	180	205
Not reported	59	88	445
TOTAL	4479	5369	6099

Source: Decennial censuses of population, 1890–1960.

out of the original Negro activities had taken place (see Table 1). This movement has proceeded sporadically and irregularly since the end of slavery, however. Five basic principles appear to have governed it.

1. Competition between Negroes and various groups of white workers, particularly the poor whites in the South and the successive waves of European immigrants in the North, has been a decisive influence. While some employers have favored the Negroes, most have not, and the whites have held the upper hand. As a result, Negroes have had to move into new employment areas rather than claim their share of the already occupied territory.

2. The slave origins of the Negro, his marginal social status, his cultural deprivation, and his deficiencies in skill and education have limited the directions of his movement. As Negroes left agriculture and domestic service they took the most unskilled, unattractive, and poorly paid occupations within other types of activities. Thus while many Negroes have obtained jobs in the construction industry, for example, relatively few have become skilled tradesmen. Many have been employed in wholesale and retail trade, but few as salespeople. Table 2 shows Negro employment in a few occupations that can be traced through most or all census years since 1890. The following tabulation shows the entire Negro employment by major occupational groups in 1959:
More than 75 percent of the gainfully employed Negroes were found in the last five groups, consisting of unskilled and semiskilled manual occupations.

3. The Negro's occupational progress has been concentrated in periods of high labor demand and low unemployment: the period of rapid economic growth from 1900 to 1908, World War I, the prosperity of 1922 to 1929, World War II, and the postwar prosperity until about 1953. In these busy times the whites were able to rise into higher-status positions, leaving room for the Negroes to enter below them; and the expansion of employment created new jobs into which Negroes could

	Employed Negroes (in thousands)	Percentage of Negro Working Force
Managers, officials, proprietors	162	2.4
Farmers and farm managers	236	3.5
Professional, technical, and kindred	303	4.5
Clerical and kindred	404	6.0
Salespeople	94	1.4
Skilled craftsmen, foremen, and kindred	390	5.8
Semiskilled operatives and kindred	1,326	19.7
Domestic servants	996	14.8
Other service workers	1,151	17.1
Farm laborers	633	9.4
Other unskilled laborers	1,036	15.4
TOTAL	6,730	100.0

Source: Bureau of Labor Statistics

move without jeopardizing or displacing their white competitors.

In periods of unemployment or economic decline, on the other hand, competition tightened up and the Negro's occupational progress halted and was sometimes reversed. Thus the Jim Crow laws and craft-union exclusivism were solidified during the depression of the 1890's. Whites took over many established "Negro jobs" during the 1930's, although overt racial conflict was held down by work relief and other New Deal social policies. These cycles of progression and retrogression are neatly indicated by the number of Negroes in the field of domestic and personal service, which has varied *inversely* with business conditions. The number increased in the 1890's, declined steadily from 1900 to the 1920's, rose during the Depression, declined again until after the Korean War, and has increased once more during the most recent decade.

4. Negroes have found their greatest opportunities in the dynamic sectors of the economy, in expanding industries during their periods of most rapid growth. They have had little

TABLE 2

Negro Employment, Selected Occupations, 1890–1960

	1890	1900	1920	1930	1940	1950	1960
Agricultural laborers	1,106,728	1,344,125	1,210,798	1,112,510	780,312	499,743	326,193
Farmers and farm managers	590,666	757,822	935,107	375,329	666,695	495,368	168,776
Clergymen	12,110	15,528	19,571	25,034	17,102	18,150	13,955
Lawyers and judges	431	728	950	1,247	1,052	1,450	2,180
Physicians and surgeons	794	1,734	3,495	3,805	3,524	4,026	4,706
School teachers	15,100	21,267	35,442	54,439	63,697	86,620	122,163
College professors			1,063	2,146	2,339	4,039	5,415
Barbers and hairdressers	16,966	19,942	31,352	34,263	28,229	43,024	46,951
Janitors and sextons			53,393	94,532	206,336	281,938	315,994
Launderers and laundresses	151,540	220,104	314,095	329,163	47,734	143,572	135,974
Servants and waiters	401,215	465,734	527,426	1,731,234	139,236	84,629	102,461
Domestic service workers					1,003,508	809,659	915,494
Housekeepers and stewards	8,104	10,596	15,161	19,865	4,156	6,220	10,811
Watchmen, policemen, firemen	2,015	2,993	5,675	7,928	10,108	15,789	24,881
Draymen, teamsters	43,914	67,585	56,714	19,566	137,121	173,911	248,276
Retail merchants	6,556	9,095	23,526	28,213	17,422	31,295	23,610
Carpenters	22,310	21,113	34,243	32,413	20,798	34,582	35,830
Masons (brick and stone)	9,645	14,386	10,606	11,701	7,370	18,003	21,738
Painters, glaziers, varnishers, paperhangers	4,387	5,782	10,386	20,447	15,664	29,335	39,145
Plasterers	4,003		7,082	13,465	7,704	17,227	18,772
Plumbers and gas and steam fitters	615	1,193	3,516	4,729	3,671	8,290	10,120
Iron and steel operatives		12,327	23,616	23,922	12,428	31,130	33,355
Iron and steel laborers			105,641	107,739	40,818	55,642	44,113

Source: Decennial censuses of population, 1890–1960.

success in breaking into stable or declining industries, particularly when the white workers have been well organized. A poignant illustration is the case of the Brotherhood of Locomotive Firemen, which removed a Negro exclusion clause from its constitution in 1964, after the railroad "work rules" arbitration had made it virtually certain that few, if any, additional firemen would ever be hired on American railroads.

5. Finally, Negro occupational progress has been unusually dependent on government, where pressure for equal treatment can be focused more easily than in private industry. The number of Negro professionals has increased most rapidly in teaching and nursing, since most teachers and nurses are hired by public agencies. The largest groups of Negroes have moved into manufacturing during periods of war. Military service itself has provided real economic improvement for many Negroes. During recent years the greatest increase in Negro employment has taken place in the civilian activities of government.

The Era of Slavery

Negroes were not, of course, engaged solely in agricultural work and domestic service during slavery. The ablest slaves were trained as skilled laborers on the plantation and in town —as blacksmiths, carpenters, masons, bricklayers, painters, shoemakers, harness makers, and so on. Some worked for their owners; some were hired out to private employers or to public agencies; some were permitted to work for themselves in return for a certain percentage of their earnings. As mining and manufacturing began to develop, the use of slaves was expanded to quarrying, coal mining, iron milling, founding, textile milling, and tobacco manufacturing. Slaves also worked on steamboats and maritime vessels, and on the railroads in every capacity except as conductors. White workers found themselves at a severe competitive disadvantage, and it is estimated that in 1865 there were five Negro mechanics in the South for every white mechanic.

Free Negro mechanics were able to hold their own in Southern cities and towns, perhaps because a vigorous and aggressive white labor force was lacking. In the North, however, the situation was quite different. There Negroes faced severe competition from immigrants, especially the Irish, who pushed them out of many common labor and personal service jobs which they had been able to acquire.

The contrasting competitive situations in the South and the North were also reflected in the political sphere. In the South,

> The utilization of slave labor in manufacture . . . before the Civil War brought to the surface the competition between Negroes and the poor whites. There was agitation against the hiring out of slaves as competitors of white mechanics and artisans. In Georgia the white laboring class succeeded in getting the legislature to pass a law in 1845 prohibiting contracts with slave and free Negro mechanics. On the whole, however, the slaveholders were able to prevent any serious restriction upon the employment of slaves in industrial occupations.[1]

The Democratic party of New York City, dominated by the Irish and supported by the Germans and other immigrant groups, opposed emancipation on the grounds that thousands of Negroes would move to the North, increasing the competition for jobs and lowering the wage rates. The antislavery movement neglected the more practical task of creating an economic future for the free Negro population in industry,[2] and free Negroes were gradually excluded from many occupations they had previously entered.

From the Civil War to World War I

With the surrender of the South, the emancipated slaves hoped to be provided with "forty acres and a mule." The Freedmen's Bureau did take possession of 800,000 acres of land and 5,000 pieces of town property, which it leased to Negroes, but most of the land was returned to the former owners after President Johnson's amnesty proclamation, and thus the Negro tenants were driven out or stayed on the property as day laborers.

As the dust of the war began to settle, most of the Negroes thus returned to agriculture as day laborers, wage earners under contract, sharecroppers, or cash tenants encumbered by a crop lien. Under these circumstances "the competition for land never became the cause for serious social conflict; as share-croppers and tenants, Negroes were restricted in their competitive opportunities and did not become landowners in sufficient numbers to threaten either the white landowners or the landless whites." [3] The restoration of ante-bellum social organization and division of labor in Southern agriculture was buttressed by "black codes," vagrancy laws, lawsuits for breach of labor contracts, and Ku Klux Klan activity. So, too, Negro domestics and those engaged in personal service continued much as before, their work being classified as unfit for whites.

But in the skilled crafts, as well as mines, factories, and docks, whites gradually moved in and Negroes were forced to give way. Since it was no longer profitable for the white masters to give them training, their skills gradually became obsolete. With the rise of craft unionism and the apprentice system in the 1865–1885 period, white artisans consolidated their hold on former Negro jobs, particularly in the building trades and on the railroads. Technological change accelerated the process of substitution, first by making the skills of the Negro increasingly obsolete and second by often rendering the work less strenuous and dirty, thus encouraging the redefinition of former "Negro jobs" as "white men's work."

Additional barriers included competition from Southern women entering industrial pursuits and the Jim Crow laws enacted during the economic depression of the 1890's. According to Arnold Rose,

> Increased use of white women in industry meant a new source of competition. It also raised a new block against employing Negroes because of the [social equality] issue. White women and Negroes cannot work together under the southern code. The

Jim Crow legislation, enacted in the 1890's, drew the color line even sharper and thus had great importance in the economic sphere.[4]

The tightening of segregation and exclusion under Jim Crow resulted not only from the desperate situation of poor whites in the 1890's, but from a political realignment in the South. Upper-class whites, fearful of Populism, cemented an alliance with poor whites within the structure of the Democratic party. As C. Vann Woodward has pointed out, the Negroes had gained new rights through a falling out between white men and now lost them through the reconciliation of white men.[5] It was also during the 1890's that liberal journalists and politicians in the North, desirous of effecting a sectional reconciliation, dropped their sympathy and concern for the Negro.

After the turn of the century American industrialism came into full flower. From an annual average of $13 billion in the last decade of the nineteenth century, the gross national product increased to $22 billion in the first decade of the twentieth century and to $40 billion in the 1909–1918 period. Total employment rose from an average of 27 million in 1889–1898 to 39 million in 1909–1918. Under these circumstances the first massive migration of Negroes out of the South began, as well as large-scale movement out of agriculture and service activities. The number of Negroes in manufacturing, mechanical, and mining occupations rose from 275,000 in 1900 to 693,000 in 1910 and 960,000 in 1920. Negroes employed in trade and transportation more than doubled during this same period, while those in domestic and personal service declined about 20 percent (see Table 1).

It was World War I that broke the social and economic fetters that had bound Negroes to the rural South almost as effectively as slavery itself, for the war created an enormous demand for previously untapped sources of labor. Business was booming as the United States supplied the Allies with weapons and materials; but combat had cut off the flow of immigrants from Europe. With labor the scarce factor in production and even before American entry into the war, Northern industries began sending labor agents into the rural South, recruiting Negroes just as they had recruited white workers in Ireland and Italy during the nineteenth century.[6]

Negroes moved most easily into expanding industries where white workers had not succeeded in setting up exclusionary barriers. They were imported as strikebreakers in coal and iron mines and in iron and steel mills. According to the census, the number of Negro operatives and laborers in iron and steel (including various fabrication industries) advanced from 12,000 in 1900 to 129,000 in 1920 (see Table 2). Other opportunities opened up—again sometimes through strikebreaking—in lumber, mining, and tobacco manufacturing, and in the meat-packing houses of Chicago, Kansas City, and East St. Louis. At the same time the process of cutting off Negroes from work in first-class hotels, barber shops, longshore jobs, skilled construction work, and railroad trades continued. Relations between the Negro and organized labor are dealt with in other chapters; suffice it to say here that "the Negro by 1900 was for practical purposes outside of the movement of organized labor." [7]

Negro business enterprise was also cultivated in this period of economic growth, but the enterprises were confined mainly to retail stores, personal service, real estate firms, and amusement establishments. These activities, some of which were lineal descendants of slave occupations, required little capital investment and were carried on within the Negro communities. Compared with white businessmen, Negroes suffered enormous competitive disadvantages, including the small scale of their enterprises, the difficulty of securing credit, the lack of good connections, the impecunious clientele, the hostility of immigrant groups in the surrounding neighborhoods, and the lack of opportunity to acquire business skills. While the number of Negro merchants rose from 9,000 in 1900 to 24,000 in 1920, this was only a tiny fraction of the Negro labor force, and meanwhile the number of Negro farmers and farm managers had declined from 935,000 to 167,000. Today it remains true that no other ethnic group participates so exclusively in a wage-earning capacity and so insignificantly in an entrepreneurial role.

World War I to 1939

The migration of Negroes to the North accelerated during World War I. After two successive waves of migration—1916–1919 and 1921–1924—it was estimated that the Negro population of the North and West had increased by at least one million.[8] Like most migrations, these resulted from the interaction of a "push" and a "pull." The push was agricultural disorganization in the cotton belt, the continued displacement of colored workers from "Negro jobs," and the sharpening of discontent among Negroes who served in the armed forces and were disinclined to return to poverty and segregation in the South. The "pull" was a kind of vacuum resulting from the curtailment of European immigration in a period of rapid industrial expansion, which was interrupted only temporarily by the recession of 1919–1920.

Most of the Negro migrants entered the unskilled, manual jobs in steel mills, auto plants, foundries, packing houses, highway construction, railroad maintenance, laundries, food industries, and some branches of the needle trades. Generally the Negroes moved into jobs that native Americans or foreign-born whites did not want or had vacated as better opportunities turned up. In 1928 it was estimated that Negroes were performing 21 percent of the unskilled labor in the building industry, 24 percent in the chemical industry, 60 percent in the tobacco industry, 14 percent in the iron and steel industry, and 39 percent in saw mills and planing mills. In the semi-skilled category, 29 percent of glass workers were Negro, as well as 42 percent of fish-packing workers and 32 percent of longshoremen.[9] Many of the migrants, of course, moved into more traditional Negro jobs in the North, particularly in domestic and personal service. In fact the bulk of the female migrants became domestic servants in Northern cities, and the number of Negro women in this occupation rose from 715,000 in 1920 to 1,036,000 in 1930.

Despite the limited character of occupational advancement, the 1920's represented a high point of prosperity for the Negro in the Northern cities. Most Negroes were working, and unemployment was no higher than among whites. This was a period of ruddy optimism concerning the future of the black businessman; it was the heyday of Dixieland jazz, which attracted thousands of whites to Negro night clubs in Harlem and on the south side of Chicago; and there was a considerable increase in the number of Negro preachers, teachers, and other professionals. But then came the collapse.

Three linked developments made the Great Depression of the 1930's particularly catastrophic for Negroes. First was the collapse of cotton agriculture in the South, second was the decline of urban employment opportunities, and third was the invasion by the whites into many of the traditional Negro jobs. The only bright spots in the picture were the relief and social welfare policies of the New Deal.

Cotton land in cultivation declined from 43 million acres in 1929 to 23 million in 1939. Negroes in every status—landowners, cash tenants, share tenants, sharecroppers, and laborers—were displaced in large numbers. Many white sharecroppers and laborers were also eliminated, but the number of white cash and share tenants remained almost constant, while the number of white landowners actually increased by about 135,000. Some policies of the government, especially the Agricultural Adjustment Administration, provided powerful financial incentives for landowners to reduce the tenant labor force; and the impact was concentrated on politically impotent Negro sharecroppers and share and cash tenants.

As the displaced Negroes flocked into the cities, industrial employment opportunities were shrinking. The burden of the Depression fell heaviest upon Negroes because they were located at the bottom of the occupational pyramid, because they were concentrated in industries sensitive to the business cycle, and because they were subject to sharper discrimination in a period of job scarcity. Under these circumstances, the now familiar differential between Negro and white unemployment appeared in the statistics for the first time. Thus the National Health Survey of 1935–1936 found, for example, that 36 percent of colored males and 28 percent of colored females were seeking work or were on emergency work, compared with 21 percent of white males and 19 percent of white females.

Much of the Negro's previous occupational progress was lost during the Depression. In particular, the number of Negroes in manufacturing, mechanical, and mining occupations fell off from 1,100,000 in 1930 to 738,000 in 1940, and the number in wholesale and retail trade declined from 398,000 to 288,000 (see Table 1). The proportion of Negro employees in manufacturing industries also declined, from 7.3 percent to 5.1 percent.

There was widespread invasion of Negro jobs by unemployed whites, often with the assistance of employers, unions, and lawmakers. Municipal licensing ordinances were revived in the South in order to drive Negroes out of barbering, plumbing, and other new occupations Negroes had entered during recent years. Otherwise displacement was concentrated in the traditional Negro jobs—waiters, porters, housemaids, elevator operators, railroad laborers, etc. In industries such as steel, automobiles, meat-packing, and coal mining, temporary layoffs and work staggering were more customary than outright discharge; and the policies of the industrial unions that already admitted Negroes militated against displacement except in line with seniority and other recognized criteria.

The work relief and other social welfare programs of the New Deal were of particular importance to the Negro because of the prevalence of destitution in Negro communities. The Federal Emergency Relief Administration reported in October 1933 that 27 percent of urban Negroes were on relief. Under the Works Progress Administration, the situation in Northern urban areas was similar, although Negroes tended to be underrepresented within Southern rural areas.

Despite discriminatory wage rates in some instances and fewer opportunities to get skilled and professional assignments, the relief agencies enabled vast numbers of Negroes to regain work habits and preserve their health. Furthermore, Negroes frequently were able to earn more on work relief than they could have obtained in private employment if jobs had been available.[10] And the comprehensive unemployment relief program of the Federal Government served as a social insurance against race riots, lynchings, and other extreme forms of racial conflict.

World War II to the Korean War

Wartime prosperity did not benefit the Negroes as rapidly as it did the whites. With a large residue of unemployed white workers—better organized than during World War I—with less need for unskilled labor, and with the historical alliance between antiunion employers and Negro migrants having been broken, the Negroes did not move rapidly into the booming defense and armaments industries. On the other hand they did gain substantially from the secondary expansion of consumer and service industries; they were in heavy demand for the less-skilled tasks in the construction of airports, military bases, arsenals, and other military projects; and they found many additional jobs in industries that had traditionally employed them, such as iron and steel, chemicals, sawmills, and meat-packing.

Although the U.S. Employment Service had a formal policy of nondiscriminatory referrals, "community customs" and employer hiring patterns were honored in practice,[11] so that Negroes were sent out only to openings where they would be likely to be hired. Then, on the ground that it was difficult to place Negroes in war industries, they were generally excluded from training programs. The inevitable consequence in many communities was severe labor shortages for war production combined with heavy Negro relief loads. As late as 1943 one author contended that more Negroes were obtaining their livelihood from relief than from any single productive occupation except agriculture and domestic and personal service.[12]

In June 1941 President Roosevelt issued Executive Order 8802, the original Fair Employment Practice regulation. The order required that future defense contracts carry nondiscrimination clauses, directed that Negroes be allowed to participate fairly in vocational training programs, and established the Committee on Fair Employment Practices to investigate and redress complaints of discrimination. Thus publicity and moral pressure were added to the increasingly powerful labor-market pressures that were pushing the Negro into the war economy.

The number of Negroes in civilian jobs increased by almost a million between 1940 and 1944, in addition to the 700,000 who entered military service. The principal movement was from agriculture and domestic service and from the ranks of the unemployed into industries. Negroes moved up in substantial numbers into semiskilled and skilled positions. Furthermore, the number of Negroes in public employment increased from 60,000 in April 1940 to 200,000 in April 1944. According to Robert Weaver, these wartime changes represented more industrial and occupational diversification for Negroes than had occurred in the seventy-five preceding years.[13]

On the other hand, despite the unprecedented shortage of labor in World War II, Negroes made very little progress outside the field of manual labor. And although they maintained their wartime gains in the generally prosperous postwar period, nevertheless at the end of the 1940's they were still largely excluded from clerical and sales occupations, professional activities, and proprietary and managerial functions—the only significant exception being the ever-increasing number of Negro schoolteachers.

The major changes in the 1940's can be summarized as follows: the number of gainfully employed Negroes in agriculture declined from 1,485,000 to 1,035,000; those in manufacturing rose from 479,000 to 998,000; those in wholesale and retail trade rose from 288,000 to 617,000; and those in professional and semiprofessional occupations advanced from 177,000 to 356,000. Finally, there was a substantial decline in the number of domestic servants—a reliable index of occupational opportunities for Negroes in other parts of the economy.

The Korean War prosperity of 1950–1953 provided the Negro with an opportunity to maintain and extend his economic gains. In fact, that period represented the apex of Negro prosperity, at least relative to white prosperity. Thus the income of male Negro wage and salary earners in 1951 averaged 62 percent of the whites', compared with 54 percent in 1947 and 55 percent in 1962. The labor force participation rate of Negro males in their early twenties (another good index of economic opportunity) reached a peak of 92.3 percent in 1953, compared with 85.6 percent in 1948 and 89.4 percent in 1964. For those between ages 25 and 34, the participation rate was 96.7 percent in 1953 compared with 95.3 percent in 1948 and 95.9 percent in 1963. The year 1953 was also the last year of relatively low unemployment among Negroes—a 4.4 percent rate for males and 3.7 percent rate for females. The corresponding rates for 1964, notwithstanding four years of uninterrupted economic growth, were 9.1 percent and 10.8 percent.

To be sure, the long-term movements of Negroes out of agriculture and out of the South have continued to operate and have accelerated greatly in recent years. The number of Negroes in manufacturing rose from 998,000 in 1950 to 1,306,000 in 1962. Those in wholesale and retail trade increased from 617,000 in 1950 to 980,000 in 1962. Substantial gains have been made in the lower levels of public administration, in nursing and nonprofessional hospital occupations, and in teaching.

But when attention is focused on the degree of integration into the economy—a concept that necessarily involves the comparative position of Negroes and whites—it seems evident that the period since the end of the Korean War has been one of retrogression rather than progress for the Negro. With overall unemployment rates generally over 5 percent, Negro workers have fallen behind the whites, notwithstanding the great energy and moral force of the civil rights movement. Only in 1964 were there glimmerings of relative improvement.

□ The Economic Status of the Negro in the Postwar Period

Statistics seem out of place in discussing a problem with such tremendous moral and ideological dimensions as the Negro's demand for economic citizenship. They cannot convey the despair of a jobless man in his eleventh month of unemployment, or the frustration of a well-educated woman confined to menial tasks, or the demoralization of a teen-ager without career prospects.

From another standpoint, however, statistics are essential in approaching a problem that is invested with such great emotional force. Absolute propositions are an indispensable basis for ideology but a poor guide for policy. Statistical propositions do show the dimensions of the problem; they do represent its magnitude and indicate the directions of change. Unless one has some grasp of dimension, magnitude, and direction, he is not in a good position to judge what can be done and what should be done.

Understanding of the Negro's employment problem and its consequences is currently clouded by optimism by some and a stylish defeatism by others. Both tendencies carry implicit statements of fact or probability—for example, that a well-educated Negro has clear sailing in the labor market, that Negroes have been slowly and gradually catching up with the whites, or that automation has eliminated the need for labor to such an extent that full employment is no longer desirable or possible; or, on the other hand, that most Negroes are unemployed and impoverished, or that most Harlem teen-agers are delinquent. The only cure for these emotionally satisfying assumptions is to have recourse to the facts.

The concept of economic integration as I use it is relative and comparative. To the extent that Negroes are proportionally represented in all the important economic activities, to the extent that they participate at all levels of occupational and professional skill, and to the extent that their unemployment experience is similar to that of whites, they can be said to be integrated. The concept thus focuses on the relative position of the Negro as distinguished from the general progress or retrogression of the entire labor force.

But have Negroes become more integrated into the economy or less so in the recent period of generally sustained economic growth with chronically excessive unemployment rates? Has the economic status of the Negro been moving toward that of the whites, or moving apart, in these last few years? Has the differential burden associated with color been growing lighter or heavier? The answers to these questions justify the judgment that Negro workers have fallen behind the whites since the end of the Korean War.

Whenever possible, this form of analysis deals with actual numbers of people rather than the more familiar ratios and percentages. The 5 or 6 percent unemployment rate, the 3 or 4 percent economic growth rate, the 4 percent full-employment target, and so forth, have become part of the general noise level, along with the size of the national debt and the Dow-Jones industrial average, and no longer stimulate a fresh response. In the analysis of unemployment, percentages conceal great differences of magnitude that one should at least be aware of. For example, the unemployment rate for Negro women over 65 is about the same as the rate for white men between 25 and 34, but in one case we are speaking of 2,000 jobless people and in the other case 262,000. Knowing the actual number of people involved also helps to put a problem in perspective and thus encourages sensible policy judgments.

Labor Force Participation

"Labor force participation" is a technical term meaning membership in the world of work. This is regarded as the normal and natural status for all healthy men beyond school age and short of retirement. Increasingly it is the choice of women, particularly middle-aged women whose children are no longer young. Not only are employed persons in the labor force, but also the unemployed, if they are out of work, able to work, and actively looking for work. If one is neither employed nor unemployed, he is out of the labor force altogether. Children, nonworking students, many housewives, unemployables, and retired persons are not in the labor force.

What is surprising and disturbing is that even in a work-oriented society such as ours, many thousands of men are outside the labor force. They are physically healthy, have attained working age, and are not in school; but because of apathy or discouragement they have never bothered to enter the labor market or have withdrawn from it in favor of idleness and underground pursuits.

The number of Negro males between the ages of 20 and 64 outside the labor force increased from 270,000 in 1954 to 405,000 in 1964.[14] It cannot be assumed that all these individuals are out of the labor force because they are alienated from the world of work in a pathological sense. There are other possible reasons for not participating in the labor force. As Secretary of Labor W. Willard Wirtz observed in his 1964 *Manpower Report,* "Statistical confirmation of the precise causes of withdrawal from the labor force have not always been possible, and hard conclusions regarding the economic pressures leading to such withdrawal has been a notably difficult task with the information available." [15] Some inferences can be drawn, however, by comparing the white and Negro participation rates and by analyzing the drop-off in Negro participation during the past decade. This will give some indication of what might be called "differential hidden unemployment"—a rough measure of the consequences of the extra discouragement facing the Negro.

Labor force participation rates show the percentage of various population groups who are in the labor market (i.e., either working or looking for work). Like practically all employment statistics compiled in recent years, the official figures on labor force participation distinguish between "white" and "nonwhite" rather than between "white" and "Negro." Aside from the fact that it is offensive to designate people in negative terms, this practice creates a difficulty, for the statistical category of "nonwhite" is not quite the same as "Negro." The difference is so small, however, that I will take the liberty—which is commonly taken by others—of dealing with them as if they were identical. The official categories will be used in the tables, but in the text I shall speak of whites and Negroes.

Table 3 shows civilian labor force participation rates for each year from 1950 to 1964. The most useful method of examining these rates is to analyze male and female rates separately. For males the trend has been downward among both whites and Negroes, but the decline has been considerably steeper among the Negroes. Older men of both races have left the labor force to about the same extent, mainly because of the spread of pension plans and mandatory retirement rules. It is among the younger men that the differences in opportunity have had the most pronounced effect. The participation rate for white teen-agers has fallen off from 50.3 percent to 41.0 percent, but among the Negro teen-agers the decline was from 56.1 percent to 37.7 percent. Likewise, for young men between 20 and 24 Negro participation rates have dropped more rapidly.

Doubtless the movement out of the labor force is partly explained by the growing popularity of higher education, but this does not explain why young Negroes have left the labor force to a much greater extent than young whites. Enrollment statistics show that 21.5 percent of white males between 20 and 24 are still in school, as compared with 9.4 percent of Negro males.[16] Furthermore, it is almost certain that a larger proportion of Negro college students are also in the labor force, since their economic difficulties are typically greater. Thus, although the picture is complicated by educational trends, it seems clear that young Negroes have suffered an increasing burden of hidden unemployment during the past decade.

Differences in school enrollment do not have an appreciable effect on the statistics of those over 24. While the participation rates for white males between 25 and 64 have not changed appreciably in this decade, those for Negro males have slowly but steadily declined. Only in 1964 was there some change in direction. Although the rate for Negro teen-age males continued to drop, those for Negro males between 20 and 65 increased for the most part.

Negro women have always worked in larger proportions than white women, not only because of the impoverished condition of the race, but also because they have often had better opportunities for steady employment as domestics than their husbands have had as laborers. But whereas labor force participation by white females increased from 31.8 percent in 1950 to 36.4 percent in 1964, reflecting the long-term movement of women into gainful employment, the rate for Negro women as a whole did not rise substantially during the period. As in the case of the boys, labor force participation among teen-age Negro girls fell off more sharply than among white girls. Again the discrepancy cannot be explained on a theory that more of the Negro girls are in high school or college, for the educational statistics show the reverse.

Among the women over 20, Negroes have higher participation rates in every age group. Furthermore, there is no tendency for those in the childbearing ages to retire even temporarily from the labor force. For example, 53 percent of the 25–34 age group and 58 percent of the 35–44 group are either working or looking for work. This situation is explained not only by the high incidence of poverty in the Negro community and the economic weakness of Negro males, but also by the large proportion of fatherless families.

In Table 4, I have made numerical estimates comparing the number of Negroes in each age and sex group who have actually entered the labor force with the number who would have been in the labor force if white participation rates had applied. The differences are shown in Column 3, a negative sign meaning proportionally fewer Negroes and a positive sign

TABLE 3

Civilian Labor Force Participation Rates by Color, Sex, and Age, Annual Averages, 1950–1964

	1950	1951	1952	1953	1954	1955	1956	1957	1958	1959	1960	1961	1962	1963	1964
WHITE															
Male	**84.1**	**84.0**	**83.6**	**83.1**	**83.0**	**82.8**	**83.0**	**82.0**	**81.3**	**81.0**	**80.5**	**79.7**	**78.6**	**78.1**	**77.9**
14–19	50.3	49.2	47.6	46.4	45.4	45.6	47.4	45.8	43.5	44.0	43.6	41.7	40.8	40.7	41.0
20–24	87.5	88.4	87.6	87.4	86.4	85.6	87.6	86.7	86.7	87.3	87.8	87.6	86.5	85.8	85.7
25–34	96.4	97.0	97.6	97.5	97.5	97.8	97.4	97.2	97.2	97.5	97.7	97.7	97.4	97.4	97.5
35–44	97.7	97.6	97.9	97.9	98.2	98.3	98.1	98.0	98.0	98.0	97.9	97.9	97.9	97.8	97.6
45–54	95.9	96.0	96.3	96.4	96.8	96.7	96.8	96.6	96.6	96.3	96.1	95.9	96.0	96.2	96.1
55–64	87.3	87.4	87.7	87.7	89.2	88.4	88.9	88.0	88.2	87.9	87.2	87.8	86.7	86.6	86.1
65+	45.8	44.5	42.5	41.3	40.4	39.5	40.0	37.7	35.7	34.3	33.3	31.9	30.6	28.4	27.9
Female	**31.8**	**32.6**	**32.7**	**32.0**	**32.5**	**33.7**	**34.8**	**34.7**	**34.8**	**35.0**	**35.5**	**35.8**	**35.6**	**35.9**	**36.4**
14–19	31.6	32.5	31.7	30.5	30.3	30.5	32.3	31.3	29.7	30.2	30.7	30.6	29.7	29.0	29.0
20–24	45.9	46.7	44.8	44.1	44.4	45.8	46.5	45.8	46.1	44.5	45.7	46.9	47.1	47.3	48.8
25–34	32.1	33.6	33.8	31.7	32.5	32.8	33.2	33.6	33.6	33.4	34.1	34.3	34.1	34.8	35.0
35–44	37.2	38.0	38.9	38.8	39.4	39.9	41.5	41.5	41.4	41.4	41.5	41.8	42.2	43.1	43.3
45–54	36.3	38.0	38.8	38.7	39.8	42.7	44.4	45.4	46.5	47.8	48.6	48.9	48.9	49.5	50.2
55–64	26.0	26.5	27.6	28.5	29.1	31.8	34.0	33.7	34.5	35.7	36.2	37.2	38.0	38.9	39.4
65+	9.2	8.5	8.7	9.4	9.1	10.5	10.6	10.2	10.1	10.2	10.6	10.5	9.8	9.4	9.9

NONWHITE															
Male	**83.3**	**83.6**	**83.8**	**83.0**	**82.0**	**81.8**	**81.8**	**80.8**	**80.4**	**79.1**	**79.4**	**78.0**	**76.4**	**75.8**	**75.6**
14–19	56.1	55.3	49.5	50.3	48.7	48.8	48.3	46.0	44.0	44.0	45.0	41.5	38.4	37.8	37.7
20–24	91.4	88.7	92.8	92.3	91.1	89.7	88.9	89.6	88.7	90.8	90.4	89.7	89.3	88.6	89.4
25–34	92.6	95.7	96.2	96.7	96.2	95.8	96.2	96.1	96.3	96.3	96.2	95.9	95.3	94.9	95.9
35–44	96.2	96.4	97.2	97.3	96.6	96.2	96.2	96.5	96.4	95.8	95.5	94.8	94.5	94.9	94.4
45–54	95.1	95.1	95.0	93.9	93.2	94.2	94.4	93.5	93.9	92.8	92.3	92.3	92.2	91.1	91.6
55–64	81.9	84.6	85.7	86.7	83.0	83.1	83.9	82.4	83.3	82.5	82.5	81.6	81.5	82.5	80.6
65+	45.5	49.5	43.3	41.1	41.2	40.0	39.8	35.9	34.5	33.5	31.2	29.4	27.2	27.6	29.6
Female	**45.7**	**44.9**	**44.2**	**42.3**	**44.7**	**44.4**	**45.6**	**45.5**	**46.2**	**45.8**	**46.3**	**46.2**	**45.6**	**45.6**	**46.0**
14–19	31.0	28.9	28.3	25.4	25.7	25.3	28.6	25.9	24.8	22.7	25.8	24.6	24.0	23.4	22.8
20–24	46.9	45.4	43.9	45.1	49.6	46.7	44.9	46.6	48.3	48.8	48.8	47.7	48.6	49.2	53.6
25–34	53.3	52.0	51.2	49.7	50.0	50.8	50.5	52.1	51.3	49.7	49.7	50.1	51.1	51.6	52.8
35–44	55.7	55.8	54.0	54.9	57.5	56.0	57.0	58.7	60.8	60.0	59.8	60.5	59.7	59.4	58.4
45–54	54.3	55.5	52.7	51.0	53.4	54.8	55.3	56.8	59.8	60.0	60.5	61.1	60.5	60.6	62.3
55–64	40.9	39.8	42.3	35.9	41.2	40.7	44.5	44.3	42.8	46.4	47.3	45.2	46.1	47.3	48.4
65+	16.5	14.0	14.3	11.4	12.2	12.1	14.5	13.6	13.3	12.6	12.8	13.1	12.2	11.8	12.7

Source: Manpower Report of the President, March 1965, Table A-4, p. 196.

TABLE 4

Effect of Different Participation Rates on Nonwhite Civilian Labor Force 1950, 1960, 1963, 1964 (in thousands)

Age group	Actual nonwhite civilian labor force		Nonwhite civilian labor force if white participation rates had applied		Difference	
1950	*Male*	*Female*	*Male*	*Female*	*Male*	*Female*
Total	4277	2498	4319	1732	−42	+766
14–19	373	209	334	213	+39	−4
20–24	618	324	592	317	+26	+7
25–34	1090	680	1135	423	−45	+257
35–44	932	604	947	403	−15	+201
45–54	737	452	743	302	−6	+150
55–64	403	198	430	126	−27	+72
65+	174	64	175	35	−1	+29
1960						
Total	4728	3116	4794	2389	−66	+727
14–19	436	260	422	309	+14	−49
20–24	564	352	548	330	+16	+22
25–34	1099	690	1116	473	−17	+217
35–44	1049	771	1075	535	−26	+236
45–54	884	645	920	518	−36	+127
55–64	538	324	569	248	−31	+76
65+	158	73	169	60	−11	+13

Sources: The 1950 nonwhite labor force estimates were calculated by applying participation rates from Table 3 to population data (U.S. Department of Commerce, Bureau of the Census, *Statistical Abstract of the United*

proportionally more. For example, among approximately 6,500,000 Negro males over 14 years of age in 1964, 148,000 fewer were participating in the labor force than would have been the case if an equal number of white males had been involved. On the other hand, there were 714,000 more Negro females in the labor force than would have been found among an equal number of white females.

The steady attrition of Negroes from the labor force since 1950 is particularly instructive. The relative deficit of male

Age group	Actual nonwhite civilian labor force		Nonwhite civilian labor force if white participation rates had applied		Difference	
1963						
Total	4802	3318	4948	2612	−146	+706
14–19	421	274	453	340	−32	−66
20–24	558	377	540	362	+18	+15
25–34	1070	749	1098	489	−28	+260
35–44	1109	821	1143	596	−34	+225
45–54	891	656	941	536	−50	+20
55–64	584	354	613	291	−29	+63
65+	168	84	173	70	−5	+14
1964						
Total	4871	3421	5019	2707	−148	+714
14–19	445	283	484	360	−39	−77
20–24	588	424	564	386	+24	+38
25–34	1074	744	1092	493	−18	+251
35–44	1101	818	1138	606	−37	+212
45–54	903	690	947	556	−44	+134
55–64	580	370	620	301	−40	+69
65+	181	92	171	72	−10	+20

States [Washington: U.S. Government Printing Office, 1964] Table 17, p. 22). Statistics on the nonwhite labor force in 1960 and subsequent years are given in *Manpower Report of the President,* March 1965, Table A-3, p. 195.

Negroes increased from 42,000 to 148,000, most of the change taking place in the final three years. Among teen-agers there was a relative surplus of 39,000 in the labor force as of 1950, but this changed to a relative deficit of 39,000 in 1964. Here is strong evidence of "differential hidden unemployment" and an extra burden of discouragement carried by the Negro males. At the same time the relative surplus of Negro females was falling from 766,000 to 714,000, and again the primary explanation lies in the fact that Negro teen-agers left the labor force (or failed to come in) more frequently than did the whites.

One evidence of economic integration, as already noted, would be a movement toward equality in labor force participation. In this respect, therefore, the period since 1950 was marked by retrogression rather than progress.

Among some of the sex and age groups, the amount of "differential hidden unemployment" bulked quite large as compared with the amount of measured full-time employment. The relative deficit of middle-aged Negro men (45–64 years of age) in the labor force came to about 79,000 in 1963, compared with 106,000 unemployed Negro males in this group. Likewise there was a relative deficit of 77,000 teen-age Negro girls in 1964, almost as many as the 87,000 counted as unemployed.

Part-Time Unemployment

Another way in which standard unemployment statistics understate the gravity of the Negro's economic problem is the practice of counting only those members of the labor force who are wholly unemployed. But many employed Negroes have casual, intermittent jobs, and it is clear that Negroes experience much more part-time unemployment than do whites.

Between 1956 and 1961 the percentage of employed Negroes in nonagricultural industries working part time (less than thirty-five hours) was never lower than 18 percent, whereas it averaged about 13 percent for white males. The incidence of part-time work was more common among Negro females also.[17]

A rough quantitative estimate of this factor can be attempted. In 1963 full-time unemployment for the labor force as a whole averaged 4,166,000, or 5.7 percent. The Bureau of Labor Statistics reveals, however, that the "proportion of labor-force time lost," including involuntary partial unemployment experienced by workers desiring full-time jobs, was 6.4 percent.[18] The additional 0.7 percent is equivalent to another 510,000 full-time unemployed. From statistics in the *Manpower Report* one can calculate that 25.6 percent of involuntary part-time workers in nonagricultural industries (588,000 out of 2,288,000) were Negro. It follows that 130,000 "full-time equivalents," representing involuntary partial unemployment, should be added to the count of 917,000 full-time Negro unemployed in 1953.[19]

Full-Time Unemployment

Unemployment rates

The most familiar unemployment statistics are those showing the percentage of the civilian labor force that is fully unemployed. Negroes have had higher full-time unemployment than whites for many years. In 1953, the last year in which Negroes enjoyed relatively good times, their incidence of unemployment was 78 percent higher than whites. Since 1955 they have regularly suffered more than twice as much unemployment relative to the size of the group. Between 8 percent and 12.6 percent of all Negro workers have been without jobs in every year since 1957 (see Table 5).

These statistics, it is true, do not bear out frequent statements that Negro unemployment is rapidly worsening under the onslaught of automation. Sensational predictions of a vast reserve among jobless Negroes are not supported by the evidence. But there is really not much comfort in the fact that after the longest period of peacetime economic expansion in our history, during which the gross national product rose from $502 billion in 1960 to $623 billion in 1964, about 10 percent of Negroes are still out of work.

Table 6 presents unemployment ratios by color, sex, and age for 1950, 1953, and 1957 through 1964. This table adds three significant points to what has already been shown.

1. The rate of unemployment is inversely correlated with age, except that it rises slightly in the case of older males. The really shocking rates are found among white teen-agers, Negro males under 25, and Negro females under 35.

TABLE 5

Unemployment Rates by Color, 1948–1964

Year	Total unemployment rate White	Nonwhite	Nonwhite rate as a percentage of white rate
1948	3.2	5.2	163
1949	5.2	8.2	158
1950	4.6	8.5	185
1951	2.8	4.8	171
1952	2.4	4.6	192
1953	2.3	4.1	178
1954	4.5	8.9	198
1955	3.6	7.9	219
1956	3.3	7.5	227
1957	3.9	8.0	205
1958	6.1	12.6	207
1959	4.9	10.7	218
1960	5.0	10.2	204
1961	6.0	12.5	208
1962	4.9	11.0	224
1963	5.1	10.9	214
1964	4.6	9.8	213

Source: Manpower Report of the President, March 1965, Table A-11, p. 204.

2. Postwar prosperity came to an end for the Negroes several years earlier than for the whites. Among the latter, employment held up well for all sex and age groups until 1958, but the Negro's economic situation deteriorated several years earlier. As R. A. Gordon has pointed out, the analyses of structural unemployment have been misplaced in time. Practically all of them have dealt with the period since 1957, but the damage was done in an earlier part of the decade.[20] The question of why the Negroes slipped backward, relative to whites, in a decade of generally full employment is still clouded in mystery.

3. The decline in unemployment rates since 1961 has been

TABLE 6

Unemployment Rates by Color, Sex, and Age, Selected Years

	1950	1953	1957	1958	1959	1960	1961	1962	1963	1964
WHITE										
Males	**4.5**	**2.2**	**3.7**	**6.1**	**4.6**	**4.8**	**5.7**	**4.6**	**4.7**	**4.2**
14–19	10.5	6.3	10.5	14.0	12.5	12.9	14.1	12.3	14.2	13.4
20–24	7.3	3.7	7.1	11.7	7.5	8.3	10.0	8.0	7.8	7.4
25–34	3.7	1.6	2.7	5.6	3.8	4.1	4.9	3.8	3.9	3.0
35–44	3.0	1.5	2.5	4.4	3.2	3.3	4.0	3.1	2.9	2.5
45–54	3.5	1.7	3.0	4.8	3.7	3.6	4.4	3.5	3.3	2.9
55–64	4.5	2.2	3.4	5.2	4.2	4.1	5.3	4.1	4.0	3.5
65+	4.4	2.1	3.2	5.0	4.5	4.0	5.2	4.1	4.1	3.6
Females	**4.9**	**2.6**	**4.3**	**6.2**	**5.3**	**5.3**	**6.5**	**5.5**	**5.8**	**5.5**
14–19	9.8	5.4	9.1	11.6	10.6	11.9	13.5	11.5	13.6	13.2
20–24	5.6	3.3	5.1	7.4	6.7	7.2	8.4	7.7	7.4	7.1
25–34	4.7	2.3	4.7	6.6	5.0	5.7	6.6	5.4	5.8	5.2
35–44	3.7	1.8	3.7	5.6	4.7	4.2	5.6	4.5	4.6	4.5
45–54	4.1	1.7	3.0	4.9	4.0	4.0	4.8	3.7	3.9	3.6
55–64	3.9	1.8	3.0	4.3	4.0	3.3	4.3	3.4	3.5	3.5
65+	2.9	1.2	3.5	3.5	3.4	2.8	3.7	4.0	3.0	3.4
NONWHITE										
Males	**8.9**	**4.4**	**8.4**	**13.7**	**11.5**	**10.7**	**12.9**	**11.0**	**10.6**	**9.1**
14–19	13.2	7.1	17.5	24.3	22.8	22.0	24.7	20.7	25.4	23.3
20–24	12.4	7.1	12.7	19.5	16.3	13.1	15.3	14.6	15.5	12.6
25–34	9.4	3.7	8.5	14.7	12.3	10.7	12.9	10.5	9.5	7.7
35–44	7.3	3.1	6.4	11.4	8.9	8.2	10.7	8.6	8.0	6.2
45–54	7.0	4.3	6.2	10.3	7.9	8.5	10.2	8.3	7.1	5.9
55–64	7.4	3.2	5.5	10.1	8.7	9.5	10.5	9.6	7.4	8.1
65+	7.0	2.6	5.9	9.0	8.4	6.3	9.4	11.9	10.1	8.3
Females	**7.8**	**3.7**	**7.4**	**10.8**	**9.5**	**9.5**	**11.9**	**11.1**	**11.3**	**10.8**
14–19	14.0	7.5	18.9	26.2	24.9	22.7	26.6	28.2	33.1	30.6
20–24	12.0	4.9	12.2	18.9	14.9	15.3	19.5	18.2	18.7	18.3
25–34	8.4	4.2	8.1	11.1	9.7	9.1	11.1	11.4	11.7	11.2
35–44	6.1	2.8	4.7	9.2	7.6	8.6	10.7	8.9	8.2	7.8
45–54	5.4	1.7	4.2	4.9	6.1	5.7	7.4	7.1	6.1	6.1
55–64	4.3	1.5	4.0	6.2	5.0	4.3	6.3	3.6	4.8	3.8
65+	4.3	1.6	4.3	5.6	2.3	4.1	6.5	3.7	3.6	2.2

Source: Manpower Report of the President, March 1965, Table A-13, p. 206.

TABLE 7

Number of Unemployed, by Color, Sex, and Age, 1950, 1960, 1963, 1964 (in thousands)

	1950	1960	1963	1964
Grand Total	3,185	3,930	4,167	3,875
Total White	2,609	3,127	3,281	3,064
Total Nonwhite	576	803	886	811
White Males	1,831	2,032	2,028	1,829
14–19	252	386	459	450
20–24	337	295	309	310
25–34	367	376	342	262
35–44	271	330	297	255
45–54	261	317	294	266
55–64	243	243	246	215
65+	100	86	80	71
White Females	766	1,095	1,253	1,235
14–19	144	253	322	323
20–24	135	161	192	198
25–34	162	197	198	179
35–44	130	190	221	217
45–54	117	185	191	180
55–64	63	87	103	106
65+	15	23	27	29
Nonwhite Males	390	508	509	442
14–19	49	96	107	104
20–24	77	74	87	74
25–34	102	117	102	81
35–44	68	86	90	69
45–54	52	75	63	53
55–64	30	51	43	47
65+	12	10	17	14
Nonwhite Females	198	295	375	369
14–19	29	58	91	87
20–24	39	54	70	78
25–34	57	63	88	82
35–44	37	66	67	64
45–54	24	37	39	41
55–64	9	14	17	15
65+	3	3	3	2

Sources: For 1950, the unemployment rates of Table 6 applied to the labor force statistics of Table 4. For 1960 and subsequent years, the number of employed persons subtracted from the labor force statistics—*Manpower Report of the President,* March 1965, Table 3, p. 195, and Table A-9, p. 201.

uneven. Employment conditions have improved substantially for Negro males over 25, but very little for the teen-agers and younger men. The position of Negro females under 35 has actually worsened. Among the white males conditions have bettered substantially for all groups except the teen-agers, and for those between 35 and 54 the unemployment rate was below 3 percent in 1964. The position of white females under 25 and over 55 was similar to that of white males in 1964, but unemployment was considerably higher for the age groups in between. Among all the groups the Negro teen-agers suffered by far the highest unemployment—the rate being 23.3 percent for males and 30.6 percent for females—this in spite of four years of continuous economic recovery and growth!

NUMERICAL ESTIMATES OF UNEMPLOYMENT While unemployment ratios are instructive for many purposes, familiarity with the actual numbers serves to provide a better grasp of the problem. Even with respect to the frightful problem of joblessness among Negro youth, actual figures provide perspective. Table 7 presents estimates of the actual number of unemployed persons in each age, sex, and color group for 1950, 1960, 1963, and 1964. In 1964 there were 728,000 Negro teen-agers in the civilian labor force and 191,000 out of work. For Negroes between 20 and 24 there were 1,012,000 in the labor force and 152,000 out of work. These figures certainly do not mitigate the severity of the problem, but at the same time they do not seem impossibly large. Surely it ought to be within the capacity of the American economy, which showed a net increase of 1,700,000 nonagricultural jobs from 1963 to 1964, to find or create employment for many of these young people.

The rise in Negro unemployment between 1950 and 1964 is apparent, particularly among the women. Some 369,000 Negro females were jobless at the end of the period, compared with 195,000 at the beginning. Those under 20 years of age experienced a threefold increase; and even in the short span of time between 1960 and 1964 unemployment among these young Negro women rose by 50 percent.

The most interesting development among males is the "re-sifting" or redistribution of unemployment between older and younger workers in both races during the past few years. After 1960 the number of jobless white males 25 or over dropped from 1,352,000 to 1,069,000, but for those under 25 unemployment rose from 681,000 to 760,000. Likewise, male Negro unemployment declined from 339,000 to 264,000 for the older group and rose from 170,000 to 178,000 for the younger. Thus many of the mature workers with established skills and seniority found their way back into jobs during the period of economic recovery in the 1960's. (For the most part, the 1963 unemployed were different individuals from those out of work in 1960.) But more and more young men lined up outside the gate. New jobs were not materializing fast enough, and these young people did not have the requisite education, skill, and personal connections to secure the jobs that did become available.

All in all, 811,000 Negroes were out of work in 1964. If their unemployment ratio had been 4 percent—the most conservative definition of full employment—the number would have been 332,000. The "deficit" of 479,000 jobs for Negroes is sufficient to create an appalling social problem. But when we take into account the rate at which the economy has been expanding, we can believe that full employment is not impossibly out of reach. It ought to be obtainable if bold and effective policies are implemented.

Measuring the special burden of unemployment associated with color brings similar conclusions. An important test of integration would be that Negroes and whites would have similar unemployment rates. These rates would differ according to sex and age, of course; and if general economic conditions were unsatisfactory, Negroes would suffer along with the whites. But they would not suffer more than the whites.

Table 8 applies white unemployment rates to the Negro labor force in 1950, 1960, 1963, and 1964. Column 3 indicates how much unemployment would have existed in each sex and age group in the absence of a special burden associated with color. These estimates are compared with the statistics of actual Negro unemployment from Table 7, and the differences are shown in Column 5.

The most important point to be observed is that the special burden of Negro unemployment became heavier as time went on. For males and females together it totaled 262,000 in 1950, 411,000 in 1960, and 468,000 in 1963. After 1960, it is true, the special burden became somewhat lighter for both males and females over 35; but this improvement was canceled out by a worsening in the relative position of the younger Negroes. It was not until 1964 that the Negro's relative position improved somewhat. The special burden of Negro unemployment dropped to 418,000, but the improvement was confined almost entirely to the males over 20. Thus the massive agitation for equal employment opportunity has not yet been very successful in building up the number of jobs available to Negroes.

As of 1963 about 500,000 to 600,000 additional jobs would have sufficed to produce a basic improvement in the economic situation of the Negro. This is equivalent to approximately one half of the annual increment in nonagricultural employment during recent years. If the Negro's special unemployment problem could be reduced at the rate of 50,000 jobs per year, a reasonably satisfactory degree of integration could be achieved in about a decade. On paper this looks easy. In practice it will be excruciatingly difficult unless (*a*) the general prosperity of the economy can be restored to the level of the early 1950's or (*b*) extraordinary measures can be taken to convert "disintegration" into integration even in the face of excessive unemployment.

Employment in Major Industry Groups

In the past the movement of Negroes out of agriculture and domestic service into other sectors of the economy has been

TABLE 8

Nonwhite Unemployment if White Rates Had Prevailed, Compared with Actual Negro Unemployment, 1950, 1960, 1963, 1964 (in thousands)

	Nonwhite Labor Force	White Unemployment Rate (percentage)	Nonwhite Unemployment at White Rates	Actual Nonwhite Unemployment	Difference
			1950		
Males					
All	4,277	4.5	192	390	+189
14–19	373	10.5	39	49	+ 10
20–24	618	7.3	45	77	+ 32
25–34	1,090	3.7	40	102	+ 62
35–44	932	3.0	28	68	+ 40
45–54	737	3.5	26	52	+ 26
55–64	403	4.5	18	30	+ 12
65+	174	4.4	8	12	+ 4
Females					
All	2,531	4.9	122	198	+ 73
14–19	209	9.8	20	29	+ 9
20–24	324	5.6	18	39	+ 21
25–34	680	4.7	32	57	+ 25
35–44	604	3.7	22	37	+ 15
45–54	452	4.1	19	24	+ 5
55–64	198	3.9	8	9	+ 1
65+	64	2.9	2	3	+ 1
			1960		
Males					
All	4,728	4.8	243	508	+281
14–19	436	12.9	56	96	+ 40
20–24	564	8.3	47	74	+ 27
25–34	1,099	4.1	45	117	+ 72
35–44	1,049	3.3	35	86	+ 51
45–54	884	3.6	32	75	+ 43
55–64	538	4.1	22	51	+ 29
65+	158	4.0	6	10	+ 4
Females					
All	3,116	5.3	165	295	+130
14–19	260	11.9	31	58	+ 27
20–24	352	7.2	25	54	+ 29
25–34	690	5.7	39	63	+ 24
35–44	771	4.2	32	66	+ 34
45–54	645	4.0	26	37	+ 11
55–64	324	3.3	11	14	+ 3
65+	73	2.8	2	3	+ 1

Sources: For 1950, the unemployment rates of Table 6 applied to the labor force statistics of Table 4. For 1960 and subsequent years, the number of em-

	Nonwhite Labor Force	White Unemployment Rate (percentage)	Nonwhite Unemployment at White Rates	Actual Nonwhite Unemployment	Difference
			1963		
Males					
All	4,802	4.7	237	509	+283
14–19	421	14.2	60	107	+ 47
20–24	558	7.8	44	87	+ 43
25–34	1,070	3.9	42	102	+ 60
35–44	1,109	2.9	32	90	+ 58
45–54	891	3.3	29	63	+ 34
55–64	584	4.0	23	43	+ 20
65+	168	4.1	7	17	+ 10
Females					
All	3,315	5.8	192	377	+185
14–19	274	13.6	37	91	+ 54
20–24	377	7.4	28	70	+ 42
25–34	749	5.8	43	88	+ 45
35–44	821	4.6	38	67	+ 29
45–54	656	3.9	26	39	+ 13
55–64	354	3.5	12	17	+ 5
65+	84	3.0	3	3	
			1964		
Males					
All	4,871	4.2	217	442	+237
14–19	445	13.4	60	104	+ 44
20–24	588	7.4	44	74	+ 30
25–34	1,074	3.0	32	81	+ 49
35–44	1,101	2.5	28	69	+ 41
45–54	903	2.9	26	53	+ 27
55–64	580	3.5	20	47	+ 27
65+	181	3.6	7	14	+ 7
Females					
All	3,421	5.5	184	369	+181
14–19	283	13.2	37	87	+ 50
20–24	424	7.1	30	78	+ 48
25–34	744	5.2	39	82	+ 43
35–44	818	4.5	37	64	+ 27
45–54	690	3.6	25	41	+ 16
55–64	370	3.5	13	15	+ 2
65+	92	3.4	3	2	− 1

ployed persons subtracted from the labor force statistics—*Manpower Report of the President,* March 1965, Table 3, p. 195, and Table A-9, p. 201.

accelerated in times of prosperity and retarded in times of labor surplus. Has the most recent period, characterized by rapid economic growth and excessive unemployment, been one of integration or retreat?

Changes in the industrial distribution of Negro employees, viewed in isolation, do not answer the question. The pattern of economic activity has been altering at an unprecedented rate. Whether Negroes are being "integrated" depends on whether they are moving into the newer types of activities *less rapidly* or *more rapidly* than the white population.

In Table 9 the numerical employment of Negroes in major industry groups is compared with the "calculated employment" that is obtained by assuming that Negroes were distributed among these industry groups in the same proportions as white workers. The resulting deficit or surplus of Negroes in each industry (calculated employment minus actual employment) is shown for 1948, 1955, and 1962. The last two columns of the table have special significance in that they indicate whether the surplus or deficit of Negroes has become more, or less, disproportionate.

These statistics throw a new light on employment trends by focusing attention on actual numbers, rather than percentages, and by taking into account the comparative experience of the two races. For example, the proportion of all Negro workers employed in finance, insurance, and real estate rose from 1.9 percent in 1955 to 2.1 percent in 1962; and the actual numbers increased from 123,000 to 149,000. But white employees are so dominant in this industry group, and their numbers increased so rapidly, that the Negroes actually fell further behind: the Negro deficit was 137,000 in 1955 and 185,000 in 1962.

Table 9 reveals a mixed picture. The relative surplus of Negroes has been diminishing in agriculture but increasing in domestic service. Negroes began to catch up in manufacturing between 1948 and 1955 but dropped further behind again between 1955 and 1962. The same was true of transportation and public utilities. In the construction industry, the scene of

TABLE 9

Nonwhite Employment in Major Industry Groups, Actual and Calculated (as White Workers Are Distributed), 1948, 1955, and 1962

INDUSTRY	PERCENTAGE DISTRIBUTION White			Nonwhite			Number of nonwhites (in thousands)			Number of nonwhites applying white distrib. (in thousands)			Surplus (+) or deficit (−) (in thousands)			Trend (toward, or away from, proportionally)	
	1948	1955	1962	1948	1955	1962	1948	1955	1962	1948	1955	1962	1948	1955	1962	1948–1955	1955–1962
Total employed	**53,434**	**56,698**	**60,749**	**5,944**	**6,496**	**7,098**											
Agriculture	12.6	10.1	7.2	21.1	15.7	11.7	1254	1020	830	749	656	511	+505	+364	+319	141T	45T
Mining, forestry, and fisheries	1.5	1.4	1.1	3.0	.7	.4	178	45	28	89	91	78	+ 89	− 46	− 50	*	4A
Construction	6.0	6.5	6.4	4.4	5.3	5.7	262	344	405	357	422	454	− 95	− 78	− 49	17T	29T
Manufacturing	28.5	28.2	26.8	18.9	19.7	18.4	1123	1280	1306	1694	1832	1902	−571	−552	−596	19T	44A
Transportation and public utilities	8.3	7.4	7.0	6.4	6.0	5.4	380	390	383	493	480	497	−113	− 90	−114	23T	24A
Trade	20.1	20.2	19.8	11.5	13.5	13.8	684	876	980	1195	1312	1405	−511	−436	−425	75T	9T
Private households	1.7	2.2	2.6	16.1	16.3	15.8	957	1059	1121	101	143	185	+856	+916	+936	60A	20A
Educational services	2.8	4.0	5.5	2.1	3.0	4.4	125	195	312	166	260	390	− 41	− 65	− 78	24A	13A
Professional services, excluding education	3.9	5.3	6.9	3.3	4.9	2.4	196	318	525	232	344	490	− 36	− 26	− 35	10T	*
Business and repair serv.	2.4	2.5	2.8	1.0	1.4	2.2	59	91	156	143	162	199	− 84	− 71	− 43	13T	28T
Other services, including entertainment	4.2	3.5	4.3	7.4	7.2	7.2	440	468	511	249	227	305	+191	+241	+206	50A	35T
Finance, insurance, and real estate	3.5	4.0	4.7	1.5	1.9	2.1	89	123	149	208	260	334	−119	−137	−185	18A	48A
Public administration	4.6	4.6	5.1	3.3	4.2	5.4	196	273	383	273	299	362	− 77	− 26	+ 21	51T	*

Source: U.S. Department of Labor, Bureau of Labor Statistics, Special Labor Force Report No. 33, "Economic Status of Nonwhite Workers, 1955–1962," Table 1, p. 2. The data for 1948 and 1955 has not been adjusted to reflect changes in the definition of unemployment adopted in 1957.

many bitter disputes over discrimination, Negro employment has become more proportional, so that by 1962 405,000 Negroes were actually employed, as compared with a "calculated" employment of 454,000. The majority of Negroes in the construction industry have unskilled jobs, however, and many are employed by nonunion contractors.

In the rapidly expanding field of wholesale and retail trade, Negroes made a notable relative gain in the 1948–1955 period, reducing their deficit from 511,000 to 436,000. But they were barely able to hold their own during the succeeding seven years. And despite the growing number of Negro schoolteachers, the deficit of Negroes in educational services has steadily increased in the postwar period, so that in 1962 Negro employment was 78,000 short of being proportional. Among the gains, the most notable has come in governmental employment ("public administration"). A deficit of 77,000 in 1948 was reduced to 26,000 in 1955 and was converted into a surplus of 21,000 in 1962. This corroborates the fact that Negroes have been particularly dependent on governmental policy as a source of economic gains.

Employment in Occupational Groups

It is essential to understand the distinction between industrial and occupational employment statistics. Educational services as an industry includes not only teachers but administrators, stenographers, and janitors. Wholesale and retail trade as an industry includes not only store clerks and traveling salesmen but managers, warehousemen, and deliverymen. Public administration includes not only government officials but postmen, chauffeurs, and gardeners. Statistics showing greater employment in these "industries" are therefore deceptive if it is assumed that they are necessarily speaking of teachers rather than janitors, salespeople rather than warehousemen, and departmental officials rather than postmen.

Occupational statistics, rather than industrial statistics, provide the best evidence of how far Negroes have come, and how

much further they still must go to attain economic integra
Occupation is not only a leading index of social status in American life, it also readily determines the level of income; the chances of steady work, on the one hand, or frequent unemployment, on the other; the likelihood of advancement; the opportunity to live in a respectable neighborhood, assuming that housing is available; the advantages that can be offered to one's children; and other highly significant life chances.

Because of the rapid growth of total employment, it was natural that the number of Negroes employed in most of the occupational categories should have increased during recent years. To evaluate the changes, however, it is necessary to compare the experience of Negroes with that of whites and of the labor force as a whole.

The most rapidly growing fields of employment between 1959 and 1964 were professional, technical, and clerical. Ne-

TABLE 10

Employment Changes, 1959–1964 and 1963–1964 (in thousands)

	1959–1964			1963–1964		
	Non-white	White	Total	Non-white	White	Total
Professional, technical, and kindred	+198	+1209	+1407	+67	+220	+287
Farmers and farm managers	− 94	− 605	− 699	−24	− 52	− 76
Managers, officials, proprietors	+ 33	+ 484	+ 517	—	+159	+159
Clerical and kindred	+158	+1183	+1341	+47	+350	+397
Sales workers	+ 41	+ 21	+ 62	+ 5	+ 95	+100
Craftsmen, foremen, and kindred	+134	+ 291	+ 425	+54	+ 7	+ 61
Operatives and kindred	+193	+ 873	+1066	+43	+375	+418
Service workers	+262	+ 954	+1216	+36	+189	+225
Unskilled laborers	−188	− 360	− 548	+11	−123	−112

Source: Calculated from Bureau of Labor Statistics data.

groes gained 198,000 jobs in the professional and technical category and 158,000 in the clerical group. But the employment gain in the manual occupations was even greater—there were 134,000 more skilled craftsmen, 193,000 semiskilled operatives, and 262,000 service workers, combined with a decline of 188,000 unskilled laborers for a net gain of 401,000 manual jobs (see Table 10). These statistics refute the commonly held view that manual labor is speedily disappearing under the impact of automation. It is true that these gains were strongly influenced by the revival of manufacturing activity during the economic recovery and that in the long run job growth will continue to be concentrated in white-collar occupations. (The Department of Labor predicts that between 1965 and 1975 employment growth will be "more than average" in professional and technical, service and clerical fields; "average" in sales, managerial, and skilled labor categories; and "less than average" in semiskilled occupations; and it predicts that the number of unskilled laborers will decline.)[21] But clearly it is erroneous to write off the manual trades.

One development in the 1959–1964 period is particularly striking. The Negroes gained 134,000 skilled trades jobs although the total increase was only 425,000, and 41,000 sales jobs although the total increase was only 62,000. This represents a sharp break with the past. Traditionally the Negroes have spread out into occupations where there was the least competition, either because manpower demand was expanding rapidly or because the jobs were too unattractive to be interesting to the whites. But the demand for salespeople and skilled tradesmen has not been expanding rapidly, and these jobs have relatively high status. That the Negroes obtained such a substantial proportion of the new jobs under these circumstances is highly significant. There seems little reason to doubt that this development reflects the influence of the fair employment principle and the impact of Negro protest.

Table 11 presents a fuller analysis of the Negro's occupational progress and retrogression from 1959 to 1964. The underlying concept is that Negroes can be considered integrated into the economy when they have an occupational structure similar to that of whites. Table 11 compares the actual distribution of Negro employment among the major occupational categories with the "calculated" distribution that would exist if Negroes had the same proportion of their work force in each category as the whites have. The relative "deficits" and "surpluses" have been computed for 1959, 1963, and 1964. The last column shows whether the trend has been toward proportionality (T) or away from it (A).

Until 1963 Negroes were losing ground in that the pattern of employment was becoming less integrated rather than more. Professional and technical employment was increasing, but not so rapidly as to reduce the deficit except in elementary and high school teaching, where Negroes have picked up 60,000 positions since 1959 and have come close to proportional representation. In the managerial and entrepreneurial fields Negroes continued to show the same weakness that has persisted throughout the century since Emancipation. The number of salaried managers did rise from 47,000 in 1959 to 72,000 in 1963, but the representation of Negroes in this type of work was still so small at the end of the period that the numerical deficit exceeded 400,000.

Negroes made appreciable gains in skilled manual trades, both in construction and in manufacturing. The number of Negro carpenters rose from 27,000 to 43,000, with other construction craftsmen increasing from 94,000 to 123,000. While employment of unskilled construction laborers fell off considerably, this had always been a Negro surplus occupation, so that here again the movement was in the direction of proportionality. The same was true of unskilled laborers in industries. It is paradoxical that the rapid elimination of unskilled jobs in recent years, a major cause of disproportionate Negro unemployment, has also produced a Negro employment structure more similar to that of whites and therefore more "integrated."

While the hiring of Negro typists, stenographers, and secre-

TABLE 11

Nonwhite Employment in Major Occupational Groups, Actual and Calculated (as White Workers Are Distributed) 1959, 1963, 1964 (in thousands)

OCCUPATIONAL GROUP	1959			1963			1964			TREND		
	Actual non-white employ-ment	*Non-white employ-ment if distrib-uted as white*	*Deficit (−) or surplus (+)*	*Actual non-white employ-ment*	*Non-whitle employ-ment if distrib-uted as white*	*Deficit (−) or surplus (+)*	*Actual non-white employ-ment*	*Non-white employ-ment if distrib-uted as white*	*Deficit (−) or surplus (+)*	*1959–1963*	*1963–1964*	*1959–1964*
										T = more proportional		
										A = less proportional		
Professional, technical, and kindred	**303**	**788**	**− 484**	**427**	**926**	**− 500**	**501**	**958**	**− 456**	**16A**	**44T**	**28T**
Medical and other health	61	135	− 74	72	152	− 80	90	157	− 67	6A	12T	7T
Teachers, except college	114	162	− 47	174	195	− 22	187	202	− 15	25T	7T	32T
Other prof., tech., kindred	128	491	− 363	181	579	− 398	224	599	− 374	34A	24T	11A
Farmers and farm managers	**236**	**316**	**− 80**	**166**	**260**	**− 94**	**142**	**262**	**− 120**	**14A**	**26A**	**40A**
Manager, officials, and proprietors	**154**	**779**	**− 625**	**188**	**831**	**− 643**	**194**	**861**	**− 666**	**23A**	**23A**	**46A**
Salaried managers	47	389	− 342	72	477	− 405	67	501	− 434	69A	29A	97A
Self-employed in retail	67	188	− 121	58	159	− 101	67	165	− 97	20T	4T	24T
Other self-employed	40	202	− 162	58	195	− 137	60	195	− 135	24T	3T	27T
Clerical and kindred	**411**	**1017**	**− 606**	**521**	**1143**	**− 622**	**576**	**1197**	**− 621**	**16A**	**1T**	**15A**
Stenographers, typists, secretaries	74	256	− 182	94	297	− 202	112	307	− 195	21A	8T	13A
Other clerical and kindred	337	761	− 424	427	846	− 420	464	890	− 426	4T	7A	2A

Sales workers	**95**	**491**	**− 397**	**130**	**499**	**− 368**	**142**	**509**	**− 367**	**29T**	**1T**	**30T**
Retail trade	61	289	− 229	87	296	− 209	97	299	− 202	20T	7T	27T
Other sales workers	34	202	− 168	43	203	− 159	45	210	− 165	9T	5A	4T
Craftsmen, foremen, and kindred	**384**	**941**	**− 558**	**463**	**992**	**− 528**	**532**	**1003**	**− 470**	**30T**	**58T**	**88T**
Carpenters	27	94	− 67	43	87	− 43	52	90	− 37	24T	6T	30T
Construction craftsmen, except carpenters	94	188	− 94	123	195	− 72	150	195	− 45	22T	27T	49T
Mechanics and repairmen	128	222	− 94	145	239	− 94	150	247	− 97		3A	3A
Metal craftsmen, except mechanics	34	121	− 87	43	123	− 80	45	127	− 82	8T	3A	5T
Other craftsmen and kindred	81	188	− 108	80	203	− 123	105	202	− 97	15A	26T	10T
Foremen, not elsewhere classified	20	128	− 108	29	145	− 116	30	142	− 112	8A	4T	5A
Operatives and kindred	**1326**	**1205**	**− 121**	**1476**	**1295**	**+ 181**	**1519**	**1354**	**+ 165**	**60A**	**16T**	**44A**
Service workers	**2147**	**673**	**+1473**	**2373**	**781**	**+1592**	**2409**	**815**	**+1594**	**119A**	**2A**	**121A**
Private household workers	996	135	+ 861	1035	152	+ 883	1010	157	+ 853	21A	30T	9T
Other service workers	1151	538	+ 612	1338	629	+ 709	1399	658	+ 741	97A	32A	128A
Unskilled workers	**1669**	**531**	**+1138**	**1461**	**506**	**+ 955**	**1481**	**509**	**+ 973**	**183T**	**18A**	**165T**
Farm laborers	632	222	+ 411	535	195	+ 340	509	195	+ 314	71T	26T	96T
Construction laborers	256	67	+ 188	203	65	+ 138	232	67	+ 165	51T	27A	24T
Manufacturing laborers	303	101	+ 202	253	87	+ 166	254	90	+ 165	36T	2T	37T
Other unskilled	478	141	+ 337	470	159	+ 311	486	157	+ 329	25T	18A	7T

Sources: U.S. Department of Labor, Bureau of Labor Statistics, *Employment and Earnings* (Washington, D.C.: U.S. Government Printing Office, May 1960), Table SA-16, p. 71; February 1964, Table A-19, p. 82; *Monthly Report on the Labor Force* (Washington, D.C.: U.S. Government Printing Office, December 1964), Table A-19, p. 30.

taries picked up considerably after 1959, the deficit was larger than ever in 1963. If Negroes had had their proportionate share of this occupation, they would have held 297,000 jobs rather than only 94,000. On the other hand there was a modest gain in the field of retail selling, notable for reasons already discussed.

On the whole, the 1959–1963 period was a stand-off at best. On the one side were the pressures for equal employment opportunity; on the other side were the retrograde effects of inadequate economic growth and a slack labor market.

The data for 1964, however, seem to show measurable progress toward integration on a much broader front. Professional and technical employment increased by over 17 percent from 1963, reducing the Negro deficit by 44,000. Negroes held their own in clerical jobs for the first time in recent years. While there was no more progress toward proportional employment in sales occupations, there was a dramatic increase in the number of Negro skilled craftsmen, and the Negro deficit in the skilled crafts was cut 58,000 in this one year. The employment of Negroes as domestic servants became less disproportionate—a real sign of progress—while their employment in other service activities became somewhat more so. Only in the managerial and proprietary field was there no sign that the relative position of the Negro was improving.

It is risky to draw confident conclusions from the record for a single year. Moreover, the 1964 data in Table 11 are based on preliminary Bureau of Labor Statistics reports with a considerable margin of error. Yet it is most interesting that this apparent change occurred at this particular time. Nineteen sixty-four was a year when the employment situation improved considerably, when the Negro's demand for equality became sharper than ever, when the Civil Rights Act became law, and when President Johnson was reelected on a platform emphasizing domestic social concerns. We will not know for some time whether 1964 was a false dawn or a true sunrise for the Negro worker. A great deal will depend on the answer. But one more fact must be noted. If 1964's rate of progress is maintained, Negroes will be fully integrated into the occupational structure sometime during the year 2000.

NOTES

1. E. Franklin Frazier, *The Negro in the United States* (New York: Macmillan, 1957), p. 594.
2. Sterling D. Spero and Abram L. Harris, *The Black Worker* (New York: Columbia Univ. Press, 1931), p. 13; Charles H. Wesley, *Negro Labor in the United States, 1850–1925* (New York: Vanguard, 1927), p. 83.
3. Frazier, *op. cit.*, p. 595.
4. Arnold Rose, *The Negro in America* (New York: Harper, 1948), p. 102. This passage summarizes a longer discussion in Gunnar Myrdal's *An American Dilemma* (New York: Harper, 1944).
5. C. Vann Woodward, *The Strange Career of Jim Crow* (New York: Oxford Univ. Press, 1957), p. 53.
6. Charles E. Silberman, *Crisis in Black and White* (New York: Random House, 1964), p. 62.
7. A. L. DeMond, *Certain Aspects of the Economic Development of the American Negro, 1865–1900* (Washington: Catholic Univ. of America Press, 1945), p. 31.
8. Spero and Harris, *op. cit.*, p. 151.
9. Charles Spurgeon Johnson, "The Changing Status of the Negro," *Annals of the American Academy of Political Science,* CXL (November 1928), 132.
10. Robert C. Weaver, *Negro Labor: A National Problem* (New York: Harcourt, Brace & World, 1946), p. 14; Richard Sterner, *The Negro's Share* (New York: Harper, 1943), p. 249.
11. See Herbert Hill, "Racial Inequality in Employment," *The Annals of the American Academy of Political Science,* CCCLVII (January 1965), 35–36.
12. Sterner, *op. cit.*, p. 214.
13. Weaver, *op. cit.*, p. 78.

14. U.S. Department of Labor, *A Report on Manpower Requirements, Resources, Utilization and Training* (Washington: U.S. Government Printing Office, 1965), p. 199.
15. *Manpower Report of the President,* March 1964, p. 30.
16. U.S. Department of Commerce, Bureau of the Census, *Statistical Abstract of the United States* (Washington: U.S. Government Printing Office, 1964), p. 111.
17. Alan B. Batchelder, "Decline in the Relative Income of Negro Men," *Quarterly Journal of Economics,* LXXVIII (November 1964), 544.
18. U.S. Department of Labor, *Monthly Report of the Labor Force* (Washington, January 1964), p. 34.
19. This calculation assumes that (*a*) the average amount of working time lost by partially unemployed workers is not significantly affected by race, and (*b*) white and Negro part-time unemployed make up about the same proportions in agricultural as in nonagricultural activities. If the second assumption were incorrect, however, the result would not change very much.
20. R. A. Gordon, "Has Structural Unemployment Worsened?" *Industrial Relations,* III (May 1964), 70.
21. U.S. Department of Labor, *A Report on Manpower Requirements, Resources, Utilization and Training* (Washington, March 1965), p. 54.

2 / Negroes in a Changing Labor Market

Charles C. Killingsworth

In their century of legal freedom, Negroes have made far greater progress toward overcoming the heritage of slavery than most reasonable men would have been likely to expect in 1865. They have greatly reduced some of the most substantial differences between them and the white population, and they have increased their average educational attainment more rapidly than the white population has. A majority of Negro families have risen above the poverty level. Moreover, great waves of migration have dispersed the Negro population throughout the nation, and more than half of them live outside the states of the Confederacy. The Negro population is now more urbanized than the white population; only about one Negro in ten remains in agriculture. Negroes have achieved some representation in every major occupational group, and their representation in higher-level jobs has increased sharply in recent years. This is the bright side of Negro history since Emancipation.

There is also a somber side. Economic equality for Negroes is still a distant goal rather than an accomplished fact. The average income of Negro families is about half that of white families. Negroes are greatly overrepresented in low-skilled and menial occupations and greatly underrepresented in the professions and other white-collar occupations. The average schooling of the adult Negro population lags almost three years behind the white average. Negroes experience much higher rates of unemployment and part-time employment than the white population. The Negro unemployment rate in the 1947–1949 period was about 60 percent higher than the white rate, and since 1954 it has been more than double the white rate, which itself has risen. There is good evidence that even these high rates have increasingly understated real Negro unemployment.

This relative deterioration of the Negro's economic position occurred during a period of slow growth in the total labor force. In the next few years the growth of the labor force is expected to accelerate, and the Negro labor force will grow even faster than the white. In 1964 Negroes were a little more than a tenth of the total labor force, but from 1964 to 1970 roughly a fifth of the additions to the labor force will be Negroes. Hence the competitive disadvantage of Negroes in the labor market threatens to increase if projected trends materialize. Jobs for Negroes could become one of the most important and difficult domestic issues of the decade ahead.

It seems self-evident that remedies for Negro unemployment must rest on an understanding of its basic causes. Unfortunately there has been little systematic investigation of the sources of Negro disadvantage in the labor market. These substantially higher unemployment rates give us some impression of the magnitude of the Negro's relative disadvantage, but they tell us nothing about causes. Racial discrimination and fewer years of schooling are frequently assumed to be among the important causes, but these factors provide an inadequate explanation for the disproportionate increase in Negro unemployment rates since the late 1940's.

Little attention has been given to the detailed structure of Negro unemployment—that is, Who are the Negroes that have the highest rates of unemployment and where are they? The answers to these questions, as will be seen, sharply contradict the common assumptions about the sources of Negro disadvantage and differ markedly from the answers to the same questions about the white labor force. The more basic question then becomes, Why is the burden of disadvantage distributed so differently among Negro workers?

Comparative unemployment rates are only one measure of relative disadvantage. Before examining those rates in detail, it will be useful to consider briefly other significant measures of disadvantage. It is also essential, before analyzing unemployment, to consider the causes of changes in the supply of Negro labor.

The Negro's status in the economy can be seen by dividing all occupations into just two groups: less skilled and more skilled. In the lower group are operatives, domestics and other service workers, and laborers and all farm workers; in the upper group are all white-collar jobs and the skilled blue-collar jobs. The results show that 78 percent of the employed Negro women and 74 percent of the employed Negro men hold jobs in the lower category, while only 39 percent of white women and 40 percent of white men have jobs in this less-skilled group. Some quibbles might be raised about this rough-and-ready kind of classification, but surely no one can dispute the generalization that even after a century of freedom, and after roughly a third of a century of the narrowing of differentials, Negroes still stand very far below whites on the occupational ladder.

□ Income Differentials

An important measure of the Negro's disadvantage in the labor market and their progress in reducing it is provided by the ratio between white and Negro earnings. There are no reliable figures for the first seventy years after Emancipation, but the Federal Government publishes reasonably good estimates going back to 1939. These recent figures make it clear that Negroes have benefited enormously from the rising affluence of American society since the end of the 1930's. In 1939 the median income from wages and salaries of Negro families and individuals was $489. In 1963 the average was $3,088. The Negro average has moved up more rapidly than the white average. In 1939 the Negro figure was 37 percent of the figure for whites, and in 1963 it was 53 percent. But it is important to note that the Negro-white earnings ratio rose to 56 percent in the 1954–1956 period. Thus there has apparently been some deterioration in the Negro's relative position in the past few years.[1]

Another important comparison is one between income ratios at different points in time. One study has analyzed changes in Negro-white ratios of median income (that is, receipts from all sources, not just wages and salaries) by region between 1949 and 1959.[2] This study shows that, for the United States as a whole, the Negro-white income ratio for men did not change significantly in that period. However, within each region there was a significant decline in the relative income of Negro men. Since the Negro-white earnings ratio in the South was twenty-five to thirty points below the other regions in both 1949 and 1959, it is clear that it was the continuing migration of Southern Negro men to regions with more favorable differentials that offset the decline in each region, considered individually. Nevertheless, the significance of the intraregional declines should not be overlooked, especially in view of the fact that Negro migration has decreased substantially in the past few years. What could account for the intraregional declines? Obviously, the rise in Negro unemployment rates relative to white rates is one factor; in 1949 the Negro male rate was about 60 percent higher, but in 1959 it was more than double the white male rate. One can also speculate that there was more extensive occupational upgrading among white men than among Negro men during this period because of the more rapid decline of the white agricultural labor force.

□ Quality Changes

Changes in the "quality" of the Negro labor force are hard to define and even harder to measure. One widely used measure is years of school completed. Pertinent data are not very reliable or complete for the first few decades of the century; comparisons can go back only to 1940. It is evident, first, that the great Negro migration of the past quarter century from farms to cities and from South to North was accompanied by, among other things, a substantial improvement in educational attainment. The improvement, especially among the younger Negroes, has been much more rapid than the improvement among whites. Thus, in the 25–29 age group, the differential in years of education fell from 3.7 more years for whites in 1940 to 1.3 in 1962. All of the progress in closing the gap had occurred, however, by the mid-fifties; since then the gain for whites and Negroes in this age group has been approximately equal—about one full year.[3]

In important ways the 1962 differential of only 1.3 years for this age group understates the differences between whites and Negroes. The great majority of the members of the 25–29 age group, whether white or Negro, have completed elementary school. The great differences that remain are in the percentages completing high school and the percentages with at least some college training. In both respects the Negroes have now attained only the levels that the whites had reached by 1940. In 1962 less than half the Negroes but more than two thirds of the whites in this age group had high school diplomas; close to 30 percent of the whites, but less than half that percentage of Negroes, had some college training.[4] It must also be borne in mind that the 25–29 age group represents a kind of "leading edge." It is old enough for virtually all members to have completed their education, but most will have done so in the recent past. The white-Negro differential in years of schooling is, of course, much larger for the *total* population twenty-five years and over. The 1960 Census reports that this differential was 2.7 years.

There is an even more significant kind of understatement involved in any comparison of years of school completed by whites and Negroes. The number of years spent in school is an imperfect measure of educational achievement. A year in an all-Negro school in the rural South is obviously not the same as a year in an all-white school in a wealthy Northern suburb. It is scarcely necessary to document the statement that, by and large, in the North as well as the South, the quality of education offered to Negroes has been greatly inferior to that offered to whites. Nevertheless, even the slum schools of the North are undoubtedly better than the Negro schools of the rural South. Therefore, while it may be reasoned that the figures on differences in years of schooling understate the educational gap that remains between whites and Negroes, they probably also understate the degree of progress that has been made in narrowing the educational achievement gap in the past quarter century. The northward migration of the Negroes has probably lowered the rate of discount that must be applied to their reported years of schooling.

□ Growth of the Negro Labor Force

Negro migration has had a very substantial effect in an unexpected direction. It has helped to increase the rate at which the Negro population has grown. During the first third of this century, the total number of Negroes was increasing less rapidly than the total population. Since the 1930's the reverse has been true. In the decade from 1950 to 1960 the white population increased by 17.6 percent, and the Negro population increased by 25.4 percent—i.e., at a rate half again as high as the white rate. Such large differences in rates of population growth have large ultimate effects, not only on the proportionate contributions of each group to the total labor force but also on age distributions and rates of entry into the labor force.

The effect of migration on Negro population growth has been the opposite of what might have been expected on a priori grounds. Migration has meant urbanization for the Negroes, and the urbanization of a population is generally accompanied by falling birth rates. But the Negro birth rate has risen sharply despite the migration of the past quarter century. The white birth rate has also risen, but by less than the Negro rate. A factor of greater importance than the higher birth rate in the growth of the Negro population, however, has been a great decline in the Negro death rate. In 1900 the death rate per thousand whites was 17, for nonwhites 25. In 1960 the white rate was 9.4 and the nonwhite was 10.0.[5] Another way of putting the matter is that since 1900 the life expectancy at birth of Negroes has almost doubled, and the differential between whites and Negroes has dropped from 14.6 years in 1900 to 6.6 years in 1960. The improvement for Negroes has been steady, but the largest change occurred in the 1940's. Two related factors were responsible. One was the urbanization of Negroes. Although Negroes everywhere get poorer medical care than whites, Negroes in cities—especially Northern cities—get more and better medical care than Negroes in the rural South. Better sanitation in cities has also been important. The other major factor has been the recent great advances in medical science. It is questionable whether this factor would have affected Negroes more than whites if the Negroes had not been moving to cities in large numbers.

The rapid growth of the Negro population in recent times has resulted in an age distribution of Negroes that is substantially different from that of the white population. Government estimates as of mid-1963 show that nearly 40 percent of the nonwhites are under 15, while only 30 percent of the whites are in that age group. About a third of the nonwhites are 35 and over, compared with 43 percent of the whites. The median age of the white population is 29.5, of the nonwhite population 22.2.[6]

Changes in the size and age distribution of a particular segment of the population have an important effect on the contribution of that segment to the total labor force. But the relationship is not simple and direct. The percentages of various age, sex, and color groups in the working-age population that are counted as being in the labor force have changed substantially over time. These percentages are called labor force participation rates. Changes in Negro participation rates relative to white participation rates have several kinds of significance. Let us first consider what the changes have been. Over the long run, and for the total population, there has been a persistent downward trend in male participation rates and persistent upward trend in female rates. In earlier years the rate for Negro men was higher than that for white men; but it has fallen more rapidly and now stands below the white men's rate. The Negro women's rate has always been higher than the rate for white women and still is. But there has been little net change in the rate for Negro women since 1948, while the white women's rate has gone up substantially.

The rate for each of these sex-color groups is, of course, an average, which conceals a great diversity of rates for various subgroups. Thus, rates for teen-agers and the aged of both sexes and both colors have been declining, which is readily understandable in terms of higher rates of school attendance and earlier retirement. The movement of Negroes from farms to cities has increased school attendance rates among Negro children faster than white rates have increased, and this explains a part of the overall changes in relationships between white and Negro labor force participation rates. But much remains to be explained. In the 25–64 age bracket, Negro men had labor force participation rates in 1948 that were not substantially different from the white men's rates. By 1964 the Negro men's rates had fallen substantially below the whites' rates. Furthermore, the school attendance rates of Negro teen-agers are still below the white rates; yet their labor force participation rates (by sex) are substantially below the participation rates of their white counterparts.[7]

Several recent studies have demonstrated that one factor which significantly influences participation rates for particular groups is the level of unemployment. When jobs are hard to find, some would-be workers get discouraged and stop looking for them, and therefore are not counted as members of the labor force. Only those who are "actively seeking work" are eligible to be counted among the unemployed. Therefore, the government's unemployment statistics tend to understate the true labor surplus when unemployment is relatively high, and the understatement tends to be greatest for the groups with the highest unemployment rates. It seems reasonable to assume, and past experience suggests, that the participation rates of a great many especially disadvantaged groups would rise if their unemployment rates could be brought down. The people who would quickly enter or reenter the labor force as presently defined if jobs become more plentiful are commonly called "the hidden unemployed." Analysis of the behavior of participation rates of disadvantaged groups in the white labor force shows that there has been a substantial increase of hidden unemployment in these groups in the past decade. What was said above about changes in Negro participation rates compared to white rates should leave no doubt that hidden unemployment has increased even more rapidly among Negroes than among whites since the late 1940's.

□ Unemployment

A realistic assessment of the Negro's labor market disadvantage requires consideration of hidden as well as officially reported unemployment. But first consider what the official statistics tell about Negro unemployment and changes in the Negro-white differential since the late 1940's. In 1947–1948 the reported nonwhite unemployment rate was a little more than 5 percent and the white rate was a little more than 3 percent.[8] In 1964 the nonwhite rate was nearly 10 percent and the white rate was below 5 percent.[9] The relative deterioration in the Negro's status occurred for the most part before the mid-1950's. The ratio had reached 198 by 1954, and since then it has fluctuated between 204 and 227. If we take this ratio as a tentative measure of relative disadvantage in the labor market, it is clear that even these figures show a marked deterioration of the Negroes' position. The deterioration has been much greater, and more recent, for teen-age Negroes. For example, in 1948 the reported unemployment rate for Negro boys was actually lower than the rate for white boys; in 1954–1955 the teen-age Negro rate (both sexes) was only a little higher than the white teen-age rate, but by 1963–1964 it was twice as high.[10]

How much more hidden unemployment is there among Negroes than among whites? Since by definition this kind of unemployment is not shown by the official statistics, we must rely on estimates. As was noted above, hidden unemployment has surely increased among whites as well as among Negroes in recent years. But since our concern at this point is with Negro-white differentials, let us ignore the hidden unemployment of whites. Let us confine our attention to men eighteen and over. We must take account of the fact that labor force participation rates vary substantially by age and educational attainment. Participation rates of Negro men in every age group were either close to or substantially higher than those of white men in the corresponding age group in the late 1940's. It seems reasonable, therefore, to assume that where male Negro participation rates today are lower than for white men in the same age and educational attainment group, there has been a differential increase in hidden unemployment among the Negroes.

Using data for March 1964, we can see what happens when the male Negro participation rates that are lower than those of white males in the same age and educational attainment group are brought up to the white rates. This "standardization" of participation rates gives us an adjusted male Negro labor force and permits us to calculate an adjusted unemployment rate for Negro men. It should be emphasized that this rate tells us only what the Negro men's unemployment rate would have been in March 1964 if the Negroes' participation rates had fallen no lower than the participation rates of their white counterparts in the same age and educational attainment classification.[11]

The official unemployment rate for white males eighteen and over in March 1964 was 4.7 percent, and the official rate for Negro men was 9.3 percent. The adjusted rate for Negro men is 13.5 percent. In other words, the differential in unemployment rates is almost doubled by taking into account the greater increase in hidden unemployment among Negro men than among white men. As was noted above, the participation rates of white women have increased substantially since the late 1940's, while the rates of Negro women have changed very little. This suggests that among Negro women also there must have been a significantly greater increase in hidden unemployment than among white women.

The significance of these findings is twofold. The more obvious point is that the current official figures greatly understate the true differential between white and Negro unemployment rates. The true Negro rate (at least for men, and probably also for women) appears to be about three times the white rate instead of twice as high. The second point is that since the late 1940's the growth of the real differential appears to have been more continuous as well as more rapid than the official figures show.

Since we seek to identify some of the important sources of this growth of the Negro's disadvantage in the labor market, we must determine where the Negro's disadvantage relative to whites appears to be greatest. The published figures show little difference between Negro men and women in this regard. There are differences by age which are significant, especially when they are adjusted to take account of the greater hidden unemployment. The unadjusted figures show that the largest Negro-white differences among men are in the 25–54 age group. But when we consider adjusted figures, we see that the greatest differentials are in the 14–44 age group. This finding reflects in part the fact that hidden unemployment among Negroes, relative to whites, is greater in the younger ages.

The most surprising contrast between Negro and white unemployment patterns is found in the differentials by educational attainment. Table 1 shows the reported differences as of March

TABLE 1

Unemployment Rates of the Civilian Labor Force, Eighteen Years and Over, by Years of School Completed, Color, and Sex—March 1964

Years of school completed	Males			Females		
	White	*Nonwhite*	*Ratio*	*White*	*Nonwhite*	*Ratio*
TOTAL	4.7	9.4	2.00	5.4	10.8	2.00
Elementary school						
0–4 years	10.4	7.7	.74	5.6	8.0	1.42
5–7 years	7.1	10.5	1.48	9.9	10.0	1.01
8 years	6.5	10.6	1.63	6.0	7.8	1.30
High school						
1–3 years	5.9	11.3	1.92	7.3	14.4	1.97
4 years	3.8	8.7	2.29	5.1	11.6	2.27
College						
1–3 years	3.6	7.3	2.03	4.5	12.6	2.80
4 years	1.3	4.3	3.31	1.7	—	—

Source: U.S. Bureau of Labor Statistics, *Special Labor Force Report No. 53*, p. A-15, table K.

1964. One might expect that the differentials would be greatest at the lower levels of educational attainment; but for both men and women the smallest Negro-white differentials are among the least educated and the largest are among the better educated. The 1960 Census figures on unemployment rates by educational attainment, color, and sex show the same general relationships.

We must immediately ask ourselves whether these relationships change when the Negro unemployment rates are adjusted, as described above, for the greater hidden unemployment in that group. We can make the most detailed adjustments by using the 1960 Census data and limiting ourselves to males. The finding is an unexpected one: the adjustments for excess hidden unemployment among Negroes are smallest at the lowest levels of education, especially among those with less than eight years of schooling; they are largest among the better-educated men. By far the highest adjusted unemployment rate is for high school dropouts. The relative differentials, on this adjusted basis (i.e., the ratio between white and adjusted Negro rates), are highest for the groups with nine to fifteen years of education. The 1964 data permit us to make this adjustment only on the basis of much broader age and educational attainment classifications, but even this cruder adjustment based on more recent figures gives us the same general pattern. As already explained, the adjustment technique which is used to estimate hidden unemployment among Negro men cannot readily be utilized to make similar adjustments for Negro women. But there is no apparent reason to believe that the distribution of hidden unemployment among Negro women differs radically from that found among Negro men, especially in view of the broad similarity in the patterns of reported unemployment rates by age and by level of education.

The regional unemployment rate differentials also provide something of a surprise. The largest Negro-white differentials are in the North Central region, and the lowest, at least for men, are in the South. The Negro-white unemployment rate ratios, as shown by analysis of the 1960 Census data, are as follows:[12]

	Men	**Women**
Northeast	2.0	1.6
North Central	2.8	2.6
West	2.3	1.8
South	1.7	1.7

The nonwhite unemployment rate was also lower in the South (7.4) than in the rest of the country (10.1). It is impossible to estimate hidden unemployment among Negroes by geographical region because the necessary data are not presently available. It should be noted, however, that Negroes are still greatly overrepresented in agriculture in the South, which suggests that we are much more likely to find underemployment than hidden unemployment there. The low earnings of Negroes in the South, both absolutely and in comparison to Southern whites and Northern Negroes, appear to support this presumption.

□ The Sources of Negro Disadvantage: An Interpretation

The analysis of Negro unemployment leads to important conclusions. The overall Negro unemployment rate has shown a pronounced upward trend since the early 1950's, both in comparison with earlier Negro rates and in comparison with contemporaneous white rates. The growth of reported unemployment among Negroes has been accompanied by a substantially greater growth of hidden unemployment than among whites. The real Negro unemployment rate is seen to be almost three times as high as the white rate when the greater prevalence of hidden unemployment among the Negroes is taken into account. We also find major differences in the structure of Negro unemployment compared with white unemployment. Among Negroes unemployment is more heavily concentrated among relatively young workers—those under forty-five—than is the case among whites. Among whites the highest unemployment rates are those of the least-educated workers; among Negroes the highest rates are at the middle levels of educational attainment, and the disparities between Negro and white unemployment rates are much greater for the better-educated Negroes. Negro unemployment rates are lower in the South than in the North or West, and the disparities between Negro and white rates are less in the South than elsewhere.

These facts challenge the conventional explanations of Negro disadvantage in the labor market. In popular discussion, racial discrimination and too little education—usually in that order—are generally taken to be the most important sources of Negro disadvantage. These are undoubtedly factors of some significance; but there is a basis for doubt that they are as important as is generally assumed. These two factors cannot explain why Negro unemployment has been growing markedly worse in recent years; why it is worse in the North than in the South; why it is worse among the young than among the old; and why it is worse among the better educated than among the less educated. Unless we can explain the growth and the present distribution of the burden of Negro disadvantage in the labor market, we cannot claim to understand Negro unemployment.

When we look back over the past quarter century, it is clear that during roughly the first half of this period labor-market conditions mitigated the Negroes' historic disadvantages. During the second half, changes in the labor market and some of the consequences of the Negroes' response to favorable conditions of the earlier years created some new disadvantages of major importance.

The labor-market conditions of the 1940–1953 period were largely determined by wars and their immediate aftermath. In a relatively short time the country moved from a condition of massive labor surplus to general labor shortage. This rapid change is frequently cited as an example of the inevitable result of an immense increase in aggregate demand in the economy. The interpretation greatly oversimplifies matters. There was indeed an enormous increase in government spending, and most of it was deficit spending. But there was much more to the story. The size of the armed forces increased by about 11 million men and women, and most of them came out of the civilian labor force. Despite a large influx of women and teen-agers, the civilian labor force was smaller in 1945 than in 1941. Unemployment decreased from 5.6 million workers in 1941 to 1 million in 1945, but civilian employment increased by only 2.4 million, and in fact was lower in 1945 than in 1942. Thus there was an increase in the demand for labor after 1940, but it was of lesser magnitude than the changes in the supply of labor.

There was also great change in the patterns of demand for labor. From 1940 to 1943 total employment in durable goods manufacturing more than doubled, and the lion's share of the increase was in ordnance and transportation equipment. Some industries, such as shipbuilding, had been low-volume, custom-order, hand-fabrication operations before the war; they were transformed into high-volume, mass-production operations. The tremendous increase in volume of output demanded and facilitated basic changes in production systems. Tasks which had been performed by skilled craftsmen were broken down into repetitive specialties that unskilled or low-skilled workers could readily be trained to perform. And the training was, by and large, paid for by the government. Probably never before in the history of the country had the opportunities been so good for workers with little skill and little education.

The greatest growth in jobs took place in the established centers of heavy manufacturing—the Northeast and North Central regions of the country, and especially in and around the large cities of these regions. The Negroes from the South went to where the jobs were. Their movements were supported by extensive recruitment efforts of factories and shipyards (also paid for by the government), and by the presence in many large cities of the North of substantial settlements of Negroes who had gone there in the 1920's when there had been a similar, though less spectacular, growth of low-skilled jobs in manufacturing.

After the war ended, a great boom began. Vast shortages of consumer goods such as automobiles and houses had accumulated, and at the same time consumers had been forced to save a large percentage of their incomes. Moreover, the great increase in employment of low-skilled workers at high wage rates had added a new stratum to consumer demand. Many families that had lived close to the subsistence level before the war could now afford some of the more necessary luxuries. A good example of this boom is the change in ratio between people and automobiles. In 1945, the United States had one automobile for each 5.4 persons, which was precisely the same ratio as in 1930. By 1953 there was one automobile for 3.4 persons, and the population had grown rapidly since 1945. Business firms were also building new plants and buying new equipment that had been unavailable or hard to get during the war and unnecessary during the preceding decade of depression. There was a great exchanging of jobs as veterans returned and women and young people withdrew from the labor force. But Negroes were usually able to hold on to the gains that they had made during the war years, especially in manufacturing industries. The boom slowed in 1949–1950, but the outbreak of the Korean War revived to some degree the labor-market conditions of the early 1940's.

Even before the end of the Korean War, Negroes were beginning to find the labor market less favorable to them than in the war and early postwar years. Probably the largest factor was the increasing flow of white men from farms into urban labor markets. Agricultural productivity tilted rather sharply upward after 1947, while the demand for food and fiber continued to grow at a slow rate; hence, white farmers began to feel the push off the land that was already so familiar to Negroes. In the 1950's the rate at which white farmers left the land exceeded the Negro rate for the first time. The movement of the whites from farming apparently was heaviest in the North Central region, which happened to be the region with the largest number of Negroes outside the South. The addition of these ex-farmers to the urban labor force, a factor of continuing importance, has increased competition for less-skilled jobs in manufacturing and the service industries.

After the Korean War ended, defense spending dropped sharply, and this drop eliminated a substantial number of less-skilled jobs in manufacturing. Government spending on defense and space exploration began to rise later in the 1950's, but changing technology made the new jobs drastically different from the simple, low-skilled jobs that were created in great numbers during World War II. Tanks, guns, trucks, airplanes, and other mass-produced items became a minor part of defense production. Atomic bombs, missiles, missile sites, radar nets, and then space ships became the major items, and such things require custom fabrication, plus tremendous quantities of engineering and scientific man-hours. The pace of change accelerated in nondefense industry as well. After 1953 total employment in all manufacturing was virtually stationary except for cyclical swings. But the job mix changed substantially, not only in defense industries but in virtually all branches of manufacturing. A persistent downtrend in the number of blue-collar jobs set in, with the greatest reductions generally among the least-skilled jobs. There was an equally persistent uptrend in the number of white-collar jobs, with the greatest increases among the most highly trained specialists. By early 1965 total employment in manufacturing was almost exactly the same as in 1953, but the number of white-collar jobs was up one million, and there were one million fewer blue-collar jobs. This change in job mix was one of the major effects of that new emphasis in technology which has been named "automation." Another change of importance in manufacturing was the movement toward decentralization of facilities. As new plants were built, many were located away from the old centers of manufacturing activity in the North Central and Northeast regions and closer to the rapidly growing markets of the West and South. Employment in service-producing industries—public utilities, wholesale and retail trade, finance, health care, government—was growing, but less rapidly in the older centers than in previously underdeveloped areas of the country.

Another labor-market factor that has come to be emphasized in some quarters in recent years is what is called "fiscal drag." It is argued that the Federal tax system has a built-in tendency to produce added revenues at a greater rate than government expenditures increase when the economy begins to move toward fuller employment of its productive resources. The result, it is further argued, is a chronic deficiency in aggregate demand—a deficiency that has been most conspicuous since around 1957. Some analysts have concluded that all of the increase in the overall unemployment rate that has occurred since 1957—or perhaps even since 1948—must be attributed to the alleged deficiency of aggregate demand. This diagnosis of the cause of excessive prosperity unemployment, especially in its purest form, is not universally accepted by students of the unemployment problem. A substantial majority of them probably would agree, however, that fiscal drag has been *one* of the important factors in excessive unemployment in recent years. The debate over the relative importance of structural changes in the economy, such as those described above, and fiscal drag as causes of rising overall unemployment levels need not be reviewed here.[13] Even the strongest supporters of the fiscal drag analysis have conceded that Negroes have "special problems" that would persist even if the general level of unemployment could be brought down by remedying fiscal drag.

The necessity for this concession can be demonstrated by the effects of the great tax cut of early 1964, which was justified principally as a measure to remedy fiscal drag. The overall unemployment rate dropped from 5.7 percent in 1963 to 5.2 percent in 1964. The latter was the lowest annual average since 1957. But the ratio between Negro and white unemployment percentages was essentially the same in 1964 (213) as in 1963 (214). We can conclude that general slack in the labor market has been one factor in high unemployment rates among Negroes, as among other groups in the labor force. But this factor has limited value as an explanation for the much greater rise in Negro unemployment than in white unemployment; and it does not explain why the patterns of Negro unemployment are markedly different from white patterns.

Let us now try to understand the Negro patterns in the light of labor market developments of the past dozen years. As we have seen, the relative disadvantage of Negroes is greatest in the North, at younger ages and at the middle and upper levels of educational attainment. There is a relationship between these categories; there are more young and better-educated Negroes in the North than in the South. Negroes in the North, and younger Negroes, are better-educated in general than those in the South and those who are older.

What are the probable sources of *lesser* disadvantage in the South? The proportion of Negro workers in agriculture in the South is much larger than in the North; it is also larger than the proportion of Southern whites in agriculture. Unemployment rates in agriculture are traditionally lower than those in nonagricultural pursuits. There is also some evidence of the survival of the tradition of "Negro jobs" in the nonfarm sector of the Southern economy. Negroes are even more overrepresented in common labor and service jobs in the South than in the North. Segregation practices give Negroes some protection against white competition for these jobs. Furthermore, the heavy northward migration of Southern Negroes has carried off a great part of the natural increase of the Negro population, which in turn has held down the competition among Southern Negroes for "Negro jobs." In the postwar years industrial development has proceeded at a more rapid rate in the South than in the North, especially the North Central region. Hence Southern whites have felt less pressure than in earlier times to take over "Negro jobs." Of course this explanation of the lower Negro unemployment rate in the South is not intended to suggest that Southern Negroes have a better life than Northern Negroes. The point simply is that economic inequality takes different forms in the two regions. This point is readily illustrated by the fact that in 1959 the median income of Negro men in the South was less than half that of Negro men outside the South.[14]

Northern Negroes, on the other hand, are much more highly concentrated in cities, and especially a few large cities, than the white population or the Southern Negro population. And, in a period of rapid changes in the labor markets of the North, Northern Negroes have been far less mobile than the Northern white population. The rate of growth of less-skilled jobs in the big cities of the North has been substantially less than the rapid increase in Negro population, and competition for the less-skilled jobs has been increased by the stepped-up migration of whites from Northern farms.

The greater relative disadvantage of younger Negroes at present can be explained in part simply by the fact that they are more recent arrivals on the scene. Most of the Negroes who got their first jobs in industry in the 1940–1953 period are now in the older age brackets. Where they have held on to such jobs, they are now protected by seniority. They also have the advantage of substantial experience in industrial employment when they must compete with younger Negroes for new jobs. Moreover, the age distribution of the Negro population tends to favor the older Negro worker. The higher death rates and lower birth rates of earlier years have greatly thinned the ranks at the upper ages, and higher birth rates and lower death rates have swollen the size of the younger age groups. To be sure, the same forces have been at work among the white population, but to a much lesser degree.

The pattern of Negro unemployment by level of education represents the sharpest departure from white patterns, and it is in some ways the most disturbing aspect of the Negro unemployment problem. More education has generally been accepted in the United States as the sure way to higher social and economic status. Why is Negro unemployment heaviest and the Negro-white differentials extremely large at the middle and upper levels of educational attainment? Some light might be shed on this important question by analysis of regional differences in unemployment rates by level of education, but the available data do not permit such an analysis.[15] Nevertheless, some causal relationships appear to be clear. Poorly educated Negroes and whites have what might be called an equality of disadvantage. Most people with only a grammar school education or less cannot qualify today for any kind of job that has a significant educational requirement. Therefore, Negroes and whites tend to compete on more equal terms for the lowest jobs in the occupational hierarchy than for the higher jobs. There is also a larger proportion of poorly educated Negroes in the South and in agriculture than in the North and in industrial jobs.

Part of the great relative disadvantage of Negroes with some high school training, high school diplomas, and college training is undoubtedly attributable to the markedly inferior quality of Negro education both in the South and the North. As the United States Supreme Court has observed, separate educational facilities are inherently unequal. The observation is valid whether segregation is the result of law and deliberate policy, as in the South, or the by-product of residential segregation, as in the North. Study after study has documented the marked inferiority of facilities, staff, and curricula in predominantly Negro schools, even in the North, as compared with predominantly white schools. And of course segregation is not limited to the grade schools and high schools. More than half of Negro college graduates have attended all-Negro colleges.

Recently there has been increasing recognition that Negro children are handicapped by impoverished family backgrounds even before they start school. The vast majority of Negro youngsters come from families with low incomes, and their parents' educational attainment is markedly below the average for the population as a whole. Figures from the 1960 Census strikingly document the close correlation between education of the parent, family income, and scholastic retardation.[16] Thus, on the average, Negro children start from a lower level and gain less than white children with the same number of years spent in school.

There is a related factor that is undoubtedly important, although it is difficult to measure in quantitative terms. The Negroes with more years of education are, on the whole, considerably younger than their white counterparts and the Negroes with fewer years of education. The overwhelming majority of the better-educated Negroes come from families in which the chief breadwinner is in a less-skilled, blue-collar job. Younger Negroes, especially in the North, do not find it as easy as their parents did to enter the blue-collar field, because most occupations in that field are either not growing or are actually shrinking. Furthermore, many of the parents feel that since their children have more education than they do, the children should not have to take the menial jobs in which the parents have spent their lives. Therefore, both necessity and aspiration push many of the better-educated Negroes to seek jobs in the more-skilled sector of the occupational hierarchy. Most jobs of this kind are white-collar jobs. In such jobs, not only intellectual ability and training but also many personal characteristics, such as manner of speech, mode of dress, deportment, and grooming, are deemed important by employers. In this regard the youngster from the white-collar family—and this is the majority of white youngsters—has an inherent advantage over the candidate from the blue-collar background. Thus, what the scholars call the low socioeconomic status of the great majority of Negro families tends to be self-perpetuating under present-day conditions. It also helps to increase unemployment among nominally better-educated young Negroes.

□ Conclusion

The purpose of this analysis has been diagnosis, not prescription. Another, longer essay would be required to outline remedies for the multiple disadvantages of Negroes in the contemporary labor market. However, certain broad implications for policy are rather obvious from the conclusions of the analysis. The first is that some of the remedies most often prescribed for Negro unemployment are likely to yield disappointingly small results. Antidiscrimination laws, higher rates of attendance at today's schools, faster economic growth, the normal operation of push-pull forces in the labor market—

none of these seem to hold the promise of substantial impact on the basic sources of Negro disadvantage. A second implication is that the mere passage of time, without the application of powerful remedial measures, will probably increase Negro disadvantage. We can find a not-so-early warning in what has happened to Negro teen-agers in the past four years. From 1960 to 1964 total employment in the United States economy increased by about 3.7 million persons; white teen-age employment increased by about half a million; nonwhite teen-age employment *decreased* slightly.[17] The point is that the trends of the past quarter century in Negro migration, birth rates, death rates, occupational shifts, and school attendance are now yielding the largest increases in Negro population in the regions and among the groups where Negro disadvantages are greatest.

The broad lines of long-range strategy are much easier to suggest than to implement: birth control; encouragement of the dispersal of the highly concentrated Negro populations in the big-city slums of the North and radical improvement of the environment of those who choose to remain in the central cities; and great improvement of the quality of Negro education, with special emphasis on preschool training for slum children. Some of the elements of this program are included in the War on Poverty and the Federal aid to education law of 1965, although—as is widely recognized—both programs are but a small beginning. And long-range programs are not enough. For the short run, remedial education, job training, and intensive counseling are approaches which are presently being developed—again on a limited scale—with encouraging results. Such approaches, essential though they are, are likely to be inadequate. Given the peculiar character of Negro unemployment—particularly its heavy concentration in the slums of the big cities—a program of job creation appears to be the only short-run answer to Negro unemployment that can be made to fit the size and shape of the problem. Some intriguing experimental projects have undertaken to train impoverished slum residents to assist professionals in the multitude of jobs involved in the War on Poverty. Some of these nonprofessional aides have been trained for work in the schools, some for counseling, some for health and sanitation work, and so on. The success of the experimental projects suggests that the shortage of trained professionals and the job shortage for slum dwellers might be eased by a single program: to hire and train the poor to help the poor.

The past half century of Negro history holds ample evidence of the adaptability of the Negro population when the economic environment provides reasonable equality of opportunity. When the nation's growth patterns and defense needs have created jobs that were open to Negroes, Negroes have migrated by the hundreds of thousands per year to get them. They have gone to where the jobs were and have lived where they were allowed to settle. In the past decade changing technology and changing regional and industrial growth patterns have made opportunity far less equal for Negroes than it was a quarter of a century ago. Death control has distorted the Negro age distribution and has intensified the overcrowding in Negro ghettos and their schools. As was inevitable in an open society, the poverty and ignorance of Negroes that were once a regional problem have now become a national problem. Despite the epic efforts of Negroes to better their lot in the past half century, their progress has been stopped while it was still far short of equality. It is time to mount a special effort of sufficient magnitude to make equality of opportunity a reality for today's Negroes.

NOTES

1. *Poverty in the United States* (Committee on Education and Labor, House of Representatives, 88th Cong., 2d Sess., April 1964), Table 18, p. 268.
2. Alan B. Batchelder, "Decline in the Relative Income of

Negro Men," *Quarterly Journal of Economics,* LXXVIII (November 1964), 529.

3. Matthew A. Kessler, "Economic Status of Nonwhite Workers, 1955–62," *Monthly Labor Review,* LXXXVI (July 1963), 780.
4. Denis F. Johnston, "Educational Attainment of Workers, March 1962," *Monthly Labor Review,* LXXXVI (May 1963), 504–15, Table 2.
5. U.S. Department of Labor, *The Economic Situation of Negroes in the U.S.,* Bulletin S-3, rev. 1962, Table 2.
6. *Manpower Report of the President,* March 1964, Table H-2, p. 271.
7. *Ibid.,* 1965, Table A-4, p. 196.
8. Kessler, "Economic Status of Nonwhite Workers," *loc. cit.,* Table 3.
9. *Manpower Report of the President,* March 1965, Table A-5, p. 197. The absolute rates for 1947–1948 are not strictly comparable with those years after 1956 because of changes in definition, but there is no reason to think that this affects the comparability of the white-nonwhite ratios.
10. *Ibid.*
11. This calculation utilizes unpublished data supplied by the Bureau of Labor Statistics. I have made the same calculation with data from the 1960 Census, which is based on a larger sample and provides finer age and educational attainment breakdowns than the B.L.S. data. The results from 1960 data are quite similar: reported unemployment rate, males 14 and over, white, 4.6 percent, and nonwhite, 8.7 percent; adjusted nonwhite rate, 13.6 percent. The adjusted nonwhite figure for 1960 is not fully comparable with that for 1964 because of the use of more detailed breakdowns and the inclusion of the 14–17 age group in the 1960 calculation, among other things. Nevertheless, the general similarity of magnitudes appears to lend credibility to the estimate derived from the 1964 data.
12. Batchelder, "Decline in the Relative Income of Negro Men," *loc. cit.,* p. 542. These ratios are for Negroes, not nonwhites.
13. An analysis of the role of structural changes, and a critique of efforts to demonstrate that these changes have not contributed to rising unemployment, is presented in my paper

entitled "Structural Unemployment in the United States," a chapter in *Employment Problems of Automation and Advanced Technology: An International Perspective,* scheduled for publication in late 1966 by Macmillan in London.

14. The median income of Southern Negro men was also less than half that of Southern white men. Batchelder, "Decline in the Relative Income of Negro Men," *loc. cit.*, p. 529.
15. The necessary data are being compiled from tapes of the 1960 Census. An analysis of regional differences is contemplated when the data are available.
16. *Poverty in the United States,* Table 25, p. 275.
17. *Manpower Report of the President,* March 1965, Table A-9, p. 201. Of course the nonwhite teen-age population increased quite substantially in the 1960–1964 period, and the labor force (as presently defined) increased by 32,000.

3 / Regions, Race, and Jobs

Vivian W. Henderson

In approaching the question of Negro employment within a Southern context, it should not be assumed that the economic problems of Negroes are confined to the South. On the contrary, it is recognized that Negro workers in other regions face many problems that are no different from those faced by Negroes in the South. Education and training deficiencies, together with employment dislocations generated by advancing technology, are sources of problems for Negro workers regardless of region or locality. The same is true in many respects with regard to the practice of racial discrimination in employment. Also, in today's highly mobile society, labor markets transcend traditional bounds of region, and job opportunities are less restricted geographically. It may appear irrelevant, therefore, to view jobs and color in a regional context.

On the other hand, it is well known that Negroes in the South have historically been confronted with problems peculiar to that region. There are regional differences, moreover, that are not just a simple matter of degree. These differences—in economic status and equality of opportunity—are significant not only for Negroes, but also for the economy of the South and the Nation, as well as for our national purpose.

The most obvious difference relates to effective implementation of the equal employment opportunity section, Title VII, of the Civil Rights Act of 1964. Since racial discrimination in employment is greater and more deeply entrenched in the South than in the North and West, where fair employment practices policy has a longer history, efforts to enforce provisions of the act must be given a greater thrust in the South if Negroes in that region are to reap significant benefits.

Also, if the same regional problem is viewed against a background of recent change in economic environments, technological advances, new manpower requirements, and labor utilization trends, implications arise regarding the pace of progress in the Southern economy. As shall be noted, the South has taken significant strides in reaching parity in per capita income with the nation as a whole. In part this has been an effect of the redistribution of the Negro population between the South and other regions, in response to the attraction of better employment opportunity outside the South. Much of the redistribution has involved the migration of low-skilled Negroes from the rural South, where they were displaced by technological advances in agriculture and farm mechanization. If employment opportunities for low-skilled workers outside the South are also diminished by technological advances, motivation for migration will in all probability be reduced. If this should happen, the South will be faced with larger numbers of Negroes seeking employment within its nonagricultural labor markets. If this occurs and Negroes are not absorbed into nontraditional areas of employment, not only will the South be plagued with larger labor surpluses, a formidable part of the region's economic problem, but its progress will be impeded in matching the economic well-being of the rest of the nation.

During the greater part of its history the South has functioned under the dual hardship of a relatively backward economic structure and a system of race relations based upon segregation. Both have had depressing effects on the economic progress of the region. The South has been the slowest growing region in the nation because it has been struggling under the handicap of an adverse business mix.[1] It has been oriented toward agriculture and relatively low-wage industries, which provided employment but were slow in generating income. Manufacturing employment, for example, was largely confined to such low-wage industries as lumber and furniture, food processing, textiles, and apparel. Consequently, whereas unemployment may not have been a chronic problem in the South, "underemployment," judged by individual incomes, has been a significant characteristic.

The South has always contained the highest concentration of the nation's Negro population. In places outside the South, Negroes have at least been able to get and hold jobs in nontraditional and nonsegregated areas of employment, even though the jobs may not have led to upgrading and promotion. In the North and the West a significant number of them have been able to penetrate jobs and industries from which they are virtually excluded in the South. Clerical and supervisory jobs in local, state, and federal agencies are examples. In the South, Negro employment opportunity is rigidly prescribed by traditions in race relations. The practice of dividing the work market into "white jobs" and "Negro jobs" has been clearly defined, and practices governing use of the Negro labor force have been reduced to observable "laws." For example, Negroes seldom work side by side with whites in the South, particularly in jobs that carry advantages in income, responsibility, potential for upgrading, and cleanliness. This is the case whether on the assembly line or elsewhere in the plant or business. Negroes rarely, if ever, supervise whites in the South, and opportunity for them to apply themselves at tasks commensurate with their skills and abilities is overwhelmingly confined to segregated areas of the economy that provide services to other Negroes.[2]

While there may be similarities in the employment problems of Southern and non-Southern Negroes, the differences are more striking. Occupation and income indices suggest that Negroes outside the South have been able to reduce the economic imbalance between themselves and whites, a tendency less discernible in the South. Poor race relations in general and employment discrimination in particular have served to postpone the closing of the economic gap between the South and the rest of the nation. There is a strong element of incompatibility between Southern racial employment practices, as well as other aspects of race relations, and economic progress.[3] Where progress has been made, Negroes have been prevented from benefiting as much as Southern whites or even Negroes in other regions.

Before turning to some of the details regarding Negro workers in the South, it is important that some of the more salient aspects of Southern economic progress be set forth and indicators of structural reorganization delineated. This will offer a meaningful background against which to explore the experience of Negroes as economic participants. Further, observation of trends may provide insight into future problems.

□ Changes and Progress in the Southern Economy

It is unnecessary to examine all the indices of Southern economic reorganization and progress. Economic progress is best evidenced by upward changes in per capita income and, to a lesser extent, in the income of families. Income determines the spending and saving power of people. At the same time it provides a measure of the earning capacity of the economy and of individual contributions to the production of goods and services. Structural changes and economic reorganization, on the other hand, are best shown by changes in industry sources of employment and income, shifts in occupational distribution of employed persons, growth in "value added" by manufacture, and characteristics of population change.

Since about 1940 the South has been moving away from a

relatively homogeneous economic structure based on agriculture toward a well-diversified economy that is organized around industries, is increasingly subject to metropolitan dominance, and has characteristics that conform closely to those of the total economy. While farming continues to occupy a significant place in Southern economic life, its relative role over the past twenty years has decreased. Since 1940, agricultural employment in the South has declined 2.5 million, or about 60 percent. Meanwhile, manufacturing employment has increased 1.6 million, or about 80 percent, and manufacturing as a source of income has increased from 19 percent to 25 percent of the total income received by civilians from current industry participation.

The change in the role of manufacturing has involved not only more factory jobs in the South, but also more diversification in employment. For example, the textile industry was once the backbone of Southern manufacturing. Before World War II it accounted for about one fourth of all manufacturing employment in the South. It is now a source of less than one fifth. More and better jobs are being created by higher-wage industries, such as the manufacture of transportation equipment, electrical and nonelectrical machinery, and fabricated metals. In the early 1940's these industries accounted for only 14 percent of all manufacturing employment in the South. In 1960, they accounted for 22 percent.

The change in the composition of Southern employment is, of course, part of a national trend. In addition to the shift from agriculture, industries are becoming more dispersed geographically. As a result, regional industrial specialization is generally decreasing, but the change has been more pronounced in the South.

The growth in the region's urban population and the drop in the number of people living in rural areas are symbolic of the decline of the South's traditional economy. The rural to urban shift is occurring among both whites and Negroes, although the tendency is faster among Negroes. Between 1950 and 1960, the number of whites living in central cities in the

South increased 26 percent, while that of Negroes increased 37 percent.

The proportion of the South's population living in urban areas was only 35 percent in 1940; 42 percent lived in rural areas on farms and 23 percent lived in rural nonfarm areas. By 1960 the proportion had increased to 58 percent in urban areas and to 31 percent in rural nonfarm areas, while the farm population had declined to 11 percent, or from about 15 million to about 4.5 million. By 1960 77 percent of the Negroes in Florida lived in urban areas; in Tennessee the proportion was 72 percent, and in Kentucky, 71 percent. In fact, in only four states—Mississippi, Arkansas, and the Carolinas—did the majority of Negroes still live in rural areas.

The South can no longer be characterized by an economic structure distinctively different from that of the rest of the country. Indeed, the Mississippi Delta farmer has less in common with a factory worker or sales representative in Atlanta than the latter has with his non-Southern counterpart. Economic growth and organization in the South will hereafter be linked to patterns of change in the total economy.

Improved employment opportunity, generated by Southern economic reorganization, is reflected in higher income. The region has reduced much of its poverty and has made significant progress in achieving a proportionate share of the nation's income. For example, in 1930 the South had 20 percent of the nation's population but only 11.7 percent of the national income; in 1963, although its proportion of the population remained about the same, its share of personal income had advanced to 16 percent. The ratio of per capita income in the South to that in the nation rose from 58 percent in 1940 to 74 percent in 1963. In current dollars, personal per capita income in the South rose from $343 in 1940 to $1820 in 1963. Even if adjustment for changes in price levels were made, the changes in per capita income estimates would still show substantial growth.

On the other hand, two facts regarding the South remain constant. First, despite improvements and economic gains, it continues to be the most depressed segment of the nation's economy. Personal per capita incomes are still less than three fourths of those in the rest of the country. Most of the nation's poverty continues to be located in Southern rural areas; the region is still plagued by large-scale underemployment; it lags in educating its population to cope with the needs of the urban economy; and traditional racial patterns in employment persist. Second, not only do Negroes in the South, as a group, constitute the most depressed part of the nation's population, but the benefits they have reaped from Southern economic progress have been minimal, particularly when compared with the progress experienced by Negroes in other parts of the country. One result of this has been the continual out-migration of Southern Negroes, with education and abilities and without them, to other regions.

□ Interregional Migration

The greatest single factor motivating population migration is economic or employment opportunity, and thus the denial of opportunity to Negroes in the South and the availability of such opportunity elsewhere has been a major cause of the regional redistribution of the Negro population.

The population of the South grew 17 percent between 1950 and 1960, although it has been losing population through net out-migration. Natural increases, an excess of births over deaths, accounted for the growth. Only two states experienced a growth in population as a result of their net in-migration rate. Florida with a rate of 58 percent and Virginia with a rate of 0.4 percent. Elsewhere in the South, more people left states than came in. The highest rate of net out-migration was 23 percent, in Arkansas; and the rates ranged from 11 to 19 percent in Alabama, Mississippi, Kentucky, and South Carolina. Net out-migration was lowest, 1.9 percent, in Louisiana; it was 6.9 percent in Georgia and about 8 percent in North Carolina and Tennessee.[4]

It is significant that most of the emigrants were Negroes.

In 1960 Negroes made up about 20.9 percent of the population of the South and about 11 percent of the nation's population. Fifty-two percent of all Negroes in the United States resided in the South, compared with 68 percent in 1940 and 59 percent in 1950. During the decade of 1940–1950 over 1.5 million Negroes (16 percent of the Negro population then) left the South and another 1.5 million (14 percent) left during the following decade. States with large Negro populations, such as Mississippi, Alabama, Georgia, Arkansas, and North and South Carolina, had net out-migrations of 15 to 35 percent in each decade. Mississippi lost the largest number of Negroes—326,000, or 30.2 percent, in 1940–1950 and 323,000, or 32.7 percent, in 1950–1960. On the other hand, the net out-migration of whites from the South was only 0.1 percent in the 1940's and 1.7 percent during the 1950's.[5]

The direction of movement of Negroes from the South has been largely to the Northern industrial states and the Pacific Coast. Between 1940 and 1950 the net in-migration rate of Negroes was 34 percent for the Northeast, 42 percent for the North Central States and 61 percent for the West; during the next decade the rates were 26 percent, 24 percent, and 39 percent, respectively. Estimates indicate that just under 1.2 million Negroes migrated to the Northeastern and North Central States and about 332,000 to the West Coast during the period 1950–1960.

The movement of Negroes out of the South has both positive and negative implications. For the greater part of the period following their removal from slavery the masses of Negroes were bound to the rural South, living in densely populated areas and dependent upon low-income agriculture for a livelihood. They were enmeshed in poverty as a result of their roles in the South's backward economy as sharecroppers and tenant farmers, and as a result of the region's enforced patterns of racial segregation. These conditions never worked in the best interest of the South. They constricted the region's markets for goods and services and kept the level of employment low. Thus, as Negroes move out of the South in pursuit of jobs created by the expansion in the national economy, the South is relieved of a sizable proportion of its low-income population.

Hence, per capita incomes tend to rise. One may surmise, therefore, that the growth in the South's per capita income cited earlier resulted in part, at least, from migration of the Negro population. Meanwhile, the absorption of Negro workers by non-Southern industries added to the total level of employment and income in other regions.

If new economic opportunity had not drained off underemployed and unemployed Negroes to other sections of the country, the South would have continued to face increasing difficulty in providing jobs for its growing labor force.

Donald Dewey[6] has suggested that since migration is largely a phenomenon of population displacement through areas of ascending wage scales, Negro workers who left the urban South for the North and the West were probably superior in economic competence, mainly through better education, to the whites who poured into Southern towns behind them. Thus, so long as Negroes are not fitted into predominately white work groups they are strongly tempted to head North and West, where isolated and dead-end jobs are at least better paid.

Estimates of educational selectivity in migration support Dewey's point. Out-migration of whites from the South appears heaviest at the lowest levels of education, while out-migration among Negroes appears lowest at these levels. For example, between 1940 and 1950 the rate of net emigration from the South of Negroes who had no education was 4 percent, while the rate increased with educational attainment to nearly 20 percent at the high school and college levels.[7] Between 1955 and 1960, the net emigration of Negro males between twenty-five and twenty-nine years of age with four years of college was 14.2 percent, compared with 7 percent for whites in the same age group with comparable education. Of all Negroes in the nation over the age of twenty-four who had completed four or more years of college, 55 percent were living in the South in 1950; by 1960, this proportion had declined to 48 percent. Also, between 1950 and 1960 the proportion of Negro professional and technical workers living in the South declined from 67 percent to 40 percent, while the proportion of Negro laborers declined only from 66 to 63 percent.

One may appropriately question whether the South will be able to continue its recent economic progress if its best-trained and most competent Negroes continue to leave and those who are less productive remain behind, adding to its labor surpluses. If job opportunities for low-skilled workers in other regions should continue to fail to expand, due to current technology and its demand for a higher-skilled labor force, the movement of such Negroes out of the South will be slowed. Consequently, competition for nonagricultural employment within the region will be stronger. This could mean that the problem of finding employment for the population will become more acute. On the other hand, if racial barriers to employment are effectively diminished and Negroes are given full opportunity to compete for jobs in Southern labor markets, the total level of employment and income in the South could be raised. Not only would there be expanded markets for goods and services, but discontent and disruption arising from a denial of opportunity to Negroes would be lessened and the South's chances of attracting and holding industries would be enhanced.

After this general outline of economic change and progress in the South, we can examine regional differences in economic opportunity for Negroes as indicated by employment and income data.

□ Income, Race, and Regions

Income is a result of economic participation; probably no other single statistical measure indicates so well the extent to which the general population is sharing in the fruits of industrial progress.[8]

The most significant improvements in the incomes of Negroes have come during the past two decades. Prior to World War II, large numbers of Negroes in the rural South were impoverished, and others in urban slums depended on the lowest-paid factory and service jobs for a living. Since 1940 the number of Negroes employed in non-farm occupations has practically doubled, from about 3.1 to 6 million. This means, of course, that more Negroes have money. Moreover, the distribution of income among Negroes has improved, and the large-scale migration of Negroes from rural to urban areas and to central cities has resulted in a significant concentration of purchasing power among Negroes. The recent economic advancement of Negroes is marked by a significant growth in their aggregate income of approximately 700 percent between 1939 and 1961. It is estimated that aggregate income of Negroes was nearly $22 billion per year, or about 5 percent of the total personal income of the nation. It is further estimated that Negro purchases account for just over $500 million, or 15 percent, of retail sales in Houston; in Atlanta, Georgia, the estimate is $306 million, or 17 percent; and in Memphis, Tennessee, about $204 million, or 24 percent.

Such advances in income and purchases, when taken as a whole, present a picture much different from that of two or three decades ago, when the Negro population constituted a relatively insignificant market for goods and services. However, these gains, along with the few made in housing, education, and occupational distribution, have led to the rather widespread assumption that the economic gap between the Negro population and the white population is constantly narrowing. Such an assumption is false, for it ignores the fact that while Negroes have been making gains, whites have gained even more.

Negroes have shown a remarkable inability to break away from poverty. The *Economic Report of the President* for 1964 indicated that between 1947 and 1962 the number of Negro families living in poverty—i.e., those with less than $3,000 per year based on 1962 prices—declined only 3 percent, as compared with a 27 percent decline in the number of white families similarly situated.[9] In 1962, 44 percent of all Negro families in the country were living in poverty, compared with 17 percent of all white families. Among Negro rural families on farms, 84 percent were living in poverty; and 85 percent of all Negro rural farm families were living in the South.

Negro families experienced about the same rate of growth in average income as white families between 1947 and 1962, although in absolute or dollar terms the growth was much greater for white families. The average income of Negro families increased by about 106 percent, from $1600 to $3300, compared with a 98 percent increase for white families, from $3200 to $6200. However, the gains made by Negro families were made during the first half of the period, and Negroes lost ground during the second half. Between 1947 and 1955, the average income of Negro families rose 58 percent and that of white families only 46 percent, but between 1955 and 1962 the income of white families rose 35 percent and that of Negro families only 31 percent.

The relatively low average income of Negro families in 1962 is in part due to the fact that about one half of all Negro families are still living in the South, where the average family income of both white and Negro populations is low; moreover, the ratio of Negro to white family income is below the national figure. For regions outside the South, this ratio was about two thirds in 1962, whereas in the South it was less than one half.

Statistics on individual incomes also show that the most significant economic gains by Negro males came before 1955. Since that time they have not progressed as well. In 1939, the average annual wage and salary income of Negro males in the United States was $460, or 41 percent of that of white males, $1112. By 1955 the figure for Negroes had risen to $2342, equal to about 59 percent of the $3986 for whites. From 1955 to 1960, the income position of Negroes relative to that of whites remained about 60 percent, but by 1962 the ratio had dropped to 55 percent.

These data are for all males fourteen years of age and over

who had wage and salary income. Among other things, they reflect higher rates of part-time work and unemployment among Negroes. But the same trend is shown by data on the wage and salary income of year-round, full-time workers. The average wage and salary income of Negroes who worked full-time during 1955 was 64 percent that of white workers. This represents a gain of 19 percent over 1939, when the ratio was 45 percent. By 1960 the ratio was 70 percent, but it dropped to 66 percent in 1961 and to 63 percent in 1962, lower than the ratio in 1955.

Trends since 1955, of course, do not obviate the fact that over the longer period since 1939 growth in the income of Negroes has been greater than that of whites, thus narrowing the relative difference in income between the two groups.

On the other hand, the absolute, or dollar, difference between white and Negro family and individual incomes has increased to over three times what it was in 1939. Thus, while the ratio of the earnings of Negroes to whites among those employed full-time increased from 45 percent in 1939 to a high of 67 percent in 1960, the dollar gap between the two groups increased from $780 to $1873; and when the ratio dropped to 63 percent in 1962, the dollar gap expanded to $2226.

This continual widening of the dollar difference is a significant dimension of the economic trap in which Negroes are caught. Relative improvements in the Negro's economic status do not adequately alter the situation. People do not spend and save percentages; they spend and save dollars. Assessments of the economic position of Negroes that are confined to acceleration concepts and percentage gains obscure the real predicament: Negroes are losing rather than gaining ground in reaching dollar parity with whites.

The rather rapid growth in Negro incomes on the one hand and the continuing expansion in the earnings gap between Negroes and whites on the other is explained by two factors. First, the earnings of Negroes have been depressed over a long period of time and were little changed prior to 1940. Thus, relatively small increments in income produce striking percentage gains. The second factor is perhaps more significant. A small proportion of Negroes are finding jobs in industries and occupations where there is stability in employment and occupational mobility. A much larger proportion of whites are acquiring the highest paying jobs in the higher occupational classifications. The gains achieved by Negroes before 1955 were related to shortages in manpower and a government wage policy which permitted wage increases only for low-paid workers. Since then, increases in wages and salaries have been greater in highly paid occupations, in which whites are concentrated, than in low-paying jobs, where most Negroes are employed.[10]

Whether the difference is reckoned in dollars or percentage points, it is clear that Negroes are at a disadvantage in securing the amenities of life at a level comparable to that of other members of the population, particularly in the South. The average individual income of Negro workers in the South is just above two fifths, 44 percent, that of whites; in other regions it is over two thirds. Moreover, full-time Negro workers outside the South earn an average of 73 to 80 percent of what their white counterparts earn. Further, Southern Negroes on the average have incomes equal to about 43 percent of the income of non-Southern Negroes, while Southern whites average about 73 percent of the average income of whites outside the South.

According to data provided by the decennial censuses of eleven Southern states, Florida was the only one in which the ratio of Negro to white income for male workers improved between 1950 and 1960. In the other states the ratio declined over a range from 3 points, in Virginia, to 13.4 points, in Arkansas. It is also worth noting that Florida was the only Southern state to experience a significant net in-migration of Negroes during the period; moreover, in 1963 Florida had the highest per capita income, $2011, of all the Southern states.

No doubt the development of space industries, as well as the movement of persons to Florida to retire, contributed to Florida's unique position.

Regional differences in economic opportunity are further reflected by data relating education and income. The average wage and salary income of non-Southern Negro males thirty-five to forty-four years of age with high school educations was $4692, about 78 percent that of corresponding white males, $5992. In the South, on the other hand, the same group of Negroes had average earnings of $3163, about 57 percent that of the $5568 averaged by their white counterparts.

If we consider occupation along with educational level, regional discrepancies still hold. Negro males outside the South, thirty-five to forty-four years of age, with four or more years of college, and working in professional and technical occupations, earned an average of $6876, 77 percent that of the average white male income, $8900. In the South the ratio was 56 percent, with Negro income averaging $4808 and white, $8534. While Southern whites in the group under consideration had incomes equal to 96 percent of those of non-Southern whites, Southern Negroes had incomes equal to only 79 percent of those of non-Southern Negroes. Such patterns prevail regardless of the age-occupation-education combination involved.

Discrepancies between the economic advancement of Negroes in the South and those in other parts of the country reflect not only the general lag in Southern progress but also a substantial lag in employment and occupational opportunity for Southern Negroes.

□ Employment, Race, and Regions

The growth in wage and salary income among Negro workers since 1940 resulted in part from improvements in the occupational structure of the Negro labor force. On the other hand, occupational advances have not come to Negroes as rapidly in recent years as they did prior to the middle 1950's;

where occupational advances were made, Negroes entered at lower levels; and the occupations they entered were characterized by low labor demand and declining importance in the economy. In contrast to earlier periods, when advances in technology were a positive force for urban Negro workers, the current manpower revolution due to technological advancement is working against them.

Before the late 1950's improvement in technology brought with it more complex machinery, some of which was operated by members of the Negro labor force. Consequently, many Negroes were pushed up the occupational ladder, even though their function or their place in industry didn't change. For example, technology revolutionized the handling of materials in industry, a function traditionally carried out by Negro workers. As concrete-mixing trucks replaced wheelbarrows, and lightweight cranes and lifting machines came into use in warehouses, the men who had handled the wheelbarrows and lifted the crates became the operators of the new machines. Negroes certainly seemed the natural candidates to operate lifting machines, conveyors, tractors, and trucks. Technological progress, however, has not served Negroes well. Not only have jobs for many workers in the coal mines and other industries been eliminated by technology, but many traditional "Negro jobs" have become "white man's work." [11] As long as a job was hot and sticky, Negro labor was used; as it became clean, comfortable, and oriented toward push-button controls, Negro labor was displaced by white. The most obvious case in point is that of food service, now handled largely by white females. As whites pursue jobs once "reserved" for Negroes, the competitive position of Negroes in the labor market becomes more disadvantageous. Negroes competing for jobs not only must overcome racial barriers but they are limited in occupational mobility by the low level to which they have been assigned in the structure of the total labor force.

When Negroes made their break with Southern agriculture and moved into urban labor markets they failed to get a real toehold. Consequently, what appeared in the early postwar period as a real prospect for large-scale movement of Negroes away from poverty and into the mainstream of the nation's prosperity has in effect been thwarted by major alterations in the economic environment and by new manpower requirements.

What happened was that many Negroes were forced out of Southern agriculture by progress in farm technology and mechanization and were pulled into the war and postwar economy by new opportunities. They were able to get and hold jobs outside of agriculture. The point is that in a full employment economy that can absorb routine labor, Negroes dislocated by technological advances had somewhere to go. This was good! The situation is different today. Sources of employment upon which the masses of Negroes have been forced to depend either are not expanding or are expanding very slowly. The Negro worker who is pushed out of Southern agriculture, who is employed in a low-skilled occupation, or who is denied opportunity to compete for higher-skilled jobs has virtually no place to go under conditions of present-day manpower demands, technological change, and structural shifts in industrial employment.

Technology has contributed substantially to curtailed employment of industrial operatives, laborers, and other manual workers. A shift to non-production workers in manufacturing and other industries has involved a sharp rise in the demand for scientists, technicians, office workers, professionals, salespeople, and administrators. New occupations have accompanied the development of new industries, such as those associated with space programs, and have also developed within existing industries.

In the long run, technological progress is an important source of industrial expansion, essential to industrial and economic progress. And over periods of time the labor force should be able to adjust to technological change. But the impact of technological progress in modern days is sharp and decisive, and adjustments to it are not spread over long periods of time. Those who adjust readily are rewarded; those who cannot do so are left behind. Moreover, labor force and unemployment patterns suggest that long-run adjustments will become increasingly difficult to achieve. Radical adjustment in manpower development is a necessity for Negroes and other groups in the economy who are disadvantaged by limited skills, education, and training and for those who are trapped in occupations of diminishing importance. In the absence of a full-employment economy (here defined to mean a job for everybody who wants a job and not just 3 percent unemployment) and large-scale manpower adjustments, Negroes cannot expect the forces of national economic growth to generate improvement in employment opportunity comparable to that of the years prior to the middle 1950's.

Three indicators provide meaningful evidence of structural transition in the economy. A brief examination of the shifts involved will suggest the special meaning they hold for Negro workers.

The economy is involved in a basic shift in employment from goods-producing to service-producing industries. In 1949, the service-producing industries—government, finance, insurance, real estate, trade transportation, public utilities, business and professional services, and household services—became the major source of employment in the economy. The proportion of the nation's work force employed in goods-producing industries—manufacturing, mining, construction, and agriculture—declined from 51 percent of the total in 1947 to 40 percent of the total in 1963. The rate of decline was only 4 percent during the ten-year period between 1947 and 1957. It was twice that during the next six years.

The year 1956 was the peak year of employment in nonagricultural goods-producing industries. Since 1956, these industries have experienced a rather sharp decline in their proportion of national employment. There has been a continual decrease in employment in mining and agriculture, and employment in manufacturing and contract construction has failed to expand.

Employment in mining declined 51 percent, from about

955,000 in 1947 to about 632,000 in 1963, a loss of 323,000 workers. Employment in agriculture declined about 3 million between 1947 and 1962, an average of about 200,000 per year; and from 1962 to 1963 employment in agriculture declined 250,000. Employment in contract construction showed an upturn between 1962 and 1963 from previous downward trends. However, neither manufacturing nor contract construction expanded beyond their postwar peaks—for manufacturing, 17.5 million in 1953 and 17.2 million in 1956; and for construction, about 3 million in 1956. The annual average employment in manufacturing was about 17 million in 1963, and in construction, about 3 million.

There is a marked trend in employment away from traditional plant and production jobs to office and nonproduction jobs. This shows up rather clearly in manufacturing, where employment has not been expanding because increases in the number of nonproduction employed were insufficient to offset the decline in the number of production workers.

Manufacturing absorbed 15.5 million workers in 1947. Just over 2.5 million, or 17 out of every 100, were in nonproduction jobs. By 1956, manufacturing employment had increased 1.5 million to 17 million workers. However, the increase was made up almost entirely of nonproduction workers. Employment in nonproduction manufacturing jobs increased 1.9 million between 1947 and 1963. A decline of over 404,000 production workers offset this increase and yielded a net increase in manufacturing employment of 1.5 million. Since 1947, nonproduction workers increased their share of total employment in manufacturing from 16.1 percent to 26 percent.

Current manpower demands attach increasing importance to white-collar occupations. In 1956, for the first time in its history, the American economy, utilized more white-collar than blue-collar workers. The share of nonfarm employment held by blue-collar workers—craftsmen, operatives, foremen, and laborers—declined from 41 percent in 1947 to 36 percent in 1963, while the share of employment held by white-collar workers—professionals, technicians, clerical workers, sales people, and nonfarm managers and officials increased from 35 percent to 44 percent. White-collar employment grew 10 million between 1947 and 1963, while blue-collar employment grew only 1.4 million.

These trends have special meaning to Negro workers. In the first place, the declining areas of employment are those upon which Negro workers have had to depend. Much of the improvement in the economic status of Negro masses resulted from their movement out of agriculture and into manufacturing, mining, and construction; and into blue-collar occupations, as semiskilled operatives and nonfarm laborers. By the same token, Negroes have had only limited success in penetrating the occupations in which employment is expanding. Their representation in the service-producing industries such as finance, insurance, real estate, trade, public utilities, and public administration has been relatively limited. The principal exception to these has been clerical employment in non-Southern state governments and in the Federal establishment outside the South, including Washington, D.C. Moreover, where Negroes have penetrated the expanding areas of service-producing industries they have been largely confined, particularly in the South, to the segregated areas of the economy, thereby being limited in range of employment and earning potential.

Changes in industrial sources of employment, as well as in manpower demands, means that employment opportunity in semiskilled and unskilled work is likely to continue to decline. The occupational structure of the Negro labor force is overwhelmingly skewed toward low-skilled occupations, and while there have been improvements, there has been no fundamental alteration beyond the significant decline in the proportion of Negroes employed in farming.

Permeating the problem is the nation's recent economic performance. In the years since 1958, a year of recession from which there has been only imperfect recovery, the economy has been unable to generate jobs in sufficient numbers to absorb the growing labor force. The labor force is expected to increase 1.2 million a year during the next few years.[12] This factor, together with dislocations in employment accompanying technological advances, preys very heavily upon Negro workers who, because of educational deficiencies and low occupational attainment, lag in making adjustments to economic transition, the effects of which are both cumulative and intense.

Continual improvements in education and in occupational achievements have not significantly altered the disadvantaged place of Negroes in the job market, especially in the South. Employment among Negro males in the United States increased by 800,000 between 1940 and 1960, from about 3.1 million to 3.9 million; and among Negro females by about one million, from about 1.6 million to 2.6 million. The increases were approximately 26 percent for Negro males and 63 percent for Negro females. The striking feature, however, is that the entire growth in Negro employment occurred outside the South. The number of Negro males employed in the South was about 2.2 million in 1940, but it had declined to 1.9 million by 1960; employment among Negro females in the South was about 1.1 million in 1940, and it had increased only 150,000 by 1960. The net effect was that total Negro employment in the South declined about 5 percent during the twenty-year period, while in other regions it increased about 1.8 million, or 147 percent.

It has already been suggested that regional differences in employment account in large measure for differences between the income of Negroes in the South and their incomes in other regions, as well as for the high rates of migration of Negroes from Southern states. Indeed, in none of the major industry categories did Negro employment in the South keep pace with Negro employment in other regions. In 1960, Southern Negroes had a smaller share of the jobs in every industry, except government, than they had in 1950. There were, of course, fewer Negroes in the South in 1960 than there had been earlier, and there were fewer opportunities open there. The situation brings up a chicken and egg question. Were there fewer jobs because of fewer people, or did people leave because the jobs were not there?

The fact is that Negroes make up only slightly less of the employed Southern labor force today, 19 percent, than they did a decade ago, with 21 percent. In each area of industry employment, the decline in Negro employment exceeds the decline in Negro labor force.

The unfavorable position of Negro workers in Southern labor markets is further indicated by their occupational attachments. The proportion of Negro males employed in white-collar occupations outside the South was 17.2 percent, two and one-half times that in the South; for Negro females the proportions were 24.5 percent outside the South and 11.5 percent in the South. (The more favorable comparison for females reflects the high number in the South who teach in the public schools.) Furthermore, between 1940 and 1960 the difference in employment ratios between white and Negro females outside the South engaged in white-collar occupations narrowed from 44 percent to 25 percent, while in the South the difference expanded from 44 to 47 percent. During the same period the difference between the proportion of white and Negro males in white-collar occupations expanded from 22 percent to 29 percent in the South while little change was shown for other regions. Generally, in comparison to the total labor force, Negroes both within and outside the South hold only a relatively small share of the jobs above the semiskilled level and a disproportionate share of jobs as household workers, and as farm and nonfarm laborers.

□ Negro Employment in the South: Two Studies

What Negroes are up against in the South is pinpointed by two recent studies conducted at Fisk University; one was on industrial employment and the other on government employment.

Industrial Employment [13]

The extent to which Negroes are disadvantaged in access to industrial jobs was indicated in a study of 372 firms holding contracts with the Federal Government. These firms, located in four Southern states—63 in Kentucky, 53 in South Carolina, 149 in North Carolina, and 107 in Tennessee—employed a total of 88,727 workers. Of these workers, 12,509, or approximately 14 percent of the total, were Negroes, while the number of Negroes in the four states involved amounted to about 21 percent of the population. These were some of the findings of the study:

1. About 27 percent of the firms had no Negro employees at all. In Kentucky, 40 percent of the firms were all white; in Tennessee, 32 percent; and in North and South Carolina, 20 percent. In other words, despite the influence of government contracts and the equal employment practices provisions of Executive Order 10925, Negro work opportunities were denied by one fifth to two fifths of Southern firms.

2. The number of Negro workers in firms that did hire Negroes throws further light on the situation. In slightly more than one third of the Tennessee firms the number of Negro employees was four or fewer. In South Carolina, 37 percent of the firms had fewer than 10 Negro workers. In North Carolina, where the average number of employees was 363, the average number of Negro workers was only about 20.

3. The most glaring disparity, in quantitative terms, was in opportunities for Negro females. In all the Kentucky firms only fourteen Negro women were employed. Only 3.5 percent of the North Carolina firms had at least one Negro female, while 76 percent had white female employees. In South Carolina 17 percent of the firms employed some Negro women while 80 percent employed white women.

Study of the qualitative aspects of employment practice reveals even more the scope of job discrimination in Southern firms. If he somehow manages to get a job in industry, the Negro employee finds himself employed at menial tasks and in a dead end situation, as indicated in these findings:

1. The dominant and consistent pattern of Negro employment in the firms studied was the heavy concentration of Negroes in the unskilled and service jobs. Among the Tennessee firms, 61 percent employed whites in jobs classified as skilled, while only 32 percent employed at least one Negro worker in such a capacity. Negro workers in skilled jobs were found in only 25 percent of Kentucky firms, and in 40 percent of firms in North and South Carolina.

2. In only about 5 percent of the firms were Negroes employed in supervisory jobs. None of the firms in South Carolina had Negroes in professional or technical jobs, and only 2.8 percent of the firms in North Carolina had Negro professional and technical workers.

3. The pattern of promotions indicated the restrictive nature of Negro employment opportunity. Of North Carolina's 149 firms, with more than 7,000 Negro workers, 58 percent had not upgraded a single Negro worker in recent experience. The same was true of 50 percent of firms in Tennessee, 44 percent in South Carolina, and 66 percent in Kentucky. Where the percentage of firms upgrading Negroes may appear favorably high, the finding is substantially qualified by the small number of Negroes actually promoted. The North Carolina report indicated that in the thirty-nine firms in which Negroes were upgraded an average of only two or three workers were involved. These experiences warrant the conclusion that on the whole, upgrading of Negro workers has been negligible.

During the fall of 1964 an informal follow-up inquiry was made in nineteen of the Tennessee firms included in the 1961 study. Seven of these had reported no Negro employees in 1961; in 1964 five of the seven had hired one or more Negroes, and one firm had hired a Negro girl in a clerical capacity. Of the twelve firms that reported one or more Negro employees in 1961, but none in professional or technical jobs, three had upgraded or hired one or more Negroes in professional positions, and one firm had promoted at least one Negro to a technical job. Of the remaining firms, three reported that they had upgraded one or more Negroes into traditionally white jobs, such as on the production line, where they worked side by side with white workers. Five firms reported no Negroes above the rank of janitor or maid, no change from 1961.

The changes indicated are breakthroughs, and no doubt important ones. Yet there has been no significant alteration of employment patterns in the nineteen firms with regard to the Negro labor force. One manager did make the point, however, that if he could expand his operations and hire new workers, Negroes would have full access to the jobs.

Meanwhile, there are isolated instances of significant change in employment practices in firms not included in the 1961 study. One such case was found in Hardeman County, Tennessee, a poor county. An electronics plant that three years ago hired no Negroes above the janitorial level now has Negro female workers working side by side with white females on the assembly line, and discriminatory signs are absent from the plant arrangements. There are about 20 Negroes out of approximately 150 employees.

Employment in Government [14]

The second study was of employment in the Tennessee state government. It involved 17,295 employees, or about 85 percent of all state employees except those working in educational institutions, and was completed in December, 1962. It offers the following examples of the problems Negroes face in securing employment in public administration in the South.

1. Of 1,216 job classifications for employees in the Tennessee state government, Negroes were found to have access to only 115, or 9.5 percent. The other 90.5 percent of the occupations in state employment were closed to them.

2. The range of occupational choice was even more limited in several departments. It was found, for example, that the Department of Highways employed over 6,000 persons during the year but only 55, or 9 percent, were Negroes, and out of 228 occupational classes, Negroes had access to only 8, or 3.4 percent. In the Department of Insurance and Banking only 9 of the 209 persons employed were Negroes; they had access to only 3 of the 91 job classes. The job classes most frequently occupied by Negroes were maid, janitor, porter, and messenger.

3. In areas of employment where Negroes could be easily

segregated in employment and serve other Negroes, they fared better. This was the case in the Department of Public Welfare and in the health services. In the Mental Health Department there were 22 job classes and Negroes were found in 17, or 73 percent. The Departments of Mental Health and Public Health together had 797 Negro workers, amounting to 65 percent of all Negro employees in state agencies.

4. Most Negroes were in jobs of low classification, in contrast to the general concentration in the high-level jobs. More than one-half of the Negro workers, 51 percent, were in unskilled jobs, compared with about 10 percent for all employees. Only 19.7 percent of the Negro workers were in white-collar jobs, compared with 65 percent of all workers. Only 1.5 percent of all Negro workers were in clerical jobs, compared with 20 percent of all workers. There were just 132 Negro professional workers in the entire state, amounting to 11.3 percent of the Negro total. Of state employees as a whole, 35 percent were in jobs at the professional level.

Government employment and public administration have been expanding and the attraction of such opportunity outside the South has been a major motivation for the migration of able Southern Negroes. A relative accessibility of clerical jobs, for example, in state and Federal agencies outside the South is a significant factor in the advantage non-Southern Negroes hold over Southern Negroes in white-collar employment.

Just as with the industrial firms, a few breakthroughs have occurred in the Tennessee state government since this study. As of the fall of 1964, about twenty Negroes had been employed in several agencies and departments in nontraditional categories.

□ Summary

This inquiry was begun with the observation that the magnitude of racial discrimination in labor markets makes it necessary to exert extraordinary efforts in the South to achieve equal employment opportunities for Negroes under the 1964 Civil Rights Act. Not only do non-Southern states have a longer history of experience with fair-employment legislation, but there is evidence of effective results.[15]

It is recognized that not all present underemployment and labor use problems pertaining to Negroes can be attributed to racial discrimination. Sometimes opportunities exist for Negroes that only a few take; and deficiencies in education and training limit the number of Negroes who qualify. Still, those in the South who do qualify for employment must usually migrate to other regions to make use of their abilities. There is little evidence that improved education has influenced in a significant way job opportunities for Negroes who remain in the South. Total employment among Negroes in the South has not increased during the past twenty years, while it has gone up almost two million outside the region. Thus the South not only loses abilities and productive potential, but it retains a disproportionate amount of unproductive and low-skilled labor, which retards the region's economic progress. There are many jobs in the South for which Negroes do qualify and from which they are presently excluded solely because of race. Opportunities for the South to upgrade its labor force and expand employment opportunities under existing Federal programs are being jeopardized by its rigid adherence to traditional racial patterns. There have been cases in Louisiana and Mississippi where communities have declined to participate in programs under the Manpower Development and Training Act solely because such participation would require them to integrate whites and Negroes in the programs.[16]

Negroes in the South are becoming more urbanized. It is apparent that, in the absence of major changes in the use of the Negro labor force, Southern poverty will be concentrated not in the rural areas but in the cities by the end of the next decade. The disadvantaged position of Negroes in the labor market is complicated by shifts in industry sources of employment and by new manpower demands; in addition, the economy has not been able to generate jobs in sufficient numbers to absorb the growing labor force. Unemployment has been expanding along with employment, and its impact upon Negro workers is more than twice that for whites. Quite obviously, therefore, an economy striving for full employment is important to Negro economic progress both in the North and in the South. Vigorous application of fair-employment policy, along with equality of education and training, are also necessary if Southern Negroes are to experience improved employment opportunities and the South is to match the rest of the nation in economic well-being.

NOTES

1. Edgar Dunn, *Recent Southern Economic Development* (Gainesville: Univ. of Florida Press, 1962), p. 8.
2. Several studies of Negro employment in the South support these generalizations. See John Hope II, "The Problem of Unemployment As It Relates to Negroes," Studies in Unemployment, Special Committee on Employment Problems, United States Senate, 86th Congress, 2nd Session; Donald Dewey, "Studies on Negro Employment in the Upper South," in *Selected Studies of Negro Employment in the South* (Washington: National Planning Association, 1955).
3. Dunn, *op. cit.*, p. 13. See also William Nichols, *Southern Tradition and Regional Progress* (Chapel Hill: Univ. of North Carolina Press, 1960).
4. United States Bureau of the Census, *Current Population Reports,* No. 247, April 2, 1962.
5. *Ibid.*
6. Donald Dewey, "Negro Employment in Southern Industry," *The Journal of Political Economy*. LX, No. 4 (August 1952), p. 279.
7. C. Horace Hamilton, "Educational Selectivity of Net Migration from the South," *Social Forces,* XXXVI, No. 1 (October 1959), p. 33.

8. Herman P. Miller, *Income of the American People* (New York: Wiley, 1955), p. 7.
9. The data used are for nonwhites. However, since Negroes make up about 95 percent of the nonwhites in the country, it is assumed that what is given for nonwhites is applicable to Negroes.
10. *Manpower Report of the President,* March 1964, p. 106.
11. Gunnar Myrdal, *An American Dilemma* (New York: Harper, 1944), p. 282.
12. *Manpower Report of the President,* March 1964, p. 17.
13. This study was conducted in 1961 by the Department of Race Relations of the Board of Homeland Ministries of the United Church of Christ at Fisk University. It was under the direction of John Hope II, with assistance by the author. See Herman H. Long, "Patterns of Negro Use in Selected Southern Industries," *Equal Employment Opportunity* (Hearings before the Special Subcommittee on Labor, Committee on Education and Labor, House of Representatives, 87th Congress, 2nd Session, January 15–24, 1962).
14. Herman H. Long and Vivian W. Henderson, *Jobs and Color: Negro Employment in Tennessee State Government* (Nashville: Tennessee Council on Human Relations, 1962).
15. See Paul H. Norgren and Samuel E. Hill, *Toward Fair Employment* (New York: Columbia Univ. Press, 1964).
16. J. Earl Williams, "The Effects of Social Institutions on Retraining in the South" (Paper given at the Conference on the Manpower Revolution and Human Resource Adjustment, Charlotte, N.C., December 9–11, 1964).

The Social Effects of Negro Unemployment

4 / Bringin' Up the Rear

Paul Jacobs

> "What's new?"
> "Nothing. Same old story. White man's still ahead, niggers bringin' up the rear."

Early every weekday morning Herman Holmes wakes to the hum of speeding auto engines and rolling tires. Holmes lives in a small frame house on a dead-end street almost at the city limits of Oakland, California, just a few hundred feet from the Nimitz Freeway. Inside the shabby, unpainted home, Holmes, a muscular, stocky, twenty-nine-year-old, dark-skinned Negro, sleeps with his wife in a tiny bedroom, their six-month-old infant in a crib alongside them. Five other Holmes children sprawl over another bed in a small room next to their parents'.

On those weekday mornings when there is still some gas left in the tank of his car and he can spare fifty cents for the bridge tolls, Holmes drives his 1958 Edsel across the Bay

Bridge to San Francisco, where his union hall is located. Holmes, who came to California a few years ago from Louisiana, is a member of the Hod Carriers and Common Laborers Union, and he must check in at the local union office every few days so that the dispatcher knows he is available for work. But construction work has been slow, and as Holmes drives across the bridge, listening to the ominous thump in the rear end of his car, he thinks back to when he was a little boy in Shreveport, Louisiana. Then he had wanted to own a café, so he could be rich and eat anything. Now he, his wife, and kids eat mostly beans, rice, and the canned apricots that Mrs. Holmes bought when they were put on sale at a very low price because the cans were bent and crushed.

Three thousand miles away, across the country, in the unincorporated town of Immokalee, Florida, at the very edge of the marshy Everglades, the Quarter starts to come alive at about the same time as Holmes awakens. The Quarter is the section of town east of the highway where the Negroes live, and the cycle of life inside it is dependent upon the growing seasons. In the spring and the late fall, when the crops are harvested, the Quarter is wide awake by 5:30 A.M., but from July to October, when there is little work to do, only a few farm worker buses load up at 6:30 near Mrs. Mac's Good Eats Café. During those hot summer months most of the people in the Quarter sleep till 8:00 or 9:00 A.M., tossing restlessly in their tiny dilapidated shacks, trying uselessly to push aside the blanket of moist heat that weighs them down.

But in rural Florida, underemployment rather than unemployment is the characteristic mode of life. Work and joblessness blend together, just as in the nearby marshes the land and water merge into one. No unemployment insurance check marks a shift to unemployment, nor is there a general relief program for which the farm workers are eligible if they run out of money.

"If you think about it, it's a miserable life," says Hewitt Howard, who owns a truck and lives in one of the best houses in the Quarter, "so I try not to think about it."

"The colored have the sorriest jobs in Oklahoma City," says the white man with a belly so enormous he can fit himself only with difficulty into the seat of his pickup truck. At the Armour Company plant he worked as a skilled cooper. Now he rebuilds television tubes, and every week or so he delivers one to Jack Johnson, a Negro who also worked at Armour and is now trying to earn a living as a television repairman.

"It was an awful shock when the plant closed," says Johnson, a slight man who wears glasses and is in his late forties. "I'd been working at Armour since 1943 and being there so long I didn't know about unemployment. I was out of work for a year and we just managed to get by. I was luckier than most of them because my car and house were paid for and the only payments I had to make was forty-one dollars a month for an improvement loan I'd taken out before I knew the plant was going to close. But the worst thing about it was that you didn't have any money in your pocket."

Fortunately, John Thompson of San Francisco never suffered from any lack of pocket money during the four months in which he was looking for a job as a computer programmer. Thompson, a six-foot five-inch Negro, just forty years of age, had been a master sergeant in the Army, earning $600 a month, until he retired in 1963 with twenty years of service. But even though he didn't suffer from a lack of money while he was jobless, he did suffer a different kind of loss: after four months of answering ads, making applications, and checking with employment services, he had to take a job as key-punch operator, the lowest classification held by any of the eighteen civilians he had supervised in the Army.

Bitterly, the ex-sergeant says, "The worst mistake I ever made in my life was leaving the Army."

Franky-Boy, who will be eighteen years old on his next birthday, will never get a chance to make Thompson's mistake. The Army won't take him. He'll fail the mental test; he can barely read and his police record is bad: Franky-Boy had been "busted" three times before he was seventeen, twice for fairly serious offenses. Franky-Boy lives in San Francisco, too, but his counterparts can be found on any street in Harlem, on the South Side of Chicago, or in any other Northern urban Negro ghetto.

It's very hard to understand Franky-Boy when he talks, and no one jammed with him in the crowded apartment where he lives speaks very clear English either. Sometimes even the boys in his gang find it hard to make out what he is mumbling as they stand on the corner discussing how to get a car or new clothes. Their conversation rarely touches on working. Instead, Franky-Boy concentrates on getting the right kind of "konk" in his hair, and he doesn't worry whether the dyed "peacock" tuft in front or the heavy grease he uses to slick it straight up in the back and the sides will upset a prospective employer.

Franky-Boy gets up around noon and doesn't bother going out to look for work. Instead, he pours some dry breakfast food out of a box, fools around with his younger brothers, watches television, fixes his hair, and in the middle of the afternoon leaves the apartment in the public housing project to meet his friends down on the street. Then they just "mess around" the pool hall until the evening, when they'll mess around some more, maybe this time with their girls in someone's apartment.

"That's all I do," says Franky-Boy, "just mess around."

When Franky-Boy, Herman Holmes, Jack Johnson, Hewitt Howard, and John Thompson are unemployed, all of them are listed in the statistical breakdowns as "nonwhite." But they have very little else in common. Their accents vary from Southern drawl to Northern abrupt; their vocabularies range from Franky-Boy's very limited typical lower-class slurring to Thompson's proper use of a far more extensive range of words, clearly pronounced. Their histories reflect a wide variety of regional differences and distinctions between family structure, education, and skills. Their work records, too, are dissimilar, their aspirations vary, and they have developed sharply different methods of translating aspirations into reality.

Even when he was a little boy growing up in San Anselmo,

Texas, Sergeant Thompson wanted to be a soldier. "I was nuts about uniforms, although I don't know why," he says, since there were no military men in his family. His father was a handyman in a gas station who also drove a wrecking car and cleaned up an auto agency showroom in town. His mother was a beautician, operating one of the beauty shops that served the five thousand Negroes who made up about six percent of San Anselmo's total population. Thompson had a sister, too, and both of them attended the same segregated high school in San Anselmo.

In 1942, when he was eighteen and had graduated from high school, Thompson enlisted in the army. For three and a half years he served overseas and was discharged in 1945 with the rank of T4. He returned home to San Anselmo, but after a few months there decided to reenlist. "I felt deep down that the Army was the only place for me to get a fair shake, the only place I could learn. I knew Texas wasn't the place for me, so I stayed in and reenlisted all the time."

Thompson's feeling about the Army as the only place he could "get a fair shake" and "learn" is shared by many other Negroes. Reenlistment rates in the Army are two to three times as high for Negroes as for whites in most classifications, including even the less-skilled ones.

In 1953 Thompson became a technical sergeant. By this time he was married to an Army librarian he had met at one of his posts. When he retired in 1963, he was a master sergeant in charge of the computer operations of the Sixth Army finance division. He and his wife, who is a college graduate, always lived on Army bases, all his friends were Army personnel, and he had lost much of the day-to-day, acute awareness of being a Negro that he'd grown up with in Texas.

"In the Army, it's all personal, the way you get along. It's not a group thing. You don't think of yourself as being in a race group. You either make it or you don't on your own."

Even now, Thompson isn't certain why he decided to retire. In the first few weeks after he got out, he wasn't very troubled about his prospects for getting a job. He and his wife, who was still working in an Army library, had to find an apartment and settle down to a civilian routine of life, and even though now they had to pay higher rents, they had no serious financial problems because he had his separation allowance and she was still employed.

Very early every morning Thompson read the help-wanted ads in the newspapers. Then he would mail out a few copies of his résumé to a list of companies using RCA computers. He mailed out twenty-five of these but only got three replies, all telling him he was overqualified for any job the company had open.

After spending another hour studying mathematics, Thompson would set out on his job-hunting routine. The search for work took him to the state employment service, which sent him out on four interviews; to the Urban League—"You always go to the Urban League," he says—to all the civil service agencies, and to the companies that advertised in the papers for computer programmers.

Slowly, he became discouraged.

I started out in good faith, but then I began to lose it. They always gave another reason I couldn't get the job. Either they said I was overqualified or they said I didn't have enough experience on their kind of equipment. Sometimes it was because I was too old and sometimes it was because I didn't have a college degree.

Sometimes the ads would call for a programmer, but when I got there they would say the job was filled. But for the next few days I would still see the ad running. Then I'd get all stirred up and think it was the racial thing, but most of the time I thought it was my age or lack of commercial experience. There was only one time I knew it was the race thing, at a bank. I went in to answer an ad with my shoes shined, my suit pressed, and I even had on a new tie. But the lady just looked at me. Those newspaper ads give you a false illusion.

By Christmas of 1963 Thompson and his wife were beginning to feel a financial pinch, even though he was getting $200 a month retirement pay. And he was getting badly worried. "I didn't know how to place my worries. I was looking for a job with a large, stable company where I would know I was going to have steady work. I wanted to hang loose, but nothing was happening to me, so I was worried."

In the afternoons Thompson would go back to his apartment and rest. "It takes three or four hours to fill out one application properly, and usually I'd be so exhausted from the tension of trying to find a job that I'd fall asleep as soon as I got home."

Then, late in the afternoon, he would drive over to the Army post to pick up his wife. They'd come home, eat, and he would read the papers again to check out the ads. After that the two of them would watch television or read some of the books and magazines scattered on tables in the apartment. Occasionally they went to the movies. They saw very few of their old friends from the Army.

Finally, in February 1964, after applying personally at more than twenty companies, Thompson heard through a friend that he might be able to get a job as a key-punch operator at a large utility company. He applied and was hired at $400 a month.

I wouldn't have taken this job if I had any choice, because for me it's like going back to a stick shift after driving automatic. But I'd been out of work since October 31st, and I couldn't stand it any more. And I don't like my job, either. It's boring. I work with four other men and none of them have either my experience or as much education as me. Now my income isn't as big as it was and I don't anticipate that it will ever be as big as it was. So I'm still worried because nothing's happening to me.

Still, Thompson is trying to make something happen to him. He's studying for civil service exams, and he keeps calling on or writing to the companies where he applied for a job as a programmer, hoping to keep his application active.

You have to keep looking up. I waited six months for my first job, so I guess I can wait for my second one. But my attitude is poor to civilian life. I can't get adjusted. The whole thing is bad. I just can't tell you. I guess it's because in the Army, I was a person and now I'm a member of a group. One day I saw a bunch of Negroes picketing the same bank where they wouldn't hire me. But I don't want to get involved with people like that. My character isn't of that kind. The worst mistake I ever made in my life was leaving the Army.

Ex-Sergeant Thompson didn't suffer very much financially during the four months that he was unemployed. And his present situation—working for less pay at below his skill level—might have been duplicated for a white ex-sergeant aged forty. But in one very important way Thompson's experience with unemployment was markedly different from that of a white ex-sergeant: unemployment forced Thompson back into realizing he was a "member of a group." In whatever way he had thought of himself during the twenty years he was in the army—as a combat soldier, as a soldier who was a computer programmer, or as a soldier computer programmer who was also a Negro—he now had to think of himself as being a Negro first.

Initially Thompson didn't become unemployed because he was a Negro, but his being a Negro affected adversely his ability to change his status from soldier to civilian worker. He became part of the statistic that demonstrates that even skilled Negroes stay unemployed longer than whites simply because they are Negro.

Like Thompson, Jack Johnson was also a twenty-year man when he became unemployed. Actually, he'd only worked seventeen years at the Armour Company in Oklahoma City when it closed down and he was retired, involuntarily. Then he learned, too, that being a Negro was a handicap in finding a new job. But that knowledge came as less of a shock for him than it had been for Thompson.

Johnson was born in Oklahoma on a sixty-acre farm that his father owned. He went through a segregated grade school in a little town near the farm and then went on to high school for one year before starting to work on the farm, helping out his father. When he was a restless nineteen, he left Oklahoma and went to Arizona, still doing farm work. From Arizona he came back home and then left again, this time to work in the California crops.

But the Depression was still on then, and farm work was slow. After vainly trying to find a job in Oakland, Johnson came back to Oklahoma City in 1940. For the next three years he worked as a dishwasher, in a garage, in a paint shop, and on a construction gang. Then in 1943 he heard that men were being hired at Armour and got a job there. He worked in the sausage manufacturing department for $.65 a hour. At the time he was the only Negro working in that department, although other Negroes were in the plant, and ten years later more Negroes were hired in sausage manufacturing.

Johnson's entire work life at Armour was in the same department, and over the years he learned to operate all the equipment that was used there. He was earning $2.42 per hour, and his life routine was as fixed as his work shift.

After work he came home to the five-room house he had purchased on a pleasant lower-middle-class street just inside the edge of the Negro area in Oklahoma City. Inside the house, family photos were hung proudly on the walls, and the suite of matched furniture was arranged for easy viewing of the television set. Three times a month he went to meetings of his Masonic Lodge, and twice a month he went to meetings of the board of ushers of his church. Every Sunday he, his wife, his son, and his two daughters went to church. Occasionally he attended union meetings, too, but as he says: "I was never very active in the union. I belonged to it, and I believed in it, but I just didn't want to be active in it."

As his children grew up, finished high school, and went on to get married or, in the case of his son, to begin a career as an Air Force enlisted man, Johnson continued working steadily at Armour. In 1946 he took a night class in radio given in one of the Negro high schools and followed that up with a two-year correspondence course. But he never could get a job in radio because he didn't have any experience, and so he adjusted himself to his routine at Armour.

Johnson, like most other workers in such situations, refused to accept the idea that his plant was going to close, even though it had been rumored in the city for a year. And after a committee set up by the chamber of commerce to investigate the possible closing had announced that the shutdown would not take place, Johnson was reassured enough to take out a loan to remodel his house. When only a few months later the plant did close down, only thirty days' notice was given to the employees.

I was surprised when the plant closed, even though I'd heard the rumors. And being out at Armour so long, I didn't know about unemployment. I thought I could get a job easy, so I didn't even worry much about making the payments for the house remodeling. I even thought I wouldn't be able to take a vacation before I started work. But I learned different pretty quick.

After the plant shut down, Johnson received $1500 in severance pay, but was ineligible for unemployment insurance because of a ruling by the Oklahoma State Employment Service that the Armour workers couldn't get their benefits until they had exhausted their severance pay at the rate at which they would have been drawing the insurance.

In his first days of unemployment, Johnson took a whole group of civil service tests for postal clerk, clerk-carrier, automobile mechanic, warehouseman, and helper. He passed the warehouseman and helper examinations, but no jobs were open. In addition, "I went all over town making applications in small packing plants. But I couldn't find anything in packing. So in October I took a job as a janitor with an insurance company at $1.05 an hour. It kinda bothered me to be getting less than fifty dollars a week after earning more than a hundred."

Johnson's difficulty in finding a new job, even at a much lower rate of pay, was a typical one for nearly all the displaced Armour workers, white and Negro, although the Negro workers suffered more severely than the whites. In the winter of 1960–1961, four to five months after the shutdown, when Johnson was washing out the toilets in the insurance building at night, 53 percent of the displaced workers were still unemployed. And only a small proportion of the men in Johnson's age bracket found any jobs within two weeks after the plant closed. So, too, just as Johnson had to accept employment at far lower wages, the average wage for Negroes working at new jobs during this period was $1.23 an hour lower than what the white displaced workers were now getting paid.

In February 1961 unemployment among the displaced Armour workers was considered so serious that the automation committee, set up under the terms of the contract between the union and the company, offered to pay part of the cost of a retraining program. Forty-six of the people who had been working in the plant when it shut down started some type of training. Johnson quit his janitorial job to take a course in auto mechanics. "I'd rather have taken electronics, but they didn't offer that."

It cost Johnson three hundred dollars of his own money for the six months' auto mechanics course. In addition, he was declared ineligible again for unemployment insurance because he had quit his janitor's job voluntarily to take the training. The automation fund paid the remainder of his tuition. After a six weeks' waiting period he was able to draw thirty-four dollars a week from unemployment insurance, supplemented by six dollars a week he earned for working on cars used in the course.

"We just barely managed to get by. The car was paid for and so was the house, but the improvement loan on the house was forty-one dollars a month, and that was hard to make. It was a good thing that the children were all grown up and out of the house."

Of the forty-six people who took the retraining courses, thirteen were Negroes. Five men started the auto mechanics course, but only three completed it, including Johnson. None of them was able to find a job as a mechanic. And so once again Johnson began his futile job hunting. Eventually he even stopped checking with the employment service. Indeed, only a very small percentage of the Armour workers got jobs through the state employment service, although, before the plant shut down, 76 percent had said they expected to get help from the employment service. After a few weeks Johnson did find work through a friend, cleaning up a movie theater. He worked from 1:00 to 5:00 A.M. every day, including Sunday, and got paid forty dollars a week. A few months later, "I got another job on a tip from a lodge member, driving a delivery truck for a printing company. That job paid me fifty-five dollars a week for five days, eight hours a day."

Characteristically, a higher percentage of ex-Armour Negroes found new jobs on tips from friends than did whites. Because of their inability to get work from the state employment service, Negroes tended to use a widespread informal network in their community to find the poor-paying and menial jobs available to them.

Ultimately, the union was successful in its efforts to negotiate an agreement with the company that provided that discharged workers could transfer to plants of the company in other locations if jobs were available. So Johnson took a job at the Armour plant in Omaha, 466 miles away from Oklahoma City, and began commuting home weekends. He was working on the loading dock, earning $2.76 an hour, and although he was "just buying the bare essentials," it still cost him $55 a week to live in Omaha, sharing an apartment with another worker. In the morning both ate cold breakfasts and then went to work. They brought their lunches and ate their evening meals in restaurants. Nights and weekends when he didn't drive the 932 miles round trip home, Johnson sat in his room watching television or went to church. "I thought about moving my wife up to Omaha, but I didn't want to do it because there were rumors going around that this plant was going to close. I was getting laid off pretty often, too. It was a lonesome time."

Ten months later he got laid off again, and this time the layoff was an extended one. Almost with relief he returned home to Oklahoma City and started looking for work there again, although he still kept in touch with the steward at Armour in Omaha in the hope that a steady job might open up there. Once again Johnson's experience and reactions to moving were typical. Initially, most of the Armour workers indicated a preference for remaining in Oklahoma City rather than moving to a company plant elsewhere. It was not until after months of unemployment or lower-paid employment that these workers were willing to move to a new community if there was a reasonable assurance they could get steady, higher-paid work.

But "everything was slow" in Oklahoma City, and so he took a temporary job, helping out in a television service place, where he was the only Negro employed. There he got eighty dollars a week and began learning to make repairs. He got laid off when the man he had been replacing returned to work. After that layoff, he got a job in a gas station for a week and was then eligible for thirty-eight dollars a week unemployment insurance for six months.

But Johnson wasn't content to just collect the unemployment insurance. Instead, while he was drawing the benefits, he took an eight months' course in electronics at the Oklahoma Institute of Technology. The course cost him $495, which he's still paying off, and he attended classes four hours a night, four nights a week. He did odd jobs, too, during this time, fixing radios to earn some money as a supplement to his unemployment insurance. When the benefits stopped, he got a job, working Saturdays, repairing televisions for fifteen dollars a day.

Today Johnson is working steadily as a repairman, averaging seventy-five dollars a week for five days of work that begin at 8:30 A.M. and end at 7:00 P.M. He gets paid on a piecework basis, and since he's still pretty slow, his income is low. On Saturdays he works at the repair shop where he began, and this fifteen dollars brings his total income up to ninety dollars a week.

Like the ex-sergeant, Jack Johnson vigorously resisted the

idea of remaining unemployed. And he is even less willing than Thompson to attribute his lowered income and desultory employment to being a Negro. Johnson isn't alone in his refusal to acknowledge that his color accounts for his present situation; only a few of the Negroes who worked at Armour said that they thought their color was a primary handicap in finding new employment. "I was forty-six when the plant closed down, and when you're forty you're over the hill already when it comes to getting a job," says Johnson.

Yet the facts are otherwise. The Negro unemployment rate in Oklahoma City is double that of the whites. And despite what Negro ex-Armour workers like Johnson say, the evidence is clear that as a group it has taken them longer to find employment than white workers in similar age groups, and they earn less than their white counterparts.

Being unemployed seemed to have less severe psychological effects on Johnson than on Sergeant Thompson, even though his joblessness lasted longer and was a much greater financial problem. One possible explanation for this is that Thompson's image of himself had become focused on his occupation, on his professional skills, while Johnson's view of his occupational identity was less significant to him. Also, unemployment did not bring with it a confrontation with Negro identity; Johnson never had the same opportunity to forget he was a Negro that Thompson did.

Unlike Thompson, Johnson's life remained inside the Negro ghetto. He left the ghetto to go to work, but he lived inside it, his children went to Negro high schools and colleges, his Masonic lodge was all Negro, and his church was a black one. The one place where Johnson might have developed more than a casual work relation with whites was in the union, but it was there that he participated the least, although usually a church and lodge activist like Johnson tends to be a union activist, too.

Down in Immokalee, Florida, a Negro has even less of a chance to ignore his color than does Johnson in Oklahoma City. The highway that separates Negroes from whites and the Texas Mexicans (who are considered white) isn't only a physical divider but represents the overall separation between the white and Negro communities. Still, Immokalee is a poor town for both the white and nonwhite farm-worker population, although it is not the worst in Florida. It was a lumbering town originally, and large scale agriculture is still a fairly new industry there. No housing is available for the migrants who come in during harvest season, and for years Immokalee was called the "Forgotten Lane." It combines low unemployment rates with low income: slightly more than 45 percent of the total population of Immokalee earns under $3,000 a year, and 40 percent of the population earn less than $2,000 a year. There are more badly dilapidated shacks made of "peckery" cypress wood in the Negro quarter than are found across the highway in the white part of town, but many of the houses in which the white farm workers live are only in slightly better repair.

That slightly-to-somewhat-better differential is a characteristic pattern in the town. The physical plant of the white high school is slightly better than the Negro school; the movie theater to which the whites go is somewhat better than the one to which the Negroes go. But both theaters are open only on occasional weekends, except during the harvesting season, when thousands of migrant farm workers, "freewheelers," descend upon Immokalee and change it into a boom town for a few months. Only one doctor, who treats both whites and Negroes, lives in Immokalee. But, as Hewitt Howard points out, the difference between the Negro and the white is that "if a colored man goes to the hospital at night, they're not going to touch him unless the policeman in headquarters in the Quarter tells them it's O.K."

Perhaps the sharpest difference between the way in which the Negroes and whites live is that all the Negroes are lumped together in the Quarter. No physical distinctions between lower and middle class exist in the Quarter, as they do over in the white section of town. In the Quarter nicely painted, well-tended houses are on the same street, sometimes even side by side with broken-down shacks tilting crazily on rotting foundations, their windows cracked, the refuse piled up in the yard next to the broken steps on which the children play, dressed in filthy clothes, their feet raw with suppurating muck sores. A high school teacher's house may be next door to the dilapidated shack of a farm worker who spends all his pay getting drunk in the wine joints on Sucker Street, the name given to the street in the Quarter that holds most of the pool halls and cheap drinking places.

During the planting and harvesting seasons, everybody in the Quarter can work, and the only people who are unemployed then are those who are too old, too young, or unwilling to go out into the fields. The work is hard and is made more difficult by the hordes of gnats that swarm around, by the "bite" of the muck, whose high acid content irritates the skin, and by the mosquitoes.

During the hot, humid summer the work slackens, and although there are always a few things to be done—clearing the fields, tearing up stumps, fixing fences—the tempo of life slows down considerably and the standard of living drops even further. During the summer months the farm workers get paid about six or seven dollars a day. Then the pay scale starts rising gradually to about twelve dollars a day during the season, although at the height of the melon harvest, skilled watermelon pickers can earn up to twenty-five dollars a day. "But you don't work many days at that speed 'cause you'll hurt all over."

During the summer months, from late May to late September, the Negroes in Immokalee get up later than they do during the other seasons. In the morning the men wander around the Quarter visiting friends, perhaps stopping in at the pool hall, a wine joint, or the drug store to find out whether anyone has heard about a construction job that was supposed to begin down in Naples. Perhaps two or three of the men will drift across the highway into the white section of town, where someone said the owner of a gas station was looking for a man to do yard work around his house.

No organized channels for finding work exist in Immokalee, except during the harvest season, when the state employment service sends in a man. But during the slack seasons finding work depends completely upon personal contact among the jobless. And the Negro women of Immokalee don't even try to find farm work during the summer, for at that time of the year, whatever work is available is usually too hard physically for the women to do. Instead, if they can afford to drive ninety miles each day, they look for domestic work in Naples, a resort town on the coast. But even this is slow, for during the summer Naples has far fewer visitors than during the winter.

No recreation centers exist in the Quarter, although the six Negro churches function as informal centers. There the Negroes attend choir practice and usher board rehearsals or deacons' meetings. For others the recreation center is the wine joint, where they can buy cheap California muscatel, sweet and heavy, fortified to bring its alcoholic content up to twenty percent. (Sweet wine is the poor Negro's anodyne; Negroes represent a major market for kosher-type sweet wines.) The number of television sets in homes seems as large proportionately in Immokalee as it is in any other part of the United States, and correspondingly, it is generally the center of the house. In Immokalee, as elsewhere, everybody seems able to visit and talk with each other while still looking and listening to the never-turned-off television.

For the teen-agers there is even less organized activity during summer vacation from school than for the adults, although there is just as much unemployment. The Negro school has no gym to play in, although there is an outdoor basketball court. The teen-age counterpart of the adult wine joint is the "piccolo joint" on Sucker Street, where the kids can dance to jukebox music and buy soft drinks if they have money. Yet petty thefts, burglaries, auto thefts, and malicious mischief, four of the most common juvenile crimes in an urban area, are much less common in a rural community like Immokalee, where there are fewer cars to steal, fewer stores in which to shoplift, fewer homes to burglarize, and more people who know what everyone else is doing.

So, too, the Negro high school in Immokalee is in much better physical condition than a de facto segregated high school in the North—the walls aren't gouged, the toilets aren't broken, and the windows in the classrooms aren't broken. And the students are quieter, more passive, less overtly hostile to their teachers and other adult authority figures. But the boys and girls who walk through the corridors of Bethune High School never get the same chance to stretch their minds as do white students who, for example, can study a foreign language. The equipment in the industrial arts classroom in the Negro school is inferior to that found in the white school across the highway, and the library has fewer books, by far, than the one in the white school. Still, more Negroes graduate from Bethune than do their counterparts in the North, but a great many of these graduates then become farm workers, entering the same pattern of low income employment, unemployment, and underemployment of their parents. One reason the Negro high school graduates in Immokalee become farm workers is that there is little alternative employment for them if they stay in the South. And although the unemployment rate among the Negro teen-agers in rural Florida is much lower than it is among Negro teen-agers in the North, the price to society is high. The Southern pattern of employment, operating in a society that itself is culturally deprived, inevitably produces large numbers of adults who are either frustrated, have low levels of aspiration, or combine both attitudes.

"Some of the biggest wine drinkers in town are the well-educated people," says one of the elders of the Negro community. "It seems like the ones that got the less education got the more judgment. When I first came here in 1950 there was one liquor store in colored town and maybe four or five beer places. Now there's so many I can't count them. And ten or fifteen years ago the colored owned some of the business places in the Quarter and now the whites do. They bought out the colored, and only the pool hall and one or two wine joints are owned by colored."

But other factors operate to differentiate between poor Negroes and poor whites in rural areas. Too many whites in the rural South still think they are masters without slaves, and until recently too many Southern Negroes still thought they were slaves without masters.

The Southern white community makes no conscious attempt to discourage certain attitudes among Negroes: whites expect Negroes to gamble, to be promiscuous, to cut each other up, to be syphilitic. Indeed, Southern whites more than expect Negroes to be this way; they want and encourage them to do so. And understandably, considering the circumstances in which so many poor Southern Negroes live—"When they get home after a day's work in the fields, I don't blame them for not being interested in my clinic," says the Public Health Service nurse—many Southern Negroes find it easy to live out the white image of themselves. Unfortunately, the white man's view of the Negro becomes the Negro's mirror of himself.

Economically, Negroes must live for the day in the rural South, for although they know that some work may be available, it will almost certainly be at a very low pay. So if they stay in Immokalee, their future is certain but dismal, their role fixed but menial. "Mostly, the colored in Immokalee are in suspense right now. But down here they realize they're colored so they don't try to do things the whites don't want them to." Instead, they leave in the hope that the city in the North will be better, not knowing that usually their dismal futures and fixed roles as menials go right along with them.

Herman Holmes brought his dismal future along with him to California from Louisiana, where he was born twenty-nine years ago. Herman was one of nine children, and he went through the ninth grade in Louisiana before his family moved to Mississippi. There Herman got in two more years of school until, at seventeen, he went into the Navy. Holmes stayed in the Navy for three years and then left. "I didn't have no rank to speak of," he says, speaking softly, as he sits in the front room of his littered but clean four-room house near the southern outskirts of Oakland. His wife sits on the sofa, next to the television, looking almost apathetically down at her youngest child, an albino baby, handicapped even more by being retarded. Mrs. Holmes is only twenty-seven, but she has six children already. But since she has nine brothers and sisters, large families seem normal to her. Her five other children are playing with a pair of broken roller skates in the little back room where they sleep.

After Holmes got out of the Navy, he worked in Shreveport, Louisiana, at a variety of "Negro" jobs he heard about from friends or his family. He delivered prescriptions for a drug store; "cut knobs out of pine wood" for a chemical company; tried hauling scrap paper for himself, but since he only made six dollars a day, he took a job as an order picker for a wholesale liquor dealer that paid $1.05 an hour. Finally, after about a year and a half, he enlisted in the Army and got married at the same time. Once again, he got out after a single enlistment. "I didn't have no education so I didn't get to do much except a little auto mechanics." By this time he decided to leave the South and move to California. He says:

> I came up here to better my condition. I have an onkel here in Oakland and I came up to work for him, heppin' him in his plumber work. When I come up here, I come alone in October. I couldn't bring the family cause my onkel he paid me only $18 a week. I lived with him but I couldn't get ahead enough to bring my family so I quit him. I got me a job then working for a maintenance company over at the army base, and that paid me $1.25 an hour. But I got laid off after three months, and then I got another job like that with another maintenance company for $1.25.

In March of the year after he had arrived in Oakland, Holmes finally was able to break through the $1.25 an hour ceiling. From March until July he worked on a construction job as a member of the Hodcarriers and Common Laborers Union. But then the job ended and he was out of work for a few weeks, until the contractor called him back again on another job, which ended the following February. He has had no steady work since then.

Soon after Holmes brought his family up from the South, they moved into the eighty-five-dollar-a-month house in which they live now. After his last layoff he drew unemployment insurance of $39.90 a week, and the family tried to live on that. The state employment service had no work for him, and neither did the private agencies he tried. Holmes discovered that it wasn't possible to live on $39.90 a week and still pay $85.00 a month rent. So he applied for help from the welfare board. "I was upset when I went on the welfare, but we couldn't make out nohow on $39.90. So the welfare give me $102.00 a month to help out the unemployment insurance. Then the unemployment stopped."

The routine of Holmes' life is a simple one. He gets back from his fruitless trip to San Francisco at about 11:00 A.M., takes the younger children out for a ride, and then goes to sleep.

Tomorrow I won't do nothing except to try and borrow some money from some friends. Maybe I can find a little mechanic work and make two or three dollars at that. Saturday nights I visit a friend's and we watch TV. I like to watch the rasslin'. I drink a little beer then, but my wife she don't drink nor smoke. Sunday I might go to church but it's just hard to say. Next week I'll go back to the hall if I got the gas money. I'm so wore out when there's no work I just come home and lay down.

The best kind of job I'd like to have is with a truck line, but that union is so hard to get into cause it's all sewed up. When I was a little boy I wanted to have some kind of business like a café. I wanted to be rich and now my kids eat beans and rice and maybe a little apricots. All I got is my health insurance from the union and we buys second-hand clothing, but when I get me some work I buys the kids some good things. But it's better here then in the South. I got me a peg here in the union hall, and I didn't have nothin' like that down there. Maybe I might be a millionaire some day, maybe somebody might die and leave me the money. That'd be good, wouldn't it?

But Holmes' future already has been charted, and nothing in the forecast indicates that he'll be a millionaire. If he remains in the construction industry his employment future is dismal, for "despite a huge increase in residential and highway construction and in industrial and commercial building in the Bay Area in the 1950–62 period, there was little change in the level of construction employment." [1] Even if Holmes wanders back into doing the kind of maintenance and janitorial work he has done in the past, it will be more difficult for him to find work in the future. "It seems likely that employment growth in these occupations will be slower in the future than it has been in the past, reflecting the use of labor-saving machinery and other economies." [2]

Holmes' dream of becoming a truck driver also is not likely to become a reality. "Over the next three years, local industries will require about 1,000 new drivers a year to meet expansion and replacement needs," but a "surplus of qualified drivers" [3] already exists. Probably Holmes will continue to be unemployed. But he will never return South. Instead, he will hang on, grimly, to that peg of his at the union hall, to the hope that brought him to California—"to better my condition."

The Holmes family will become increasingly dependent upon the welfare agencies. A succession of men and women from those agencies will pass through the household, all lumped together as "the investigator." And the children will grow up not knowing what it is to have a father who goes to work every day. Instead, they will see their daddy discouraged into apathy, sitting around the house, watching television, sleeping on a sofa, or puttering around in the weedy yard where a 1958 Edsel with a snapped drive shaft slowly turns into junk.

And one of the children in the Holmes family might grow up to be like Franky-Boy, who can hardly be understood when he talks.

Franky-Boy was born a loser, or at least with very few possibilities of even becoming a winner. His father abandoned his mother before he was a year old; since that time a succession of men have passed through his mother's life, leaving behind six half brothers and sisters.

When he was a little boy, Franky-Boy never heard the phrase "Once upon a time," for no one ever told him a fairy tale. The focus of family life in the apartment was today; tomorrow had no reality for his mother beyond whether the man snoring heavily in her bed that night would be there the next day or whether her sister would be well enough to take care of the children so she could go out to work as a domestic and supplement the welfare allowance. No one read to Franky-Boy from a Little Golden Book, for his mother could hardly read the newspapers.

Inside all the apartments where Franky-Boy grew up, no one knew or cared very much about what was happening on the outside, and Franky-Boy's first contacts with that world came when the investigator from the welfare office paid a periodic and perfunctory visit to the apartment. Franky-Boy got educated in the street, long before he went to school. It was in the street, not in the home, that his values were shaped, because his mother lost control over him when he was about five. By then he was out in the street alone; his mother was working, and there was no child-care center where Franky-Boy could be left until his mother came home. It was in the street he learned that the Man, the white world, was not to be trusted, and it was in the street that he learned to split the scene, to disappear as soon as he saw the enemy, the police, cruising by in their cars.

As a child Franky-Boy learned to steal. To him stealing was not so much a way to gain status as it was first a childhood game and then an adolescent one, like stickball or baseball is to other kids. The first game Franky-Boy learned was from his brother, who showed him how to steal pennies and nickels from his mother's friends' pants. Then he learned how to steal candy in the grocery store and then went on to steal small toys from the five and dime. Later, as a teen-ager, he learned how to steal cars and how to mount a foray into a department store, scattering frightened shoppers as his menacing gang rushed through the aisles, grabbing useless items from the counters. And always his routine games were breaking windows in the school building, gouging the plaster from the walls of the recreation center, and maybe slashing a few tires.

Jail meant nothing to Franky-Boy, and he learned how to behave there long before he first got inside one. He learned to stay cool when the cops picked him up, to lie coolly, to pretend ignorance coolly, to accept arrest coolly, and to get through the increasing sentences coolly, too. Franky-Boy knew that only after you were eighteen and got sent to real prisons instead of juvenile halls did you have to start worrying about breaking the law.

One of the very few things Franky-Boy *did* learn at home was sex. In the crowded apartments where he always lived, sex was as close to him as his mother's bed. So Franky-Boy learned very early to associate the sounds of sex with pleasure. He learned, too, when his fifteen-year-old sister became pregnant, that the woman had to pay more of a penalty for sexual pleasure than a man.

When Franky-Boy was little, he never announced with childish pride and hope for approbation, "When I grow up, I'm going to be a fireman." In fact, no one ever asked Franky-Boy what he was going to be when he grew up. But he did learn, pretty quickly, to give the right answers to that question when, later, social workers and school teachers, impatient with him because of his latest arrest, would say, "Don't you want to be something?" "Sure, man," he would answer. "I want to be a jet pilot."

Sometimes, too, Franky-Boy thinks about how it would feel to be Godzilla, the huge killer gorilla, rampaging through the cities, killing all the whites, for the one thing that Franky-Boy does know, without any doubt, is that he's black. And when he gets into a fight with another Negro and starts screaming, "You black bastard, I'll cut your nigger balls off!" he is cursing himself, too.

Very little that Franky-Boy learned in school interested him. When he was little and in the early grades, he might have been helped into normal channels, for Franky-Boy was reasonably bright then. But no one can expect a little boy to hold back by himself the strong forces pushing him into delinquency, for neither at home nor in the street were there any strong counterpressures. He rarely did his school homework, and no one pushed him into studying. Instead, he sat in class becoming more apathetic year by year but getting promoted anyway because it was easier for the teacher to get rid of him than keep him back. Soon he began cutting school, and by the time he was fifteen he was already a repeated truant. And when he wasn't out of school because he stayed away, the school principal kept him from class by suspending him for misbehaving. His school record wasn't helped either by the weeks and months he spent in juvenile halls and Youth Authority jails after he got caught breaking open the cigarette machine in the all-night laundromat, stealing a car, and then breaking probation by drinking.

By the time Franky-Boy was fifteen he was ready to leave school. "It's a real drag, man," and when he was sixteen, he just stopped going. No one seemed to care very much, either. Gradually Franky-Boy learned how to fill the hours in the day that most people fill with work.

After he gets up at noon and eats a cold breakfast, he has a brief quarrel with his mother about money. Then he watches television for an hour or two. It doesn't matter terribly much to him what he sees, as long as it doesn't require any effort on his part to understand what's happening on the screen. That means he never looks at news programs, and he automatically turns to a new channel the moment a discussion program fills up the screen with people talking. He likes action on the screen: cowboy movies, war pictures, and any program that shows school principals having trouble with students.

Late in the afternoon, after he's had enough of television

or looking at a comic book, Franky-Boy takes off for the street. Then in his fantasies he becomes a movie monster, Godzilla breaking up the world or maybe the Red Fox, the cool one, with a dyed tuft of crinkly hair sticking up from his head and a loose swagger, ready, man, anytime, for anything. And when he finds his friends, his gang, lounging around in front of the pool hall, he slides into the group, willing to take part in whatever happens next.

What does happen next depends upon a variety of circumstances. Perhaps the boys will shoot pool if a few of them have enough money to pay for the time. Perhaps they'll move over to the understaffed rec center, looking for some action or a quiet corner for a crap game. Perhaps they'll stand around and lie to the younger kids about the rumble they had with the Egyptians or the Conquerors or the Sabines. Then, when it gets dark, they can pile into someone's car and head for the drive-in. There, over greasy hamburgers, lots of french fries with catsup, and cans of beer passed around among them, they'll talk and argue about the things that most interest them: sex, clothes, cars, and getting money.

Maybe the evening will be filled with a party at someone's house, where there's a record player, girls, and more beer or wine. At the party Franky-Boy will be spoiling to get into a fight with "that stud who's trying to make it with my girl," but someone will get between them. Then they'll go off into the night again, back to the drive-in or just cruising around to check the action, always keeping a wary eye out for the police. Franky-Boy is out on probation, which means he ought not to be drinking beer and riding around in cars. Maybe later that night a couple of the boys will make a score in a liquor store and come back with money and whiskey that they'll share with the gang, for sharing is an important value in the group. Then they might adjourn to the recreation center, where the door can be broken into easily and the mats from the gym piled into the small room with the battered ping-pong table in it. And under the table, Franky-Boy and his girl go into a frantic embrace. At 3:00 A.M. he's home in the apartment again and flops down into the bed he shares with one of his kid brothers. Another day has been filled up.

Franky-Boy is more than just unemployed. Unlike Thompson, Johnson, Howard, and Holmes, Franky-Boy has never been employed. He has no sense of occupation, no idea that jobs serve such long-term purposes as raising living standards and making possible a better education. Instead, a job is only a way, and not a very good one at that, to end, temporarily, an immediate need for money.

One component of normal identity in America—a job—is still missing from Franky-Boy's life and has been missing during his important adolescent years. That vacuum is filled with acquiring the identity of the cool Negro, unabashed by arrests, antisocial in behavior, for whom membership in and acceptance by his group is as important as it is to the high school girl, desolate because a favored club turned her down. Franky-Boy must project himself in the terms that his group thinks important, and so he won't give up his "peacock," the red-dyed tuft aggressively sticking up from his kinked hair, his orange shirt with the tab collar, the tie pin holding down the nonexistent tie, the pointed shoes, and the black hat with the very thin brim, a brim that is an essential part of his vision of himself.

This does not mean that all delinquent Negro teen-agers are unemployed or that unemployment among Negro teen-agers necessarily leads to delinquency. Some of the teen-agers Franky-Boy played with in the street years ago as a child never became delinquents. But it is obvious that Franky-Boy's life has been skewed toward delinquency and crime by his having grown up in a community where unemployment and the absence of occupational identity were the dominant mode of life for the men.

That skewing began when he was born into a disorganized family, dependent on relief and relatives. In such homes the income per person is lower than that in the families of nondelinquents. Few businessmen head up the ghetto delinquent's family, and if the Franky-Boys have fathers, the men work at unskilled outdoor jobs. The families of delinquents like Franky-Boy include more people unwilling to work than are found in the families of nondelinquents, and, finally, delinquent children have a higher percentage of fathers with very bad work habits than are found among the fathers of nondelinquents.

Families with domestic problems produce more delinquents than those where stable relationships prevail, and here, too, a Negro family such as Franky-Boy's is more likely to produce delinquent children than the white one. A higher proportion of Negro families are broken for reasons of domestic infelicity, a higher percentage of illegitimate children are born to Negro mothers, more Negro families are headed by a woman, and more Negroes are bound by common-law marriages.

And since the social and economic conditions in which delinquency develop more easily are the characteristic milieu into which more poor Negroes than poor whites are born, the proportion of Franky-Boys in the Negro population is going to be higher than the proportion of white juvenile delinquents in the white community.

Perhaps some of this discrepancy, which is characteristic of urban cities in the North, is due to the police, who are more likely to arrest Negro juveniles than whites for the same offenses. But even taking into account the possible bias of the police, the fact still remains that there are proportionately more Franky-Boys in the Negro communities than in similar white ones.

Why shouldn't there be? In the absence of both occupational identity and some reasonable income or job, what role is left for Franky-Boy to assume but one the white man expects—the Negro delinquent? What the white and Negro middle-class worlds do not understand about Franky-Boy is that unemployment and delinquency are normal, integral parts of his relationship to the white world. The identity of the *Negro* delinquent is what distinguishes Franky-Boy from his white counterparts, equally poor, equally unskilled, equally unemployed, and equally without a sense of occupation. They, like Franky-Boy, may also have been born into a jail, but they can get out more easily, for his prison is almost escape-proof. Its bars are the color of his own skin. The white seventeen-year-old with the same kind of family history as Franky-Boy's has a better chance than Franky-Boy does of breaking out of the jail, only because his skin is white.

One thing does disturb Franky-Boy about his present status: the fact that his mother and the family are on welfare. Franky-Boy and his friends display no hesitation in admitting and discussing their jail records, but they are reluctant to concede that their family income is derived from the welfare bureau. Being on welfare means, to them, that they are in a dependent status, while getting arrested is one of the few ways independence can be demonstrated.

And just as participating in a civil rights demonstration wasn't "in character" for Sergeant Thompson, it isn't in character for Franky-Boy or his friends. "Me get up there and march around in front of all them people? Man, you got to be crazy to do things like that!" But unlike Sergeant Thompson, who understands there is a connection between such demonstrations and his experience but rejects it, the abstract aims of the civil rights movement have no meaning in the context of Franky-Boy's life. He may know that Martin Luther King somehow is fighting "the Man," but he doesn't know or care very much what the fight is all about, since it is all very far away from him and his needs.

If Franky-Boy doesn't become an adult criminal, he may become an intermittent jobholder—another Herman Holmes—by the time he is in his early twenties. At present, a combination of forces pushes up Franky-Boy's chances of getting some employment as he grows out of his teens. He knows that if he breaks the law, he'll go, not to the Log Cabin, but to San Quentin. He may make a girl pregnant, and her family will force him to marry her. His mother may shove him out of the apartment because he isn't bringing in any money. And perhaps more importantly, one or two older friends, helped in turn by their older friends, will have found some kind of job by then. They will get Franky-Boy a job, too, maybe working with them in the small shop that undercoats and paints cars.

Gradually his goals might change enough so that he'll leave the group which is now so important a part of his life, to be replaced there by another, younger version of himself. Slowly he might begin to develop a few tenuous connections to society. He may start voting occasionally in elections, although with less frequency than either Negro middle-class or white lower-class people, because of a reluctance to register for voting or at the employment service: putting down your name and address lets the police and the bill collectors know where to find you, and Franky-Boy won't even bother looking for a job that requires being bonded. "I'm not bondable," he says.

The tragedy of America is that Franky-Boy's chance comes so much later for him than it does for a white boy in a similar position, that his desire for independence wasn't understood enough when he was younger to have been converted into something useful, and that the sense of community he has with his gang has been dissipated in delinquency. Perhaps if there had been a child-care center where his mother could have left him, perhaps if he had not been automatically promoted in school when he shouldn't have been, perhaps if the recreation center had a bigger staff, perhaps if the state employment service was given a bonus for making difficult placements instead of being penalized, perhaps if there were more jobs for teen-age Negroes, perhaps then Franky-Boy might have been able to better and more quickly overcome the handicap of being born into a disorganized Negro life. But, as Franky-Boy would say, "Yeah, man, that's right, and if my grandma had balls, she'd a been my grandpa."

Franky-Boy and the increasing number of his counterparts in the urban Negro ghettos of the North are both the product and the cause of the sharpening racial-economic crisis the country faces. Slowly, the Negro in America has been moving from the status of slave to that of a free man. But the rate of progress is dangerously slow, because an ever-increasing segment of the Negro population stagnates, cut off from participation in the movement away from slavery, toward a new identity. And even those skilled and educated Negroes who are beginning to have an identity linked to occupation or professional status rather than race are uncertain about their roles.

"For once in my life, I'm the right color at the right time," says the young Negro social scientist, sardonically. "I've got more job offers than I can handle. I can take my pick of two foundations, three government agencies, and half a dozen universities. But whichever job I take, I'll still wonder whether I'm being hired because they think I'm good or because I'm the kind of Negro everybody wants to hire right now."

The young man's doubt about himself rests on the new nepotism of color practiced by American society toward those Negroes who fit the modes of the dominant white society. But because it *is* a nepotism of color, it still reflects the disability of every Negro, whether he be a Ph.D., a computer programmer, a packinghouse worker, a farmhand, a laborer, or a delinquent kid, in dealing honestly with the white world: in the significant employment relationship all of them are handicapped, to varying extents, by being Negro. The handicap may be only a psychic one, as it is for the social scientist, or it may be a very tangible one, cutting him off completely from work, as it does for Franky-Boy. But whichever it is, it makes unemployment a more common social disease and a more pernicious one among Negroes than among whites. And all of society pays the costs of this social disease; costs which will rise more and more as unemployment continues to debilitate Negro workers and their families.

NOTES

1. State of California, Department of Employment, *Manpower Resources, San Francisco Oakland Bay Area 1960–1970* (San Francisco, 1943), p. 17.
2. *Ibid.*, p. 43.
3. *Idem.*

5 / Sex, Status, and Underemployment of the Negro Male

Kenneth B. Clark

The traditional status of the Negro in American life is determined by the work he has been permitted to perform. For the American Negro, occupational status and human status have been one from the time of slavery up to the most recent civil rights protest. The slogan of the March on Washington in August 1963, "Jobs and Freedom Now," was not only a demand for equal employment opportunities but an assertion of the Negro's desire for acceptance as a total human being. In demanding that the opportunities for mobility and free competition in the economic and job market be opened to him, the Negro is also demanding to be included in the American Protestant ethic that constructive work is the basis of human dignity and provides the basis for one's manhood. He is in fact demanding that that myth be discarded which was essential for the support of human slavery and its successor, racial discrimination—the myth that the Negro was less than human and that his subhumanity had to be dealt with by a castelike restriction to certain occupations.

But so far the Negro has not been successful; his demands have not been fulfilled. In an "affluent society" the Negro is still the victim of greater rate of unemployment than whites. What is even more significant in this whole area of occupational status is the fact that those Negroes who are employed are, for the most part, restricted to menial jobs which clearly limit dignity and self-fulfillment. In England the voluntary acceptance of the subservient role by the working-class Englishman gives the individual the power, or the illusion of power, to change; but inferiority of occupational role based on skin color reduces the actual and psychological chances of mobility or hope because skin color cannot be changed. In America the system tends to tie menial status to color, and escape seems futile.

The present bleak occupational predicament of the Negro will probably be reinforced in the future if present trends are not counteracted by massive and realistic corrective programs. Former Secretary of Commerce Luther H. Hodges stated in an address at the Equal Opportunity Day Dinner of the National Urban League on November 19, 1963:

> In our total economy, white-collar jobs, which generally require more education, already outnumber our blue-collar jobs. This trend will continue. And, today, even our factory jobs are largely closed to applicants who lack a high school diploma. . . .
>
> Negroes, to a very large extent, have been excluded from the white-collar occupations which, since 1947, have accounted for 97 percent of the total increase in United States employment. Only one-sixth of all Negro workers are in white-collar jobs today, compared with nearly half of the white work force. . . .
>
> This is not only tragically unfair to Negroes, it is an intolerable loss of talent to our society and to our national economy.

Exclusion of Negroes from apprenticeship training programs conducted by the better-paying skilled craft unions is a well-known and documented method of relegating Negroes to unskilled and low-paying jobs. Roy Wilkins, executive secretary of the National Association for the Advancement of Colored People, stated in his introduction to *The Negro Wage-Earner and Apprenticeship Training Programs: A Critical Analysis with Recommendations*:

At present there is a broad exclusion of Negro youth from major apprenticeship training programs jointly conducted by industrial management and labor unions in the North as well as in the South. For many occupations the only way a worker can be recognized as qualified for employment is to complete the apprenticeship training program. This is true for the printing trades, among machinists and metal workers, the various crafts in the building and construction trades industry and many others. The role of the labor union in these occupations is decisive because the trade union usually determines who is admitted into the training program and, therefore, who is admitted into the union. This results in a loss to the entire economy when basic human resources are not utilized. This discrimination directly relates to the future status of Negro wage earners throughout the United States. Given a continuation of present rates of advance, it will take Negroes 138 years, or until the year 2094, to secure equal participation in skilled craft training and employment.[1]

If the Negro seeks economic mobility and human dignity through the path of education, the persistent problems of racial discrimination and exclusion continue to reduce his chances of success. A key factor in the restriction of the Negro to the status of an underemployed proletariat, whose lack of skills will soon result in his exclusion from an increasingly automated economy, is the pervasive inferiority of the education provided for Negro children and youth. The pattern of discrimination, exclusion, rejection, and humiliation that conspires to contain the masses of Negroes in their menial occupational roles is perpetuated by subjecting them to segregated and invariably inferior education. Substandard education makes it difficult, if not impossible, for Negroes to compete on equal terms with others for skilled or managerial jobs, even if discrimination were not a reality.

The economic value of education is quite different for Negroes than for whites in America. Those Negroes who manage to overcome the handicap of inferior elementary and secondary education and press on to higher education are by no means assured that this will result in equality of status or economic opportunity. While the picture of the Negro college graduate working as a porter might not be as true today as it was in the 1930's, it is still true, as Herman P. Miller points out, that,

> The income gap between white and nonwhite *widens* as education increases. The lifetime earnings of nonwhite elementary school graduates are 64 percent of that received by the whites. At the high school level this ratio drops to 60 percent and among college graduates it is only 50 percent. *The fact is that in 1959, the average nonwhite with four years of college could expect to earn less over a lifetime than the white who did not go beyond the eighth grade.*[2]

This discrepancy is found not only in the South, but also in Northern, Midwestern, and Western states.

Constrictions on the occupational, educational, and economic status of Negroes become a powerful, damaging force that permeates almost every facet of life and becomes psychologically tied to intimate aspects of the self. The burden seems to fall with particular force upon the Negro male. He has little or no power to change his inferior status, and his entire life is dominated by the reality of his position. Not only does he have a menial job, but he becomes, therefore, a menial person. He sees himself as not quite human and is fixed in this role by his job and his skin.

Antidiscrimination and equal opportunities legislation have not alleviated the condition. Where legislation is in effect, job discrimination persists, only in a more subtle form. One must assume, therefore, that the manner in which covert discrimination operates makes it relatively immune to the laws that have abolished its cruder manifestations. In addition to rigorous enforcement of legislation, techniques must be used that are as subtle and as pervasive as the social evil they seek to overcome. One effective step would be to educate the public on the very real economic and human consequences of banishing the Negro male to the rigid status of an underemployed and explosive underclass. Although the human consequences of this problem are dealt with here, the economic and pragmatic effects are clear and inextricable.

While the Negro male is emasculated by educational and occupational discrimination, there is evidence that society as a whole is more willing to accept the Negro female. Approximately 55 percent of Negro college students are female in contrast to the nationwide pattern in which 60 percent of college students are male.[3] Dale L. Hiestand has pointed out that during the twentieth century, "the proportion of Negro women workers in semiskilled jobs and in the white collar fields has grown steadily and substantially." [4] His data also support the conclusion that proportionately more Negro women than Negro men have moved into the white-collar occupations.

These data are all the more devastating in a society such as ours where it is impossible for females to work in occupations of low status without a major loss in their general status. In our society, ordinarily, females are considered of lower rank than males. When the Negro male sees the Negro female in a relatively higher status, his loss of dignity is greatly intensified. He finds himself inferior not only to white males but to Negro females as well. He is in double jeopardy.

In every situation the Negro female appears to have priority of status. Consequently, any relationship between male and female is fraught with tension—in courtship, in domestic decisions, in discipline of children. Denials or attempts to obscure this condition merely highlight its pathos.

Theories to the effect that all American males are dominated by the female do not alter the basic predicament of the Negro male. The emasculation of the white male by his female generally involves her desire to have him attain status symbols in order to enhance her own status. When a woman insists that her husband ask for a raise, she operates, nevertheless, within the framework of male dominance. She accepts society's judgment that male status is superior. She believes, in effect, that she can attain status for herself only through her husband. Even the most emasculating females function in these terms, dominating males in order to have them compete more effectively for status. This can destroy the male, but it supports the prevailing principle of masculine social and economic superiority.

The pattern of relationship within the Negro family is deeply affected by this imbalance of relationship between the sexes. The Negro male often loses the ability to function as a father and a husband.

In our society, rightly or wrongly, the relationship between the male and female, even in the most intimate matters, is influenced by status. This is a truism often ignored. Males of high status are generally more desirable to females than males of lower status. Even the lower-class female gains psychologically if she is admired or possessed by a male of slightly higher status. On the other hand, lower-class females are fair game for all males. It is understood that the male will use his masculine superiority to gain higher economic status, higher occupational status, and sexual priorities. A male who seeks a better job, makes more money, and achieves a better education becomes more attractive to the female.

The Negro male is exposed to the values of white society, but he has not been permitted to function in terms of these values. He does not hold a status superior to the female, and neither can she, unless she is extraordinarily naïve, hope to manipulate him in the status climbing accepted by white middle-class society. She is aware of the fact that moving upward is related to the color of skin, from which there can be no escape. She also knows that the male has little choice, but this does not prevent her from feeling some contempt for the male who cannot provide the protection and dignity which the white male appears to provide for his female. She, too, has accepted white middle-class values. For the male this acceptance leads to resentment, self-doubt, and self-hatred.

Related to this complex pattern is the number of successful Negro females, particularly in show business, who have married white males. They argue that they are required to do so because there are so few Negro males with whom they have anything in common. They imply that they have outgrown the Negro male. One can infer that they believe that no Negro male could bring them any additional status. Once having demonstrated a successful break through racial constraints, they reach a level of prominence which would be threatened by public association with a Negro male. Generally, Negro males do not have comparable status.

Even the successful Negro male may seek association with white females in quest for even higher status. But he has more barriers in his way than do Negro females who associate with and marry white males. He faces the open resentment of usually more powerful white males, the bigotry of the masses of whites, and the inability to counter this resentment either by superior power of his own, unless he be a wealthy professional or an extraordinarily talented entertainer or prize fighter. Negro females are considered the property of, and fair game for, "higher status" white males, while white males consider white females their exclusive property, not to be shared with "lower status" Negro males. This perspective is consistent with the general assumption that males have rights of possession of females and its specific application in the area of racial status.

Basically, the position of the Negro male makes it difficult for the Negro female to respect him in terms of the standards which this society considers important—material possessions, economic status, symbols of privilege, well-furnished homes in good neighborhoods, fashionable clothing, private schooling. Such things, obviously, are not available to unemployed or menially employed lower-class persons. If the Negro female is to respect the Negro male, she often has no choice but to respect him solely in terms of his qualities as an individual, without the support of material success. This is a difficult basis for interpersonal relations among the privileged individuals of our culture—and is no less difficult among the underprivileged.

The Negro female may ultimately learn to judge the value of

her male almost solely in terms of his male prowess. One can surmise that such evaluation of a male by a female or vice versa must lead to an ephemeral relation. A relationship based primarily on sexual gratification cannot be enough; it is essentially an escape. Genuine relationships must be reinforced by other factors, such as the ability of the male to provide for and protect his female—to furnish the material basis for a stable and mutually gratifying life. But the Negro female has little choice but to be satisfied with transitory benefits. In the case of the most socially marginal Negroes, respect can be based on such resources as who is the most accomplished sexually, who is the toughest guy on the block, who has the most explosive temper, who is the shrewdest slickster. These stereotypes are substitutes for real power, a pseudocompensatory power rooted in a precarious economic situation and reflecting tenuous personal relationships without reinforcement by society.

The Negro male is aware that he does not bring to the female the basis for respect that white males provide. Caught in this predicament, he can either submit to it and be totally menial in relation to the female, as well as on his job, or he can seek the escapes of the stereotyped, shiftless buffoon or the accommodating Negro, thereby intensifying the basic problem. He may seek escape through wine or narcotic addiction, removed from any direct exacerbating ego involvement with women or engage in spasmodic sexual exploration in which he seeks immediate gratification without sustained responsibility. For any sensitive man it would appear to be psychologically unbearable to remain in a situation with a female in which sexual gratification cannot be buttressed by symbols of status or power. Some Negroes may seek a resolution, or masking, of this predicament by exaggerated use of superficial masculine traits, such as a propensity for dalliance, taunting, hostility, and irritability and an adolescent preoccupation with the conquest of a number of females. Still others may seek satisfaction in exhibitionist displays of dress and flashy cars or in a flamboyant shrewdness in marginal or antisocial activities. The common denominator of these devices is the avoidance of situations in which he would expose himself to himself and to his female as the powerless individual that society has made him. He cannot bring evidence of real worth and substance to a relationship with a woman because of the reality of his inferior occupational and economic status. Insidiously his menial job status has produced the psychological reality. He has been taught effectively that he *is* inferior. He knows he is inferior and he knows that his woman knows it, and no matter how he tries to disguise it, he cannot help her compete for middle-class symbols of status.

The situation is even more threatening when it involves children. The Negro who cannot fulfill his responsibilities as a male, as defined by middle-class standards, cannot face his children without shame and humiliation. He feels required to escape from the family or to resort to one or many compensatory patterns. Under these conditions the child does not associate a masculine role with sustained responsibility. All too often escape from familial responsibility or promiscuity or hostility seems to be what is expected of the man and therefore of the boy who is to become the man. The child cannot be expected to understand the reasons, the dynamics, for the behavior of his father. To him it is merely the way of life. Rejection by his father becomes part of what is believed to be his role. Interestingly enough, many children with absent fathers idealize them in a kind of dreamlike image of their strength and prestige. These are the children society may refer to as illegitimate and consider a burden imposed on the welfare rolls by ignorant and immoral mothers. But very often the father stays away knowing that he can only bring poor wages to his family and shame to himself if he lives at home, but that his family will receive funds for dependent children if there is no father in the home. The economic rewards of broken family life match his own psychological needs for avoidance of a responsibility he cannot sustain.

One of the most devastating things a teacher can do to a lower-class child is to ask him: "What does your father do?"

Such an inquiry, harmless enough in middle-class society, creates tremendous anxiety in the child. The child often responds with sheer fantasy, exaggerating his father's occupation, claiming that he is a policeman or a fireman or a clerk, or in another job that seems to the child to convey status. Almost never will he admit that his father is a porter or a dishwasher or an elevator operator. Rarely will he admit that his father does not live at home unless he disguises his absence by saying he is dead. The more intelligent the child, the more likely he is to use the defense of fantasy to cover his own humiliation.

The Negro male, therefore, is required to face the fact that he cannot protect his children or be the agent through which they will be adequately fed or clothed or educated. What appears to be irresponsibility or neglect by the absent fathers can be seen rather as the anguished escape of the Negro male from an impossible predicament. He cannot function effectively as a husband and father, so he often does not function at all. Even his presence would not be significantly different from his absence. If he were present and unable to protect his wife and child, there would be psychological torment and the inevitable explosion into aggression. The additional tragic predicament of the Negro male is that his powerless status tends to be self-perpetuating. What the Negro boy learns first is that to be Negro and male is to be menial—and to be menial is to be defeated in the competition for socially desirable status and its constructive rewards. When these avenues are blocked, the individual must seek other avenues for attaining that minimal status essential for human life.

Programs designed to end poverty, no matter how enthusiastically generated, will fail unless they acknowledge the realities of the interrelationship between job discrimination and the psychological damage associated with the menial status of the Negro male, as well as the effects of these upon the stability of the Negro family. Unless these conditions are faced, understood, and remedied, one can expect nothing other than perpetuation and extension of the social and personal pathology associated with American racism. The emasculation of the Negro male is implicit in his exclusion from the opportunities to be a meaningful part of the American economy. It not only leads to waste and tragedy for him, his women, and his children, but remains a major threat to the apparent affluence and stability of the American society as a whole. By denying the Negro the right to share in its affluence, society not only condemns the Negro to tragedy but also nurtures the seeds of its own destruction.

NOTES

1. Herbert Hill, *The Negro Wage-Earner and Apprenticeship Training Programs: A Critical Analysis with Recommendations* (New York: NAACP, 1960).
2. Herman P. Miller, *Rich Man, Poor Man* (New York: Thomas Y. Crowell, 1964), p. 155 (Italics H.P.M.)
3. Kenneth B. Clark and Lawrence Plotkin, *The Negro Student at Integrated Colleges* (New York: National Scholarship Service and Fund for Negro Students, 1963), p. 25, and R. E. Iffert, *Retention and Withdrawal of College Students,* United States Office of Education Bulletin, 1958, No. 1 (Washington: U.S. Government Printing Office, 1957), p. 8.
4. Dale L. Hiestand, *Economic Growth and Employment Opportunities for Minorities* (New York: Columbia Univ. Press, 1964), p. 46.

6 / Culture, Class, and Family Life Among Low-Income Urban Negroes

Hylan Lewis

Family organization and child rearing among Negroes in the United States are not, to use a phrase of Ralph Ellison's, "a hermetic expression of Negro sensibility." They are, rather, parts of the same forces that have shaped contemporary society and culture in the United States. E. Franklin Frazier demonstrated brilliantly how the family among Negroes, rooted as it is in human nature, "may take protean forms as it survives or is reborn in times of cataclysmic social change." [1]

In a paper written for the 1960 White House Conference on Children and Youth, I suggested that

> not enough is known about the dynamics of present family forms and functions and about the behavior patterns which are distinctly urban products. . . . The forms, as in the case of the family headed by the female, may be the same but the context in which they fit and function has probably changed in important details. Knowledge of [the historical] background is necessary but not sufficient to explain and understand the Negro family . . . in the changing cities of today.[2]

This study has two purposes: first, to illustrate some of the faulty ways in which the terms "culture" and "class" are used to describe and explain family behavior of low-income urban Negroes; and, second, to present some findings and illustrative materials from a study of low-income families in the District of Columbia.[3] These findings and materials accent further the belief that family forms and functions among Negroes in today's cities are understood best, and dealt with best, as products of contemporary urban life.

I

The term "culture" is now widely applied to numerous dimensions and components of the behavior of aggregates, groups, and persons. Like "class," with which it is frequently used in combination—and often interchangeably, it seems—"culture" is sometimes used in an actuarial fashion to describe and predict the life chances of individual, aggregates, and groups. At other times it is used to describe and explain social and physical conditions; and at still other times it is used to describe and to explain the objective and subjective characteristics, the conscious and unconscious behavior, and the character of individuals and groups associated with these life chances and conditions.

"Culture" is used variously to refer to the living conditions, the chances of improving socioeconomic status, and the personality attributed to members of low-income families and to residents in low-income areas. Too frequently some of these things are described, and even defined, in terms of one another. That they are related would hardly be disputed; however, the precise nature of the relationships and their implications for family life among Negroes, for example, are not made clear.

The linkage of culture and class in itself makes for problems: "culture differences and social stratification vary independently. They can neither be reduced, nor can they be equated." [4] And David Riesman aptly suggests that "cultural differences, no matter how forcefully they may strike the ear, the eye, or the nose, are not necessarily connected with character differences of equal significance." [5] For example, some of the things frequently referred to as cultural and class differences in the child-rearing behavior of low-income Negroes, and that are seen as significant differences, are probably better seen as temporary gaucheries, or perhaps gaffes, in acting out valued aspects of the culture of the wider society.

A possibly serious consequence of starting with the assumption that the low-income Negro family is a cultural type, particularly when deviant behavior is involved, is indicated in Potter's comments about studies of national character:

This inclination to take culture as a given factor and to explain character in terms of the culture without very much consideration of the forces which determined the culture . . . is a limiting factor which in the last analysis could interfere with the deepest and fullest understanding of society. The determinants of the culture must themselves be introduced fully and carefully into the analysis.[6]

The constant and basic danger is that the loose use of the term "culture" in explanations of family life among Negroes can easily encourage situations where "pseudofacts have a way of inducing pseudoproblems, which cannot be solved because matters are not as they purport to be." [7] An illustration is taken from a prominent sociologist's address on urbanization problems:

In the case of the Negro, now, it is not a problem of Americanization, because the Negro has been an American citizen, on the average, considerably longer than the white person in the United States. It is a problem of acculturation, however, because the movement represents essentially a movement of people with a primitive folk culture from the rural slum south, to the urban north and west, or to urban areas within the south.

The process of acculturation is one of the most difficult a human being can experience. . . . It requires time—time measured in human generations rather than years. . . .

Let us illustrate a few of the problems. A Negro in the Mississippi Delta tosses his empty whisky bottle or beer can in a cotton patch, and what difference does it make? But on the asphalt pavements of a city it can make a difference aesthetically and with respect to safety.[8]

None of the key assertions made above about the relationship between culture and the behavior of urban Negroes is an unqualified fact. One ignores the considerable extent to which urban Negroes of the first, second, and third generations are represented in the statistical indications of the problem behavior unevenly distributed among low-income persons that is categorized frequently as lower-class behavior. Social disorganization in some major urban centers is by no means limited to the recently arrived representatives of "a primitive folk culture from the rural slum south."

Social science knowledge and experience indicate that the process of acculturation—assuming that this is the key problem—may or may not be difficult; and that it may or may not require "time measured in human generations rather than years." The degree of difficulty and the amount of time involved vary, and the rate at which differing aspects of differing cultures is taken over varies, even when the two cultures involved are disparate and alien, as is not the case here. It makes a difference in what we seek to know, and to change, about the lives and the life chances of low-income urban Negroes if we assume that their behavior primarily reflects either the lack of acculturation of the migrant or the imperatives of a Negro lower-class culture.

The last illustration suggests important questions that need to be answered: In the search for cultural differences that *make* a difference in family living and child rearing, how is the salience of tossed whisky bottles figured? How really significant is this trait in comparison with church attendance, latch-key children, illegitimacy rates, and housing availability and costs, for example? Do lower-class persons toss the empty whisky bottles or beer cans on the streets because of a significant difference in shared norms, because they do not know any better, or because they know better and do not care? And what distinguishes their behavior from that of other American litterbugs? Assuming they do not know any better, how long would it take them to learn not to? And what would be needed to properly cue and reinforce the preferred custom—or is it a habit?

Among the unplanned effects of the linkage of the term "class" with the term "culture," as seen in the popular circulation of the term "lower-class culture," are the tendency to select the more colorful, dramatic, "different"—but not necessarily significant—traits and to encourage invidious and double standards of judgment. The inclinations to condemn or to condone, to denigrate or to romanticize, get in the way of accurate description and interpretation of family and neighborhood life among contemporary low-income urban Negroes.

Some students of persons who are termed lower class frequently insist on having it both ways: On the one hand, there is the frequent assertion that such people are characteristically inarticulate, noncommunicative, which can be taken to mean either that they have little to say or that they do not have the native or "cultural" equipment to do so. On the other hand, when representatives from this category do talk, there is a disposition to raise serious questions about what they say, particularly when it is inconsistent with their behavior or with assumptions about the mainsprings of their behavior. Of course, either or both of these allegations may be objectively true. The point is that neither low or inadequate communication nor a gap between professions and behavior is a class trait.

First, there is a question as to how much the differences in behavior reported and perceived are reflections of the methods used and how much they are due to the class and culture of the subjects.

Second, "pretend rules"—reflections of what A. L. Kroeber called "the trick of professing one thing and doing another" [9] —are probably common to all individuals and groups, regardless of class and cultural placement: "They [societies] vary chiefly in what they are inconsistent about." [10] According to Kroeber, we should not feel too harshly about some of the gaps themselves: "Professions after all mean standards and ideals; and it may be better . . . to have standards and fall short of them than not to have them." [11] Whether or not this is a sound position, there is still the key question: Are the things that Negro parents are inconsistent about, for example in their child-rearing behavior, reflective of class and cultural differences? And if they are, why?

A summing up of some of our concerns about the ways in which culture and class are sometimes used to describe and to explain the child-rearing behavior of low-income people[12] would stress dangers arising from:

1. Confusions about the meanings and uses of culture and class, and about the kinds of dimensions of behavior to which they might be appropriately and usefully applied;

2. Questionable extensions of assumptions and of limited data; and what is probably more serious, the partial and garbled versions that filter into other fields and into popular thinking;

3. Tendencies toward perception of culture and class as fixed and "determinative"—as the inflexible arbiters of life chances as well as behavior;

4. Preoccupations with culture and class that divert not only the consideration of the forces that affect them, but also divert consideration of the probabilities, the pace, and the direction of changes in them;

5. The urge to order, under one general rubric, varying and frequently disparate behaviors, or aspects of them. In at least some instances these behaviors might best be understood and dealt with as lacking in the coherence and consistency of cultural systems and all that this conception connotes;

6. Tendencies to impute to a total category, such as the lower class, the depreciated, and probably more dramatic and threatening, characteristics of a segment of that category;

7. Underestimation or exclusion from attention of the range in behavior: "for some problems the range rather than the mode may be the crucial datum";[13]

8. Tendencies to oversimplify complex behavior, frequently obscuring the fact that people today, in Aldous Huxley's words, tend to be "multiple amphibians living in a number of worlds at once";

9. Misplaced emphasis on differences, to the exclusion and underemphasis of basic similarities that derive from the same general culture. Some of these differences are of questionable significance and tenacity, while the similarities might be the keys to understanding behavior, and to programing change. Best results might come from leading to the child-rearing strengths of individuals and groups, rather than to their perceived weaknesses.

II

In the discussion that follows, some of the data and propositions that accent these concerns will be presented.

Family and community field reports and family ratings of the families studied in the District of Columbia yield indications of underestimated diversity and range in the child-rearing behavior of low-income families. There is variability in the degree and quality of parental concern about children's health, education, and welfare demonstrated among the low-income families studied. Evidences of positive concern and a willingness to sacrifice for children, despite deprivation and trouble, are found in a good proportion of the families. Mrs. R., a low-income parent with a limited education, provides one illustration of a combination of these elements.

Mr. and Mrs. R. are the parents of eleven children, nine of whom are living at home. They have lived in Washington less than three years. Recently Mrs. R. remained in jail for two weeks while awaiting trial for assaulting her husband. Her minor children were placed in Junior Village[14] when she was taken to jail. Excerpts from the mother's account of the experience and of the manner in which she weighed personal and family alternatives follow:

You know, I didn't have to stay in jail those two weeks. I could have paid forty dollars for bail and gotten out, but I just kind of felt that I'd stay there for a while. I just thought I'd be better off.

I had seventy-three dollars on me because I had the rent money. One mind told me to pay the bail and the other mind said no. So when they told me I could make one telephone call and asked me who I wanted to call, I told them to just call the rent man and tell him to come and get the rent and I would stay in jail.

The rent man came and got it that Tuesday. I was glad I paid the rent, as we had to have a place to stay when I got out. The only thing that worried me while I was in jail was the children. I worried about them, as they have never been separated from me before. When I got out of jail my husband came for me and asked me if I didn't want to come home and fix something to eat for the children. I told him, "No, I just want to get the children," and I kept right on from the jail out to Junior Village to get them. They had been taken good care of there, but there won't be no more separations. The next separation will just have to be a death separation because I know I won't do anything like that again. . . .

I have always treated my husband nice and tried to help him. I also tried to share. When I have worked I have given him money when he needs it. I don't drink and I told him that if he can't control his drinking then he shouldn't drink. I didn't like him out there in the yard acting ugly in front of all the neighbors. . . .

Before I go back to jail I'll leave. This is the first and last time I'll go to a place like that. Not to jail. Not to be locked up. But I did get some relief in that place. Somehow you don't mind it when you've been listening to cursing day and night. It worried me to be away from the children so long but I did get some rest. I got tired of sitting around there and asked for some work to do and they put me in the laundry. The matron was sorry to see me go because I was such a good worker.

Our materials and analysis indicate that parents who show a high degree of concern as well as parents who show a low degree of concern are found both among families receiving public assistance and those which are not, among one-parent and two-parent families, among recently arrived families, and among those either native to Washington or long-time residents in the city. Distinguishable are parents with high concern who demonstrate it in their behavior, parents with considerable verbal concern who exhibit inconsistent or contradictory behavior, and parents who express little or no concern and are extremely neglectful.

Field reports have documented the impression that regardless of the quality of active concern about their children, parents, with few exceptions, do not prefer or approve the circumstances in which they now live and in which their children are being brought up. Even in the case of the most neglectful parents, the evidence points to the fact that they ascribe no virtue to neglectful behavior in themselves or in others or to neighborhood disorganization and poor housing. If there is any suggestion of approval, it smacks of perverseness, defiance, bravado, or desperation of the I-don't-care type.

The field materials of the Child Rearing Study lend support to the proposition that these low-income urban parents tend to show greater conformity to, and convergence with, middle-class standards in their verbalizations of values—in what they say they want (or would like to want)—than in their actual behavior.[15]

It was suggested earlier that some things that are statistically true about child-rearing forms, circumstances, and activities may be quite misleading clues to the complex child-rearing behavior of low-income urban Negroes.

III

Gross statistics and descriptions of family social structure among low-income urban Negroes provide at best partial and limited indications of the dynamics of child rearing. Following are some propositions that are pertinent to this assertion, and that have come out of our study on child-rearing practices among low-income families in the District of Columbia.

1. The amount and the implications of the diversity among

Negroes in low-income urban families are too frequently overlooked or underrated in popular and scientific thinking.

2. Negro family behavior, and especially those with low income, is marked by a shifting back and forth between, and a compartmentalizing of, selected aspects of poverty and deprivation and of adequacy and affluence.

3. Much low-income family behavior has a strongly pragmatic cast, essentially nonclass, noncultural (or transcending class and culture, as currently used) in its derivations.

4. The answer to the problem of family disorganization is not one of inculcating marriage and family values in young couples; there is ample evidence that they exist. The critical test is to find ways and means for the young adult male to meet the economic maintenance demands of marriage and family life.

> Since the job is a crucial determinant of where and how the family fits in the society and of the effectiveness of its claims on many of the society's rewards, probably the most important single clue to the quality of change in the Negro family and on the community [in which Negroes live in any numbers] is . . . in the job picture . . . for the male.[16]

The evidence suggests that Negro mothers from the low-income category, as much as any mothers in any category of our population, want and prefer their men to be strong and supportive in marriage, family, and community relationships. There is no need to invoke a mystique of the matriarchy to explain low-income, female-headed child-rearing units when we take into consideration the economic pressures of late twentieth-century urban living upon the young adult Negro male, and especially the ways in which these alter the choices open to low-income women and men.

Related to these key propositions about child rearing among contemporary urban Negroes are several factors, the most important of which are:

1. The contrast found in many low-income urban Negro

families between the parents' verbalizations about their own childhood and life values and the actual behavior of these parents;

2. The crucial nature of the family cycle—the age of parents in relation to years married and the number and ages of children;

3. The relationship between the lack of child-rearing options and the early and differential effects of extra-family influences on low-income families;

4. Indications of pressures toward early social weaning (independence training) among many low-income Negro families, particularly those with large numbers of minor children;

5. Indications of pressures both inside and outside the family that operate on some parents to diminish confidence in their ability to control children who are not yet adolescent, sometimes as young as five and six;

6. Some of the presumed freedom of lower-class children to move outside the household and freedom from parental control reflecting the results of either early independence training (early social weaning) in large families or the urban child's success in wresting this freedom from overburdened, confused, and sometimes inadequate parents.

Presented next are some materials that suggest the complex nature of the relationships between behavior and conditions, and professions and preferences, among low-income urban Negro parents, drawn from field notes of two field workers, Camille Jeffers and Elliot Liebow, who did participant observation, the first as a resident in a public housing project and the second with "street corner" young male adults. In the first set of illustrations, two Negro male adults indicate something of their slants on themselves, their families, and life.

Although the present condition and outlook of each of the men is different, their expressions share the marks of human inconsistency and voice strong preferences for recognizable goals of the greater society. In the first set of excerpts from field documents, a semiliterate thirty-year-old construction worker expresses himself on a variety of subjects, including himself.

Sonny has been in Washington nine years. During this period he has been married and separated and fathered eight children, three on his wife and, by his account, five others on five different women.

On education and "being somebody":

[Sonny is talking about a man the field worker (FW) and he had met]

SONNY: That's what I ought to be doing. I ought to be in his place . . . dressed nice, going to school, got a good job.

FW: You make more than he does.

SONNY: It's not the money. . . . It's position, I guess. He's got a position. When he finish school he gonna be a supervisor. People respect him. . . . Just thinking about people with an education and position gives me a feeling right here [touching his stomach].

FW: You're educated too, Sonny. . . . You have a skill, a trade. You're a cement finisher. You can make a building, pour a sidewalk.

SONNY: That's different. Look, can anybody do what you're doing? Can anybody just come up and do your job?

FW: I don't think so.

SONNY: Well, in one week I can teach you cement finishing. You won't be as good as me because you won't have the experience but you'll be a cement finisher. That's what I mean. Anybody can do what I'm doing and that's what gives me this feeling. . . .

Suppose I like this girl. I go to her house and I meet her father. He starts talking about what he done today. He talks about operating on somebody and sewing them up and about surgery. I know he's a doctor cause of the way he talks. Then she starts talking about what she did. Maybe she's a boss or a supervisor. Maybe she's a lawyer and her father say to me, "and what do you do, Mr. Washington?" . . .

You remember, at the court house, Lonnie's trial?

You and Jim Marshall was talking in the hall? . . . You remember, I just stood there listening. I didn't say a word . . . because I didn't even know what you were talking about. That's happened to me a lot.

FW: Hell, you're nothing special. That happens to everybody. Nobody knows everything. One man is a doctor, so he talks about surgery. . . . But doctors and teachers don't know nothing about concrete. You're a cement finisher and that's your specialty.

SONNY: Maybe so, but when was the last time you saw anybody standing around talking about concrete?

*

Sonny turned away from a TV drama involving a young Mexican boy and his father to say that if he had a million dollars he would travel all over the world and learn a lot of things "like you and those people at the museum." [The field worker asked why this was important to him. (Sonny had earlier accompanied the field worker to visit a museum that he had worked on as a construction worker but had never been inside after it was finished.)]

SONNY: Well, I think about my oldest boy [about nine] a lot. I want to be a big man in his eyes. If he's out on the street playing with some kids and one boy say, "My daddy's a lawyer," I want my boy to be able to say that his daddy is a big man too. It's too late for that now. I can't hardly read or write but I still want to learn things.

On being a parent, in wedlock and out of wedlock:

We were sitting in Dickie's Grill and Sonny was recalling the circumstances in which Hattie had told him he was the father of her unborn child. "When a woman says it's your baby, you just got to go along with her."

Later, we talked about Linda, the mother of his youngest child. He said that when Linda told him she was pregnant, she said she knew an old woman who would get rid of it for fifty dollars: "You're a married man, you can't help me."

"You have the baby," Sonny told her, "I'll do what I can."

I [the field worker] asked whether the fifty dollars had anything to do with it. He said the money had nothing to do with it. "Everybody should have a chance. My mother didn't get rid of me like that, so why should I do that to somebody else? That wouldn't be right. . . . When he grows up, maybe he be a doctor or lawyer. He come to me when I'm old. He say, 'You help me when I was little, now you old and I help you.' "

Shirley, the white waitress and co-owner of Dickie's Grill, joined us for a beer. Shirley, who lived alone and was five months pregnant, said she was making arrangements to put her baby up for adoption because she wouldn't be able to give the baby the care, time, and attention he had a right to. "It wouldn't be fair for me to keep it," she said. "I know I'm doing the right thing." When she left I asked Sonny if he thought Shirley was doing the right thing.

"No. If you got a baby and you got to scuffle, you scuffle. You don't give him away. Suppose it's a boy. A boy always likes a older head. Suppose he starts going out with this woman. He say he an orphan—is that what you call it?—and she say that she had a baby once but she give him away. Then they find out that she's his mother." ["Do you know anyone that's happened to?"] "No, but I've heard about it."

*

Sonny had just confessed to me that he had been lying about his wife and children living with him. He said his wife had left him in November, 1960. "It was all a lie, Ralph, but I love my wife. When I go to bed at night she's with me and my kids are too and deep down in my heart I believe she's coming back. I really believe it. And if she do, I'm going to throw out all these other women and I'm going to change my whole life."

*

Sonny and I [the field worker] were idling in the poolroom.

"Children learn from their parents. If you want them to do right, you've got to do right. If you go around drinking and cussing in front of them, they'll come up drinking and cussing. If a man can't help drinking and cussing, that's O.K., but when he comes home he can't do it in front of the children." ["What else do you do to teach them the right thing?"] "I hit them sometimes. That's important to help them know right from wrong. But you can't let them keep on doing bad things and then whip them for things they did a long time ago. You got to whip them when they done it so they'll know what it's for. . . . Sometimes they ain't going to listen if you don't whip them."

Presented next are the roughly parallel comments of a twenty-eight-year-old man who has been in Washington six years. He is married and the father of two children.

On being somebody:

I believe in religion. I live by the Book. . . . I don't drink; it just never appealed to me. I don't gamble and I don't stay out late or run around. I work hard. . . . I always save some pennies from every dollar.

*

I live for wants. I don't fool around. I see something I want, I get it. When I go to the Safeway, if I see a steak marked five dollars and I want a steak, I turn it over, look at both sides, and if I like it I buy it.

*

I live for today . . . but I keep an eye on tomorrow, too. When I go to bed, my wife knows that if I don't live till morning she got ten thousand dollars for herself and the kids.

If I die, flowers won't do no good. . . . All I want is a plain box. Let someone say, "He was a good man," then put me in the hole, cover me with dirt, and let me go.

My wife's check goes straight to the bank. We don't even look twice at it. And we save something from my check too if we can.

When I get paid, we sit down together with pencil and paper and we write down how we're going to spend the money. Everything gets written down, everything. We even write down the sixty or seventy cents I'm going to put in that pinball machine right there. I don't drink, I don't gamble, and I don't stay out late or run around. I work hard and that's relaxation for me.

*

Next year, or the year after that, we're going to buy a house with a piece of ground, maybe out in Virginia. I don't like being next to somebody else and neither does my wife. . . . We want to be by ourselves.

On marriage and the family:

I want my boy to have everything I didn't have. I want him to have everything he wants, within reason. . . .

You can't give a kid too much. You can't give a kid too much loving or anything. There's no such thing as too much for a kid.

*

Sometimes it's good to take a switch to a kid until he's ten or eleven years old. I ain't taken a switch to either one of mine in a year and a half, but I'll do it if I thinks they needs it. But not after they're ten or eleven. When a boy gets that old, it starts getting hard for him to cry. If you take a switch to him and he don't cry, he starts thinking he's tough, and taking a switch to him just makes him hard.

*

You got to talk to children, to explain things to them.

*

When my little girl gets up in the morning, the first thing she wants to do is eat. I tell her no, that she got to take a bath and then she can eat. I don't make her get dressed all the way. I tell her she can set at the table in her underwear if she takes her bath, and while she's doing that I put on the water for oatmeal or something.

*

You gotta know when to see what they're [children] doing too. Sometimes my boy gets to tearing up the Sunday papers. He knows he ain't supposed to do that, and sometimes I don't let on I see him doing it. Then I looks surprised and I say, "Somebody tore up the Sunday paper. Why don't you put it in the trash," and that's all there is to it. A kid needs that sometimes.

*

[Children] got to know when you're just fooling around and when you mean business. Most of the time my kids know just from my tone of voice or the way I look whether I'm playing around. They know they gotta listen to me when I ain't playing around.

*

When Dick's eight-year-old son came home from school crying and explained that he had been beaten up by some bigger boys, Dick told him he didn't want him to come home crying from school. He was to return to school the next day, and if the boys bothered him again, he was to stay and fight hard as he could and do as much damage to them as he could. And if he was beaten, he was to do the same thing the next day and the next.

To be discussed next—in the context of our interest in examining the complex relationships between behavior and conditions and professions and preferences—are aspects of the consumption behavior of low-income families living in public housing and the contrasts between the present living conditions of three young mothers and the present living conditions of the parents and siblings of these mothers. Camille Jeffers' reports, made during fifteen months of participant observation as a working mother resident in public housing, provide the illustrative materials and impressions. The first concern the use and value attached to home furnishings.

Young families who are just setting up their households and making new purchases show strong interest in home furnishings. The thing that distinguishes one household from another is not so much the taste displayed but the quantity and quality of the furnishings. Tastes are determined by the current vogue—modern furniture, pole lamps, the pair of matching living room lamps, portable bars, and colored telephones. Whereas any one apartment may not have all of these, there are usually enough "conspicuous consumption" items, particularly among the young families, to suggest awareness of and attempts to conform to current vogues and standards in furnishings. Many of the families appear to be preoccupied with fixing up their homes. Emphasis is placed on color schemes, and many change from drapes in the winter to cottage curtains in the summer.

The television set is almost universal; the sets are frequently the types with the largest screens. The record player is almost as universal as the television and is frequently part of a radio-TV-phonograph combination. Record collecting is a common hobby, with frequent exchange of latest acquisitions among friends.

A furnishing which is highly valued but appears infrequently is a rug. A feature of the field worker's apartment which drew frequent comment from visitors was the fact that she had rugs on the floors. Onc visiting mother said with a sigh, "Some day I'm gonna have a rug." This same mother borrowed a 9 by 12 cotton rug from a friend whose husband was in the service to prepare her apartment for her own husband's return from the service. The field worker commented that these incidents startled her into realizing that much that is taken for granted by middle-class people is beyond the horizon of many apparently would-be middle-class but low-income families.

Beneath the surface of modern furniture, hi-fi's, and record players there are often glaring gaps in furnishings—a lack of dishes, linens, scrubbing paraphernalia, irons, and the like. This seems a paradox in light of the presence of heavy, relatively expensive pieces. The answer lies in part in the fact that heavy goods are easily obtained on credit, whereas expendable items are characteristically bought for cash. This reflects a problem for many low-income families: after paying the installments on the major furniture items, buying food and clothing, and paying rent, there is not much left for other purchases.

The initial interest in the family background of some of the young parents was stimulated by close observation of contrasts and inconsistencies in the behavior and attitudes of a neighbor of the field worker. Seeking to know and understand her better led to contacts with her outside family. Experiences in this instance encouraged similar follow-ups with other families. These help to throw light on questions about why some of the young parents are like they are, as well as to give strong intimations about their future chances and behavior.

Discussed here are three mothers—all natives of Washington and in their mid-twenties. Each mother married while in high school, following pregnancy. Each marriage has been unsatisfactory. Two mothers have four children below six years of age. One of these mothers' husband is in the service; the other is separated from her husband, has one out-of-wedlock child, and was pregnant again by the same man. This second mother received public assistance. The third mother has two children, ages four and five. She lives with her husband and was then pregnant with a third child.

Each of the mothers is from a family in which there were several children. One is the oldest of six children, another the oldest of five, and the third the middle child of five. In each instance the parents of the mothers are living together, with some of the younger children still in the house. In each instance both parents of the mothers have generally always worked in service occupations with civil service status.

The noteworthy thing about the parents of each of these mothers is that they are all upwardly mobile homeowners, despite large families. For example, within the last five years one family has moved into a detached eight-room house in a middle-range income area. Another moved into the same area because of the "rowdiness of the housing project children" in the neighborhood in which they formerly lived. In discussions about their parents, all three mothers appear to perceive their parents as strongly motivated to acquire new and better things—a car, a house in a higher status neighborhood, new furniture. And the mothers seem to perceive themselves as casualties of this parental motivation. One said that she did not think her family should have "sacrificed" her for a car.

Another, in almost identical words, said she did not think her parents should have "sacrificed" her for a house. The mothers see themselves as having gone without adequate food and clothing while their parents were making efforts to move upward, as having been pressed into substitute mother roles with younger siblings while their mothers worked. None has a close relationship with her own mother. With indications of resentment they see their younger siblings as having lives and opportunities much better than theirs were. The younger brother of one is now a college sophomore.

The parents of the mother with illegitimate children are very critical of her; yet it appears that this mother is more actively concerned about her children's affectional needs than her parents were about hers. The father of another mother has never forgiven his son-in-law for getting his daughter pregnant while she was in high school; his daughter sees herself struggling with little success to develop a kind of "togetherness" in her family that she says she did not have in her home as a child. The third mother's parents appeared to be so tightly budgeted in their expensively furnished new house that they were obviously reluctant to feed their daughter's four hungry children during an extended Sunday visit. In contrast is the occasion when this same daughter shared scarce food supplies for several days with the two-year-old child she took in when a mother and five children were evicted.

A paradox is present in situations of this kind if parents striving to "get ahead"—to acquire the visible signs of better living and to get into a better neighborhood to bring up their children—wittingly or unwittingly sacrifice a child, or children, in the process.

In these families—those of the young mothers in public housing and of their parents in middle-income residential areas—the operation of class and cultural factors is complicated. In a sense these are very knowing families. They straddle deprivation and poverty *and* the better life and new affluence. Many of the wants and ways associated with each condition are familiar to the families of both generations. What each does about the wants and ways associated with these conditions, or can do about them—and why—are different matters.

The materials and analysis of the Child Rearing Study point to wide variety in the styles of individuals and families. They show that all low-income people are not lower class in orientations to life and in showing the preferences conventionally ascribed to this category.

Walter Miller's influential conception of lower-class culture holds that although it is not exclusive to lower-class people, the "female-based" household is a cardinal trait:

> . . . the way of life . . . is characteristic of a substantial portion of . . . our population defined as "lower class," [and] the material applies most accurately to that subsegment of this group whose family system centers around the "female-based" household. . . . If we take 40% of the households within this to be "female-based" units, we obtain an estimate of about 15% for the "hard core" lower class group.[17]

According to this formulation lower-class culture is in its clearest form in lower-class "female-based" households—roughly estimated as including one in six lower-class persons. This leaves considerable room for variation among the other 85 percent of the lower class and for considerable dilution of lower-class culture in the rest of the lower-class population.

Our field experience in Washington suggests that it is highly questionable that all or even a substantial majority of the low-income (lower-class) "female-based" households among Negroes are responsive to and supporters of a distinctively organized or integrated way of life. On the contrary, there is an indication of alternate and of mixed styles of living among low-income, "female-based" households in the Negro and other segments of the low-income population in contemporary urban centers. There are differing styles of lower-class family behavior; and action programs should be geared to differences within this "female-based" segment, and to similarities of low-income family behavior to adequate-income family behavior. Different types of low-income Negro families often live side by side in the same neighborhood or area, but that is often practically all that they do, or want to do, together. Still, much community organization and block work assumes that because these people live in the same area this in itself provides a basis for developing a viable and organized community.

The diversity and lack of consensus that characterize some locales in which the poorer members of the lower-income category live are suggested in the impressions of a staff anthropologist who spent a summer studying a one-block low-income conclave:

The scope and intensity of my observations were insufficient to justify generalization about the social position of those whose conduct of life is conspicuously disorganized in terms of the standards of the larger society and of their own immediate needs. Such persons include the men who are unable to hold a job and support their families and the perennial ADC mothers who exist in a kind of serial polyandry. I do not know to what extent and in what areas of activity such persons are accepted and rejected by their neighbors. Acceptance, especially for the women, is certainly greater than in the larger urban society, but some censure and a larger portion of pity is to be found in the attitudes and behavior of most respondents toward these "disorganized" persons.

Is there a representative Upton Square resident? In a sense there is not, since individuality and idiosyncrasies of character flourish there as they do not, at present, in conformist middle-class society. It can be stated, however, that most Upton Square men and women work hard, or fairly hard, for little material reward, judged by general American standards, and that they lead relatively circumscribed lives.

What are the goods that they obtain or wish to obtain from life? As stated earlier, I cannot venture to generalize about areas and modes of satisfaction, nor about the levels of aspiration, except to say that the former, although various, center to a considerable—to me even somewhat surprising—extent around life; and the latter are more in evidence than some sociological studies of the working class would lead one to expect. An Upton Square parent certainly hopes that his children will avoid "getting into trouble," but the aspirations of my respondents for their children were not limited to this negative hope as were those of the "hard core" proletarians reported in Walter Miller's Boston study. It must be said, however, that Upton Square parents appear to be as baffled by their adolescent children and neighbors as are their fellow Americans in many kinds of communities and status levels.[18]

Our Washington family and community materials indicate that the behaviors observed in the varying low-income families were not generated by or guided by an urban lower-class "cultural system in its own right—with an integrity of its own." This is not meant to suggest that there are no differences other than income between this category and the adequate-income category of the population, or that there are no modalities in the characteristics and in the behaviors of this segment. On the contrary, we reconfirm that there are several modes or styles of family living and child rearing rather than a single or basic mode or style among urban Negroes. We are especially impressed by the range of behavior within the low-income category of Negro families.

The behavior of the bulk of the poor Negro families appears as pragmatic adjustments to external and internal stresses and deprivations experienced in the quest for essentially common values. A seeming paradox is that affirmation of, if not demonstration of, some of America's traditional virtues and values in their purest form is found to be strong and recurrent among even the most deprived of Negro families. Our view is that it is probably more fruitful to think of different types of low-income Negro families reacting in various ways to the facts of their position and to relative isolation rather than to the imperatives of a lower-class or significantly different ethnic culture. It is important that we do not confuse the basic life chances and actual behavior of the contemporary Negro parent with his basic cultural values and preferences.

Our experience suggests further that the focus of efforts to change should be on background conditions and on precipitants of deviant behavior rather than on the presumably different class or cultural values operative in child-rearing behavior among Negroes, and particularly low-income Negroes. The way to remove the threat of the problem behavior of low-income Negro families is not likely to be found in a kind of functionalism or cultural relativism, or in sealing off persons who are presumed to be most inclined to exhibit such behavior; nor is it to be found in getting low-income urban Negro families in general, or a segment of them, to revamp what is presumed to be their culture.

NOTES

1. E. Franklin Frazier, *The Negro Family in the United States* (Chicago: Univ. of Chicago Press, 1939), p. xii.
2. Hylan Lewis, "The Changing Negro Family," in Eli Ginzberg, ed., *The Nation's Children,* Vol. I: *The Family and Social Change* (New York: Columbia Univ. Press, 1960).
3. A project sponsored by the Health and Welfare Council of the National Capital Area and supported by Mental Health Project Grants, 5-R11-MH 278-5, from the National Institutes of Health, U.S. Public Health Service, Department of Health, Education, and Welfare. The formal title is "Child Rearing Practices among Low Income Families in the District of Columbia"; the working title used is "Child Rearing Study."

   A considerable portion of this chapter is adapted from an unpublished position paper, "Culture, Class and the Behavior of Low Income Families," that was prepared for the Conference on Lower Class Culture, sponsored by the National Institute of Mental Health, Research Utilization Branch, and the New York State Youth Commission, in New York City, June 27–29, 1963.
4. M. G. Smith, "Social and Cultural Pluralism," in *Social and Cultural Pluralism in the Caribbean: Annals of the New York Academy of Sciences,* LXXXIII (Art. 5, January 20, 1960), 770.
5. David Riesman, "Psychological Types and National Charac-

ter," *American Quarterly,* V (1953), 330; cited in David M. Potter, *People of Plenty,* Phoenix Books edition (Chicago: Univ. of Chicago Press, 1960), p. 11.

6. Potter, *op. cit.,* p. 62.
7. Robert K. Merton, "Notes on Problem-Finding in Sociology," in Merton, *et al.,* eds., *Sociology Today: Problems and Prospects* (New York: Basic Books, 1959), p. xv.
8. Philip Hauser, "Rapid Growth: Key to Understanding Metropolitan Problems" (Address to the Washington Center for Metropolitan Studies, May 5, 1961).
9. A. L. Kroeber, *Anthropology* (New York: Harcourt, Brace & World, 1948), p. 272.
10. *Ibid.*
11. *Ibid.*
12. Our data collection was guided by a definition of low income. The income ceiling was based on the minimum-comfort workingman's budget for a family of four in Washington, D.C. All of the low-income families included in the study population would undoubtedly be placed in the lower class by any of the objective criteria currently used.
13. Oscar Lewis, "Personality Characteristics—Discussion," in F. L. K. Hsu, *Aspects of Culture and Personality: A Symposium* (New York: Abelard-Schuman, 1954), p. 38.
14. A public institution for the emergency care of neglected and dependent children.
15. Hyman Rodman's notion of "the lower class value stretch" is relevant here: Hyman Rodman, "The Lower Class Value Stretch" (Revision of a paper read at the annual meetings of the Eastern Sociological Society, April 1961 [mimeographed]; published in *Social Forces*). See also Elizabeth Herzog, "Unmarried Mothers: Some Questions to Be Answered and Some Answers to Be Questioned" (Paper presented at the Eastern Regional Conference, Child Welfare League of America, Baltimore, March 1, 1962).
16. Hylan Lewis, "The Changing Negro Family," *loc. cit.,* p. 136.
17. Walter B. Miller, "Cultural Features of an Urban Lower Class Community" (mimeographed), n.d., pp. 13–14.
18. Richard Slobodin, " 'Upton Square': A Field Report and Commentaray" (Child Rearing Study, Health and Welfare Council of the National Capital Area [mimeographed], 1960, p. 13).

The Means and Expressions of Protest

7 / Civil Rights Strategies for Negro Employment

August Meier

Historically speaking, civil rights groups have been slow to attack the problem of Negro unemployment. In their early years each of the major Negro protest organizations—the National Association for the Advancement of Colored People (NAACP), founded in 1909, the Congress of Racial Equality (CORE), founded in 1942, the Southern Christian Leadership Conference (SCLC), founded in 1957, and the Student Nonviolent Coordinating Committee (SNCC), founded in 1960—attacked discriminatory laws and the most overt forms of racism, such as disfranchisement and segregation in places of public accommodation. As time went on, each of these organizations added the problem of employment to its sphere of activities, but only since 1961 has employment become a principal focus of the Negro protest movement. The problems arising out of the poverty of the Negro masses—the problems of jobs, housing, and education—have now moved to the center of the stage, and they will almost certainly be the paramount concerns of civil rights organizations in the future.

☐ Beginnings, 1910–1930

In the light of recent developments, it is ironic that the earliest major organization to concern itself primarily with the problem of Negro employment was an agency commonly considered conservative, one which probably could not be described as a protest or civil rights organization until the "Negro Revolt" swept the country in the 1960's. I refer to the National Urban League. The League was founded in 1911, two years after the NAACP, as a coalition of three philanthropic groups interested in the economic and social problems of the underprivileged Negroes then first migrating to Northern cities in substantial numbers. Its founders were businessmen and professional people oriented toward social work and philanthropy. Most of them were allied with the conservative or accommodating wing of Negro leadership, then headed by Booker T. Washington, the founder of Tuskegee Institute in Alabama. Washington rose to prominence when conditions were rapidly deteriorating for Negroes, especially in the South. The period was characterized by lynchings and race riots, disfranchisement and Jim Crow laws, peonage on cotton plantations, and the rise of the discriminatory American Federation of Labor (AFL). Washington preached a program of thrift and industry, self-help, and racial solidarity that would elevate Negroes to middle-class status and thus "earn" for them the recognition of their citizenship rights. Basically, the Urban League hoped to increase Negro employment by improving the quality of Negro labor. Labor efficiency became a shibboleth to the League, for it accepted Washington's belief that discrimination in industry was due largely to lack of skill and careless work habits among Negroes. Like Washington, League officials stressed on the one hand the importance of Negro self-improvement and the virtues of skill, hard work, and thrift, and on the other hand a tactful and diplomatic approach to powerful whites. The organization therefore concentrated on "selling" Negro labor to white employers. Its methods were those of conciliation and gradualism. It trained Negro workers and held conferences with employers in order to demonstrate that Negro labor performed well. It assumed that once this was proven, economic discrimination would diminish or disappear. The League saw its basic role as one of creating an understanding between Negroes and white employers; most of its funds came from industry, and prominent white philanthropists were active in League affairs.

In its early years the Urban League did two major things. It operated as an employment agency and it created associations of Negro workers in order to train them in the more efficient performance of their tasks. The League hoped to see Negroes enter the more highly skilled jobs, but economic realities dictated that its efforts be directed toward maintaining the Negro's foothold in menial positions. Thus the pioneering New York branch of the League formed organizations not only of Negro mechanics, but also of elevator men, bellmen, pullman porters, and chauffeurs in order to improve the quality of their work. During World War I, when it had grown to half a dozen affiliates in Northeastern and Middle Western cities, the League naturally stressed the placement of Negroes in war industry.

During the prosperous 1920's, as the number of local Leagues grew, the organization's work expanded. It instituted an annual "Negro Industrial Week" to propagandize the value of Negro labor to businessmen, and in 1930 it initiated an annual "Negro Vocational Opportunity Campaign," aimed at encouraging high school and college youth to prepare themselves for better grades of employment. Vocational guidance, in fact, became a major activity of the national League's industrial department. Local Leagues continued to teach Negroes to be good workers. The Atlanta League, for example, proudly described how it trained janitors to be better janitors before referring them to jobs. Year in and year out the most consistent activity of the Leagues throughout the country was referring Negroes for job openings in industry and in domestic and menial labor. As a matter of fact, many local Leagues were basically employment agencies. Still, modest successes were registered by both national and local Leagues in persuading employers to open to Negroes jobs previously closed to them.

One serious problem that faced the League from the beginning was the attitude of organized labor to the Negro worker. Since white workers commonly regarded Negroes as hostile competitors, organized labor was, with some notable exceptions, an even greater bar to Negro industrial employment than were employers. Yet it was clear that without admission to labor unions the Negro's path to most skilled jobs would remain closed. In 1918 the League and the NAACP jointly conferred on the subject with Samuel Gompers and other representatives of the AFL. In 1920 and in 1925 the League communicated again with the AFL, but the AFL blandly asserted that it did not discriminate. Consequently the League, while urging the acceptance of Negroes into unions and encouraging Negroes to join them where possible, often found itself compelled to side with employers.

The problem became acute with the closing of war industries after World War I. In 1919 the League's annual conference passed a set of resolutions that endorsed the principle of collective bargaining, but in view of realities urged Negroes to proceed cautiously in seeking admission to unions. Negro workers were further advised to work as strikebreakers only where a union excluded them from membership; to organize with white men where conditions were suitable; and where such a course was not feasible, to organize themselves to bargain with employers and organized labor. This statement was broad enough to permit the autonomous local Leagues to proceed as they deemed best—to endorse and work with unions, to refer Negroes to employers as strikebreakers, or to remain neutral. The national League, it should be emphasized, encouraged Negroes to join unions and opposed strikebreaking. In 1925, in cooperation with the New York labor movement, it established the Trade Union Committee for Organizing Negroes. This committee achieved a few results, but was disbanded after a year and a half.

Local Leagues were less sympathetic than the national office to the notion that Negroes could expect much from organized labor. This attitude was partly due to the fact that their financial donations came mainly from influential businessmen, who also sat on the boards of local Leagues. Thus the national League supported the organizing drive of the Brotherhood of Sleeping Car Porters, but the Chicago League, which received an annual contribution from the Pullman Company, opposed it. In some cases, during the twenties and early thirties, local League officials deliberately supplied strikebreakers to employers. This action was due to more than desire for financial support; the officials were convinced that organized labor could not be trusted. Time and time again, AFL unions had organized plants that had a substantial percentage of Negro workers, only to freeze out the Negroes later and become lily-white organizations. Local League officials justified the use of their industrial departments to supply strikebreakers by reasoning that after a successful strike, Negroes would be eliminated by the union. In addition, it was hoped that gains in job status won by Negroes during a strike would be maintained after it; unfortunately this rarely occurred. The strikebreaking activities of local Leagues have often been criticized as reflecting the upper-class bias of their leaders, and in part they did. Yet the record of labor was such that local League officers, desperately attempting to secure job opportunities, inevitably tended to aid anti-union employers. Operating in a milieu where their achievements could at best be limited, local League personnel were placed in a cruel and tragic dilemma. In general then, the League's endorsement and encouragement of Negro entrance into labor unions remained largely a verbal commitment; in the context of the times it is hard to see how it could have done differently.

Unlike the conciliatory Urban League, the National Association for the Advancement of Colored People was founded as a protest organization by Negro and white liberal opponents of Booker T. Washington. Its program of securing the Negro's constitutional rights through propaganda, legislation, and court action was considered incredibly radical at the time. During the first two decades and more of its existence the NAACP handled labor problems in the same way it dealt with other kinds of discrimination. It was not concerned with finding jobs—an activity it left to the Urban League—but with protesting, on the basis of civil liberties, against discrimination by government, by unions and, less often, by private employers. There was no concerted attack on any of these matters, not even on the question of union racism, though the NAACP, like the League, several times communicated with the AFL in an attempt to discuss the question. Like the League it was consistently rebuffed.

The NAACP investigated and tried to ameliorate specific complaints about employment whenever it could. In 1921, for example, it called the attention of the Department of Justice to cases of Southern peonage. Its most notable successes were achieved in instances where a particularly egregious act of discrimination committed by a Federal agency was brought to its attention. But the problem was vast and the Association's resources were limited, so there were only isolated cases of NAACP intervention. Moreover, employment problems were a distinctly subordinate part of the NAACP's activities, which centered on disfranchisement, segregation, and lynchings.

More radical than either the NAACP or the Urban League was the group around A. Philip Randolph and Chandler Owen, who edited the *Messenger* magazine between 1917 and 1928. This group of socialists insisted that the only solution to the Negro workers' problems lay in united action with white labor. They appealed to organized labor to admit Negroes and exhorted Negroes to join unions. The magazine was published in New York, where the socialist-oriented needle trades and clothing unions provided a unique milieu that afforded at least some justification for the hope of united Negro and labor action. But the only real success the *Messenger* group could claim was the organization of the Brotherhood of Sleeping Car Porters.

□ Depression and New Deal, 1930–1940

The economic catastrophe of the 1930's caused a sharp shift in the character of the work of the racial advancement organizations: The critical economic problems of the working class received far more attention, and the approach to these problems was modified.

The Urban League found its employment bureaus helpless, and its industrial secretaries across the country came to concentrate on intervening with New Deal agencies to secure fair treatment for Negroes in the apportionment of jobs on public works financed with Federal funds. Even before the election of Franklin D. Roosevelt, the League had made representations against gross exploitation of Negro workers on the War Department's Mississippi River flood control project, and against the exclusion of Negro workers from the construction of Boulder Dam. The NAACP, whose annual reports between 1928 and 1931 had ignored the problems of Negro labor, in 1932 and 1933 conducted major protest campaigns in regard to these two matters, and like the League it worked to protect Negro interests in the New Deal agencies. During the early New Deal period, the Association's efforts in this direction were generally undertaken as part of a coalition of twenty-two racial and interracial organizations known as the Joint Committee for National Recovery, which did especially notable work in protesting against discriminatory provisions in the codes being drawn up under the National Industrial Recovery Act.

But the most dramatic type of activity on the employment front during the early years of the Depression was a form of what is now described as "direct action," conducted for the most part by groups outside of the well-known national organizations. This activity consisted of "Don't Buy Where You Can't Work" campaigns designed to obtain clerical and sales jobs in white-owned stores in Negro neighborhoods. The first of these campaigns occurred in Chicago, where, three or four years before the crash of 1929, the Negro community was already experiencing a sharp reduction in employment that foreshadowed the Depression. The campaign was initiated there in 1927 by the local Urban League but was soon taken over by a militant weekly, the Chicago *Whip*. Picketing and boycotts had signal success. With the coming of the Depression this technique spread to New York, where a self-styled Muslim, Sufi Abdul Hamid, started a campaign that was later taken over by middle-class leadership; to Washington, where the work was done under the aegis of a group known as the New Negro Alliance; and to Richmond, Cleveland, and other places, where it was led by NAACP branches. Success was spotty and Negro leadership was divided, for it was argued that if whites employed the same tactics, Negroes would lose more jobs than they gained. It is noteworthy that the beneficiaries of these campaigns were not the masses but the children of middle-class Negroes, who sought sales jobs because of the scarcity of other types of employment.

During the early thirties neither the NAACP nor most local Urban Leagues had supported the AFL's union expansion drives, conducted under Section 7A of the National Recovery Act, for Negroes were unsure of the motives of organized labor. The NAACP suspected that, consistent with its past practice, the AFL was planning to use Section 7A to eventually exclude Negroes from jobs they already held.

In the middle thirties, however, came the rise of the Congress of Industrial Organizations (CIO), whose racially egalitarian outlook made the NAACP and the Urban League more sympathetic toward the labor movement. The League organized numerous workers' councils in over a hundred cities as a device for educating workers in the principles of trade unionism, and in some cases even secured the admission of Negroes from these councils into AFL craft unions. However there was no unity of opinion on this matter of endorsing the industrial unions either in the League or in the NAACP. For one thing, there remained for some time a widespread feeling among Negro leaders throughout the country that the CIO was too radical. The NAACP national board was split on the question. For example, only after considerable debate did the liberal members obtain permission for the president of the United Automobile Workers (UAW) to address the NAACP convention in Detroit in 1937. The difficulties encountered by the NAACP in shifting from its traditional program was epitomized in a crucial decision taken in 1935. By that time the legal department had begun to develop through court litigation a series of precedents against labor union discrimination. But the NAACP decided to abandon this line of action and to devote most of its slender resources to the campaign against school segregation.

On the other hand, considerable pressure was put on the NAACP by some relatively radical intellectuals, both on its board and off, and especially by a group at Howard University. Some of these intellectuals were among the leaders in the formation of the National Negro Congress in 1936. The Congress was a coalition of a wide variety of fraternal, religious, labor, and civic groups, designed to fight for Negro advancement, especially on the economic front. The Communist Party came to be the real driving force behind the Congress, but this did not become evident until later, and many non-Communist notables were connected with it. At that time, the Communists were attempting to form a united front on a progressive (as opposed to a radical) program, joining with socialists, liberals, and other "petit-bourgeois elements." The Congress cooperated closely with left-wing trade unions. It agitated on behalf of A. Philip Randolph's resolution calling for the outlawing of race bias in the AFL. In 1940, when the Communists openly asserted their control over the organization, most of the non-Communist groups and individuals ended their affiliation. But it had provided an important platform for the articulation of the broad range of Negro protest in the period, with major emphasis on union affiliation and a labor point of view.

Pressed from the liberal and radical left, the NAACP gradually came to embrace the industrial unions. The final step came during a strike against the Ford Motor Company in 1941, on the eve of United States entry into World War II. Responding to the appeal of UAW leaders, who promised to correct discriminatory practices within the union, the executive secretary of the NAACP personally joined the picket line and circled the River Rouge plant in a sound truck, urging Negro strikebreakers to come out and join the strikers. A number did so, and the consequences were as momentous for the NAACP as for the UAW. For the next decade and a half the idea of securing racial advancement through an alliance with the industrial unions was a cornerstone of NAACP strategy.

□ World War II, 1940–1945

With the rise of defense employment that began in 1940, the NAACP and Urban League again changed tactics. Each in its own way exerted pressure to open opportunities for Negroes in aircraft and other war industries and at military installations. The League, whose program was concentrated in the employment field, undoubtedly accomplished far more than NAACP branches, even though the United States Employment Service took over much of the League's job-referral function. The League worked to secure entrance of Negroes into government training programs for war industries, and in several cities was even able to secure the admission of a small number of Negro workers into the highly discriminatory building trade unions.

However, the most dramatic, and in long-range effect, the most important, activity on the employment front during the war years came from A. Philip Randolph, the president of the Brotherhood of Sleeping Car Porters. In 1941 he threatened a mass march of 10,000 Negroes on Washington if President Roosevelt did not act decisively to ban discrimination in the defense industries and the armed services. The NAACP and Urban League leaders were at first cool toward the idea of mass action of this sort, but once the idea caught fire, they gave their support. The march was called off only after Roosevelt reluctantly issued an executive order establishing a Federal

Fair Employment Practices Committee. Though the FEPC lacked enforcement powers, it established a precedent for considering job discrimination a denial of civil rights, and paved the way for the fair employment practices laws passed by a number of states after the war and by the Federal Government in 1964. And though the march was not held, the threat of it foreshadowed the future in two fundamental ways: it suggested the crucial importance of economic problems to the Negro protest movement (as distinguished from the conciliatory Urban League), and it was deliberately based on mass action by the Negro working class.

□ The Postwar Era, 1945–1960

In the decade and a half following World War II the Urban League once again modified its strategy. It was the League's belief that the Federal Government performed the referral of employees for routine jobs better than the League could. Therefore the League emphasized placing Negroes in jobs that members of the race had never held before. In 1947 it instituted a "Pilot Placement Program," under which well-qualified Negroes would be placed in positions previously closed to them, with the expectation that if they were successful other Negroes would be employed in similar jobs. Some very well-known corporations participated in this program. Unfortunately, the result was all too often merely token employment of overqualified Negroes, as the League itself complained. In other areas, the League expanded its vocational guidance program and it was able to secure the cooperation of industrial personnel in initiating formal college career conferences. In 1949 the League convinced industrial employers to conduct job interviews at a Negro university for the first time. It also established a liaison with labor leaders, and it consulted with officials of government agencies. But basically its program continued to be oriented toward convincing businessmen that employment of Negroes was both good ethics and good business.

The most remarkable innovation in the postwar years was the development of the NAACP's labor program. After the war, and through the middle 1950's, NAACP cooperation with the industrial unions was at a high level. After the war, at the request of its membership, the NAACP established a labor department responsible for investigating and exposing discriminatory employment practices in government and business. During the late forties it concentrated on attempting to secure policy changes in the government and in firms with government contracts, and on trying to obtain legislation that would benefit Negro workers. It attacked cases of discrimination in government agencies. It was instrumental in securing President Truman's executive order barring discrimination by the government and by companies holding government contracts. It persuaded the Department of Labor to take its first halting step toward integrating Negroes in Federally financed apprentice training programs. (However, apprenticeships are controlled by the craft unions, and consequently, despite instances of local victories, apprenticeship training programs to this day have remained generally impervious to sustained NAACP attacks.) The NAACP also cooperated with other groups in obtaining the passage of state and municipal fair employment laws. It organized a small labor committee consisting of certain influential trade union officials, and through them it eliminated some instances of discrimination both in the AFL and the CIO. It worked closely with organized labor in the fight against antilabor legislation in the Eightieth Congress, and urged President Truman to veto the Taft-Hartley bill. And for the first time the Association took an active interest in the plight of migrant agricultural workers, attempting to secure government intervention to improve their condition. This has continued to be an interest of the Department of Labor, and during the 1950's the NAACP was instrumental in obtaining some improvements in Federal policy. But the exploitation of these migrant workers remains a major scandal.

At the turn of the decade, the NAACP labor department

was reorganized, being officially assigned three major goals: to eliminate race restrictions in the hiring, training, and promotion of Negroes; to secure equal rights for Negroes in trade unions; and to develop trade union support for the NAACP civil rights program. In carrying out this mandate the labor secretary worked directly with unions, with industry, and with state and city fair employment units.

Beginning at the close of the 1940's the NAACP assigned a liaison person to work closely with local branches and with unions to further NAACP-labor cooperation, and this work was now expanded. The Association's labor program was an institutionalized expression of the belief that racial advancement would come largely through a Negro-labor alliance. During the flurry of CIO organizing drives in the early forties, some branches had worked with the industrial unions to recruit Negro workers, and this practice was now revived. In some factories where Negroes formed a large proportion of the work force, the labor secretary, in cooperation with local branches, organized a bloc Negro vote for the CIO union in the NLRB elections. At times unions requested, and received, the help of the labor secretary and a local branch in convincing Negro strikebreakers to leave their jobs. In this manner, the NAACP assisted not only several CIO unions, but also the United Hat Cap and Millinery Workers, the International Ladies Garment Workers, and others in the AFL.

Some unions made substantial financial contributions to the NAACP. The Association tried to work *with* unions to end their discriminatory practices, assisting in setting up workshops and conferences on fair employment, and in establishing civil rights departments. Beginning in 1952, it began to attack the question of separate seniority lines in Southern industry. These were provisions written into union contracts that allocated specific occupational categories to Negro and white workers, thus keeping Negroes out of skilled jobs regardless of their abilities or their length of service. The NAACP received the support of the national leaders of the Oilworkers International Union on this question, and as a result thousands of jobs in Southern oil and chemical industries were opened to Negroes. A few years later, the NAACP worked with the UAW to eliminate this type of discrimination in certain automobile plants in Michigan and in St. Louis, and since 1960 it has made some progress in the Southern pulp and paper industry.

In addition, the NAACP made determined efforts to break down discriminatory practices of both unions and employers by filing complaints with President Eisenhower's Committee on Government Contracts. However, it was only at the end of the decade that even slight progress was made through this tactic, most notably in the aircraft industry. Also at that time, the legal campaign against Southern school segregation having been won, NAACP lawyers began again to attack racist unions in the courts. On the local level, the NAACP, exerting pressure through state or municipal fair employment units, occasionally secured the admission of Negroes into apprenticeship training programs.

The method of increasing job opportunities by gaining concessions from employers was an Urban League specialty, but the NAACP also engaged in it from time to time, beginning in the late forties. After mid-century, the Association experimented with picketing and other forms of unpleasant publicity when negotiations were unsuccessful. In a few instances, most notably at the Philco Company plant in Philadelphia in 1952, it was able to open up hundreds of job opportunities with these tactics.

The merger of the AFL and the CIO in 1955 was followed by a slowing of progress on the problem of union discrimination. The merged labor federation, despite the existence of a civil rights committee, seemed more characterized by the old AFL attitude than by that of the former CIO. This situation led to increasing Negro disillusionment with labor unions. Negroes were no longer willing to accept the discrimination that plagued even the most progressive industrial unions. Toward the end of the decade, the situation worsened as a result of the tightening labor market. With fewer available jobs and declining membership rolls, unions were less likely than before to open new opportunities for Negro workers. In response to this situation, the NAACP first attempted to negotiate directly with labor leaders; when this failed, the NAACP in 1959 finally attacked the racists in the AFL-CIO openly. While still friendly with the more egalitarian unions such as the UAW, the United Packinghouse Workers, and the United Rubber Workers of America, the NAACP generally became more critical of organized labor, and the old dream of securing racial justice through an alliance with the industrial unions faded.

During the 1950's the Congress of Racial Equality (CORE), which from its inception in 1942 had pioneered in the use of nonviolent direct action as a weapon against race discrimination, began to attack employment bias. Until at least the latter part of 1961, CORE's attention was devoted almost exclusively to desegregating places of public amusement and accommodation. But in the late 1950's it experimented with direct action techniques (picketing and boycotting, or "selective buying") in attempting to open up new job opportunities. How much direct action was applied in agitating for employment during the 1950's is a question that awaits painstaking investigation. There was of course a tradition of such action stemming from the "Don't Buy Where You Can't Work" campaigns of the thirties. But these had been limited to picketing and boycotting for jobs in retail stores located in Negro areas. One of the earliest cases of picketing for employment outside the ghetto was a mass demonstration, in 1939, at the New York World's Fair, organized by a coalition known as the Greater New York Coordinating Committee. After World War II there was sporadic picketing and boycotting of white-owned stores in Negro neighborhoods; beginning in the early 1950's, the NAACP occasionally picketed manufacturing concerns; in 1958 the threat of a combined direct action project by the NAACP and CORE secured the employment of Negroes as sales clerks in department stores in downtown St. Louis; and in the same year, CORE conducted what may have been the first *boycott* of an *industrial* firm, in its successful campaign against a St. Louis bread manufacturer. Nevertheless, despite scattered victories, at the end of the decade direct action was still distinctly a weapon of secondary importance in the struggle against employment bias.

By 1960 the NAACP, the Urban League, and CORE were all in some degree attacking the employment problem. The League concentrated on the problem of industrial opportunity. The NAACP's labor department was one of many NAACP activities, but it was an activity that was vigorously conducted. CORE's interest in the question was minimal, paradoxically, in view of the prominence of socialist-oriented people among CORE's founders and early participants. Both the Urban League and CORE concentrated on gaining concessions from employers—the League by conciliatory negotiation, CORE by direct action. The NAACP was largely, though not exclusively, concerned with the problem of fighting trade union discrimination. The NAACP and the Urban League carried on the most extensive work, and their approaches, though overlapping to some extent, generally complemented rather than competed with each other.

□ The Civil Rights Revolution, 1960–1964

Since 1960 dramatic changes have occurred in the character of the Negro protest movement and have led to sweeping modifications in its approach to the quest for equal job opportunities.

The developments were prefigured by the rising tempo of direct action during the late fifties. The most famous instance is the Montgomery, Alabama, bus boycott of 1955–1956, which propelled Martin Luther King to international fame. In 1957, King organized the Southern Christian Leadership Conference (SCLC), which sought to coordinate direct action movements in various Southern cities. The student sit-ins of 1960–1961 and the formation of the Student Nonviolent Coordinating Committee (SNCC) in 1960 gave the civil rights movement a new edge of militancy and galvanized the older organizations. Both SCLC and SNCC have remained Southern organizations, though they utilize the nonviolent direct action tactic pioneered by CORE. CORE did not establish itself in the South in a substantial way until 1961.

The competitive rivalry that developed among all the civil rights groups further enhanced the militant, immediatist character of Negro protest. The NAACP, among whose branches direct action was previously a peripheral activity where it was employed at all, at times has become deeply involved in direct-action demonstrations, while also continuing its work along legal and legislative lines. Even the Urban League has become more militant in tone. Among the organizations engaged strictly in direct action—CORE, SCLC, and SNCC—there are differences in style. SCLC has a tendency to engage in a few highly dramatic demonstrations, most notably the Birmingham demonstration of 1963. Southern members of CORE and SNCC tend to be "true believers," more spontaneous than any of the others. However, there are Northern activists who are every bit as militant and self-sacrificing as those in the South, and there is a wide range of types in all organizations. There are certain militant NAACP branches that heartily subscribe to "taking to the streets," while other NAACP branches are completely opposed to such activity. Differences between the organizations are not solely due to matters of tactics and strategy. Often, in fact, personality clashes appear more important than ideological disagreements in explaining the rivalries among various civil rights groups. Usually, however, these interorganizational conflicts, which are especially strong on the local level, have helped rather than hindered the movement. For each organization, in trying to outdo the others in the competition for funds and prestige, engages in more constructive effort toward achieving racial equality than it would otherwise. And when it is important that they do so, the various organizations usually manage to cooperate on joint projects.

The civil rights movement has not only become more militant since 1960; it has also become more of a mass movement. The alienated urban slum dwellers have been stirred by the Negro Revolt: they have shared in the "revolution in expectations" that has occurred among American Negroes since the middle 1950's. But the "dream" of which Martin Luther King speaks so eloquently has remained for most of them more than ever, as the poet Langston Hughes has put it, "a dream deferred." Raised hopes have been met only with the same old bleak prospects of chronic unemployment, rat-infested tenements, and overcrowded and inferior schools. By 1963 it was evident that in a number of communities some of the lower class, many of whom are chronically unemployed, were becoming involved in the movement—and were not always remaining completely nonviolent. The degree to which the lower classes actually participate in the civil rights movement is one that calls for further research. SCLC, CORE, and in particular SNCC attempt to enlist the active participation of the "man in the street," but it is difficult to assess the effectiveness of this practice. Some of the most militant CORE chapters are made up of urban slum dwellers but there are also militant CORE chapters with a very middle-class membership. On the other hand many NAACP branches have a predominantly working-class membership, including certain branches that are quite properly criticized for ignoring the interests of the masses. Often the members and leaders of a CORE chapter and an NAACP branch, or of an SCLC affiliate and an NAACP branch, appear to be drawn from similar strata of society; the differences appear to lie in the kinds of personalities each group tends to attract, or in idiosyncrasies in patterns of local leadership. In general, it may be said that CORE and SNCC are more militant than the NAACP and more self-consciously concerned with the problems of the Negro masses—a paradoxical situation in view of the fact that both CORE and SNCC include many middle-class white militants, while the NAACP is almost entirely run and financed by Negroes.

Concurrently with these developments, a growing emphasis

was placed on economic problems. There are several reasons for this. For one thing, as disfranchisement and segregation in public accommodations were being eliminated, it grew clear that the economic status of the masses was the root of the whole problem facing the Negro community. Second, as the movement became more of a mass movement, it naturally tended to articulate the needs of the working classes. The ironic result was that the most militant elements in the protest movement came to the conclusion reached by the conservative founders of the Urban League—that the economic problems were central.

Since 1960 the NAACP labor program has been expanded along the lines laid down in the late fifties. Greater emphasis has been placed on the development of legal weapons against biased labor organizations, and in a new stratagem the NLRB was asked to decertify such racist unions. After President John F. Kennedy established his Committee on Equal Employment Opportunity, the NAACP filed numerous complaints against unions and against companies with government contracts. As a result of the representations of the NAACP labor department before this Committee, many new job opportunities in aircraft firms have become available, the historic pattern of discrimination in the Southern steel industry has been broken, and the employment practices of Southern textile and tobacco factories and paper and pulp mills have begun to change. Probably the greatest victory of the NAACP labor department came in 1961, when the Lockheed plant at Marietta, Georgia, hired over two hundred Negroes in skilled categories, bringing to a conclusion a four-year campaign against the company and against the International Association of Machinists, which for many years had maintained a segregated local at this plant.

The NAACP also began extensive use of direct action techniques to secure fair employment, though not all of its branches favor this type of activity. Following the victories in the 1960 lunch-counter sit-ins, in which many NAACP youth councils and college chapters participated, local NAACP units, such as those at Durham, North Carolina and at Savannah, Georgia, employed similar direct action to obtain from dozens to hundreds of jobs in drug stores, variety stores, and other retail outlets. In 1963 the NAACP demonstrated against building trades unions in New York, Philadelphia, Cleveland, Pittsburgh, and other cities, but the "less-than-token" accomplishments of these demonstrations did not break the general pattern of discrimination. On the other hand, in 1964, as a result of demonstrations in forty-one cities from Buffalo, New York, to San Francisco, the NAACP compelled General Motors to employ Negroes in secretarial, managerial, professional, and supervisory capacities for the first time. The NAACP's labor activity is still but one aspect of its broad program; but outside of the Urban League it is the only racial advancement organization to employ a specialist in the area. On the local level, CORE chapters are more consistently interested in employment opportunities than are NAACP branches, and have obtained a greater number of openings, but the labor department at the NAACP's national office has secured thousands of new job openings for Negroes (often through large-scale direct action campaigns). In addition, it has the most varied, and in some respects the most sophisticated program for combating job discrimination of any civil rights group, being the only one that employs legal strategy and tactics.

The NAACP has not been alone in its accelerated campaign against racism in trade unions. In the spring of 1960, Randolph established the Negro American Labor Council (NALC) to fight discrimination from within the AFL-CIO. Its board consists chiefly of Negro members of unions, and it has affiliates in a number of cities. Perhaps its most important activity has been organizing Negro caucuses within unions. The most dramatic fruit of this practice was the election of a Negro to the international board of the UAW in 1963. The Trade Union Leadership Council of Detroit, which accomplished this, is the NALC's most active affiliate. It has also eliminated racial entrance bars in eighteen of the nineteen construction unions in Detroit, and has organized a program for training Negro youth to qualify them for apprenticeship openings.

In examining the leading nonviolent direct action organizations and local direct action groups, it is interesting to note that SNCC, the most militant of all of these, has done relatively little in the employment area. This is not because SNCC is unconcerned about the problems of the masses. On the contrary, SNCC workers in general have greater psychological identification with the masses than do most active people in other civil rights groups, with the exception of members of some CORE chapters. Moreover, SNCC has been the most successful in securing the active participation of working-class people. But SNCC has concentrated its activity in the hard-core areas of the Deep South, where the fight against disfranchisement, not to mention public accommodations, is still to be won.

SCLC affiliates and CORE chapters have become very active in campaigns against job bias, and their work has been supplemented by local *ad hoc* groups, often led by ministers. One of the outstanding cases involved Philadelphia clergymen, under whose leadership selective buying campaigns opened 3,000 jobs for Negroes in consumer-goods industries between 1960 and 1963. Less successful were the Brooklyn ministers who in 1963 demonstrated against discrimination in the building trades; like the NAACP and CORE they foundered on the rock of union intransigence. In the South, one can point to a number of efforts, including the highly successful "Operation Breadbasket," sponsored in Atlanta by SCLC and local ministers, which opened up many white-collar clerical and sales positions in 1963. Since 1961, CORE chapters have given increasing emphasis to the employment situation. By 1963 this issue had become their major concern, and the only issue on which practically all of them worked consistently.

During the years 1960–1964 there has been an evolution in direct action strategy against job bias. The power of the boycott became very evident during the sit-in campaigns against variety and drug stores in 1960–1961, and once the lunch counters were open, it was natural that there would be efforts in many Southern cities to secure employment in such stores, and later in other downtown businesses that had a significant proportion of Negro customers. It is important to point out that these selective buying campaigns differed from the "Don't Buy Where You Can't Work" campaigns of the 1930's in that they were directed at downtown stores also patronized by whites. This development was in part made possible by the growing purchasing power of Negroes and by the rising proportion of Negroes in the central core of urban centers, both trends leading to greater dependence on the Negro market by downtown businesses. A further change in tactics occurred in 1963, especially in the South, with the appearance of the tendency to package all sorts of demands, economic and otherwise, into one thrust for "Freedom Now." Generally this approach did not prove especially successful as a technique for improving job opportunities, and it was soon dropped.

The first type of business to receive the attention of the activists of the sixties was the retail establishment—the variety store, the downtown specialty and department store, and the chain food store. Once these had changed their policies, civil rights groups moved on to other types of firms. Generally they picked as targets those businesses that are most sensitive to pressures from direct actionists because they manufacture consumer goods, because they are regulated by public commissions, or because, for other reasons, they are seriously concerned with their public image. These categories include telephone companies, gas and electric companies, milk and bread companies, and banks. CORE has been pre-eminent in dealing with these types of companies. It has, moreover, specialized in obtaining semiskilled jobs, requiring a minimum of training—jobs for which high school graduates can easily qualify. It has been unusually successful with banks in many parts of the country. For example, in Boston one bank alone agreed to hire over two hundred Negroes in a wide variety of job categories. And the agreement CORE made in the summer of 1964 with the Bank of America, in California, was a major victory that provided for the hiring of 8,000 Negroes in a twelve-month period.

Direct actionists have been slow to apply their techniques to heavy industry, as firms in this area are less susceptible to consumer boycotts and to loss of a good public image. It is true that the NAACP is working with increasing success through the President's Committee on Equal Employment Opportunity, and that the Urban League has achieved many notable advances with such companies. But for the most part, direct actionists have not attacked firms of this sort. As late as the end of 1964 the Newark, New Jersey, chapter of CORE appeared almost unique in its policy of practically ignoring food chains and other retail outlets, and concentrating on major manufacturing enterprises. The chapter has achieved some significant successes, and the future will almost certainly witness more of this kind of activity.

By late 1963 and 1964, the lessons derived from direct action were evident to business as well as to civil rights groups. Consequently the very threat of a demonstration was often sufficient to bring about a settlement. On the other hand, although there was something of a rapprochement between the more progressive unions like the UAW and the Negro protest movement, the events of 1963 clearly demonstrated that direct action techniques were of very limited usefulness when applied to highly racist craft unions such as those in the building trades.

Because of their histories and structures, the various civil rights groups which employ direct action have varying styles of operation. The NAACP, although it utilizes direct action in many branches and on certain projects sponsored by the national office, still places a great deal of reliance on legal action and on pressure exerted through government agencies. The likelihood that it will be the threat of decertification by the NLRB that will break down the barriers to entrance to the skilled craft unions suggests the continuing importance of the

NAACP's legalistic tactics. Because of the central role of the labor secretary at the national office, the NAACP's attacks tend to be somewhat more coordinated around the country than those of other organizations. Partly for the same reason, and partly because of its emphasis on filing complaints with the President's Committee, the NAACP deals to a great extent with top management levels of national concerns. CORE, SCLC, and local groups depend exclusively on local direct action. Of these only CORE is a national organization, but it finds that large corporations prefer to deal with the issue on a piecemeal basis, making changes when local community pressures warrant them. Thus, CORE chapters, with their high degree of autonomy, initiate their own action programs. There is a tendency, however, for a successful campaign by one chapter to be imitated by others. During 1963–1964, for example, many CORE chapters concentrated on banks, with signal accomplishments from California to Massachusetts.

Since 1962 the direct action movement, particularly CORE's, has stressed not token representation, but rather the theory that special consideration is required to compensate for past discrimination. Agreements now often carry definite stipulations that among new personnel hired a disproportionate number will be nonwhite until a fair representation of Negroes is achieved. For example, CORE's agreement with the A & P food stores in New York City in 1964 provided that during the next year ninety percent of new employees would be nonwhite. This figure is unusually high, but it is representative of the insistence of direct actionists that there must be compensatory or preferential treatment of Negroes until a reasonable balance of white and nonwhite employment is achieved.

Curiously enough the idea of compensatory employment policies originally came not from CORE militants but from the Urban League. New conditions have brought a marked change in League tactics, and beginning in 1961 it became far more aggressive. League leadership projected dynamic new slogans such as "compensatory employment" and proposed a "domestic Marshall Plan" to help unemployed and deprived Negroes overcome the serious disabilities resulting from three centuries of deprivation. The Negro masses, the League holds, must be given special treatment that will prepare them to compete with others on a level of equality. Merely to decree equality by law will not correct the grave imbalance created by the past. Genuine equality cannot be achieved if Negroes lack the training and skills to make use of new opportunities. Therefore, the League holds, a special effort must be made in employment, education, manpower retraining, youth motivation, and family strengthening to bring deprived Negroes to the point where they will not be at a disadvantage in competition.

Employers, pressured by militants from CORE, NAACP, and other groups, have increasingly turned to local Urban Leagues for help in obtaining Negro recruits. So sudden was the awakening of the business community that at first many Leagues were embarrassed to find themselves unable to fulfill this function. The national League met this situation by creating a "Skills Bank," a roster of people with skills needed by industry who in the past had found no use for their training because of employer bias.

The League's years of traditional alliance with business have now paid off for both the League and the civil rights movement as a whole. League officials, who formerly were "liked" by businessmen because they appeared to "understand" the businessman's "problems" when it came to employing Negroes, are now in a position to speak bluntly and to demand rather than supplicate. Both nationally and locally, League officials can now exert strong pressures upon business by pointing out the folly of not following League recommendations. The Urban League does not itself participate in direct-action demonstrations, but nationally and in most of the local Leagues it recognizes their value. By staying out of the streets, the League retains the confidence of business; at the same time it is in a position to interpret most effectively to the business community the programs and goals of the more militant groups. The national League and the more effective of the local

Leagues are of definite assistance to the more militant organizations, although the militants frequently are unaware of this fact. At the same time the pressure of the militant groups makes business more appreciative of the League, and thus enhances the effectiveness of the League's operations. The legal pressures which the NAACP uses along with other techniques similarly serve to bolster the efforts of both the Urban League and the direct action organizations.

The varied approaches of the different organizations, particularly the direct action strategy, have in the years 1961–1964 created substantial increases in job opportunities for Negroes. Yet clearly the continuing high rate of Negro unemployment suggests that all of the techniques and organizations put together have not been able to solve the problem of mass Negro unemployment. There is, in fact, some evidence that civil rights organizations have come to believe that direct action has its limitations; that it cannot by itself end the economic problems of the masses. This is true even of CORE, the pioneer in nonviolent direct action. Civil rights groups have become increasingly convinced that only changes in Federal economic policies can get to the heart of the problem of structural unemployment. Consequently there has been increasing discussion, especially in CORE and SCLC, of the thesis that the civil rights organizations should get directly involved in partisan politics in order to secure government intervention in solving the enormous economic and social problems that Negro poverty and deprivation present.

The pre-eminence of direct action among the tactics of civil rights organizations may well be over. As this chapter is being written (December 1964), most of the civil rights organizations seem unsure of their future strategy, uncertain of what techniques would now be best to use. The course of the movement has proven so unpredictable in the last few years that it is not possible to say with any degree of confidence what direction the strategy of Negro protest is likely to take in the coming months and years. One may hazard the guess, however, that we are likely to witness the evolution of a pluralistic strategy to solve the problems of the masses; a strategy including legalism, various types of direct action, involvement in partisan politics, and whatever other tools may appear to hold some promise.

□ Conclusion

Over half a century ago the philanthropists and social workers who founded the National Urban League had seen that the economic status of Negroes was the fundamental problem. Closely associated with Booker T. Washington, most of them shared his naive assumption that if they increased their economic efficiency, unskilled Negro workers would be accorded their rightful place in the economic system. The Urban League's founders hoped that such preparation for economic participation would ultimately lead to the acceptance of Negroes by their fellow citizens, and to the disappearance of other forms of discrimination. By an interesting ironic twist, history has proven these philanthropists wrong and at the same time has brought other racial advancement groups to endorse their emphasis on economic conditions. Unlike Washington and his Urban League friends, Negro protest leaders started out by attacking disfranchisement and segregation directly, and, with some conspicuous exceptions, regarded economic problems as a secondary order of business. But the very success of the protest movement in securing the franchise and the destruction of segregation laws made it plain that the economic problems facing Negroes could not be solved simply through the achievement of constitutional rights, and that these economic problems were vital in any consideration of the race's future. At the same time, the protest movement's achievements on the issues of franchise and segregation gave Negroes the organizational and political power to mount a really effective attack on employment discrimination.

So today, instead of an accommodating conciliatory organization, dedicated to the thesis that Negroes must prove their worth to their employers, we have a broad movement of protest organizations, ranging from the Urban League to SNCC and employing a wide variety of strategies and techniques, putting the responsibility for conditions squarely on the shoulders of American whites. In the course of the last half century, the Urban League and the Negro protest movement have been transformed; indubitable progress in opening up new employment opportunities has been made, but Negro unemployment and the related problems of education and housing remain as the major problems with which each of the civil rights organizations will be grappling, each in its own manner, in the future.

CHICAGO, ILLINOIS
December, 1964

BIBLIOGRAPHICAL NOTE

The evolution of NAACP and Urban League policy is best approached through their published annual reports. Three works of Depression vintage contain much valuable information, though they are critical in tone: Sterling D. Spero and Abram L. Harris, *The Black Worker* (New York: Columbia Univ. Press, 1931); Horace R. Cayton and George S. Mitchell, *Black Workers and the New Unions* (Chapel Hill, N.C.: Univ. of North Carolina Press, 1939); and Ralph J. Bunche, "The Programs, Ideologies, Tactics and Achievements of Negro Betterment and Inter-racial Organizations," a research memorandum prepared for the Carnegie-Myrdal study of the Negro in America, 1940 (copy available at Schomburg Collection, New York Public Library). A superb and unique study of the activities of a local Urban League is to be found in Arvarh E. Strickland, "The Chicago Urban League, 1915–1956," unpublished dissertation (Urbana, Ill.: Univ. of Illinois, 1962). Recent strategy of the Urban League can be studied in the speeches of Whitney M. Young, Jr., copies of which have been printed by the League, and in his *To Be Equal* (New York: McGraw-Hill, 1964). The NAACP involvement in the Ford Motor strike of 1941 is dramatically recounted in Walter White, *A Man Called White* (New York: Viking, 1948).

The Bunche memorandum and Claude McKay, *Harlem: Negro Metropolis* (New York: Dutton, 1940), contain good discussions of the "Don't Buy Where You Can't Work" movement. The point of view of the *Messenger* group must be studied in the pages of the magazine itself. The pamphlets and broadsides issued by the National Negro Congress, including the proceedings of its conventions, may be consulted for information about that organization. Herbert Garfinkel's unusually perceptive study, *When Negroes March* (Glencoe, Ill.: Free Press, 1959), and "March on Washington Movement," *Proceedings of Conference Held in Detroit, September 26–27, 1942,* were the sources used for the March on Washington Movement.

The activities of CORE, SCLC, and SNCC are less well recorded. Their news releases and their respective publications—*CORElator, SCLC Newsletter,* and the *Student Voice* are of some help. H. Lees, "The Not-Buying Power of Philadelphia's Negroes," *The Reporter,* XXIV (May 11, 1961), 33–35, is an interesting account of a major selective-buying campaign led by a local group of ministers. Nat Hentoff, *The New Equality* (New York: Viking, 1964), contains some helpful information on recent developments, including the work of the Detroit Trade Union Leadership Conference. The work of the NALC itself was studied through materials in the files of A. Philip Randolph. Articles in the New York *Times* and the Washington *Post,* 1961–1964, have also been helpful in arriving at the generalizations in this chapter.

However, the printed sources are of limited usefulness at best, especially in dealing with organizations other than the NAACP and the Urban League. Much of the material for this article, especially for the more recent years, was obtained from interviews and from personal observation as a participant in the civil rights movement. Interviews with the following people provided much valuable information and helpful insights: Julian Bond, public relations director of SNCC; Robert Curvin, Northeastern regional vice-chairman of CORE; Herbert Hill, NAACP labor secretary; Norman Hill, former program director of CORE; Floyd McKissick, national director of CORE; Clarence Mitchell, head of the Washington Bureau of the NAACP and formerly its labor secretary; John Morsell, assistant to the executive secretary of the NAACP; Guichard Parris, director of public relations of the National Urban League; Marvin Rich, formerly community relations director of CORE and now director of the CORE Scholarship, Educational and Defense Fund; Bayard Rustin; Miss Bernice Wilds, secretary to A. Philip Randolph; Reverend Andrew Young, executive director of SCLC; and Whitney M. Young, Jr., executive director of the National Urban League.

Finally, I acknowledge with appreciation the information and criticisms that came from two colleagues also working on the history of twentieth-century Negro racial advancement and protest organizations: Elliott M. Rudwick, professor of sociology, Southern Illinois University, and Arvarh E. Strickland, of the history department, Chicago Teachers College.

8 / Riots, Ghettos, and the "Negro Revolt"[1]

William F. Soskin

□ Fundamentals in Understanding the Negro Protest

The problem of discrimination is one of the enduring tragedies of the human race. It may be linked, perhaps more than we acknowledge, to the evolutionary quirk that has combined in each human being a highly developed cortex and an emotion-regulating system that is at least half a million years more primitive, so that in quiet contemplation we create the noblest of ideas, but when aroused or frightened we respond with primitive irrationality.

Whatever the root of the problem, it is worth reminding ourselves that it is not only American citizens, not only white men, not only Christians who persist in wantonly exploiting and demeaning some of their fellow men. Discrimination has been practiced by Brahmans and other high-caste Hindus against untouchables in India, by the Watusi against the Bahutu in Africa, by European Jews against Yemenite Jews in

Israel, by people of Spanish ancestry against those of Indian ancestry in Central and South America, and by many other groups. We are not excused by this situation; it should only make us more mindful of our great obligation in searching for a solution and of the great contribution to mankind a solution would present.

It is also worth reminding ourselves that poverty is among the most deadly of cultural cancers, and that its destructive effects, either short-term or long-term, produce the same behavior in men of all races. One needs to read only a little of the history of Paris or London in the early days of the Industrial Revolution, or of New York City a century ago, or to look at the slums of large cities anywhere in the Western world to find parallels for some of the demoralizing conditions in today's Negro ghettos. Poverty-stricken, unemployed, demoralized white men—and women—also tend to engage in rioting, violence, and self-degradation.

Let us now look specifically at our own present situation. Fundamental to the understanding of the so-called "Negro problem" is the realization that there is no *single* Negro problem. The difficulties faced by Negroes in the U.S. are many, complex, and varied. The differences in Negro problems are geographic, economic, political, social, and educational. The problems faced by the urban Negro are different from those of his rural counterpart. Issues and priorities are different in the North and in the South; for the middle class and for the lower class; in the eyes of youth and from the viewpoint of their elders; for liberals and for conservatives.

In some parts of the Deep South, for example, housing may be reasonably integrated although public services and facilities have been rigidly segregated, whereas in the North, schools, facilities, and services may be integrated in principle but *de facto* segregation exists due to the segregated housing pattern. In parts of the North, breaking the union barrier may be a significant issue; in parts of the South Negroes see integration of unions as a threat to the hard-won privileges they enjoy in their all-Negro locals, and as courting potential domination by white majorities. In the South the Negro's efforts at reform have often met with massive and violent resistance, in the North with devastating indifference.

Middle-class urban Negroes have a legitimately paramount concern for housing and education. They press for more "room at the top" in business and industry and in the professions. More and more, those who have moved furthest toward a status parallel with whites face a new ambivalence: Is striving for "cultural whiteness"—the complete assimilation of all of white society's values, mores, styles, and goals—in the best interests of the Negro? Why should he not proudly develop his own identity and culture, one compatible with those of the whites but preserving and cultivating distinctively Negro features?

By contrast, lower-class urban Negroes are far more concerned with immediate significant improvements in job security and income, in their second-rate schools, and in slum housing, as well as with obtaining some relief from the barrenness and hopelessness of their daily existence. Whereas the middle-class Negro is searching for his "best fit" in a multiracial society, the lower-class Negro is asking merely to be let in at long last.

These differing concerns and goals produce a variety of local and national organizations with clearly differing and sometimes conflicting strategies and objectives. Only one monumental basic fact links Negro to Negro in a common brotherhood: that their skin color is the incriminating mark by which a "democratic" white society singles them out for unending exploitation, humiliation, and degradation.

Another fundamental that must be grasped is the magnitude of the present psychological gulf between many whites and nonwhites. The growing anger of the more vocal Negroes, fanned and fed by a growing impatience, comes as a surprise to whites who live comfortably and peacefully, far removed from the major Negro centers. The Negro and *his* problems never impinge on their thinking, their world, their smooth-running democracy. For them sit-ins, stall-ins, and Freedom Rides are evidence of irresponsibility, of unreasonableness, of lawlessness, of radicalism, reinforcing all the myths about Negroes that they have learned to believe. If such whites do come face to face with the Negro world they discover in themselves an entirely new response: fear. They sense the Negro's envy of the "privileged caste"; they sense some of his bitterness. They sometimes see the flaring anger that injustice breeds. They realize for the first time how far most Negroes have been forced into a world apart, a culture so unfamiliar to the average white that it could as well be in a foreign land. And in this alien world they discover a complement to the white man's rejection: the Negro's distrust. For the failure of the white man thus far to deal honestly and fairly with his nonwhite fellow citizens has bred a suspicion so deep that very few whites are ever trusted. And out of the recognition of this distrust springs an unreasoned and often unacknowledged fear.

The people who know this perhaps best of all are the young whites currently working in the Freedom Movement. Sometimes the ambivalent attitude of their young Negro co-workers in the Mississippi COFO project in the summer of 1964 was hard to conceal ("If any heads get smashed down there this summer, I hope it'll be that blond rich kid's, not mine"). At least in the beginning, some Negrocs felt the whites had joined the dangerous venture "for kicks." This pervasive distrust was recently reflected in a feature article in *Ebony* magazine on the ten white men Negroes trust most.[2] Not respect, not admire, but *trust*. The gulf that exists is wide and deep. Bridging it will not be easy.

This lack of trust is closely related to another fundamental that must be understood by anyone trying to assess the current protest. A large part of the Negro community is no longer responsive to pleas for continued gradualism. This segment is finally tired of being praised for its patience—to be blunt, it is sick and tired. Leaving aside radicals and liberals, more and more moderates are now convinced that it is futile to appeal any longer to the white man's conscience, to his sense of fair play. In the white man's system of values, they say, fair play is for playgrounds—white playgrounds—and patience is a quality best cultivated in the tranquility of an all-white suburbia.

All things considered, the number of Negroes who are willing to wait a little bit longer is surprisingly large; they are found mostly among those whose circumstances have become at least tolerable. But these are being steadily eclipsed by the great majority, who find their lot in life more and more precarious and unbearable. This majority, long apathetic and inarticulate, is now accumulating the necessary numerical strength and motivation, the necessary organization and leadership, and the necessary assortment of acceptable and effective techniques for pressing the campaign. It wants equality now, justice now, "Freedom NOW!" And a considered evaluation indicates that the present pressure will only grow stronger and more insistent unless it is appropriately relieved.

Finally, it is necessary to understand the one objective and the one underlying complaint shared by most Negroes, whatever their differences. White officialdom has always been quick to praise the Negro for his progress (thereby implicitly shifting the full burden of responsibility for improvement onto the Negro alone). But what is well-known now in the Negro community is the distinction between *absolute* and *relative* progress. The Negro's earnings rise, but the white man's rise faster; his educational opportunities improve, but the white man's improve faster; his housing improves slightly while the white man's improves greatly. It is an end to "second pickin's," the closing of the gap, "democratization of the spoils," and a full and equal share in the rights, privileges, and opportunities of the "American way of life" that is the main objective of these excluded Americans.

□ Currents of Change in the Negro Community

Perhaps not since the twenties and the Back to Africa movement of Marcus Garvey and his followers has public attention been focused so steadily on the concerns of the Negro. The unending reform efforts of the Negro everywhere, the legal victories large and small, the riots, the martyrs, the emergence of new ideologies, and the shattered hopes, all of which are the daily preoccupation of the Negro community, are experienced by White America only as surprising, puzzling, and somewhat annoying disturbances that seem to occur unpredictably. Occasional bloodshed is remembered, occasional court decisions are recalled, but in the mind of the white public individuals like the late Father Divine and Malcolm X, Joe Louis, Cassius Clay, and Sammy Davis, Jr., have been far more familiar over the years than the quiet and significant achievements of the NAACP.

Yet profound changes have been remaking the Negro in America. In a country racing headlong from a rural to a rural-urban to an essentially urban society, Negroes have far outpaced whites in making the transition. In 1900, 77 percent of the Negro population lived in rural areas; by 1960, 73 percent were city dwellers. In 1900, 90 percent lived in the South. At present nearly half of all city-dwelling Negroes live in the North.

This great, silent northward migration continues unabated. From 1950 to 1960 the net migration of nonwhites from the South was approximately 1.5 million. During that decade California alone showed a net gain of over 350,000 nonwhites; New York, over 280,000; Illinois, nearly 190,000; and Michigan, over 125,000. Most of the urban white population feels, but does not fully understand, the steadily changing racial "mix" that is slowly relieving strain in some parts of the country while creating new pressure points in others, and obviating the basis for old fears in one area while creating urgent new problems in others.

The shift of Negroes from rural to urban living is accompanied by a seemingly omnipresent shortage of housing, a mounting need for more and better schools, and increasing pressure for jobs. Slum houses grow steadily older and more dilapidated; overcrowding continues unrelieved in the spreading ghettos. Indeed, it has been estimated that if all families were forced to live as densely crowded together as the Negroes in our larger ghettos, the entire population of the United States could be accommodated in three of New York City's five boroughs.

No matter how much national income rises throughout the years, the median family income for nonwhites remains shockingly far below that for whites. What is even more discouraging to Negroes is that a marked difference exists regardless of educational level. The estimated lifetime earnings of a Negro high-school graduate is lower than that of a white with only an elementary education. The estimated lifetime earnings of a Negro with five or more years of college and university education is about equal to that of the white high-school graduate. Meanwhile, unemployment rates continue to rise faster for Negroes than for whites.

In addition to the demographic and economic forces at work, significant social, political, and psychological changes are in process. The great move to the cities, by bringing large numbers of the least educated, the least articulate, and the most vulnerable Negroes into close proximity, has begun to give the Negro community a cohesiveness that it never before could claim. These people are now more easily mobilized, less easily intimidated. Among the majority, the idea of a flight back to Africa is dead. The subservient, passive accommodation once preached by Booker T. Washington is scornfully called "Uncle Tomism." The third course, that of seeking redress through the courts and by legislative action, regarded as extremely radical in the twenties, yet pursued so successfully over the years by the NAACP, is now considered too slow and conservative as a prime mover. The NAACP's progress seems far more impressive to whites and to the Negro middle class than to those who live in the ghettos and daily feel the squeeze of privation. Among them an old idea is gaining new life as an explanation for their plight. It is in many respects as fallacious as the white man's myth of Negro inferiority, but to the Negro his own explanation is just as appealing, just as plausible. It is simply this: that the Negro is intentionally kept in a subservient, disparaged, and deprived state by the power structure of the white community—its banks and business houses, its educational system, its city, state, and Federal officials. All are thought to be engaged in an unspoken conspiracy to keep the Negro down, to divest him of his constitutional rights, to maintain him in a state of relative ignorance and political impotence in order to exploit him economically. This theme was not invented by Malcolm X, the Black Muslims, or the Black Nationalists; and it is no evidence of a Communist plot. The idea has been around a long time, but now it is more widely shared, and people are beginning to speak their minds more openly.

Add to this simplistic explanation the elements of joblessness, evidence of exploitation by merchants and slumlords, the complex issues of police brutality and the dispatch with which law enforcement officials appear to solve Negro crimes, and the ever-present evidence of drug traffic in the slums, and one can see the sources of reinforcement for this idea. It is as plain to the ghetto Negro as racial inferiority is to the comfortable middle-class white businessman. Clearly, these two entrenched attitudes are on a collision course.

□ The "New Negro": Leadership and Organizations

The new orientation in the important Negro communities of such major cities as New York, Chicago, Detroit, and Philadelphia is having a pronounced effect on organizations, leadership, and spheres of influence. Not very long ago, Negro leadership was the prerogative of a small elite, sons of long-established families and usually graduates of the distinguished old Negro universities, or at least men who "finished off" there after graduating from Harvard or Yale. Men who could talk to the white man, eat in his home, sit in his councils. Men who could speak for the rank-and-file Negro, even though they had never lived in his midst.

Today, this pattern is changing. Formerly esteemed spokesmen now find themselves accused of being Uncle Toms by lower-class Negroes. Those most often consulted at the White House and in other high places are sometimes considered betrayers, who have sold out to the so-called white power structure. The authority of the old national "Negro Establishment" is being eroded away.

In the process, the South has once more emerged as an autonomous and significant center of Negro leadership, ending a hiatus begun by the collapse of the Southern Negro Youth Congress in the late forties. The Southern Christian Leadership Conference (SCLC) and the Student Nonviolent Coordinating Committee (SNCC), both Southern groups, have revived a bold and effective civil rights campaign. On a cold December evening in Montgomery, Alabama, back in 1955, a tired Negro seamstress named Rosa Parks declined to give up her seat and move to the back of the bus on the Cleveland Avenue line. This action by Mrs. Parks, whom one Negro writer has called the most important seamstress since Betsy Ross in the struggle for liberty in America, led to a boycott of the Montgomery transportation system by the city's 50,000 Negroes that lasted for months. In 1957, SCLC came into being under the leadership of Rev. Martin Luther King, Rev. Fred Shuttleworth, and others. In 1960, SNCC was formed to coordinate the reform efforts of students in Southern Negro colleges. Quickly spreading across the South, with headquarters in Atlanta, these two new organizations counterbalanced the much older, Northern-dominated NAACP (founded in 1909).

The newer Southern organizations mobilized Negroes to action. Within a month after the first student-organized sit-in, the movement had spread to thirty cities in seven states, and 1300 demonstrators went to jail. In Albany, Georgia, in 1962, roughly 2000 were arrested; in Birmingham, 3300. Since then, Birmingham, Montgomery, Albany, Monroe (Georgia), and more recently Selma (Alabama), have become unforgettable names to other nonwhite peoples all over the world. The ready acceptance of this new leadership in the South has posed a challenge to the leadership and pre-eminence of the older, Northern-centered organizations.

A younger Northern organization, the Congress of Racial Equality (CORE), founded in 1942, has also challenged the conservative NAACP. Under the vigorous leadership of one-time NAACP program director, James Farmer, it took the initiative on the Freedom Rides through the South and remains a major force in the civil rights campaign. In the North, more and more, the spark and drive is being supplied by grass-roots leaders in the ghettos. Most notable among these are young Negro college students, themselves products of the teeming city slums, who know first-hand the privations of their families and neighbors, who speak the language of the ghetto and are not ashamed of it, who stay and share in the community's travail instead of trying to escape it, and who, therefore, are much more effective mobilizers and shapers of opinion than elite leaders could ever hope to be.

Pressed by the initiative of these newer and more militant organizations, the NAACP has been forced to re-examine its organization and progress. The rift within the NAACP between prominent old conservatives and aggressive younger activists has already produced significant internal changes. To lessen the control of socially prominent conservatives and to open new channels for the emergence of strong local leaders, the NAACP is encouraging the organization of multiple autonomous chapters in the larger cities.

Many of the new Negro leaders have been called radicals, and some of them undoubtedly are; no one can doubt that there is a radical component in the current protest movement. Lerone Bennett, Jr., senior editor of *Ebony* magazine and author of "The Black Establishment," has tried to contrast the characteristics of the older, more conservative elite (the Establishment) with those of the element he calls "activists":

> Establishment ("in") style can best be understood in comparison with activist ("out") style. Activists seek a *showdown;* the Establishment seeks an *accommodation.* The Establishment says it

is necessary to *reduce* racial tensions; activists say it is necessary to *raise them* to the highest pitch.

Activists *denounce* white people; the Establishment *appeals* to their sense of fair play. Activists call for a *revolt;* the Establishment calls for a *conference.* Activists appeal to the *masses;* the Establishment appeals to *"the better people."* Activists *march;* the Establishment *confers;* Activists *demonstrate;* the Establishment *negotiates.* Activists *demand;* the Establishment *resolves.* Activists are *radical* (in the Latin sense of the root); the Establishment is *conservative* —militantly so.[3]

While sharp in its delineations, like any mere dichotomy this one obscures at least as much as it clarifies. In simplifying, it lumps together issues and processes that do not belong together. The fact is that a number of quite different kinds of organizations voice the Negro's discontent and they by no means all bear the same relation to the current protest.

□ Organizational Alignments and Goals

There are four distinct groups within the Negro protest movement. Two of these, one centering around the NAACP and the National Urban League and the other around CORE, SCLC, and SNCC, agree on one general goal—an end to discrimination and segregation—but differ in tactics. The third group, the Black Nationalists, has a diametrically opposed general goal—complete separatism—and is stridently antigovernment in political posture, as well. The fourth group, made up of politically extreme organizations, is also antigovernment, but one of its two branches also works with and supports the first two major groups in civil rights actions, while the second renounces collaboration and sometimes seems to be pursuing the course of avowed political revolutionaries.

The first group, consisting of the NAACP and the Urban League, backed up by a vast network of local Negro "uplift" organizations, believes that the Negro's rise to full and equal citizen status requires a long, unceasing effort. Their policy is to have the laws of the land rigidly enforced, to work away at discrimination in business and industry slowly but steadily, to encourage Negroes to seek more and more education, and in general to work gradually and firmly on a wide range of Negro problems. The effectiveness of this program over the years has been remarkable, but the years have been long, longer than many Negroes seem able to bear. This group continues to hold the strong support of many older liberal Northern whites and of most upper-class Negroes, but its strength is diminishing among younger white liberals and, for the present at least, among angry young Negroes everywhere.

The second group is spearheaded by CORE, SCLC, and SNCC. These are the activists, Northern and Southern, who have adapted Gandhian passive resistance into effective nonviolent tools such as sit-ins, boycotts, and peaceful protest demonstrations. Their goals are the same as those of the first group, but they want action, action *now*. Eschewing reliance on prayer and patience, they are quite convinced that white society will do nothing that it is not forced to do, that white community leaders will act only when faced with a serious disturbance of their peace and profits. Laws, they say, may remain unenforced for decades, but an effective demonstration or boycott produces quick results. The movement appeals to millions of Negroes because it allows them to act now in a lawful and nonviolent way, and to see in their own lifetime some demonstrable relief for themselves and their children. CORE, SCLC, and SNCC work sometimes in concert and sometimes along independent but parallel courses. The latter two organizations are especially strong among Negroes in the South, and all three enjoy firm support from younger Northern liberals of both races.

Both of these complexes, one led by the NAACP and the Urban League and the other by CORE, SCLC, and SNCC, are dedicated to a very simple, self-evident proposition: as citizens under our constitution, Negroes have a right to full participating membership in society. The United States of

America is their country, their government—they want only an equal opportunity to live in peace and dignity in their native land. Not all restive Negroes feel this way. The Black Nationalist organizations, best known through the publicity received by the Muslims and the late Malcolm X, constitute a third group, one with quite a different viewpoint. While the first two groups strive for an equal place within American society, the Nationalists want out. Rather than integration, they espouse complete separatism. Many, perhaps most, seek to identify with Africa, and refer to themselves as Afro-Americans. The Muslims go a considerable step further than other Black Nationalists, developing an equally racist antithesis of the white supremacy doctrine. Elijah Muhammad and his followers have preached the doctrine of Black superiority. For the Muslims, Allah—God—is a Black, and Negroes are His chosen people. Uncompromisingly antiwhite, Muslims hold that contact with the degenerate white man has degraded the Black ("Negro" is an unacceptable term to Muslims), that there is no possibility of peaceful coexistence of the two races, and that the Black must seek a separate home, whether here or in Africa, in order to purge and protect himself from contamination by an evil white society. The Muslim attack on failures of Christianity has had a telling effect on Negro Christian congregations throughout the country.

In the large Negro centers of the North the Muslims claim thousands of converts who no longer regard themselves as citizens of the white man's state. The militancy with which the group strives to defend itself from what it regards as an alien, evil government makes it difficult for an outsider to distinguish between defense and offense in its teachings and practices. The wedding of a religious dogma to a political objective further complicates the assessment of the Muslim movement. As a religious organization, it has found deep respect in some parts of the Negro community. It has inspired thousands of Negroes to an austere religious life. It has conferred some degree of dignity and self-respect on believers who had nowhere else to seek it, and to many nonbelievers these are positive features. On the other hand, the hate it engenders is deeply troubling to other Negroes and whites alike.

Given the avowed objectives of the organization, it is unlikely that the Black Muslims will contribute in any constructive way to the furtherance of the goals of the larger Negro community. Its most recent history—including the brutal murder of Malcolm X, long its most effective recruiter, the rumors of scandal beginning to swirl around its leaders, and the recent reports of violence and intimidation in some of the local mosques—suggests that the movement is losing some of its appeal in the Negro community.

It would be foolish and false to believe that among the extremists in the Black Nationalists there are none eager to incite violence. The existence of a militant group of "Blood Brothers" among Negro youths in Harlem has been publicized, but never proved. The most that can be said is that some Black Nationalists proselytize actively among Harlem's youth, and there can be little doubt that the proselytizing carries a heavy overtone of incitement to violence.

The Muslims aside, most other Black Nationalist groups are small, local organizations. In Harlem there are perhaps twenty or more such groups, unrelated except in sentiments. Because of their segregationist position, Black Nationalists play a very little role, if any, in the civil rights and freedom movements; but they are a continuing source of ferment in the Negro community, and of late they seem to have been rather effective in arousing teen-agers.

Finally, there is a fourth distinct group, small, but certain to catch the public eye and possibly distract it from the main groups. It is the kernel of Negro political extremism. No national movement that has its roots in the problem of poverty or that concerns itself with social, political, and economic inequities can fail to attract and involve political extremists of the left and the right. The left offers help with an ulterior motive; the right screams dire warnings with an equally ulterior motive. The labor movement right up through the thirties faced this same problem. At times, it drew strength from the presence of political radicals, with their zeal and industry. On the other hand, it suffered a great deal of public distrust because, through the presence of these elements, adversaries tried to discredit the entire movement as a political conspiracy. Whether the Negro protest movement wants them or not, some extreme left-wing white and Negro groups appear to be there, self-invited, seeking advantage where they can and offering unsolicited help wherever they can because social unrest and mass dissatisfaction are fertile climates for recruiting.

On the extreme radical left of the Negro protest movement are a number of small groups. Two of them have been described by William Worthy, the Revolutionary Action Movement (RAM) and Uhuru (the Swahili word for freedom). Both are said to be blatantly revolutionary, and both are firmly aligned with Mao Tse-tung's political philosophy, which has given a new turn to the proletarian struggle by shifting it from poor versus rich toward a worldwide struggle of nonwhites against whites. More apparent in the Negro protest, at least in the North, is the active participation of persons aligned with the New York-based Progressive Labor Movement (PLM), which quite openly espouses the idea of a Marxist-Leninist revolution in the United States. In addition to PLM, Students for a Democratic Society (not to be confused with Students for Democratic Action) and some small Trotskyite and Socialist groups are also active to some extent.

With this degree of complexity in the Negro protest, it is easy to see why fears, distrust, and confusion arise in the white community. Yet it is probable that the number of all the Black Nationalists, including the Muslims, does not match the membership of the White Citizens Council and the Ku Klux Klan, and that the numbers of political radicals of the extreme left are counterbalanced by the white reactionaries of the extreme right. Most Negro leaders and the overwhelming majority of the Negro community, however, are keeping to a much less extreme course. It is for the rest of us in a democratic society to listen always with attentiveness and restraint in order to distinguish between the mere adventurers in change and the citizens with a just complaint or a vital new idea.

□ The Harlem Riots of 1964

The relationship between the activities of organizations and events in community life is not always apparent to outsiders. The Harlem riots of 1964 are a case in point. That they were not entirely a spontaneous outbreak of purposeless lawlessness is still not understood by many in the white community. That they were denounced by leaders in the mainstream of the civil rights movement makes them appear an even more puzzling phenomenon. Examining their antecedents in a psychological context may help to shed light both on the riots themselves and on the complex currents of thought and action that exist in the large Negro urban centers.

Violence is a tactic fervently disavowed by every responsible leader in the movement. Despite the thousands of arrests, the scores of recent church burnings, and the murders and brutal beatings, the major organizations in the Freedom Movement hold resolutely to a policy of nonviolence. What then can be made of the riots that occurred in half a dozen Northern cities in the summer of 1964? [4]

Startled whites have asked, Why did they happen? The real wonder is that more of them did not occur. For one thing, it can hardly be denied that they were expected to occur. In 1963, the Freedom March on Washington had served as an outlet for frustrations in the Negro community, but in 1964 no such event was planned, and from winter on through early spring Negro and white leaders alike were intoning warnings about the "long, hot summer." Police departments prepared for it; newsmen wrote about it; TV programs discussed it; lecturers in auditoriums and churches across the country talked about it, seemingly in dread mixed with a hopeful expectation that someone would do something. At times these warnings took on the cast of irresponsible incitement.

But for a more significant factor one has only to look to youth gangs and the uses to which adults can put them. In both the North and South youth gangs constitute a volatile element equally unpredictable for white and nonwhite leaders. In the South, inspired by the fervor of the White Citizens Council and the model of the Ku Klux Klan, gangs of white youths spoil for trouble, local "heroes" in the service of white supremacy. In Northern ghettos the preachings of Muslims and other Black Nationalist groups fan the emotions of Negro youth gangs until they are willing soldiers in a "heroic" fight against oppression. The emotional tinderbox created by hate campaigns against whites is easily touched off in a congested, crime-ridden area where crowds of aimless, unwanted men walk the streets as a daily reminder to any youth of what lies in store for him. The feeling of injustice runs deep in Negro youth, and desperate hopelessness, too. Those who can see a constructive way out seize upon it; those who cannot want to strike back in any way possible. And there are always some adults around to goad and encourage them, just as there are in white communities.

The Harlem riots did not flare up out of nothing. They had a history, and however futile and misguided, they also had a purpose. Harlem youth gangs had been having stepped-up "trouble" with whites for some time. Intergang fighting is said to be diminishing there, and while this is partly due to the effectiveness of youth workers, it is also due to the emergence of a common outside enemy—"Ofay," "Whitey," "Mr. Charlie," "The Man." In 1963, during the winter preceding the riots, some Harlem youths stabbed and killed a merchant's wife and brutally beat her husband; a young white missionary, Brother David, was murdered in the streets; a white female social worker was slain while walking with a Negro co-worker. That spring there were several instances of Negro gangs terrorizing white subway riders, and during the same period a small band of youths viciously attacked an old white fruit peddler. The peddler was killed, and in the ensuing encounter with police an adult Negro was badly beaten and later lost one eye—giving rise to a widespread charge of police brutality toward Negroes.

The entire community of Harlem has a history of concern over police brutality, and such events remain fresh in the minds of Harlemites, police as well as residents, long after the news is off the front page. Because they remain fresh, they are an ever-ready source of fuel—for the police on the one hand, for residents on the other. This latest charge was rekindled on several subsequent occasions. Mothers voiced it when they demonstrated for the placement of a traffic light near a school, and it came up again during a protest to obtain a new play street. The people of Harlem fear the charge of police brutality, and the least responsible elements exploit it. Handbills go out. People become aroused.

It is in this context that one must examine the slaying of James Powell and what it meant. Powell was a young Harlem teen-ager. One day in the summer of 1964, as he was on his way along the street with some friends, it is said that he taunted a white building superintendent, and that the man in turn sprayed him with a water hose. In an angry exchange, Powell reportedly threatened the man with a weapon, a knife. Minutes later he was fatally shot by an off-duty white police lieutenant who tried to apprehend him. Shot and killed —by a *white* officer. Whitey's officer. The white man's "enforcer." Although, after a long and careful investigation, a mixed jury downtown completely exonerated Lt. Gilligan, uptown on the streets of Harlem there was an insistent angry charge of "Murder!" "Police brutality!"

And on the heels of the exoneration came Jimmy Powell's funeral.

The essential requirements for a riot are a crowd and some occasion for arousing feelings, and Jimmy Powell's funeral met them. There was a meeting about Powell and Gilligan that whipped up feelings, and, in connection with the funeral, there was an extra contingent of police nearby. When the crowd poured out of the meeting, someone apparently shoved someone who shoved back.

The mounting tension of weeks and months snapped, and in an instant the melee was on. James Powell, police brutality, Whitey, joblessness, the Ku Klux Klan, Medgar Evers, four young girls killed in an unsolved church bombing . . . all of it poured forth in one great, ugly flood of outrage. Against the police. Against City Hall. Against employers who won't hire Negroes and slumlords who won't repair hovels and merchants who exploit black people, against white supremacists who murder civil rights workers and . . . And in the chaos, the junkies, the winos, the down-and-outers and the plain lawless ones with little interest in politics or human rights gathered from Seventh Avenue and its shabby tributaries to make what profit they could in looting while the police were distracted elsewhere.

Early next morning handbills were passed through the streets in certain sectors, urging Harlemites to organize block brigades, to place barricades in the streets, to prepare for another engagement with the police. Fortunately there were few takers, but the inciters, despite pleading from other leaders, could not be dissuaded from holding another mass meeting that evening. After more inflammatory speeches, a Black Nationalist "priest" led a group of youths through the streets on a march to the nearby police station, ostensibly to demand that the Police Commissioner arrest Lt. Gilligan at once, on a charge of first-degree murder. As the marchers approached the station, the police erected a barricade. But the barricade itself was an incitement to the aroused youths. They were here to confront the Commissioner, to demand "justice" in the Powell case. Now, only twenty-four hours later, they were face to face with the oppressor again, with many scores to settle. In minutes the second night's riot was on.

Whatever it is—aimlessness or "sport" or some other motive—that prompts white youths to rumble at summer resorts, the Harlem riots were hardly of the same making. And while the outbreak was repudiated by most of the civil rights workers and citizens who live and work in Harlem, one cannot fail to see that what happened there in August, 1964, was deeply rooted in community affairs and that it was not an act of hoodlumism but an insurrection—shortlived, but deeply disturbing nevertheless, because each successful incitement eases the way for the next.

The seriousness of the youth situation in Harlem, Bedford-Stuyvesant (a section of Brooklyn, N.Y.), and other similar areas cannot be overestimated. Beyond the other factors in slums that are conducive to lawlessness—the high percentage of broken families, the ever-present examples of crime and corruption, joblessness, and the daily struggle for existence; the easy availability of "pot" or "Mary Jane" (marijuana); and the meaninglessness of presently available educational experiences—the growing anger toward white society that exists among the least-educated Negro youths poses a grave problem for others besides the police.

It should be clear to all that among the most prejudiced, white as well as nonwhite, in the North and South alike, blind hate incites men and their sons to the most heinous crimes. Brutality begets brutality. No longer, in this day of television, is the murder of a Negro in the South unrelated to next week's violence along Seventh Avenue in Harlem or South State Street in Chicago. No longer is continued job discrimination in the white community unrelated to the activities of marauding teenagers in the Negro community, since it is translated directly and repeatedly by adults to youths in the ghettos. The Klan rides that still terrorize Negroes in the South are finding a new, politically inspired counterpart that is beginning to terrorize whites in the North.

The pattern of violence takes different forms in the North and South. In Harlem the attacks on whites are most often the work of youths still in, or barely out of, their teens; in the South white attacks on Negroes appear often to be the work of mature men, heads of families. In the North the choice of white victims during the past few years fall in no particular pattern, almost as if chosen by whim: a merchant, a female social worker, a young missionary, an office worker, a schoolboy; in the South the victims are Negroes prominent or active in civil rights work. In the South the killings are planned acts of intimidation, in the North impulsive acts of retribution.[4]

□ HARYOU-ACT—A Faltering Prototype

Just as riots reflect some of the negative forces at work in the large Negro centers in the urban North, other developments less well known to the white community reflect the positive, constructive endeavors, and from these too the white community can learn something of the scope of the problem and the difficulties ahead. HARYOU-ACT is such an endeavor; it merits examination.

In Harlem and in its sister community, Bedford-Stuyvesant, far too many young people are feeling, "Talk don't get you nowhere." Increasingly, they believe that no white men, no officials, are to be trusted, their own self-seeking politicians perhaps least of all. Harlem's *Amsterdam News* has editorialized bitterly that every new government project in Harlem is basically only another scheme by some local Negro group to pay its members fancy salaries. Any man, white or Negro, who gets money from Washington is by that very fact discredited as having been bought off by the white power structure. To maintain any leadership status in Harlem one has to demonstrate to the community his ability to walk tough and talk tough to "The Man"—"The Man" in City Hall, "The Man" in police headquarters, "The Man" in Washington.

Yet there is no mechanism through which Harlem can speak to "The Man" with the clear voice of local authority. Harlem is like a city without a government, where only the policy racketeers and dope peddlers have a well-disciplined organization. Many of the young people feel themselves outside the city government, and divide their allegiances among scores of independent leaders, each secure in his own little fief.

There is so much wrong in Harlem, so much that needs doing, that the question is not where to begin, but how. Among the hows, the foremost is how to bring about some coordination of effort, some unified planning, and an administrative organization strong enough to survive the first outraged howls of all the special-interest groups that live off and profit from Harlem's present condition.

Harlem needs immediate relief from the dreadful overcrowding maintained by the steady northward migration. It needs relief from rent costs that are, although lower than many rentals in white areas, still not commensurate with the lower incomes of Negroes. It needs a greater money influx, and more Negro-operated businesses and services to keep that money circulating longer in the Negro community; for, as matters now stand, dollars brought into Harlem flow straight back out into the white community through the predominantly white business establishments. Harlem needs more and better police protection, for its residents are no less fearful than white people of crime and violence, whether committed by Negroes or by whites. And Harlem needs jobs—new jobs for its unwanted men, and steadier jobs for those frequently unemployed.

For its children Harlem needs better schools, appropriately adapted curricula, more nursery schools, more teachers, and facilities for special tutoring to help overcome the educational gap. It desperately needs a vast increase in summer camp facilities—Federally financed, if city funds and private philanthropy cannot carry the burden—to take more children off the teeming streets during the long summer months. It needs better health services. It needs more public recreation facilities, because with the discriminatory differential in earning power and family income, Harlem families cannot afford to purchase for recreation what many white neighborhoods and families easily provide for themselves.

For its youth Harlem needs educational, social, and economic opportunities at least vaguely approximating those available to young people across the ghetto border, in white man's territory.

Harlem is a testing ground for government efforts to improve conditions in Negro ghettos, and Harlem Youth Opportunities Unlimited (HARYOU) several years ago undertook the major task of tackling some of the basic problems there. Originally conceived as a modest project of the Harlem Neighborhood Association, HARYOU gradually grew in size and scope into an independent organization. With a broadly representational local board of directors and with encouragement and financial aid from private, city, and Federal sources, it undertook a systematic two-year study of the needs of Harlem youth.

Under the inspired and capable leadership of Dr. Kenneth B. Clark, professor of psychology at City College of the City University of New York, a comprehensive community action program was designed. The program reflected a massive, tightly reasoned diagnosis of the trouble spots. It contained a number of highly imaginative proposals for dealing with education, recreation, job training, and other problems. Of critical significance in this whole planning operation is the extent to which Harlem youngsters were involved in collecting the data, evaluating it, and formulating proposals for remedies. Teenagers—called HARYOU Associates—conducted surveys and street interviews, canvassing the community's opinion, assessing its attitudes, searching out its perceptions of Harlem's needs. Then followed months of discussion, with the young people themselves actively proposing solutions, debating alternatives. Out of it all came an impressive document, *Youth in the Ghetto: A Study of the Consequences of Powerlessness and a Blueprint for Change*. Over 1500 copies of the 600-page report have been circulated, and for Harlem residents who would find the tome tedious or incomprehensible the substance was distilled in comic-book form, thousands of copies of which were distributed throughout the community.

The program called for the establishment of large numbers of nursery schools where children would be given an early start on language skills and culturally enriching experiences, which Harlem home life often cannot provide.

To help pupils bridge the gap between levels of achievement in Harlem schools and in schools elsewhere, the report proposed a vast tutorial program in which older and more advanced students are paid to furnish after-school tutorial assistance to those having difficulty.

There was a proposal to upgrade the quality and quantity of the teaching staff in Harlem schools, to revise markedly certain aspects of the school curriculum, and to introduce every available advanced teaching procedure. Harlem schools, it was felt, should be better equipped and better staffed than white schools in order to compensate for the handicaps under which children grow up in ghettos.

Because such organizations as Cub Scouts and Boy Scouts seem singularly inappropriate to the needs of ghetto youth ("How can you have a Cub Scout cook-out on your lawn, when there isn't a lawn in Harlem?"), HARYOU proposed to develop a uniformed Cadet Corps. Models for the Corps already exist in Harlem; it can be related to the daily life experiences of Harlem boys and tailored to the limits of their resources. ("For kids who rarely see a forest, learning about deer tracks doesn't make much sense; on the other hand, a merit badge for spelling or school achievement serves a real purpose.")

Beyond these, HARYOU proposed to offer youth special opportunities for developing creative talents in dancing, music, film-making, dramatics, and the like.

To provide older youth with some experience in business and commerce, HARYOU proposed to open several commercial enterprises, such as a sporting goods store, a coffee shop, and others, to be operated by HARYOU trainees.

On the whole, HARYOU's plan was the most formidable any Negro community has ever undertaken in trying to cope with the "gap." The small team of Negro professionals who initiated and directed the planning—besides Clark, much credit is due to Cyril D. Tyson, Kenneth E. Marshall and James A. Jones—represented an unusual pool of talent. The outcome of their effort constituted a significant departure from conventional social-agency approaches to community problems.

Several weaknesses were evident from the outset. With its large budget, HARYOU was an attractive plum and target.

Its board was simply not powerful enough to withstand a serious assault from outside. After two years of intensive study, planning, and negotiations with prospective underwriters, on the eve of its acceptance HARYOU became the object of a political fight, which was waged, significantly, entirely within the Harlem community. Dr. Clark, the main architect of the plan, and its guiding force through the entire period of planning and negotiation, finally withdrew. Today the program is known as HARYOU-ACT, reflecting a merger with another Harlem program of considerably narrower scope. ACT was a Federally financed program, sometimes loosely described as a "domestic Peace Corps," in which college-trained Negro youths were recruited for community work in Harlem. The program was sponsored by Rep. Adam Clayton Powell, who was instrumental in effecting the HARYOU-ACT merger.

Possibly a second weakness in HARYOU-ACT is its self-imposed isolation from the white community. In part, such independence is forced upon the organization by the attitudes, not only of the young people in the community, but of some adult groups as well. HARYOU-ACT's success or failure hinges in important measure on the extent to which it can attract and involve Harlem youth. Many of these youngsters share in the general distrust of whites, and even if they do not, might easily, in the present climate, expose themselves to the epithet "Uncle Tom" for participating in an interracial project. Besides, those already involved want to show the world what the Negro can do on his own, given half a chance, and to them the idea of an all-Negro staff is a real source of inspiration.

Yet with a project of this size and scope there seems reason to question whether the Negro community entirely on its own can martial a large enough staff of sufficient caliber to bring the program to a successful conclusion. Learning by doing is a laudable way to develop administrative, managerial, and policy-making skills, but at this level it can also be an unnecessarily wasteful and expensive way. Learning by trial and error has yet to demonstrate its superiority over guided learning where complex skills and experience can be transmitted verbally.

Furthermore, a high degree of autonomy will leave HARYOU-ACT vulnerable at the times when it needs allies. Already in its brief existence this has proven to be the case. For the future one can predict periodic attacks, and the board of directors still lacks adequate ties with prestigious institutions that could defend it.

How HARYOU-ACT will fare "under new management" remains a judgment for the future, but the problems of Harlem are evident also in Chicago, in Cleveland, in Los Angeles, and in other major cities where similar projects will undoubtedly emerge. The Negro communities need help, desperately, and under the Poverty Program there is every likelihood of their getting long overdue aid. But money alone is not enough in these communities. They lack oranization. They lack comprehensive planning: HARYOU-ACT did not and could not concern itself with issues like housing, health, and crime. They lack a large enough pool of administrative and professional skill. To these lacks the Federal Government must give special attention; it must be prepared to offer counsel and resources both before and as it pours money into local projects.

□ Conclusion

In the course of his struggle to achieve human dignity and freedom the American Negro has trudged along many roads. He has tried prayer and supplication, to no earthly avail. He has tried subservient accommodation; the role was intolerably degrading. He has repeatedly considered withdrawal from the white man's world, an impractical solution. And he has tried the law. When hopelessness was greatest, the law was one route by which some progress could be made. Now new leaders are exploring with an entirely different strategy: firm and direct confrontation that forces the white community to take cognizance, to *act*. The eagerness of Negroes and the reluctance of whites in this confrontation is posing fundamental problems for individuals, for communities, and for governments.

For the immediate future one can foresee an ever-quickening pace to civil rights activities as leaders and organizations vie for position. There will be conflicting pressures on both citizens and governments as different Negro groups pursue their separate strategies. For at least the next decade we shall all be pressed, white and nonwhite alike, into a deeper examination of issues and their implications as we explore solutions. Already a number of problems have reached critical proportions.

Violence, for example, has already reached the explosive point in both the North and the South. Unlike police jurisdiction, reactions to violence are not confined by state boundaries. What happens in the South or East sets patterns for what might happen in the Midwest. If the law is to be observed in one section, it must be observed equally in all. We must also ponder the danger in equating law-enforcement with white power and authority. In much of the South, the white man *is* the law and to be against the white man is to be against the law; similarly, in Northern ghettos, to be against the white man is to be opposed to the law: the one is the embodiment of the other. It might not be so if the Negro community had more people of its own race responsible for maintaining law and order.

Education is another example. Urging Negro drop-outs to return to the schools that they left in the first place out of frustration or dissatisfaction seems a pointless effort. The curriculum and practices in predominantly Negro schools demand immediate re-examination and revision if we are not to sacrifice still another generation of Negro youth.

Job training for young Negroes will be at best a temporary delaying tactic unless new jobs are created. As A. Philip Randolph has noted, opening up all the unions in the country would simply have the effect of democratizing unemployment a bit.

Employment—meaningful employment and not merely "made" work—must be found for the masses of unoccupied adult Negro males. And there is no more imperative need than that of exploring new ways of supporting mothers and children in fatherless Negro families. The present regulations, which virtually oblige Negro fathers who are employed irregularly to desert their families to make the mother and children eligible to receive public assistance, are an evil, a tragedy, and a public shame.

Remedial efforts in Negro communities will require the development of whole new quasi-government structures, and the training of young Negro professionals to man them. At present, opportunities for the training of such men do not exist.

Furthermore, the programs of these quasi-governmental agencies are bound to generate opposition in some quarters. If a HARYOU-ACT, a Mobilization for Youth, or a Woodlawn Organization undertakes to involve the community in neighborhood improvement projects, and if as an outgrowth a rent strike develops, what position will the sponsoring city and Federal governments take?

These are a mere smattering of the questions and issues that face us. There are no ready solutions at hand; we face a long test of our tolerance for unstructured experimentation and exploration.

With respect to prejudice, let us acknowledge now that it will endure. There is no more possibility of legislating universal amity than of guaranteeing happiness. But amity is clearly different from rights, privileges, and opportunities, and can it not be now agreed that henceforth these at least must be shared equally by all citizens?

And are we not obliged finally to recognize the truth in the opening sentence of the Birmingham Manifesto: "The patience of an oppressed people cannot endure forever"?

NOTES

1. This chapter was originally prepared in slightly different form as a 1964 staff report for the Office of Planning, National Institute of Mental Health.
2. *Ebony,* April 1964.
3. Lerone Bennett, Jr., *The Negro Mood* (New York: Ballantine Books, 1964), p. 69.
4. As this book goes to press, the special committee appointed by Governor Brown of California to investigate the causes of the 1965 Riot in the Watts section of Los Angeles has announced the near completion of its report. From all indications, there will be no startling revelations of an organized plot. Rather, Watts, too, seems to have been an expression of intolerable frustration too long smoldering and too long unheeded by the surrounding community.

9 / The Economics of Protest

Michael Harrington

I

The Negro in America is the victim of a formal, institutionalized racism, but this system of open discrimination is confined primarily to the South. There it has been under vigorous attack by the integration movement. With the Civil Rights Act of 1964, it has become for the most part illegal under Federal law, and some, but by no means all, of its practices have actually been changed through voluntary compliance with the law.

The Negro in America is also the victim of an informal system of racism that exists North, South, East, and West. Its mechanisms are economic and social: a labor market that keeps Negroes at the lowest levels of income and skill, a housing market that confines them to racial ghettos, and an educational process that produces more drop-outs than high school graduates.

As A. Philip Randolph summarized the historical background in his speech to the 1964 Convention of the Negro American Labor Council: "Negroes are second class citizens because while the Civil War emancipated them from the chains of chattel slavery, it never transformed them into free workers in the labor market or free citizens in public life."

This brutal reality affects every aspect of Negro life. It doubles the disadvantage of color with the misery of poverty. It invades the intimacy of family life and even maims the individual personality and spirit. And this economic and social plight both goads and limits the organization of Negro resistance to racism.

It has long been recognized that the conditions under which a group lives and works help shape the way in which it acts collectively. To take a simple, familiar example, European country life erupted into peasant *Jacqueries,* while European city life brought forth strikes, the institution of unions, and socialist parties. And indeed, in the domestic social movement that preceded today's Negro Revolution—the tremendous expansion of labor organization in the 1930's—the conflict between the AFL and the CIO involved, among many other things, rival sociologies. What were the organizational potentials and capacities of the assembly-line way of life?

As Joseph G. Rayback put it in his *History of American Labor,* the CIO of the thirties realized that "American industry was no longer work-shop industry and that the typical American worker was no longer a skilled worker. . . . While the foreign born, the semi-skilled and the unskilled had accepted their lot in silence, in the twenties this docility began to change. The inferior workmen began to recognize that they constituted an overwhelming majority of the labor world and that they were a potential power." [1]

There are obvious similarities between the rise of union militancy in the thirties and of race militancy in the fifties and sixties. But how far does the analogy go? Is there a cohesiveness in Negro daily life that is the equivalent of the solidarity engendered by the mass production experience? And if changes in the economy and the character of the work force are an important clue to the rise of the CIO, what do the present trends in the same area portend for the Negro movement?

These questions must first be placed in a historical context. There are links between the changes in Negro social and economic conditions and the evolution of Negro organized resistance. Once some of these relationships are established, it is possible to make educated guesses about the future. Certain economic trends would result in social conditions that would make the organization of Negroes on their own behalf much more difficult; others would be an incentive to the growth of the civil rights movement. And all this becomes something more than an exercise in analytic imagination when one realizes that those future economic realities are to a considerable degree subject to the present political will. This line of inquiry is not new, and it is useful to establish at the outset the range of the theories that have already been argued.

In recent years, the intensification of civil rights militancy has given rise to the theory that Negroes constitute a unique social phenomenon, a dynamic force that can revolutionize the entire nation as well as solve the issue of race. This view is often encountered in the young, radical generation of civil rights activists. It has been put in scholarly form by S. M. Miller, among others. Miller sees the Negroes as part of a "new working class" whose rebel consciousness is formed by the double indignity of racism and poverty. In this view, the passivity, the *lumpen* character, often ascribed to those at the very bottom of the economic scale is canceled out or modified by race consciousness: "Usually, the long-term economically depressed are unlikely candidates for a dynamic political movement, but the race ethnic dimension, as well as the economic factor, is propelling the poor, whether Negro, Mexican-American or Puerto Rican." [2]

There are some theorists who would make Negroes into an essential element of a new radical power, a black substitute for the white, Western proletariat that failed. So in *One Dimensional Man,* Herbert Marcuse talks of a "revolutionary" "substratum of outcasts and outsiders, the exploited of other races and other colors" that is to help remake the world of the advanced societies.[3]

Perhaps the most surprising advocate of this view of the special political vocation of the Negro is Senator Richard B. Russell of Georgia, the leader of the segregationists in the upper chamber. In a 1963 CBS–TV interview, Russell complained that the 20 million poorest whites are worse off than the 20 million poorest Negroes because they lack the "articulate" leadership of the Negroes and few of them vote.[4]

At the other extreme, there is the view that Negroes, because of the chaotic conditions of life that the economy imposes upon them, will find it extremely difficult to sustain a prolonged and organized assault on racism. Because of the growing dimensions of the struggle since the Montgomery bus boycott of 1955–1956, this thesis has not been advanced recently in its "pure" form. Hardly anyone would agree with Richard Wright's terrible moment of pessimism (and it was a moment, not a final judgment) when he wrote in 1945:

> White America has reduced Negro life in our great cities to a level of experience of so crude and brutal a quality that one could say of it in the words of Vachel Lindsay's *The Leaden-Eyed* that:
>
> It is not that they starve, but they starve so dreamlessly, It is not that they sow, but that they seldom reap, It is not that they serve, but that they have no gods to serve, It is not that they die, but that they die like sheep.[5]

Yet, it is important to consider the *degree* to which the economics and sociology of racism impede, rather than stimulate, resistance to racism. This approach follows a line of investigation opened up by E. Franklin Frazier in the twenties. In his essay "La Bourgeoisie Noire" [6] Frazier attempted to explain why Negroes at that time were not as revolutionary as many radical white theorists thought their plight should make them. Frazier felt that the internal class structure of Negro life, in which the upper stratum aspired toward bourgeois assimilation and the lower stratum was still excluded from industrial work, had kept Negroes from making a militant challenge against their bondage.

There have been enormous changes since Frazier wrote, not the least of them the rise of a mass civil rights movement. And yet there is still substance to his insight. For, paradoxically, the cruelties of racism, formal and informal, have driven Negroes to both protest and passivity. Or, to put it another way, white America's crime against the Negro has organized him for resistance—and disorganized him into hopelessness.

The Black Muslims are particularly conscious of this latter reaction because their roots are among the ghetto poor and workers. Thus, the late Malcolm X said:

> We perfected the art of humility and politeness for their sake . . . but at the same time we treated our own women as if they were mere animals, with no love, respect or protection. . . . We were supposed to be part of the "Christian Church" yet we lived in a bitter world of dejection . . . being rejected by the white "Christian Church." In large numbers we became victims of drunkenness, drug addiction, reefer smoking, in a false and futile attempt to "escape" the reality and horror of the shameful condition that the Slavemaster's Christian religion had placed us in.[7]

Malcolm X put his point so bluntly—in the mouth of a white his words would probably be regarded as racist stereotyping—because he believed that his teachings could overcome this disorganization. But the issue is far beyond any solution by religious conversion, by Malcolm or anyone else. It involves massive economic and social determinants, and it is my purpose to discuss the ways in which these could help shape the future of Negro organization and protest.

The thesis of this analysis is:

1. that the direction of Negro migration over the past sixty-five years or so, from South to North, from agriculture to industry, created the economic and social basis for increased Negro participation and militancy in the civil rights struggle;

2. that automation grievously threatens this pattern if it continues to be introduced at the price of chronic high rates of Negro unemployment;

3. that the increasingly unfavorable position of the Negro in the labor market is thus not simply an attack upon his individual livelihood but an assault on the very structure of Negro life itself, aggravating every disintegrative factor and making resistance and organization extremely difficult;

4. that changing this economic position is thus a collective necessity of the civil rights movement as well as a desperate individual Negro need;

5. that the accomplishment of this transformation requires the reversal of profound economic trends and can only be done by a massive intervention of the public power; and this kind of action will only be forthcoming if there is a new political majority in the United States, which means that the 10 percent Negro minority must of necessity seek allies to that end.

The most important social and economic change for the American Negro has been the migration from the rural South to the cities of both South and North. As a result of this transition, Negroes progressively extended the popular basis of their Freedom Movement and increased its militancy. And although this development did not rescue the Negro from his relative position in society—he went from the lowest status in the Southern countryside to the lowest status in the urban areas—it did create new kinds of communities and organizations. In this context of modest and utterly inadequate change, the economic and social trends of the past sixty-five years did more to help than to hurt the Negro movement.

In the rural South, where the large majority of Negroes lived after the Civil War, the Negro was "a landless peasant without the tradition of the European peasant which binds the latter to the soil." [8] The great organizational achievement of this period was the continuation of the Negro church; there was no civil rights movement in the modern sense of the phrase. This was the time in which Booker T. Washington was hailed by both black and white for urging Negroes to accommodate to a segregated way of life.[9]

When Washington was challenged early in this century, the opposition did not come from the Negro masses but from the "talented tenth" of the Niagara Movement and the NAACP, and from their white allies. The Negro intelligentsia had entered American history, not the sharecroppers. And it was of considerable significance that the NAACP was founded at a conference in New York City. The event symbolized the transfer of Negro leadership from the South to the North, a situation that was to persist for half a century.

After World War I, a new fact of Negro economic and social life expressed itself in Negro organization. Between 1880 and 1900, Southern Negroes began to move to Northern cities in increasingly greater numbers.[10] At the war's end, these new communities provided the mass basis for Marcus Garvey's nationalism. New York was the stronghold of that movement; Chicago, Detroit, and Pittsburgh were also important centers. Even more important than the shift in geography was the change in the social class of the Negro protesters. They were Southern Negroes who had become Northern, urban, and poor. They "were becoming disillusioned about the City as a Promised Land. This provided proof for Garvey's argument that America was the white man's country." [11] It was under these circumstances that the Negro masses appeared in the Negro struggle for the first time since the Reconstruction.

Negroes were, of course, hit by the Depression. In a city like Chicago, the "Fat Years," 1924–1929, had been the most prosperous in the Negro community's history.[12] Nearly three-fourths of the Negro men and half of the Negro women were at work. But for them these good times were only relatively good: they worked at dirty, low-paid jobs. So, paradoxically, the New Deal disaster relief engendered by the Depression sometimes involved great gains for Chicago Negroes. The WPA and other programs "eventually provided a bedrock of subsistence which guaranteed food and clothing. The ministrations of social workers and wide education in the use of public health facilities seemed actually to have raised the level of health in the Black Ghetto during the Depression years." [13]

The organizational history of the Negro movement during the entire period between the two world wars reflects this new urban environment. The popular base of the movement was broadened, and Negro demands were going beyond such basic matters of life and death as an anti-lynching bill. A. Philip Randolph emerged as a major force oriented toward a radical alliance of white and black labor. The system of industrial unions in the CIO brought considerable numbers of Negroes into the labor movement for the first time. In the March on Washington Movement of 1941, Randolph was able to concentrate this new organizational power into an effective, if short-lived, instrument of mass protest, which secured the first Fair Employment Practices order.

In the 1930's, the Northern Negro had switched from Lincoln Republicanism to F.D.R. Democracy. Out of this political development and organizational experiences like those just described, there came a new perspective, a civil rights strategy defined in broad social terms. Thus, in 1945 Drake and Cayton concluded their *Black Metropolis* with some anticipation of "Things to Come" and saw the hopes of Negroes as dependent upon that New Deal hero, "the Common Man."

At the same time as these new kinds of protest appeared, the NAACP was profoundly affected by the changes in Negro life. Its membership base was extended well beyond the Negro intelligentsia. Urban workers and Southern sharecroppers were recruited along with the Negro middle class.[14] Yet, the extent of actual mass participation in NAACP activities should not be overemphasized. The NAACP branches remained for the most part "tax bases" for the national organization.[15]

During World War II, the quasi-colonial economy (agriculture and raw materials) of the entire South was altered in the interest of national defense. Industry emerged as a new force, and this trend was accelerated by state and local development plans in the postwar years. At the same time, the fields of the South were becoming modernized and the need for agricultural labor was declining. Between 1940 and 1959 so many Negroes left the rural South that by the end of this period sharecroppers and impoverished farm families were predominantly white.[16]

By the fifties, approximately sixty percent of Southern Negroes were living in cities.[17] Thus, they were no longer widely dispersed, easily subject to terrorization or mired in the general backwardness of the countryside. And like those who had left the rural South for Northern cities, they became more militant in the process. However, this was a migration within the area of formal segregation, and not a flight from it. As a result, the first target of the awakening Southern movement was discrimination in public accommodations.

In 1955, Rosa Parks defied the Jim Crow regulations on a bus in Montgomery, Alabama. Her action set off a wave of protest and direct action in the South that continues to this day. And eventually this struggle led to the Civil Rights Act of 1964, which confirmed by law what Negroes had been asserting through civil disobedience.

The man who symbolized this new movement, the first major Negro leader since Booker T. Washington to be based in the South, was Martin Luther King. Unlike Northern leaders, King could not draw upon the talents and resources of Negroes in labor and in political groups. For although the urban South was an economic step up for the Negro, he was still subject to a poverty crueler and deeper than that encountered in the North. The main institution supporting Negro protest was the church. This was true in 1955 in Montgomery at the beginning of King's public career, and it is true of his Southern Christian Leadership Conference to this day.[18]

However, it would be a mistake to think that this Southern church was the same one that had grown up under slavery and after the Civil War. The move to the city had transformed religion along with everything else. The fervid, other-worldly spirituality of the hopeless days of Babylonian exile in the rural South was no more. Now the concerns were secular and political.[19]

The other organization that came out of the upsurge of Southern protest was the Student Nonviolent Coordinating Committee. Initially, SNCC was a broad federation for Southern youths, mainly but not exclusively Negro, who had electrified the nation with the sit-in demonstrations of 1960–1961. SNCC had a collegiate base; its partisans were members of or aspirants to the middle class. On occasions, a generational debate broke out between the SNCC militants who wanted to carry the direct action on to a clear victory and older leaders who seized at opportunities to negotiate. In this case, what was involved was not simply the impetuosity of youth and the prudence of age, but the psychological and political difference between young people who grew up in cities and their elders who had been formed by the old, agricultural South.

After the enormous initial successes of SNCC, it became increasingly a staff organization (by 1963, it had a budget of $160,000).[20] Involved in this change in SNCC's activity was a strategy and a sociology, which came most dramatically to the fore in the incredibly courageous assault against racism mounted by SNCC in Mississippi.

Throughout the organizational history of the civil rights movement, the rural South had played a minor role. SNCC determined to change this pattern and to appeal to the poor in the countryside. These people were seen as having the dynamic for political and social change. With mock voter registrations and elections in Freedom Schools, with the formation of the Mississippi Freedom Democratic Party, and with other activities, SNCC, in uneasy alliance with the NAACP, CORE, and SCLC, made serious inroads into the traditional passivity of the rural Negroes. But real and basic problems remain. It is still not at all clear that the rural Southern Negro population can sustain political and direct action activity at an intensity comparable to that of the rights movement in the cities. In any case, the initial impulse for the Mississippi development came from the new, not the old, South; from the students of Atlanta, Nashville, and Birmingham rather than from the farmers of the Mississippi Delta.

Finally, the North, which had led the struggle for half a century, now followed the initiative coming from the South. In the sixties, there were Northern sit-in demonstrations for jobs and housing, rent strikes, the gigantic March on Washington of August 1963, school boycotts, and other direct actions. CORE, for example, which had pioneered in the American application of nonviolence without becoming a major civil rights force, grew from 15,000 members in 1959–1960 to 77,000 members in 1963–1964.[21] And that group's philosophy shifted from an emphasis on a trained cadre of nonviolent activists toward mass action.

Eventually, the new Southern and Northern protests came to be called a Revolution. New leaders appeared, challenging the established spokesmen, charging that the ghetto poor were being ignored.[22] As one observer sympathetic to the new and rebellious currents put it, "The passive Negro, who trusts that God and the NAACP will salvage his dignity while he concentrates on avoiding trouble, is rapidly becoming extinct."[23]

In summary, then, over more than half a century, the urbanization of the American Negro and his entry into industry has widened the mass base of participation in the civil rights movement and intensified its militancy. The actual gains in living standard have been modest by absolute standards and less than modest when compared to the white advance. Yet these gains provided the basis for new organizational forms of resistance. Negroes had concentrated themselves in cities, had developed modern attitudes and skills, and had come into contact with the labor movement in some areas. On this economic and social base, by 1964 Negroes had created the most important American thrust for social change since the rise of the CIO in the thirties.

II

In the sixties another trend became discernible. The evidence indicates that it began during the fifties and that it was at work during that period of growing militancy and organization. Even as Negro aspirations were rising higher and higher, the economic and social trends which had furthered the rise of the contemporary civil rights movement began to reverse their direction. For half a century, things had been getting relatively better (again it should be noted that this is only true within the miserable context of racism). Now it was quite possible that they would steadily worsen.

The impact of this negative situation was not immediately felt by Negro organizations. On the contrary, when it was realized that, for all the talk about equality, Negroes were suffering increasing economic discrimination, the immediate effect was to galvanize the movement to action. If the deterioration of the Negro's social and economic position were to continue over a long period of time, it would not only be a personal tragedy for millions of individual Negroes, but a social catastrophe that would accelerate the disintegration in the structure of Negro life and thus severely limit the possibilities of Negro organization.

In exploring this point, there is no intention of trying to document a fatalistic pessimism. The exact opposite is the case. Since the dangerous economic and social trends that now threaten the future of the Negro struggle can be made subject to democratic political action, the conclusions of this analysis underline what can be done now while there is still time.

The new economic fact that threatens even the modest social and economic gains made by Negroes up until now is, of course, automation and its impact upon the labor market. Through no fault of his own, the Negro is in one of the worst possible positions to face this development.

The geographical distribution of the Negro population today defines three different styles of Negro life. In 1960 there were 18.9 million Negroes in the United States. Of these, 11.3 million were living in the South, 3 million in the Northeast, 3.5 million in the North Central States and one million on the West Coast, primarily in California. And in the South, 60 percent of the Negroes were living in cities, 40 percent in rural areas.[24]

In the United States as a whole, Negro income was 52 percent of white income in 1959. In the Northeast, the range was from a high of 74 percent of white income in Pennsylvania to a low in New Jersey of 65 percent; in the North Central States, from Indiana's 79 percent to Missouri's 68 percent; and in California the figure was 70 percent. The Southern high point, 61 percent in Kentucky, was lower than in any non-Southern state; and the low, 32 percent in Mississippi, is almost unbelievable when one considers that white income in that state is itself quite low.[25]

The poverty of the rural South makes it impossible for people there to finance their own self-organization. This is why urban-based (and in terms of fund-raising, primarily Northern-based) organizations like the NAACP, SCLC, SNCC, and CORE have been key to developments there. In 1960, the Bureau of the Census reports, the median annual income for Mississippi Negroes on farms was $474.[26] As a result of the hopelessness of this economic situation, plus the impact of mechanization in the field, there has been considerable emigration. Between 1950 and 1960, for instance, the Negro population of Mississippi declined 7 percent, and the loss was particularly severe among those in the 20-to-34 age group and those from the countryside.[27] This has the effect of taking some of the most dynamic individuals, the potential leaders, out of the struggle.

In the urban South, economic conditions are much better than in the rural areas. Yet poverty is still the basic and overwhelming fact. In the Urban League analysis of the Bureau of Census figures, the Southern cities had a much higher percentage of Negro poverty than the Northern cities. In Richmond, Miami, Louisville, Jacksonville, Atlanta, New Orleans, and Memphis, between 41 percent and 51 percent of the Negroes were poor (the Federal Government's poverty criteria were used). All of the Northern cities had a Negro poverty rate below the 41 percent level, and in the best of the major population centers, Los Angeles, "only" 23 percent of the Negroes were poor.[28]

The urban North is the best economic and social setting for

Negroes. Incomes are higher than in the South. And if one takes the Urban League study's extremely modest definition of middle-class status—a family income of over $6000—then 39 percent of the Negroes in Los Angeles, 36 percent in Washington, and 35 percent in Chicago are in the middle class.[29] Yet these facts cannot obscure the position of the Northern and urban Negro at the bottom of the economic pile. Nor should they detract attention from the possibility, even more ominous, that Negroes are now being pushed backward relative to the rest of the economy.

During World War II, with full employment, a labor shortage, and the necessities of defense, the Negro made his greatest gains relative to whites.[30] These gains, coupled with the new political consciousness of the thirties, had important organizational functions. They made action seem feasible at the same time that they revealed the gap between Negro aspiration and reality and stressed a common interest in closing it. And these attitudes are some of the classic elements that drive people to protest and resistance.[31]

If, however, an unfavorable long-term economic and social trend erodes the present gains, locking Negroes even more securely within the poverty of the ghetto, then the sense of hope will disappear and with it one of the conditions needed for constructive action. When this menacing pattern first began to show up in the fifties, the Negro reaction was not passivity but protest and anger. This eventually led to the March on Washington in 1963, which had full employment as a major civil rights demand. And this kind of response can continue for some time. But in the long run, if the economic and social trend continues, there is a likelihood of paralysis or violent and aimless individual action.

Under the present circumstances, however, Negroes are not able to solve these economic and social problems unaided. The disadvantages in education and skills that white America has imposed upon black are an important factor. They make many Negroes unfit for the new economy. The racial ghettos are profound miseducators, usually more influential than the schools themselves. The Negro child is often the classic victim of the drop-out cycle: he arrives at class on the first day educationally retarded by one or two years; during his first three years he is not taught to read, write, and count, and thus he drops even further behind; by the age of nine, attending school has become to him a way of marking time, since it is by then impossible to make up all the lost ground; and at sixteen he may legally leave school.

As a result of this pattern, the Urban League reports that in Los Angeles, which had the *lowest* percentage of Negro drop-outs over twenty-five years of age, the rate was still 55 percent! [32] This is true at a time when the educational and skill requirements of the economy are increasing. Thus, between 1949 and 1959 unemployment increased in every age group for those with less than a high school education, and decreased for those above that level.[33] And these statistics do not take into account those forced out of the labor market altogether. Negroes were, and are, concentrated in the educational groups that suffer most from change, and also in those occupations most vulnerable to automation.[34]

These are some of the reasons why the Negro percentage of the white wage declined between 1949 and 1959.[35]

What if these patterns were to continue? They need not do so, of course, since it is possible to subject automation and unemployment to democratic controls and direction. But what if this were not done? How would it affect the perspective of the Negro struggle for equality in the United States?

Such a development would exacerbate all that is disintegrative in Negro life. If this took place, the resultant suffering would be more likely to lead to passive withdrawal or destructive violence than to the development of a revolutionary movement or the expansion of the present civil rights organizations. The Harlem riots are a grim case in point.

Negro teen-agers are among the prime victims of automation and of the current patterns of demand in the labor market. They suffer the highest rates of unemployment in the nation and have gained the least from the various Federal training programs.[36] This intolerable fact was a major element in the upheavals in the Northern ghettos during the "long, hot summer" of 1964. Perhaps the most interesting analysis of the situation comes from the FBI Report on the riots.[37] It is a persuasive document: Precisely because it minimized the role of Communists and other groups, and emphasized the social pathology of the slums, it must be taken as something more than a routine police statement.

According to the FBI, "The evidence indicates that aside from the actions of minor organizations or irresponsible individuals, there was no systematic planning or organization of any of the riots." Or, to put it in the terms of this essay, the riots were not a result of Negro organization but a function of disorganization.

One of the leaders who was in Harlem throughout the riots, attempting to argue for nonviolence, was Bayard Rustin. Rustin had been the effective organizer of the massive March on Washington of August 1963, and he had received support in that enterprise from the streets, and even the bars, of Harlem. But he reported that neither he nor any other Negro leader or organization (the Black Nationalists included) was in even basic communication with the rioters.

Clearly, the majority of the people of Harlem did not riot. The FBI describes those who did: "While adult troublemakers incited the riots, the mob violence was dominated by the acts of youths ranging in age up to the middle twenties." This is precisely the group with the highest unemployment rate and the least hope. Even though their plight is extreme and desperately in need of collective action and resolution, these young people are so demoralized that they are outside the constituency of any of the Negro organizations. Their response, understandable as it is, given the circumstances, will not change their lot. And that is the essential tragedy.

It is conceivable that the American economy could produce an even larger number of such young people. Indeed, there are many indicators which now point in this direction. Under such circumstances, the long-term pattern of the past sixty years would be partially reversed. Rather than increasing their absolute standard of living and occasionally making gains relative to whites, Negroes would be slipping back in the labor market. And this fact could severely contract the potential for mass Negro organization.

The young are a dramatic, obvious example of some of the most negative possibilities. But they are not alone. For even with the gains made by the Negro in this century, the heritage of slavery and the discriminatory reality of Emancipation have built many instabilities into the very structure of Negro life. These will be reinforced by an increase in unemployment; and they too will make organized resistance all the more difficult.

The particular situation of the Negro family is well known. As Frazier put it:

> The widespread disorganization of family life among Negroes has affected practically every phase of their community life and adjustments to the larger white world. Because of the absence of stability in family life, there is a lack of tradition. Life among a large portion of the urban Negro population is casual, precarious, and fragmentary. It lacks continuity and its roots do not go deeper than the contingencies of daily living. This affects the socialization of the Negro child.[38]

The main, current reason for this problem lies within the economy. Negro women in cities have always been able to get steadier jobs, usually as domestics, than the men. In New York in the early 1960's, Negro women had a median income 93 percent that of white women; for Negro men, the figure was 68 percent.[39] This often meant that a man was capable of being a biological but not an economic father. It led to matriarchal relationships—to a high number of impoverished Negro families with women at the head—and its effects upon children were a factor in the 1964 riots.

Here again, if the economic trends described earlier in this section are not changed, then the material basis of Negro family life will become even more insecure. There will be whites of good intentions who will murmur at how unfortunate it is that there is so much illegitimacy, desertion, and promiscuity in the Negro ghetto without realizing these phenomena are social products of racism rather than personal sins.

This is one of the reasons that the "self-help" analogy going from the Negro present to the immigrant past fails. The European ethnic groups came to America culturally intact and with a community spirit; their lack of education was not decisively against them since the unsophisticated economy had a tremendous need for sheer muscle power; and they did not face a disability as profound as that of color. By contrast, Negroes have been subject to the most virulent race prejudice. The slave traders had consciously set out to destroy their ties to Africa and to institutions like marriage as well. So, as James Baldwin has poignantly recorded, the Negro who comes into contact with Africans sadly realizes that he is American.

For historical and economic reasons, then, Negroes had less of a chance at real community than any other group in the nation's history. Automation might deepen this disability. The experiences of youth, marriage, and family might be made increasingly mercurial.

Finally, one other item should be added to this inventory of factors affecting the structure of Negro life (which is illustrative and by no means exhaustive). The three different Negro styles of life—the rural South, the urban South, and the urban North and West—are dynamic, for it is a typical Negro experience to move from one style of life to another. In New York City, for instance, the Negro population increased 290,000 in the forties, and 340,000 in the fifties.[40] Part of this increase can be attributed to a relatively high birth rate. Yet the fact remains that in 1960 one half of the nonwhite population of the city over twenty years of age had come from the South.[41] Ralph Ellison caught the emotional heart of this statistic when he spoke of Northern Negroes "shot up from the South into the busy city like wild jacks-in-the-box broken loose from our springs—so sudden that our gait becomes like that of deep sea divers suffering the bends."

Such an experience is unsettling under the best of circumstances. It will become even more so if this transition from South to North ceases to be a step up and becomes a journey into an impossible labor market. In other words, the entire benign and positive impact of the Negro migration experience could be changed along with all the other aspects of life.

These, then, are a few significant examples of how the continuation, or intensification, of the present patterns of Negro unemployment, and particularly youth unemployment, go much deeper than the individual tragedies or even the sum total of them. These economic and social trends constitute an attack upon the very structure of Negro life, a strengthening of all that is disintegrative and anti-community. Consequently, they hold out the possibility that Negro America could have shrinking human resources with which to meet accelerating problems.

And clearly, such an analysis challenges some of the more simplified theories in which the poorest Negroes will take over the role once assigned in radical vision to the revolutionary workers.

And for all the tremendous gains that have been made by the civil rights movement, there is a very real sense in which the options remain as Drake and Cayton defined them twenty years ago. In 1945 they wrote:

> The fate of the people of Black Metropolis—whether they will remain the marginal workers to be called in only in times of great economic activity, or will become an integral part of the American economy and thus lay the basis for complete social and political integration—depends not so much on what happens locally as on what happens in America and the world. Given widespread postwar unemployment, the Negro may again become a chronic relief client. . . . This, too, depends not so much upon Chicago as upon the possibility of America's achieving full employment in the postwar world and on the development of a world program for emancipating the Common Man.[42]

How this situation is resolved will affect, not simply the personal fate and psychology of Negroes, but the hopes and potential of the most dynamic and important social movement in the United States since the thirties.

III

The foregoing analysis has policy implications for both Negroes and whites.

First, from the point of view of the civil rights movement itself, the assumption that adverse economic conditions will, over a long period of time, increase militancy is most questionable. Therefore, one of the main responsibilities of the Negro struggle is a concern with the question of full employment. And this is an "integrated" task, for it is clearly impossible to provide jobs for Negroes while leaving whites behind. The issue will be resolved on a national basis or not at all.

The creation of full employment will take the expenditure of large amounts of money in a planned fashion.[43] And it will require the winning of a political victory in Washington, since the Federal government is the only possible power that can direct such an effort. The decisiveness of these economic and social questions should, in turn, point the civil rights movement toward the politics of alliance. A lunchroom can be integrated by Negroes acting on their own; perhaps even a few jobs can be won on a construction site by direct action; but the achievement of full employment requires the mobilization of a political majority.

And the key to this is a union between the civil rights and labor movements.

It is obvious that such a union is more easily stated than achieved. Precisely because the past decade has been marked by chronic, high unemployment, many tensions have developed between unionists and Negro activists. White workers, fearful of automation, have regarded Negro demands for work as threats to their livelihood. In this they have often been seconded by their leaders and reinforced by the racial prejudice that still suffuses the entire society.

If this split were to deepen, it would have the most reactionary effect on American life and would preclude the creation of a political majority capable of winning full employment for black and white worker alike. In 1964 the overwhelming majority of the labor leaders and rank and file understood this possibility and joined in a coalition with Negroes to defeat Goldwater. This development took place partly because many trade unionists were more fearful that Goldwater would take their jobs than that the Negroes would. In other words, a disaster was averted but the issue of the "white backlash" was by no means resolved.

To bring Negroes and labor together on a permanent political basis, something other than fear is needed. And that programmatic basis for an alliance is the recognition of a common interest in full employment. In 1965 there were some signs that Negro leaders were understanding this point more and more. Martin Luther King gave support to several strikes and organizing drives, and the "summit" meeting of Negro leaders called by A. Philip Randolph endorsed many of the economic proposals of the AFL-CIO. On labor's side, there were attempts to prepare for the implementation of the Fair Employment sections of the Civil Rights Act of 1964.

And yet, there is no point in exaggerating the ease of creating this alliance. Both subjective prejudice and objective economics pose serious obstacles to it. Still, the fact remains that without such a unity, the ten percent Negro minority will be politically incapable of winning the economic legislation that is so crucial to both the individual and the Negro movement. And the unions cannot carry *their* program if they set themselves against the most moral and appealing force for social change in the United States. The way of the labor-Negro alliance is certainly a difficult one, but it is the only way.

Finally, what is being described here is not an economic policy based on *noblesse oblige* toward the unfortunate Negroes. It is integrated action in the name of all the American people. The massive social investments in housing, schools, hospitals, and transportation systems would not only provide jobs for the black and white poor but would constitute a positive response to the general crisis of the American city. And investments in the human care of human beings—in teachers and teacher's aides, in social workers and indigenous, nonprofessional organizers—would relate to the qualitative development of a society that is in sight of the solution of the quantitative problems.

In current political language, Negroes could be hired along with their fellow citizens to work at the building of a Great Society.

And if this country does not do these things, it is about to inflict one more terrible wound upon the Negroes of America. For chronically high unemployment and the coming problems of automation strike at the potential of both the individual Negro and the Negro community. It would be an unpardonable irony if the economics and sociology of racism could thus subjugate the emerging American consensus in favor of integration.

NOTES

1. New York: Macmillan, 1963, p. 346.
2. S. M. Miller, "Poverty and Politics," in Irving Louis Horowitz, ed., *The New Sociology* (New York: Oxford Univ. Press, 1964), p. 297.
3. Boston: Beacon, 1964, p. 256.
4. Quoted in Nat Hentoff, *The New Equality* (New York: Viking, 1964), p. 222.
5. Richard Wright in the introduction to *Black Metropolis*, by St. Clair Drake and Horace R. Cayton (New York: Harcourt, Brace, 1945), p. xxxiv.
6. In V. F. Calverton, ed., *Anthology of American Negro Literature* (New York: Modern Library, 1929), pp. 379 ff.
7. Quoted in C. Eric Lincoln, *The Black Muslims in America* (Boston: Beacon, 1961), pp. 69–70.

8. Frazier, "La Bourgeoisie Noire," *loc. cit.*, p. 381.
9. Unless otherwise noted, this résumé of the history of Negro protest relies on E. Franklin Frazier, *The Negro in the United States,* Revised Edition (New York: Macmillan, 1957). In particular, see Chapter 20.
10. *Ibid.*, p. 174.
11. *Ibid.*, p. 259.
12. Drake and Cayton, *op. cit.*, p. 77.
13. *Ibid.*, p. 386.
14. Tom Kahn and August Meier, "Recent Trends in the Civil Rights Movement," *New Politics,* III, Spring, 1964.
15. James Q. Wilson, *Negro Politics* (Glencoe, Ill.: Free Press of Glencoe), p. 282.
16. Herman P. Miller, *Rich Man, Poor Man* (New York: Thomas Y. Crowell, 1964), p. 70.
17. *Ibid.*, p. 85.
18. The description of SCLC is taken from Martin Luther King, Jr., *Why We Can't Wait* (New York: Harper, 1964).
19. Nathan Glazer and Daniel Patrick Moynihan, *Beyond the Melting Pot* (Boston: MIT Press and Harvard Univ. Press, 1963), p. 25.
20. Alexander Heard, "The South Ahead," in Avery Leiserson, ed., *The American South in the 1960's* (New York: Praeger, 1964), p. ix.
21. Report of the National Director, 22nd Convention, July 2, 1964.
22. See, for example, Louis Lomax, "The Crisis in Negro Leadership," in *The Negro Revolt* (New York: Harper and Row, 1962 [Signet Edition, 1964]), p. 160 ff.
23. Lincoln, *op. cit.*, p. 229.
24. Miller, *op. cit.*, pp. 85 ff.
25. *Ibid.*
26. Quoted in COFO Paper No. 1, *The General Conditions of the Mississippi Negro* (Jackson, Miss., 1963; mimeographed), p. 1.
27. *Ibid.*
28. *Urban League Report,* November 17, 1964 (mimeographed).
29. *Ibid.*
30. Miller, *op. cit.*, Chapter 6.
31. Martin Oppenheimer, "White and Black," *The Massachusetts Review,* VI (Autumn–Winter, 1964–1965), 215 ff.

32. *Urban League Report.*
33. Charles Killingsworth, "The Automation Story," in Charles Markham, ed., *Jobs, Men and Machines* (New York: Praeger, 1964), p. 38.
34. Tom Kahn, *The Economics of Equality* (New York: League for Industrial Democracy, 1964), Chapter 2.
35. Miller, *op. cit.*, pp. 86–87.
36. *Manpower Research and Training* (U.S. Department of Labor, 1964), p. 27.
37. New York *Times,* September 27, 1964, p. 82.
38. Frazier, *The Negro in the United States,* p. 636.
39. Glazer and Moynihan, *op. cit.*, p. 30.
40. *Ibid.*, p. 25.
41. *Ibid.*, p. 26.
42. Drake and Cayton, *op. cit.*, p. 767.
43. See, for example, Leon Keyserling, *Progress or Poverty* (Washington: Conference on Economic Progress, 1964).

IV

Employers, Unions, and the Negro

10 / How Management Views Its Race Relations Responsibilities

George Strauss[1]

What is management's responsibility in the area of race relations? Does management in a free enterprise system have any responsibility other than to stay within the law and to maximize profits? And if management does have an added responsibility, is it enough to be scrupulously colorblind and always to select and promote the best man? Or should management go further, actively seeking Negro applicants to offset the previous discrimination against Negroes with some sort of reverse discrimination that favors them? If so, to what degree? In 1963 U.S. Steel was attacked for its alleged failure to use its influence to reduce segregation in Birmingham, Alabama. Does management have any responsibility to change community values? The purpose of this chapter is to discuss some of the problems management faces as it deals with civil rights pressures in the middle 1960's. It will not provide a detailed description of what management has done in this area, for this is the subject of another chapter.

A little background is necessary. My main point of reference is the San Francisco Bay area. San Franciscans enjoy the self-image of a cosmopolitan, highly tolerant community. Until recently San Francisco's minority problem was primarily Oriental (and in the past Orientals were subject to at least as much discrimination as Negroes are now). But the Negro population of San Francisco grew fifteen-fold in the period 1940–1960. Lack of jobs and the feeling that the community's performance was not consistent with its values led to a series of demonstrations and incidents of civil disobedience. These in turn led to arrests, convictions, and jail sentences, but also contributed to a widespread breakdown of discriminatory job barriers.

Along with these events have come some very substantial changes in managerial attitudes and behavior. With various degrees of reluctance, a broad range of managers have taken on the responsibility of eliminating discrimination. Some have engaged in tokenism and have dragged their feet, but others have taken on the difficult task of integration with sincerity of commitment and with a strong desire to show that business can do the job without government interference. The details are discussed in Chapter 11; the intent is what is important here.

This chapter, then, is concerned with managers' responses to a changing environment. It is a case study of how management's vague concepts of social responsibility are translated into action. It shows how a managerial group, placed in a new situation, first fumbles but eventually develops a response to new conditions. We will look in turn at the basic values management brings to bear on the problem; at the reasons for the apparent contradictions between beliefs and performance; at the impact of recent pressures; and at management's dilemmas as it decides whether to be colorblind or whether to take "affirmative action" to increase its Negro employment. The final section presents a natural history of integration and discusses some of the problems personnel directors face in introducing policies of integration.

□ Basic Managerial Values

Naturally, managers do not approach the race relations issue in a vacuum. They bring with them values they have developed over the years. Some of these are common to members of the American upper and middle class generally; others are more specific to management. Thus the reaction of managers to Negroes' demands for jobs is undoubtedly affected by their reaction, as citizens, to Negroes' demands for desegregated housing or their reaction to Negro riots in the big cities. The job battle is just one front (though perhaps the most important one) in the great Negro Revolution of the 1960's.

We will look at just two sets of values here: (1) the increasing acceptance by many executives of the concept that management has a social responsibility beyond profit maximization, and (2) the tendency to make the managerial process more "rational" and "objective" in the long run.

Social Responsibilities

With the rapid advance in the size and influence of American industry, a vigorous debate has begun over its proper responsibilities toward the community as a whole and toward employees and customers. Management has always felt some responsibilities, particularly to employees. The early textile manufacturer of New England, for example, often provided elaborate opportunities for his "charges" (typically young girls) to worship God and to obtain an education. Even the worst of "robber barons" often provided housing facilities and distributed Christmas gifts and other forms of largess to his employees. This was personal rather than corporate charity, and gifts, rather than rights, were bestowed.

Corporate objectives are less clear than once they were. Increasingly managers look upon themselves as professionals, and as such concern themselves with "ethics." At least for publication, they seem to worry about social obligations. Growth, share of the market, and company (and managerial) prestige are partially supplanting the goal of maximizing profits, and some managers claim that their function is to act as trustees for a number of interests (some of which admittedly conflict). It is not uncommon for managers to talk of their role as mediators between stockholders, employees, and customers, rather than solely as representatives of the stockholders. Though it can be argued that under law management's sole obligation is to maximize its stockholders' profits, few managements make this argument—and this is more than just a matter of public relations.

The close interrelationship between business and society seems to be more clearly recognized by businessmen today than it was before the Great Depression and World War II—and this is true even in industries not closely affected by government purchasing and government regulatory commissions. Many businessmen are beginning to develop a sense of a special responsibility—call this *noblesse oblige* if you like—to behave in the interests of the national welfare. It is increasingly accepted that, in a world where economic planning is the norm, the right to manage can be maintained only to the degree that social responsibility is accepted.

Naturally, managers differ in their interpretation of their social obligations. Many think primarily in terms of lobbying for their special interests. Some see themselves as protecting free private enterprise from left-wing conspiracies. Still others think in terms of preserving the status quo. Liberals might prefer that businessmen stick to making profits and stay out of the public arena. Yet it seems reasonably clear that managers are beginning to feel a social obligation that goes beyond enriching themselves and their companies. They feel that their corporations should at least function as good citizens. For some, this merely means adjusting to community values, but many go beyond this to assert that managers should take the initiative in solving social problems. Specifically, in the light of recent events a significant number of managers have come to the conclusion—on the intellectual level at least—that management, as a group, has an obligation to help solve the Negro problem, even though some of this thinking is still in terms of giving contributions to Negro colleges rather than providing jobs for Negroes.

Rational Decision-Making

Fredrick W. Taylor's concept of scientific management contributed to the development of management professionalism (as, of course, did the separation of ownership from control). Scientific management, a rather primitive approach, which did not progress beyond flow, motion, and time studies, has given way to management science, which makes use of sophisticated mathematical techniques and complex computers. But the emphasis is the same: to make decisions on as objective a basis as possible.

The contrast between the views of professional management and those of the small businessman on this subject is very strong. The small businessman typically feels under an ethical obligation to do special favors for his friends; to him it is only right and proper that the better jobs be reserved for his sons.[2] The ideology of professional management is very different. Though nepotism, apple polishing, and office politics undoubtedly continue to exist in big business, these are universally condemned as unethical. The norm of behavior is quite clear: rewards and benefits should be distributed on the basis of merit alone. To an ever-increasing extent personnel decisions are subject to rules rather than to individual discretion. Individual rewards are determined on the basis of objective criteria rather than on the basis of personal relationships. Though the purpose of this is to make better decisions, a result is also to make more impersonal ones. In Weber's terms, universalism is replacing particularism.

Personnel men, for example, have devised an elaborate paraphernalia of selection techniques, including aptitude, achievement, and personality tests (all carefully checked for reliability and validity), weighted application blanks, group oral interviews, and the like. All of these are designed to make selection a more rational, less subjective process, and so to establish procedural safeguards that will minimize personal bias, favoritism, and other nonobjective influences. The entire procedure has an aura of science, and has been much influenced by psychological research.

□ The Conflict Between Creed and Deed

Assuming that most managers do feel a sense of social responsibility and do believe that individuals should be treated on the basis of individual merit according to rational, objective criteria, why up till now have so few Negroes been hired in any but the most menial positions? A great deal of hypocrisy exists, but we need a more probing explanation. As Myrdal suggests, the clash between ideology and practice in this country is unusually acute in the area of race relations. Certainly management's vague concepts of social responsibility did not become operational until outside pressures made them so. At least three reasons can be given for management's failures to translate its feelings into action:

1. Obligations toward Negroes are relatively low on management's perceived list of obligations.

2. Few managers see themselves as discriminating or treating Negroes unfairly.

3. In some cases top management's policy is not translated into action at lower levels.

These reasons are in part mutually reinforcing; in part they are inconsistent. Yet one should not expect a logically consistent ideology when management's position has rarely been well thought out and is normally affected by a host of conscious and unconscious influences.

Low Priority of Obligation

Though management does recognize moral and social obligations, purely business obligations usually come first. Until recently, management tended to view its obligations toward Negroes as existing primarily on the eleemosynary level, and to compartmentalize these obligations from purely business ones. Though many managers—particularly in personnel departments—may have felt a moral obligation to hire Negroes, they also felt a practical obligation not to stir up present employees or customers. Since there were real fears (some of which were justified) that introducing Negroes would lead to "trouble," the practical obligation came first.

In any case, businessmen can devote only a limited amount of time and attention to social obligations, and as a consequence they tend to rank these in a rough order of priority. Any obligation to treat Negroes in a nondiscriminatory fashion had a lower priority among social obligations in most businessmen's minds than did the obligation to maintain a safe working place, to help redevelop Main Street, to push the Community Chest over the top, or to work for a Republican victory.

Modern organizational theory has rediscovered the old saw that it is the squeaking wheel that gets the grease. Though management may try to solve problems on a rational basis, it doesn't attempt to solve all problems at once; instead, it tends to go from crisis to crisis, and the span of attention given to any one problem may be fairly short. To obtain acceptance of Negro employees, management is required to give up some of its limited supply of time and energy; in the past, other problems seemed more urgent. As a clergyman put it, business leaders "always felt a moral obligation to be nondiscriminatory. Only recently have they realized how important this is."

Management's concept of social responsibility is strongly influenced by its perception of what the public wants. Management would like to be socially responsible, but normally only to the extent that this is noncontroversial. Managers want to be considered good citizens, but being a good citizen may mean adjusting to the community's values rather than trying to change them. Until recently managers believed that, on the whole, the community wanted discrimination.

Certainly there has been a tendency to look upon the obligations of race relations as ones that can be satisfied easily (often by what Negro leaders call "tokenism"), and to give up any attempt at integration when the opposition becomes strong. Many managements assumed that all that was required was a pious statement, or a symbolic gesture, and then the job was done. As a *Fortune* article put it, "The fact that so few firms are carrying out their commitments under the Plans for Progress program does not necessarily imply that the signers are insincere; it does suggest a lack of realism on their part about what they have to do to carry out the program." [3]

Non-Perception of Discrimination

Prior to the recent furor over employment practices, few managers considered themselves discriminatory or irrational and subjective in their selection policies. Most managers had given very little thought to the problem, but assumed that they were objective. Certainly, few Northern businessmen have justified a refusal to hire *qualified* Negroes. The problem was that of defining qualification. At least unconsciously many managers felt that certain jobs were not suited for Negroes, just as some jobs are not suited for women or for old men. There was a great deal of blindness or selective perception here—which Myrdal calls the "convenience of ignorance"—and even intellectual laziness and moral cowardice. Management just did not see the Negro applicant as a potential skilled tradesman, salesman, or executive. This view was easy to maintain because there were in fact very few qualified Negroes, and because even these few realized there would be little point in applying for such positions.

Recent government and Negro action group pressures have forced management to re-evaluate its perceptions—to give some conscious thought to those ideas it has always taken for granted—and to apply some really rational, objective standards to the selection process.

Poor Communication

In some cases discrimination has occurred because a sincere top management policy opposing discrimination has not been implemented at operating levels. Certainly, such policies are not self-enforcing. In most cases they represent a sharp contrast with past practices, and many employees tend to resist them if they can. Since there is conflict between creed and deed in this area, and pious platitudes are so frequently uttered, it is understandable that many employees are uncertain whether new policies are to be taken seriously.

Lower management is subject to a great deal of pressure—to maximize production, to minimize labor expense, to maintain quality, to eliminate grievances, to prevent accidents. Many of these pressures are mutually inconsistent: for example, an increase in production usually means higher labor expense and the possibility of increased accidents. The smart subordinate learns what is really important, and tries to "get by" in other areas. In the past no one really cared if lower management engaged in discrimination.

The problem is more complex, however, than just poor communication or relative priorities, as the following example may illustrate. This case, which was reported by a Negro investigator for a government civil rights agency, involved the president of a hundred-employee company who was an active member of the Urban League board of directors, a generous contributor to the United Negro College Fund, and a pillar of the community. A charge of discrimination was made against this company, and upon investigation it was discovered that it had but one Negro employee, a janitor. All hiring was done by an elderly female personnel director who openly stated that she didn't believe that Negroes were "suited" for the kind of work in which this company engaged. Since she had never received any instructions to the contrary, she had assumed that this was also the policy of her boss. When apprised of this situation the president expressed what the investigator felt was genuine surprise and indignation—he had been told that no qualified Negroes had even applied—and in the next few months several Negroes were employed.

This case can be explained in a number of ways. One can ascribe it to the failure of the company president to set a clear-cut company policy, to inform the personnel director what this policy was, and to see that the policy was carried out. Yet more than this is involved, for here was a case of functional blindness, of compartmentalizing social obligations from business obligations. It is hard to believe that if this executive really wished to apply his social philosophy to his own company he would not have engaged in some sort of investigation to determine why it was so lily-white.

Poor communication is one of the reasons why discrimination persists, but there has been poor communication because of the low priorities attached to this area of company policy. When management really wants to get something done it does more than issue a statement or make a token gesture.

□ The Impact of Recent Pressures

Recent pressures have brought the problem of Negro employment to the forefront of management's attention. Though management's reaction hasn't always been rational and objective, it has had to give the problem some conscious thought. It is hard to ignore a chorus of chanting CORE pickets at your front door. These pressures also helped translate moral obligations into practical necessities and raised the Negro question quite a few notches higher in management's scale of priorities. For a number of companies, race relations have been among the most important problems of 1964.

Finally, these pressures and associated governmental actions have spelled out in much greater detail the social and moral obligations of businessmen. Those businessmen who believe that their only obligation is to stay within the law now know that the law forbids discrimination. Those who wish to remain "good citizens" now know that the standards set for them by the more articulate representatives of society call for them to hire an appreciable number of Negroes at all levels of organization. Those who want to "go along with public opinion" know that it has changed considerably in the last ten years, though some see evidence of a recent backlash.

In many cases, the fact that outside agencies have established standards has made it easier for companies to implement their own policies. To those who object to the introduction of Negroes, management can now say it has no choice but to do what the government (or even civil rights groups) has told it to do. These pressures have strengthened the position of those who support hiring additional Negroes, and it has at times almost silenced those who opposed them.

In addition, there is a certain tendency among management groups to follow the leader. Personnel policies follow fads (witness the successive popularity of training courses in human relations, communications, in-basket techniques, and T-groups). In San Francisco, employers associations play an important role in setting industrial relations policies. Personnel directors who looked upon integration as primarily a moral problem see no inconsistency in waiting for the employers' associations to set the policy. Once the pattern is set by the associations or by leading firms, other companies follow, because it is the thing to do. Certainly many companies have found it easier to react to pressures than to be leaders.

The requirement of government contract agencies (and Negro action groups) that employers take a periodic census of the number of Negroes employed, by level and occupation, provides management with what is sometimes called control data. Executives can no longer plead lack of awareness of what is happening in their own organizations (and American management always pays greater attention to a problem once it can be stated in terms of numbers). Though there is little discussion of quotas as such, many companies behave as if, in fact, they had a quota to fill.

The Nature of the Pressures

The foregoing factors provide only the context within which the pressures operate. Nothing is as significant as the pressures themselves. There seems to be little question that without them change would have occurred with glacial slowness.

Change has been most rapid in those industries subject to pressure—that is, those which have contracts with the Federal Government (primarily in aerospace and electronics) and those which are most subject to picketing and sit-ins on the part of Negro action groups (primarily consumer service industries).

According to personnel men in defense industries, the government's pressure has been continuous, and growing in intensity. Militant civil rights leaders, on the other hand, claim that the government has been rather ineffective and that its agents are easily hoodwinked. Personnel men say that at one time there was a substantial difference in the diligence with which various government agencies enforced fair employment practice rules; many departments apparently looked upon this as an unwanted task. Most recently enforcement has become more uniform and, some claim, "the pressure has become vicious." Not only is there the threat of losing a contract, there is also the major burden of being investigated and the constant nuisance of submitting reports.

The civil rights groups in San Francisco picketed the industries where their pressures were most likely to be effective: retail trades, automobile dealers, drive-in restaurants, and hotels. Only a handful of locations have been actually subject to picketing, but to avoid this pressure many other organizations have scurried around to find qualified Negro employees.

Relatively little mention was made by personnel officials of the California State Fair Employment Practices Commission. Doubtless some companies have changed their practices in order not to be cited before this commission, and there seems little question that it has played a useful role in educating managers and in helping them in difficult situations. One might argue, however, that the Commission has been more effective in mediating pressures than in generating pressure on its own.

□ Management's Reactions to Pressures

Management's reactions to these pressures has not been as simple as some of the foregoing might suggest. With few exceptions there has been no sudden realization of guilt, a cry of *mea culpa,* and then a major effort to make up for past faults.

Recent pressures have come to management as a shock, as they did for all of white America, for what was once enough is no longer enough. To the extent that management believed that it did not discriminate, it resented having its good faith and integrity questioned. "A company can get real emotional," one observer commented, "when it has a standard hiring procedure, based on tests, and it is charged with discrimination when it turns a Negro down. It feels the same way the university would feel if a Negro charged discrimination when he failed the entrance exam."

Civil rights groups select large, prominent firms for their picketing, perhaps in part because they feel that firms concerned with their reputations might be more likely to give in, and in part because a settlement reached with such a firm would have greater value as a precedent. Yet, according to personnel people, some of these very firms have previously been leaders in effecting integration. Understandably, this leads to considerable bad feeling. Some managements harbor resentment toward civil rights groups because they feel that they have already made an arrangement. Thus one personnel director told a militant civil rights group that it didn't have to see him because he had already worked out an arrangement with the Urban League. He was quite upset when told that the Urban League did not speak for this committee. Similarly, some managements have been resentful when concessions, at one time considered great advances, are now questioned as inadequate. They sometimes feel that the Negro leaders are being ungrateful. "Regardless of what you do for them," a personnel director complained, "it is not good enough." (But a government representative commented, "Some employers want a new badge or a gold star every time they hire a Negro.")

Companies do not like being called to account for what they feel is not their own failing but the illness of society. They dislike being the battleground in a war they feel is not of their own making. Nevertheless, reluctantly (but in some cases with determination), many have begun to accept responsibility for this nasty problem that has been thrust upon them. Management finds itself in the unhappy predicament of having a waif left at its door. Though it denies paternity, it will feed the infant; it may even give it top priority (particularly when it screams "Daddy").

Thus management's sense of obligation to do something about the Negro problem is far more deeply felt than it was in the past. But from management's point of view this is not an enforceable obligation—it is something like giving money to the Community Chest, and there is a good deal of resentment against the efforts of outsiders, whether the Government or civil rights groups, to tell management what to do. Instead management feels that the elimination of discrimination is its own responsibility, and one that it will handle in its own way.

There is considerable feeling that business should not botch up the Negro question the way it did the union question in the 1930's. It is thought that if business does not take the lead, then the government and civil rights groups will be able to place restrictions on business policy that business will never be able to remove. "If we don't take the responsibility here and handle it our way," a top executive commented, "we will create a monster that we won't be able to handle in the future."

There is some disagreement among managers as to the wisdom of negotiating and signing contracts with civil rights organizations. A number of management groups have done this—and have indicated that the pressures were such that they had little choice in the matter. "You ask me about signing," a personnel director commented. "There is a matter of principle here. Of course, we shouldn't sign. But we've got an obligation to our stockholders. We just can't let a bunch of pickets hurt our business."

Other managers feel that signing is a serious mistake. They do not propose to give a self-appointed group the right to bind companies with a contract. Having already given one outside organization, the union, the right to question their activities, they do not propose to do it again.

The tactics of civil rights leaders have bolstered the determination of some managers to keep outsiders from interfering. It is easy for managers to view this leadership as a bunch of wild men, bearded beatniks who seek trouble for its own sake. The emotional, insensitive approach of the civil rights advocates cannot help but breed counter-emotion on the other side.

"I hope I never have to go through tension like that again," a personnel director commented on the period during which his industry was negotiating with civil rights groups. "Our top executives would meet together day after day. There was table pounding, throwing of paper on the floor, and people yelling 'We can't let those niggers push us around.' You know, as a result, there are a lot of liberal people among the executive group—some of whom used to give money to Negro organizations—who are going to vote for Proposition 14 just as a way to get back at them." [4]

Yet with so many opportunities for white racial prejudices to be inflamed, the surprising thing is that company people have remained so temperate—not only in public statement, but generally also in private conversation. I was impressed on a number of occasions by personnel men who would make a strong, emotionally loaded comment about the opportunism and irrationality of civil rights leaders—and then tempered their statements with "Of course, I understand how they feel."

In many ways the sit-down strikes of the 1960's aroused the same emotions as did the sit-downs of the 1930's. Once more management denied that the problem was serious and insisted that it was one the company should handle alone. Once more management showed great resentment of outsiders and felt their tactics were inadmissible. Once more management had to face idealistic, undisciplined young agitators who were much more effective in rabble-rousing than in contract negotiations. The difference—and this is all to management's credit—is that this time management has reacted in a generally calm and mature manner.

□ Colorblindness or Affirmative Action

There is considerable question as to how far management should go in the acceptance of greater responsibility. Actually, management has a spectrum of choices. It can be neutral and colorblind in its policies. It can step up efforts to recruit Negroes without lowering hiring standards. It can pick Negroes for job vacancies even though they are not the best qualified applicants, as long as they meet minimum standards. It can provide special training for those who don't meet minimum standards at the moment but might eventually be qualified. And it can lower its present standards to accommodate those who will never meet even these minimums.

Generally speaking, two positions are most prominent. Some believe that it is enough to be colorblind and scrupulously impartial. Others feel their companies should take affirmative steps to recruit and hire Negroes. (There are those, of course, who still support discrimination. In San Francisco this is not an articulate group.)

Colorblindness

Of the two groups, those who believe in colorblindness, or neutrality, are the more emotional in support of their belief. They recognize the legitimacy of the nondiscrimination argument, perhaps admitting that they had been discriminating inadvertently in the past, but they feel that discrimination in favor of Negroes is just as unfair as discrimination against them. Members of this group will do what is just, but they believe that as businessmen they have little responsibility for solving social problems. They state their willingess to apply the same personnel policies to people of all colors, but refuse to lower their standards to benefit any group. They feel that their internal personnel policies will be distorted if applied as a remedy for social injustice. Thus, if their past policy has been to hire at the bottom, they refuse to make an exception to hire Negroes at higher levels.

There is little question that the application of antidiscrimination rules to joint union-management apprenticeship programs has led to a raising of standards—for example, requiring high school algebra for admission—thus, on paper, making it even more difficult for Negroes. (In practice these rules have helped a bit.) Further, there are a good many double standards here —one standard being, as a personnel director put it, "just FEPC talk," while the other is applied to relatives and other favored groups.

Perhaps the policy of neutrality in fact masks conscious or unconscious discrimination. Nevertheless this policy is rationally defensible—and, from the point of view of those who support it, morally defensible as well.

Affirmative Action

The demands of Negro action groups and government contract agencies call for affirmative action to "promote equal job opportunities." The simple colorblind approach of nondiscrimination, acceptable only a few years ago, has given way to "equal employment opportunities," and the emphasis is not on vague *opportunity* but on concrete *employment*. The pressure today is for employers to hire significant numbers of Negroes at all occupational levels and to take whatever measures may be necessary to achieve this end. "The official position of the government is getting close to reverse discrimination," one personnel director observed, and another added, "They bring all the pressure they can." [5]

Affirmative action is demanded because colorblindness rarely results in integration. "You can post an equal employment sign for a hundred years," the director of an employers' association remarked, "and a hundred years from now there will still be no change in the work force." The limitations of colorblindness are well known and will be only briefly repeated.

1. The mere existence of a nondiscrimination policy does not result in qualified Negroes applying for work, even when they are available. The traditional recruitment channels—word of mouth, relatives of present employees, union hiring halls, better (*i.e.* white) schools and colleges—rarely affect Negroes. Even when Negroes hear of vacancies they seldom apply for jobs that past history has taught are not open to them.[6] If Negro applicants are to be obtained it is necessary for companies to make special efforts to reach them.

2. For a number of jobs now opening up there are few, if any, trained, qualified Negro candidates. If Negroes have never had the opportunity to gain experience or training, obviously there will be no experienced or trained Negroes available. Educational requirements tend to preserve racial imbalance because of the relatively low proportion of Negro high school and college graduates. Negroes have often failed to take advantage of the educational opportunities available to them when these opportunities have not been linked to potential employment. Even so-called objective intelligence and aptitude tests may contain a built-in cultural bias that tends to reduce their effectiveness as a predictor of Negro ability.

Thus, if a company is to hire any Negroes at all for some jobs, it must lower or drop its requirements of experience, education, or training, revamp or eliminate its testing procedures, and—if qualified Negroes still cannot be found—provide training so that Negroes can obtain these qualifications. The key question, to cite a commonly heard phrase, is not whether a man is *qualified* but whether he is *qualifiable*.

Does affirmative action require hiring Negroes who will remain unqualified even after training? That is, does it mean hiring someone who will never meet acceptable standards? Perhaps this is required, but none of those interviewed mentioned such a problem.

Affirmative action does require census-taking to determine the number of Negroes in various departments. Some companies have honestly felt that such polls would violate government antidiscrimination regulations, and there is a good deal of inconsistency in this area, according to civil rights agencies and progressive groups. Companies are supposed to know the number of Negroes they employ, but are not to make any mention of color on individual personnel records.

Does affirmative action mean reverse discrimination? This is largely a semantic question. Those who are committed to the principle of integration normally use the euphemism "affirmative action" in public, but in private admit that they mean reverse discrimination, at least in the sense that opportunities are granted to Negroes that are not made available to whites, and that where two candidates are equally qualified the Negro will get the job.

Though reverse discrimination "may run counter to the established order of labor and management relations and the neat ethical concepts by which personnel managers have been guided for the past half-century or so,"[7] nevertheless the manager who is committed to integration doesn't seem to worry. The concern with reverse discrimination comes from those who believe that colorblindness is enough.

Reverse discrimination comes easier because the granting of preference to favored groups is not completely unknown to management. In making purchases, many companies grant favors to companies that buy from them. In the personnel field, preference has long been given to senior employees, even in non-union companies. (And civil rights groups are in effect asking for a form of seniority to offset the "seniority" long enjoyed by whites.) Some companies limit their hiring largely to those recommended by current employees. At least lip service has been given to providing special attention to veterans and the handicapped; in fact, veterans' preference is required in the civil service.

□ The Natural History of Integration

Interviews suggest that many companies have had roughly similar experiences in dealing with recent pressures. Let us examine the typical pattern, noting that there are many, many deviations from it.

Before Application of Pressures

Minority group members were hired in some categories by numerous companies long before the present civil rights agitation. (In California these minorities at first were overwhelmingly Oriental.) Certain jobs have been traditionally reserved for minority group members since before the Civil War, and a few jobs have been made available by socially minded employers.

Racial barriers to Orientals began to decline quite rapidly in the Bay area after the war. In some companies Orientals have now found jobs in a wide variety of departments. In fact, some department heads actually prefer Orientals. The prevailing pattern, however, is still for minority group members to be concentrated in certain departments, and, in the case of Negroes, usually in the lower-paying jobs.

The Coming of Pressures

Outside pressures have hit companies at various times. Some were affected by the World War II FEPC; others still have not felt their impact.[8]

Outside pressure generates pressure within management. It reinforces the view of those who support integration, and weakens the position of those who oppose it. Usually staff people are the ones most willing to support integration. Professional people, particularly those in personnel, advertising, and research are often more liberal in their social and political thinking than are other members of management. Staff professionals feel economically more secure and less afraid of automation. Consequently, there are companies with a higher percentage of Negro chemists, engineers (and even secretaries) than of Negro production workers.

Line managers are too busy for staff's social theorizing. As far as subordinate line officials are concerned, integration is another (and unnecessary) nuisance that is bound to stir up trouble. From their point of view, it is easier to operate with homogeneous departments consisting of people with the same sort of backgrounds.

Steps Toward Integration

Progress toward integration normally follows a series of stages. These stages do not follow one after another automatically. In fact there is a tendency for "plateauing," that is, for a company to halt at one stage and to progress no further until there is a renewal of outside pressures.

The first stage is the issuance of a policy statement or the signing of a pledge. As we have seen in itself, this may be almost meaningless.

The next stage is the hiring of a Negro. In the past, the first Negroes hired were brought in for low-paying jobs. Some companies now regret this. If a Negro is brought in at a high-paying level, the shock is felt just once: there is a presumption that all jobs will eventually be integrated. There is no such presumption when a Negro is brought in at the bottom, and the battle must be fought again and again as Negroes move up the ladder.

The third stage involves "leap-frogging"—bringing a Negro into an entirely different kind of job, often one with considerable public exposure.

Stages two and three involve a good deal of handpicking—handpicking of departments where resistance will be least, and handpicking of Negroes who will be good workers and win easy acceptance.

The final stage, and often the most difficult one, is the introduction of a significant number of Negroes through all occupations and departments in the organization.

Along the way management will normally go through a stage of colorblindness, decide that this is not enough, and then decide to take positive steps to recruit Negroes. Eventually it may engage in various forms of reverse discrimination. Besides deciding on these policies, it must face a number of practical problems.

Practical Problems

Personnel men report three sorts of practical problems in dealing with integration. These are: (*1*) winning acceptance of Negroes by various groups within the organization; (*2*) recruiting qualified Negroes; and (*3*) applying personnel policies to the Negroes recruited.

Winning Acceptance

Management must win acceptance for minority employment from at least four groups: (*1*) subordinate line management, (*2*) rank-and-file workers, (*3*) the union, if any, and (*4*) customers. I will comment on the first three only.

1. SUBORDINATE LINE MANAGEMENT As suggested earlier, there may well be opposition to integration from members of line management who feel this policy is at best an added burden and one that is likely to lead to employee unrest. Actually, line management is more fearful than is justified: new Negro employees are often accepted more easily than had been expected. Nevertheless, supervisors of the first departments to experience integration are likely to feel put upon; consequently they drag their feet and otherwise resist the new policy.

All reports indicate that if integration is to succeed, management must take a firm no-nonsense position. Stories like the following are often heard: During a meeting that a company called to announce a new equal employment policy, one supervisor stated that he would submit his resignation as soon as the first Negro was placed in his department. The top executive present countered quickly, "If your resignation is submitted on that ground, it will be accepted immediately." This stilled all opposition.

Personnel texts have preached for years that the function of the personnel department should be merely to recruit and screen new employees, and that line management should make the final hiring decisions. An effective integration policy often requires that selection be centralized in the personnel department. A retail chain still has an unsatisfactory integration record, largely because it believes that taking the right to hire away from store managers would be too damaging to their morale and motivation.

II. RANK-AND-FILE WORKERS Resistance from the rank and file does occur, though it is usually less than expected. The Negro demand for jobs now held by whites has added to the general insecurity caused by increasing automation and chronic unemployment. In addition, some companies require less of Negroes for promotion than they do of whites, thus contributing to a feeling of favoritism. All this tends to exacerbate already existing prejudice.

Work group resistance seems to be strongest at two points: when the first Negro is introduced into a department, and then when so many Negroes are introduced that the whites feel themselves becoming a minority. At this stage many whites seek to transfer out, and other whites resist being transferred in.

III. THE UNION The role of the union on the job is discussed elsewhere in this book. Let it be noted that in spite of the liberal beliefs of many top leaders, union policy itself cannot be too far in advance of the rank and file. Resistance is particularly strong where the union operates a hiring hall and union members are out of work.

According to some personnel directors, unions constitute the single greatest road block to integration (other than the shortage of qualified Negro job applicants). Dealing with unions requires great tact, as union leaders sometimes try to set up a bargaining situation in which the company is expected to make economic concessions in order to win acceptance for Negroes (thus forcing management again to decide how high a priority it wishes to assign to integration).

Recruitment

Understandably, when companies look for missionaries who are to be the first Negroes in a given department or in the entire company, they seek someone who is really outstanding in terms of technical ability and social skills.[9] Naturally there are only a limited number of really outstanding people; the cream has now been skimmed off, and companies who are newcomers to integration must accept second best.

There is a shortage of even "adequate" Negro candidates in many occupations for which previous training is required. Traditionally, Negroes with professional and craft skills have found it as hard to find jobs as have those without skills—and some have found it even harder. Today, unless all my respondents are wrong, the picture is dramatically different for many trained Negroes (at least outside the building trades). There are a significant number of occupations in which a Negro has a better opportunity to find a job than does a white worker. Good Negro secretaries, according to a number of reports, are worth their weight in gold.

Negro action groups give first priority to placing Negroes in high-paying, high-prestige positions. Negroes with college degrees in business, engineering, or the sciences are very scarce. Placement officers from the better colleges report that the demand for Negro graduates far exceeds the supply.

Since most companies have had little experience recruiting in the Negro community, organizations such as the Urban League have found themselves in the novel position of having more job openings than they are able to fill. The State Department of Employment has substantially increased the number of its Negro placements. A number of San Francisco companies have helped finance PACT, a Negro organization founded for the purpose of placing minority group members in white-collar and managerial positions (as well as to help them establish small businesses). And some companies now employ full-time specialists charged with recruiting Negroes from Negro colleges and elsewhere. In a sense, companies are now required to use the same imagination in recruiting Negroes that they used to recruit all applicants during World War II.

As the pressures to hire Negroes mount, and as the limited supply of trained Negroes gets progressively more depleted, company hiring standards for Negroes are dropping rapidly. Some companies have tried to be colorblind, using all kinds of objective selection techniques. But most companies subject to substantial pressures have been forced to abandon colorblindness for various kinds of affirmative action. In the policy described as, "If merit and ability are equal, the Negro gets the job," the word "ability" has been stretched considerably in application. In practice, Negroes are often hired if they have only the minimum qualifications.

And these minimum qualifications are dropping all the time. A company trying to fill a job that normally calls for a college graduate with four years of accounting settled for a junior college graduate in bookkeeping (with the expectation of providing this man the necessary additional training on the job)—a privilege that would not be extended to a white man. A retail store, after failing to find a college graduate to fill a management position, took one of its own employees who had had some college experience and paid half of his college expenses while he finished up. A large company set the passing score on its entrance examination ten percent lower for Negroes than for whites—and this seems quite common.

Personnel Policies

Negro action groups are not satisfied with obtaining jobs just at the bottom rung of the ladder; they want Negroes to be employed at all levels in the organization, and particularly in management. This creates additional problems for companies that traditionally have hired people at the bottom and promoted from within. If Negroes are moved up at the same slow rate as whites, it may be years till they appear at higher levels. Yet promoting them rapidly creates hosts of serious morale problems. If there must be favoritism, personnel directors feel that it should be at the hiring stage rather than in promotion. As a consequence, in some companies the tradition of promotion from the ranks has been broken.

Discipline represents another problem area. Line managers report that Negroes are more likely to flout rules or slow down on the job. The line managers' perception may be distorted by prejudice, but nevertheless personnel directors feel this is a problem. Some Negroes are seen to exhibit a chip-on-the-shoulder attitude, to be lazy, to break rules, and to ignore many of the niceties of middle-class manners and behavior.[10] A certain number of Negroes may seek special privileges and yell "discrimination" when these are denied.

In any case, a good deal of adjustment is required all around, and these problems complicate the personnel director's life. Certainly personnel directors today are sensitive to any personnel incident that involves a Negro. They report being especially careful in discipline cases, both to avoid charges of discrimination and to ensure that line management has not been prejudiced.

The whole equal opportunity program has reduced management's flexibility—in a manner somewhat analogous to what happened with the coming of the union. In dealing with unionized employees, personnel men were already extremely careful to document their position and to follow the rules in all cases involving promotion, transfers, discipline, or compensation. In dealing with Negroes, they must show equal care in all these areas and also in the area of hiring (unions have generally not placed restrictions on employers' freedom to hire new employees, except where hiring halls have been maintained). For non-union companies all this comes as quite a shock. For unionized companies this is merely an extension of a familiar problem, but the personnel director must cultivate a new set of relations with people who have not learned the fine art of collective bargaining.

Negro pressure groups, by creating the right-to-be-hired in addition to the pre-existing right-to-be-treated-well-after-being-hired, have made the personnel process increasingly inflexible and bureaucratic. To take an example: As the result of the "Cadillac sit-in," a civil disobediance demonstration held on the premises of a large San Francisco auto dealer and resulting in an agreement on the part of the San Francisco Motor Dealers Association to promote minority employment, the Association requested its members to fill out a form in quadruplicate for every job vacancy (one each for the union, the Mayor's Committee on Human Rights [now the Human Rights Commission of San Francisco], the state employment service, and the dealer) and another set each time a man was hired, giving the reasons for his employment. These forms, as well as all job applications, are to be kept on file in case outside groups wish to inspect them.[11] What a difference between this and the highly informal procedures typically followed by dealers in the past!

□ Conclusion

This chapter, it should be emphasized, is based primarily on conversations with representatives of management. It deals with problems as they see them. Furthermore, my discussions took place in a geographical region that is proud of its tradition of tolerance; therefore the opinions expressed may not be typical of American industry generally. Yet, to the extent that pressures in other communities have been less severe than in San Francisco, this report may be a forecast of things to come.

The picture I get from my vantage point is perhaps distorted, but it suggests that during the last two years some very significant changes have occurred in personnel policies and practices affecting Negroes. Government and Negro action group pressures have pushed many large employers past colorblindness to affirmative action. Job opportunities for qualified Negroes have dramatically improved, and the main problem now seems to be that of raising the level of Negro education.

True, integration is still far off. If outside pressures die down, there may well be another period of "plateauing," but there seems little doubt that the Negro action groups have so far won a substantial victory. For better or worse, Negroes are receiving special attention and often favoritism. The process of correcting the gross inequity of anti-Negro discrimination is doubtless creating some inequities in terms of internal company personnel policy. Personnel people are faced with some severe moral and practical dilemmas as they seek to accommodate affirmative action to sound personnel administration.

NOTES

1. I wish to express my thanks for useful criticism to Baughn Blakenship, Earl Cheit, John Hislop, Sidney Ingerman, Arthur M. Ross, and Barry Silverman.
2. Representatives of both union and management in the construction industries openly proclaim the virtues of nepotism with a frankness that would be inconceivable in large publicly controlled corporations. This factor explains in part why civil rights groups have made relatively little progress in the construction industries.
3. Charles E. Silberman, "The Businessman and the Negro," *Fortune,* LXVIII, No. 3 (September 1963), 99.
4. Proposition 14 was a proposed amendment to the state constitution, submitted to the California electorate, that would have outlawed legislation against discrimination in housing.
5. The decision by a hearings examiner of the Illinois Fair Employment Practices Commission ordering Motorola to cease administering a general ability test to job applicants because it discriminated against "the hitherto culturally deprived and disadvantaged groups," since "its norm was derived from the standardization of advantaged groups," was viewed as a straw in the wind by personnel men. In his order the examiner asked the employer, if he chose to replace the test, to "adopt a test which shall reflect and equate inequities and environmental factors among the advantaged and culturally deprived groups." *Myart and Motorola, Inc.* Charge No. 63C-127, 55 LRR 373 (February 26, 1964, Illinois Fair Employment Practices Commission, Hearing Examiner Robert E. Bryant). Since this article was written, the commission order has been set aside by the Illinois Supreme Court.
6. Of course, as the word gets around the Negro community that

a company is hiring Negroes, we may expect more Negroes to apply.

7. George Schermer, "The Demands for Equal Rights," in Jerome W. Blood, ed., *The Personnel Job in a Changing World* (New York: American Management Association, 1964), p. 328.
8. According to government sources, there are small employers who are still not aware of the existence of antidiscriminatory legislation.
9. At one time individuals with light skins were preferred. Now those with dark skins have an advantage, if anything.
10. The chip-on-the-shoulder attitude, if it does exist, may represent a natural reaction to what is perceived as a hostile atmosphere. The claim of laziness and other faults may reflect either stereotypes on the part of management or the fact that in the Negro culture there is no tradition that hard work pays off.
11. According to a recent charge by Frank Quinn, Director of the Human Rights Commission of San Francisco, "a great majority" of the employers have failed to file these statements. "Publisher's Point," *San Francisco,* VIII, No. 2 (February 1966), 6.

11 / Industry's Racial Employment Policies

Herbert R. Northrup

The racial employment policies of American industry have undergone a profound change in recent years. This has been partly due to a slow evolution dating back to World War II, or perhaps even earlier. Nevertheless, a great deal has occurred in the last two years due to the same forces that resulted in the passage of the Civil Rights Act of 1964. These include the increasing activity of Presidential committees on racial employment in the defense industries and the activities of state Fair Employment Practices Commissions.

This chapter examines the nature of the change and how it has occurred. Although based upon examination of a limited segment of American industry, it is the product of observations over a twenty-five-year period. Moreover, the companies examined have been those which are taking the lead in providing employment opportunities for Negroes, and which are in a position to affect most substantially the total racial employment policies of American industry.

□ Employer Racial Policies in the South

Southern industry may be divided into two general groups insofar as historic racial employment policies are concerned. In the first group are those industries that were in the South prior to the Civil War, and in the second group, those that came South in the late nineteenth century and later. The Negro had a place in the first group, typified by the tobacco industry. Negroes had been employed in this industry since its inception in Colonial times, and they still comprise a large segment of the work force. Until recently, the pattern of this industry was one of a racial occupational segregation that kept contact between the races at a minimum. Negroes did the stemming and other processing operations, while whites took over the manufacturing. Thus, while the Southern mores of the early part of the century were satisfied by the confinement of Negroes to non-machine, non-manufacturing jobs, Negroes did have at least one-half of the jobs.

But if Negroes were confined to non-machine jobs in the tobacco industry, they were virtually excluded by the textile industry, which set the pattern for new manufacturing industries in the South from the 1880's until the beginning of World War II. The textile industry was brought South as part of a move to lift the economy out of Reconstruction difficulties. It served as a source of both capital and employment, and as a means of solidifying an alliance between the Southern planters' oligarchy and the populous group of poor whites. The oligarchy provided jobs for the whites excluding the Negro from the work force and maintaining the socioeconomic and political *status quo*. The racial industrial and occupational pattern was thus established. Until World War II, Negroes continued to be excluded from industries which migrated to, or developed in, the South, or else were confined to the most menial tasks.

At the same time that the textile industry began its Southern migration, the segregation laws first came into existence. One cannot read those laws and examine the conditions under which they became effective without realizing that one of their prime purposes was to differentiate the Negro labor product and make it more expensive than that of the whites. If the employment of Negroes requires extra toilets and drinking fountains, it is obviously more expensive to employ Negroes; if the employment of Negroes requires segregation, and if segregation is not easy to maintain, it is again obviously more expensive to employ Negroes. If Negroes are forced to live in ghettoes on the outskirts of town and forced to ride in uncomfortable segregated transportation, then it is more difficult for Negroes to obtain work and to come to work, and their ability to supply a labor product is adversely affected.

□ World War II and the Postwar Era

World War II marked the beginning of a change in the thinking and habits of American industry insofar as the employment of Negroes was concerned. The need for Negro labor was obvious to all but the most obdurate thinkers and practitioners. In addition, World War II marked the beginning of effective agitation on the part of Negroes for equal employment. This added a new dimension to industry's thinking, because such agitation challenged the traditional view that it was too troublesome (and hence bad economics) to hire Negroes. Moreover, the agitation was extremely effective because it was pressed upon a government that was not only sympathetic at the executive level, but which during the war was the principal, and often only, customer of industry. As a result, Negroes were hired in substantial numbers in many defense industries. Although they were, for the most part, concentrated in unskilled jobs, some significant gains were made and some changes developed in corporate policy which lasted beyond the war. In other cases, of course, the change proved temporary.

One of the most notable accomplishments after the war was the stand taken by the International Harvester Company, which sincerely attempted to integrate its plants, both North and South.[1] In the immediate postwar period, however, the International Harvester experience was not typical in the South. Many corporations reverted to older policies. A large multi-plant manufacturing company that expanded in a number of areas established several plants on a lily-white basis. Other companies employed only Negro janitors. The traditional mores of the South seemed still to be dominant.

In the 1950's, and especially toward the middle of that decade, one began to sense a change in the attitude of large corporations that had established subsidiaries or branches in the South. Particularly significant in industries selling directly to the public was the feeling that a "Negro market" existed, and that here was a potential that had not been tapped. Moreover, these industries became aware that there was communication between the ever-growing Negro population in Northern cities and members of their race in the South.

In addition, other industries, headed by individuals who valued the public images of their organizations, were becoming increasingly concerned that a significant percentage of Americans were growing up without any knowledge of, interest in, or ideas of support for American industry. They began to realize that contributions to Negro college funds, or employment of Negroes in the North, might not be enough.

□ The Effects of the School Controversy

The changing attitude of businessmen toward the employment of Negroes in the South was given a significant push by the controversy over segregated schooling. For the most part, industry did not consider that this fight was its own until mob action and the threat of closed schools became a reality. To Southerners desirous of improving economic conditions in the South through industrialization, and to industrialists who wanted to locate a plant in the otherwise inviting areas of the South, the imminent blow-up over schools raised some very serious questions. These came to a head when Governor Orville Faubus of Arkansas closed the schools of Little Rock rather than submit to integration. What happened as a result is best described by the man who headed the Little Rock, Arkansas, Industrial Development Corporation for over a decade, Mr. Everett Tucker, Jr. He had been instrumental in bringing an average of five new plants a year to the Little Rock area between 1950 and 1957, ranging in value from $100,000 to over $3,000,000. In 1957, prior to the outbreak of violence in September, he had been able to report that eight new plants had been installed. Three and a half years later not a single new plant had come in. Said Mr. Tucker:

> It's sort of an insidious thing. The principal damage comes about when you don't even know that it's happening to you. You just don't hear from the XYZ Company that it's on the prowl for a new plant location. You never hear from them; they are not going to write you and say, "We were going to look at Little Rock, but now we're not." [2]

The fact that Little Rock (and all Arkansas) was wiped off the map of approved industrial locations by the major American corporations in 1957 can be attested by this writer from personal knowledge and experience. No intelligent industrialist will knowingly locate a facility in an area where strife can disrupt production. Any industry that sells a consumer product would be foolish indeed if it located a plant in an area where the potential for becoming caught in racial turmoil was great.

There are, in addition, more fundamental reasons why racial strife and a threat to the educational system destroy the potential of an area for industrial development. The modern corporation today is looking for plant locations that provide the type of educational and cultural atmosphere desired by their key professional and managerial personnel. This is particularly important in such industries as electronics, which stress research and development; and this is why strong statements were made by executives of General Electric and Westinghouse Air Brake in opposition to the schools closing in Virginia. For example, Dr. Louis Rader, then manager of the

General Electric plant near Waynesboro, Virginia, and now a vice-president of the company, pointed out that he might lose up to one fourth of his key personnel if the schools in the area did not remain open, and that it would be virtually impossible to recruit replacements of comparable character.[3]

In a similar vein is this comment made in 1958 by Thomas Meloy, then president of the Westinghouse Air Brake subsidiary, Melpar, Inc.:

> I, personally, have had my part in building an industry from a few dozen people to well over 4,000 in Northern Virginia. It is now an important asset to the communities on which it draws. Of the 4,300 people in my company, over a thousand are of professional level, that is to say, engineers of various types, such as electronic, chemical, mechanical, aeronautical and civil, and mathematicians, physicists, metallurgists, and other specialists. The other three thousand-odd employees consist of technicians, machinists, draftsmen, technical writers, assemblers, and office personnel.
>
> Of the thousand professional personnel, all but a very few came from the outside, and the majority from the North where school standards were much better. Our greatest problem in persuading them to come here was the lack of desirable schools.[4]

Once the issue was joined and the battle decided in Virginia, other states in which industry has had a strong influence, notably Georgia and South Carolina, have proceeded toward integration without the demagogy and difficulties that have characterized the situation in Alabama, Mississippi, and, earlier, in Arkansas. It is undoubtedly significant that the steel industry in Alabama does not sell to the consuming public and, at least until recently, has seen little reason for a social consumer orientation.

Opposition to the closing of schools on racial grounds is, of course, not the same thing as employing Negroes in one's own plant. Nevertheless, the stand taken by industry on school closing is illustrative of changing attitudes toward the racial composition of the labor force. Despite the antagonisms among whites and Negroes that were generated by the school controversy, it was during this period, the late 1950's, that in-

dustry began a significant turn-around in racial employment policies in the South. The same large multi-plant company that was mentioned before as starting lily-white plants after World War II made a determined effort to begin the integration of its work force in the South. Negroes were employed on assembly lines and as skilled employees where they could be found, and in more than one plant, the Negro office worker appeared for the first time. Serious consideration was given at corporate headquarters to the need to increase Negro employment throughout the country, and emphasis was laid on satisfactory racial and educational situations in locating new plants. A satisfactory racial situation was specifically defined as including the lack of any interference in the fair employment of Negroes, and in the complete integration of in-plant facilities such as lunchrooms, toilets, and drinking fountains.

□ The Kennedy-Johnson Period

With industry already receptive to fair employment, the proposals developed by the Kennedy and Johnson administrations met little opposition. The late President Kennedy greatly strengthened the President's Committee on Equal Employment Opportunity. Following the precedent set in the Eisenhower administration, the Vice-President was named chairman of this committee. Mr. Johnson proved a vigorous leader in this capacity. The committee had a large staff and aggressively sought to further Negro employment. This enabled several companies, particularly those in the South, to use the existence of the committee as a means for furthering fair employment; and it forced many others throughout the country to abandon non-compliance, or token compliance, as a policy. Among the notable contributors to improved Negro employment during the Kennedy administration's first years was the Lockheed plant at Marietta, Georgia, near Atlanta. By actively recruiting Negroes for the wage and salary levels, it was able to place qualified Negroes in jobs throughout the plant at supervisory, white-collar, professional, and lower and middle managerial levels.[5]

Mr. Johnson added a wrinkle all of his own—which most of the one hundred largest corporations (including Lockheed) have accepted. That is the Plans for Progress Program. Under Johnson's aegis, representatives of the leading corporations of the country were called down to Washington and asked to sign pledges to actively further the employment of Negroes and other minorities. The plan was gradually extended, and 268 firms, employing well over 8,000,000 people, were participating by August 1964.[6] As early as the end of 1963, for the 103 companies which were participating at that time, total employment increased from 3,900,000 to 4,250,000, or 7.6 percent, while nonwhite employment went up from 200,000 to 241,000, an increase of 20.5 percent. The number of salaried positions rose from 1,900,000 to 2,020,000, or 2.1 percent, while those held by nonwhites increased from 29,000 to 43,000, or 47.7 percent.[7] Continued improvement was reported as of July 1964.[8]

The progress of the Committee was, of course, part of the general progress at this time. The Bureau of Labor Statistics, for example, was able to report early in 1964 that there had been a noticeable increase in white-collar employment for Negroes.[9]

Western Electric Experience

Plans for Progress companies have, however, led the way. Data for the Western Electric Company, the manufacturing arm of the Bell Telephone system, show a continuing increase in Negro and other nonwhite employees, even in the face of a slight drop in general employment. This has been accomplished by a conscious program of recruiting Negroes, under specific orders from the top officers of the company. Western Electric has had to seek channels for recruits that it had not heretofore utilized.

Specifically, communication has had to be made with the Negro community to convince people to apply. This, companies often find, is hard and discouraging work. Negroes are often fearful of leaving the accepted avenues of travel to look for jobs. Once the word gets around, potential employees do apply. Meanwhile, the experience of those already on the payroll, their treatment, and their opportunities for promotion, all determine the number of future applicants. Western Electric made it the duty of its managers to further Negro job opportunities, and placed the controls in the hands of its central personnel function.

The Period Preceding the Civil Rights Law Period

Of course, not all companies are Plans for Progress companies, nor are all gains attributable to this program. Nevertheless, it was the particular genius of President Johnson in bringing groups together that gave the management of major American corporations a specific goal in which most of them believed, and which they felt was good for their businesses and for the country—that Negroes should be encouraged to obtain better opportunities for jobs.

The demonstrations, outbursts, and counterdemonstrations that occurred late in 1963 and in 1964 emphasized the soundness of the Plans for Progress Program. It was now definitely good business to avoid trouble and to employ Negroes, and companies set out to do it. In the words of a sardonic observer: "Since the demonstrations began, Negroes have suddenly popped up all over the eastern part of the country as bank tellers, secretaries, and in similar white-collar jobs. Everybody has his Negro out front where he can be seen." [10]

Negro college graduates became the most sought after of the job seekers. Negroes with specific qualifications, such as engineers or accountants, found themselves especially rushed. Programs were set up at industry's expense in most major cities, often in conjunction with branches of the National Urban League, to recruit or to train Negroes in a variety of jobs from machine operators to salesmen and from office clerks to computer programmers.

Much more than token employment has been involved. Even in the South the color line has broken down. Reynolds Tobacco Company, for example, has led the way in ending the racial occupational segregation of the tobacco industry. Today in Winston-Salem, North Carolina, Negroes and whites work side by side at the same jobs, and there are Negro supervisors, some of whom direct white workers. In such areas as Greenville, South Carolina, the rigid color line of the textile industry has begun to disintegrate—a notable accomplishment in an industry in which there is tremendous worker hostility and an historic managerial policy toward exclusion of Negroes.

□ The Impact of the Civil Rights Law— Some Cases in Point

The passage of the Civil Rights Act of 1964, with provisions for fair employment effective in July 1965, is likely to have little impact on the racial employment and personnel policies of major American corporations in the North. Years of living with state fair employment laws, Federal Government committees and programs, and a belief at top management levels that Negroes deserve opportunities have already conditioned their policies and motivated their practices. In the South, however, despite much progress, there is much that this law can affect. The following three cases illustrate different methods that have been tried to meet the stresses inherent in the implementation of non-discriminatory employment policies.

The Case of the Recalcitrant Accountant

Mr. F. M. Jones was regional manager of the Southeastern regional accounting department of the Vehicle Chemical Company. Like most large companies, Vehicle had joined the Plans for Progress Program. Vehicle had employed Negroes in factory work for many years, and some years before had begun to integrate its New York, Chicago, and other Northern offices. In the South, however, it followed the company practice of most Northern industries by not bringing Negroes into office work except as porters, janitors or in other menial positions.

When Vehicle signed the Plans for Progress commitment, however, it took the matter seriously and so advised its regional managers, including its Southern regional office in Georgia. Jones, the manager of that office, was a Southerner, but he realized that the time had come for integration. He placed orders with employment agencies, talked to Negro ministers and the local Negro college, and soon had an attractive list of personnel. He was able to find an excellent girl to be a bookkeeper in the credit department, as well as additional persons who could be trained from the stenographic pool and eventually be secretaries. He decided to act without further delay.

First of all he had meetings of his office personnel and explained what had to be done, stressing not only the need of the company to comply with this program before it was forced to by the impending equal opportunity law, but also, as a sincere churchgoer, emphasizing the moral issue involved. His ideas were well received, and the persons he hired, who were obviously qualified and determined to do a good job, aided the smooth transition.

Everything seemed to be going quite well at the end of the first two weeks, and Jones was obviously pleased with himself for having done a good job in a difficult situation. But then he learned that William Moore, the number three person in the office, had been making disparaging remarks about the new bookkeeper, who was obviously qualified and whose deportment had been exemplary. For example, at lunch hour Moore regularly started off on the theme that "he never thought he would see the day when he had a nigger working in the same office with him."

Jones called Moore in and very carefully, with much obvious pain—for Moore was an excellent producer and had been a personal friend of Jones for some years—once again told Moore that the change was permanent, that there could be no backtracking, and that the company was only fulfilling its moral responsibility. He did not belabor the economic consequences of failure. He felt he had turned Moore around.

For the next few weeks things seemed to go along all right. Meanwhile, Jones found and hired additional Negro personnel and had already made up his mind that the girl in the credit department would receive a promotion if things continued to go well. It never occurred to Jones to back down in his determination to make integration work. He was therefore shocked when he received evidence that Moore had not changed, but had merely become more subtle—and more vicious—in his opposition.

Once again he called Moore in, and this time in a gentle but firm manner he pointed out to Moore that his reaction was understandable to Jones as a Southerner, but that it was nevertheless emotional, and out of place in the modern world. He said further that the Vehicle Company had no choice in the matter, that it had to go along with integration. He also pointed out that if Moore was ever going to be a manager, he would have to face up to such problems in a rational manner, and that if he did not, he could hurt the relationship of the company with its suppliers, or its customers. Finally, he said that if Moore could not in good conscience go along with this policy, he (Jones) would have to assume his responsibility by forcing Moore to resign. A month later, there was no sign of any change in Moore's attitude or behavior. Though reluctant to do so, Jones was forced to fire him.

In retrospect, Jones thinks he failed because he was unable to straighten out a man whose work performance had been very good; but he still has been unable to think of any other course of action. He gave a full report to his superiors and warned them that they might expect some White Citizens Council reaction, but there was none.

How Not—But Successfully—to Integrate

The South Texas plant of the Widespread Metals Company had been lily-white since its construction in 1937. There were no segregated facilities because there was no need for them. For many years, the plant had been highly profitable. Organized by the United Steelworkers of America, employee relations were, on the surface, amicable, but, like so many that developed in the lush post-World War II period, were based on steady concessions and "pay-outs" to the union by a succession of plant managers and personnel directors, who pushed production out of the door regardless of the long-run consequences.

By 1961, however, competitive materials had steadily eroded the profit position. As new plant management sought to cut unnecessary costs, and indirectly to take away side-bar concessions to the union, relations between the plant and the local union grew strained. As time went on, the personnel manager, trained under the old regime, grew uncomfortable under the stricter practices and no-concessions policy of the new management.

Meanwhile, the company was becoming increasingly conscious of its vulnerability to charges of discrimination, with attendant bad publicity and possible loss of government contracts. Directives and policies warning against discrimination began emanating from the safe confines of New York staff headquarters. It was at this stage that the plant personnel manager, knowing that his job was in jeopardy, decided on a dramatic act. He, single-handedly, would integrate the plant, just as he (in his own mind), single-handedly, had kept labor peace. That he might not be able to buy his way out as he had done formerly, even if the new regime were willing to use the old tactics, did not seem to occur to him.

To his credit, the personnel manager did a good screening job, using the state employment service and doing his own interviewing. He lined up six capable young Negroes with excellent backgrounds and hired them for starting assembly line jobs. He then arranged for them to report for work on a Tuesday, when both the plant manager and the union district representative would be attending a Community Chest meeting. No company or union official, supervisor or foreman knew what was taking place. The surprise was complete.

The six Negroes reported and the plant was promptly seething. The assistant plant manager and the local union president reached the plant manager and union district representative almost simultaneously at the meeting. The latter accused the former of luring him to the meeting to get him out of reach, finding it difficult to believe that the integration move was made without his knowledge.

Back at the offices of the plant and the local, the plant manager and union representative took charge. The former quickly got to his line foremen and told them that, since integration was company policy, there could be no back-off, despite the manner in which it was handled. The district representative, after finding no company support for his suggestion that the Negroes be sent home, told the local officers that any strike would be illegal and against the international union policy.

The plant managed to run through the day without major incident. The next day the plant manager began a series of meetings of small work groups throughout the plant. He told each that integration was government, company, and union policy. He emphasized that no one's job was in jeopardy. And he stated that if there were any violence or threats the perpetrator would be summarily discharged, noting also that the union circular stated that there would be no union appeal for such activity. To his supervisors, he again reiterated that it was their obligation to make integration work.

The firm stand of management (and union support) made integration work. Two weeks later the personnel manager left for a new job at a competitive company—a job to which he was committed before he integrated the plant. He was replaced by a firm adherent to a tough but fair policy. Much unrest followed as the company successfully brought the plant under its control—but the unrest was never racial in origin.

Authoritarian Accomplishment vs. Human Relations Attitudes

A major manufacturer ordered its plants to integrate in the South in late 1963. One Southern plant was headed by an authoritarian Southern gentleman who received his orders and carried them out. He called his plant superintendents together and said, "Gentlemen, we have these instructions to integrate and we are going to do it. There will be no difficulty, it will just be done." A superintendent spoke up and remarked that he was a Southerner and just did not think he could work in such a situation. "That's fine," said the plant manager, "we will give you two weeks' pay." The superintendent changed his mind. Another superintendent said, "What will happen if some of the men get in a fight with these new colored recruits?" "I'll fire the people who are fighting, I'll fire their foreman, and I'll fire the superintendent of the group."

Integration took place speedily and without incident. "We don't like it, but we are living with it," one superintendent told the writer.

In another plant of the same company, the man in charge was a well-trained graduate of a human relations-oriented business school. He saw the integration task as a fine case study for his alma mater and invited a team of professors to observe and to advise him. He began a long education process, hired local sociologists, consulted with the branches of the Urban League and the NAACP, and carefully indoctrinated all his people. The result was a walkout, much difficulty, problems of supervision, and general turmoil. The job of integration still remained to be accomplished six months later, but the manager had by then been replaced.

In musing over his experiences after leaving this job, the former plant manager wondered whether he would not have been wiser to concern himself less about attitudes and more about controlling behavior. "I was let go for not doing the job," he told this writer, "and it finally dawned on me that when I am in charge, I should take charge and manage."

A Word about Small Business

For small business there is, however, a different problem. In the South the small businessman who wants to comply with the law is up against a potential backlash of his white customers.[11] In addition, most small businessmen look at the exemptions under the act for 100 employees the first year, 75 the second, and 50 the third, and feel they have plenty of time. Their day of reckoning is, of course, coming. The small business can be the most solidly hurt by a Negro or white picket line over racial employment problems.

Moreover, many small businessmen lack the sympathy for fair employment found in the executive of the large corporation. Emotionally they are on the other side. They regard the law as just an intrusion into their rights; they do not want to live closely with people of another race, for in a small business a manager does live closely with his employees. The great impact of this law on small business will not be felt for several years, but small business, especially in the South, has a long way to go before it is ready to live with it.

In the North the problem is not so serious, for small companies have been living with fair employment laws for some time. Nevertheless, most of the state commissions have not had the staff or the ability to enforce the law upon the small businessman. With the additional pressure of a Federal bureaucracy they may succeed, and the small businessman in the North will find that he, too, has an obligation under the law. which in many cases has yet to be met.

□ Problems Ahead

The great problem facing the Negro who seeks employment is, of course, his lack of training. There is competition today for Negro workers who have skills, and no one has a better chance for a job than the Negro engineering graduate. Companies that have traditionally hired Negroes now find they have difficulty getting the high-caliber employees they once recruited with ease.

Yet with all these advantages, Negroes in this country may once again face disappointment, for the equal opportunity law is no substitute for qualification. The big job ahead is not equal opportunity but motivation and training. The great majority of Negroes are not trained for industry's requirements, and far too many, as a result of years of discrimination, do not have the necessary education or motivation. It remains to be seen whether we possess sufficient social knowledge to alter these conditions so that Negroes can be hired. Otherwise they and their leaders may attempt to convert fair employment into preferred employment—to attempt, like the novelist James Baldwin, to punish today's white workers because yesterday's were not fair. If such is attempted—by quota, by pressure, by a government bureaucracy—industry's reaction to the equal opportunity law will stiffen, and the present inclination to cooperate will change. The favorable climate augurs well—but abuse in the name of underprivilege can dramatically alter this.

NOTES

1. John Hope II, *Three Southern Plants of International Harvester Company,* selected studies of Negro Employment in the South (Washington: National Planning Association, 1953).
2. Quoted in Helen Hill Miller, "Private Business and Public Education in the South," *Harvard Business Review,* July-August 1960, p. 77. See also W. H. Nicholls, *Southern Tradition and Regional Progress* (Chapel Hill: Univ. of North Car-

olina Press, 1960), pp. 114–15, 118–20; and New York *Times,* January 9, 1961.

3. Quoted in Miller, *op. cit.,* p. 81. For statements by Radar and others, and the effect of business leadership in ending the Virginia school crisis, see *ibid.,* pp. 81–84; and Nicholls, *op. cit.,* pp. 117–18.
4. Miller, *op. cit.,* p. 81.
5. See *Business Week,* April 13, 1963, pp. 90–96.
6. Data for Plans for Progress graciously supplied by Mr. G. William Miller, Chairman of Advisory Council, and President, Textron, Inc.
7. The President's Committee on Equal Employment Opportunity, *Plans for Progress, a First year Report by the Plans for Progress Advisory Council,* August 1964.
8. From statistics compiled by the Plans for Progress Program and the President's Committee on Equal Employment Opportunity.
9. U.S. Department of Labor, Bureau of Labor Statistics, *Monthly Report on the Labor Force for April 1964* (Washington, D.C.), p. 7.
10. Bernard McCormick, "The Insurrectionist," *The Greater Philadelphia Magazine,* June 1964, p. 83.
11. For cases in point see "Dixie Diehards," *Wall Street Journal,* August 27, 1963, p. 1.

12 / Negro Employment in Birmingham: Three Cases

Richard L. Rowan

The research in this article was conducted during the summer of 1964 in one of the most highly segregated cities of the South—Birmingham, Alabama. Although the Birmingham racial employment situation has been analyzed previously,[1] the earlier surveys did not delve deeply into policies and changes in individual or key companies.[2] However, since the companies studied here are the most important manufacturing firms in the area in terms of both size and influence, the results obtained for them also indicate the general trend of Negro employment in the city. In order to gain information on and understanding of the employment problems of Negroes in this controversial location, interviews were conducted with business, civic, and union people, and available records of the relevant parties were examined. Three companies—two in the basic steel industry and one in the aircraft industry—were studied in depth.

Several questions were considered: What is the current race-relations environment in the city? What changes have occurred in the past decade in the proportion of Negroes to whites in the population, the labor force, and education? What jobs do Negroes hold and what factors have been responsible for changes that have occurred? What are the company policies in regard to recruiting, selection, training and promotion of employees? What has been the work experience of Negro employees? What role has the union played in eliminating segregation at the workplace, and what has been the role of management in community matters pertaining to race relations?

□ General Background

Birmingham, Alabama, is a comparatively young city. Founded in 1871, it naturally became an iron and steel center in an area where coal, iron ore, and limestone were found in abundance.[3] Today it is one of the largest industrial cities in the Southeast and the hub of the thirty-fifth largest metropolitan area in the U.S.

Race Relations

In November 1962 Birmingham citizens voted, in a protest movement, to change the form of city government from a three-man commission (including a mayor) to a mayor-council organization. The three-man commission included two arch-segregationists, Eugene "Bull" Connor and the mayor, Art Hanes. Both men wanted no change in the city government and attempted to defeat the reform movement, known as "The Citizens for Progress," by making speeches attempting to link it to integration. In one speech, Connor claimed that "they want to integrate your city." [4] In spite of the remarks and appeals made for the status quo by the segregationist forces, a change was voted. A new mayor and a nine-man council were elected on April 2, 1963, and directed by the Jefferson County Circuit Court to take office on April 15, 1963.[5]

The election was protested by the incumbents, and the case went before the Alabama Supreme Court, which ruled, on May 23, 1963, in favor of the mayor-council government. During the period April 2 to May 23, 1963, Birmingham had a twin government. The three-man commission refused to relinquish office and leave City Hall, while the newly elected officials waited for court decisions to give them the power to take over. The commission remained at their desks in City Hall; the new group moved into temporary offices at the other end of the building.

During this chaotic period, when no real community leadership existed, the Rev. Dr. Martin Luther King came to Birmingham and announced that the city would be the desegregation center of the nation. Demonstrations and protest marches followed, and Dr. King and hundreds of Negroes were arrested and jailed. It was at this time that Birmingham was projected into the national limelight as a city of terror. Policemen using dogs to break up riots were shown on front pages of newspapers across the country. In the absence of a city government in office, there was no way to deal with the racial problems that had arisen. Communication did not exist between the races until a few business leaders met and formed a committee to resolve the disputes.

The demonstrations left a bitter feeling with the white community, city officials, and many white businessmen. The newly elected mayor of Birmingham announced on the day he took office that he was "sympathetic toward racial problems here," but when asked if he would open the door to Dr. King, he replied, "I would not and would not to anyone who would violate the law." [6] The mayor has insisted, however, that his office is always open to *local* citizens, either Negro or white. Almost all leaders in the companies and unions interviewed look upon Dr. King as an agitator. This feeling is based on the belief that Dr. King acted irresponsibly by demonstrating in Birmingham when there was no city government in office to cope with the situation.

Since the new mayor took office, biracial committees have

been formed and there is indication of progress. A committee known as the Community Affairs Committee contains a biracial subgroup named the Group Relations Subcommittee. The charge of this group is stated as follows:

> The task of this committee will be to restore public communications, to define the specific problems and to recommend alternative courses of action for city agencies and civic organizations. Its constant goal must be to reduce both the immediate and the underlying problems in order that all citizens of the city may have fair opportunities, equal treatment before the law, and a fair enjoyment of municipal facilities and services.

The subcommittee includes Negro and white, conservative and liberal, and integrationist and segregationist members. Perhaps the most vital characteristic of the group is that it serves as a means of communication between the races. The subcommittee has not always been pleased with the mayor's action on recommendations it has made, and many citizens also feel that although the mayor was wise to establish this group, he has been too reluctant to move on certain issues. One problem area on which both white and Negro members of the subcommittee would like to see action taken is the employment of Negro policemen. The Group Relations Committee has insisted that Negroes be hired, but the mayor has considered this action impractical from a political point of view. The mayor calls the members of the committee "eager beavers; they want to get ahead and do things." [7] A Birmingham newspaper put the issue in the following perspective:

> Birmingham long has needed Negro police, not because anyone demands it but because they will be useful in curbing crime. We have long said so. The mayor has a duty to be positive and to assure the entire community of a will to do these things that should be done. This willingness to act has seemed missing. Birmingham *must* have leadership.[8]

No doubt there is a real fear on the part of the mayor that overly rapid action may lead to a return to office of "Bull" Connor, which would aggravate already unstable race relations.

Population

Birmingham refers to itself as the "Magic City," due to the miraculous growth in its population between 1880 and 1910, when it increased from 3086 to 132,685. Recent decades, however, have not been marked by significant increases. The total population of the Birmingham Standard Metropolitan Statistical Area (Jefferson County) in 1960 was 634,864. Of this figure, 65.4 percent were white and 34.6 percent Negro. The Negro population was heavily concentrated within the city limits of Birmingham, where almost 40 percent of the population was Negro; however, in several outlying areas, including the industrial towns of Bessemer, Fairfield, and Dolomite, over 50 percent of the population was Negro.

The overall trend in Negro population has been downward, dropping from 37.3 percent in 1950 to 34.6 percent in 1960 for the metropolitan area as a whole; however, for the Birmingham division the drop was only from 39.9 percent to 39.7 percent.[9]

Labor Force

The total civilan labor force for the Birmingham Standard Metropolitan Statistical Area in 1960 was 231,819. Between 1950 and 1960, it increased by 8.1 percent, 18,709 persons, while the population fourteen years of age and over increased by about 7.3 percent, by 32,211. All of the gain in the total population for the ages fourteen years old and over was in the white group, which increased from 259,925 to 296,310, while the nonwhite group (almost entirely Negro) decreased from 145,145 to 140,971.

In 1950, the civilian labor force was 64 percent white and 36 percent nonwhite, whereas in 1960, 69 percent was white and 31 percent was nonwhite. Over the decade from 1950 to 1960 unemployment increased for both white and nonwhite workers, but the rate of unemployment for nonwhites has remained more than twice that for whites.[10]

Manufacturing has been the most important source of employment in Birmingham over the years for both Negroes and whites, and in 1960 it provided jobs for 27.8 percent of all white workers and 25.6 percent of all Negro workers. Within manufacturing, the most important area of employment has been in primary metals industries—at blast furnaces, steel works, and iron and steel foundries. It is estimated that 60 percent of the employees in the steel industry are white and 40 percent Negro. Table 1 reflects the importance of the iron and steel industry in Birmingham's employment picture.

TABLE 1

Nonagricultural Wage and Salary Employment, Birmingham Standard Metropolitan Statistical Area (Averages, in thousands)

Industry	1955	1957	1959	1961
TOTAL	193.9	207.2	196.6	195.6
. . .				
Manufacturing	62.7	70.2	60.5	56.9
Durable Goods	51.3	58.2	48.8	44.8
Primary Metals	29.5	31.8	26.0	26.5
Blast Furnaces & Steel Works	21.8	23.7	19.2	19.7
Iron and Steel Foundries	7.1	7.5	6.6	6.7

Source: Based on data obtained from the Alabama State Employment Service, Department of Industrial Relations, Birmingham Office, Birmingham, Alabama.

Education

The city of Birmingham entered its first year of rather broad integration in the public schools during the 1964–1965 academic year. Prior to that, the school system was operated on a segregated, "separate but equal" basis. Table 2 compares Negro and white school facilities in 1963:

TABLE 2

Educational Facilities, 1963

	City of Birmingham		Jefferson County	
	White	*Negro*	*White*	*Negro*
Elementary Schools	50	42	43	22
High Schools	8	5	11	7
Total Enrollment	37 377	33 678	40 611	17 286
Number of Teachers	1 391	1 057	1 406	551

Source: Birmingham City Directory, 1963, p. XXVIII. In the 1964 City Directory figures are not broken down on the basis of Negro and white.

In 1950, 7190 Negroes out of a population of 109,860 had completed four years of high school, whereas in 1960, 11,938 out of a population of 107,045 had attained the same level. Four years of college had been completed by 1620 Negroes in 1950 and by 3185 in 1960. These gains raised the average number of school years completed by Negroes from 6.4 in 1950 to 7.6 in 1960.[11]

The foregoing statistics covering population, labor force, and education provide a background for studying some specific companies in the Birmingham area.

□ Company Studies

The company studies that follow highlight the various approaches taken by Birmingham businessmen and union leaders in relation to equal employment opportunity.[12] Information pertaining to each of the companies is presented under the following headings: Employment-Manpower Utilization; The Employment Process; The Work Experience; The Union and the Contract; and Community Matters. It is hoped that this somewhat rigid format will emphasize the similarities and dissimilarities in the work undertaken by those under study.

Company I

Company I, a small company in the basic steel industry, has been in Birmingham since the mid-1930's. Even though it is a subsidiary of a national firm with headquarters in the North, the management has been predominantly Southern. The president of the firm has held various positions during thirty-five years with the company in Birmingham.

Employment-Manpower Utilization

WORK FORCE The present employment in the company is approximately 1000, including 470 Negroes and 530 whites. Negroes do not serve in supervisory positions; a company spokesman stated, "They do not possess the necessary educational background and knowledge." Most Negroes perform relatively unskilled or semiskilled work.

FACTORS INFLUENCING CHANGE A combination of management policy—with union cooperation—and government pressure through Executive Order 10925, has been responsible for recent changes in employment practices in the company.

Prior to 1962, the company had a segregated employment and promotion system. Strict departmental seniority rules allowed white employees to progress up the promotion ladder, while Negro employees were confined to rather menial tasks in segregated departments or subdepartments. The union contract specified that promotions (for whites) would be made on the basis of (a) ability, (b) physical condition, and (c) seniority, and that (c) would govern when both (a) and (b) were equal. A large number of grievances were filed by the union as a result of these arrangements, and the company many times was hard put to prove that (a) or (b) were unequal when they promoted a man with less seniority. Cases arose where a man would advance to a certain point in the department and become "frozen" there because he did not have the ability to move up. If he was not frozen, he was promoted into a position for which he was unqualified, and difficulties arose.

In order to eliminate grievances, the company decided to administer tests to all white men who applied for jobs, to make sure they were qualified enough to move from the lowest to the highest positions without having to be frozen in the middle. In 1952 these tests became a part of the pre-employment program for all whites, but were not administered to Negroes. Consequently, between 1952 and 1962 the company developed a group of highly screened white employees and a group of nonscreened Negro employees. When the company signed its agreement with Executive Order 10925 in 1962, one of the problems it inevitably faced was the integration of promotion ladders.

In the process of making changes, the company admits that it made some mistakes. For example, Negroes were asked to take qualifying tests—designed by a group of psychologists, including one from a Negro school, from the colleges in the area—to determine how they would stand in relationship to white employees. This appeared unfair to Negroes, especially since they were asked to take the tests while already employed, whereas whites were tested before employment. As a result of complaints, the company abandoned plans to make the tests retroactive. In the future, the tests will be administered to both Negroes and whites upon application for employment.

It appears to management that the tests will result in fewer jobs for Negroes in the immediate future, since it is unlikely that they will be able to compete favorably with whites. Desegregation also means, then, that Negroes may have to forego jobs that were available in the past. Formerly they were hired to do "Negro work," which required little or no training. When a Negro presented himself for employment, he was not asked to pass an examination, hold a high school certificate, or otherwise demonstrate his ability to learn and progress. He understood that he would take his place in a segregated work environment where he would remain for his working life. Nor did the company open opportunities to Negroes that would enable them to go beyond a certain level in the plant.

There is no such thing as "Negro work" any more, and each man hired is expected to have the requisite qualifications to move to the top of his department. Although this will mean better opportunities for Negroes hired in the future, those who were hired prior to the introduction of employment standards may still find the doors to many jobs closed to them.

The Employment Process

RECRUITING AND SELECTION The company has not hired extensively in the past decade. Recruiting has been done through the Alabama Department of Industrial Relations and through the company's own media. Selection for whites from 1952 onward has been done through testing, whereas between 1952 and 1962 Negroes were not tested at all. At the present time, tests are administered to all prospective employees as part of the company's selection program.

PROMOTION POLICY Strict departmental seniority is still in operation, but segregated subdepartments have been eliminated. In the future all employees will be promoted on the basis of seniority, providing the ability and physical condition of candidates are equal.

TRAINING AND EDUCATIONAL FACILITIES There are no formal training or apprenticeship programs offered by the company, although some effort has been made to assist or train Negroes assigned to jobs requiring new skills. In certain cases, Negro employees have been given special consideration while they overcome deficiencies.

WAGES There is no difference in the wages paid to white and Negro workers performing the same jobs. Wage rates range from approximately $2 to $4 an hour and follow the pattern set by the large steel producers in the area.

The Work Experience

PERFORMANCE ON THE JOB The company feels that there is no noticeable difference between the performances of Negro and white workers. This view is consistent with that of other companies in the area.

RELATIONS BETWEEN WORKERS Historically, good relationships existed between Negro and white employees. Seven or eight problem cases have resulted from integrating the work forces, but no major incidents have been reported. Prior to integration, management informed all supervisors and foremen of the proposed changes, and notices were posted in the plant. The transition has been orderly for the most part, and management does not anticipate major problems even though it says "some trouble can be expected in the period of adjustment."

SERVICE AREAS "White" and "Colored" signs have been removed from all service areas, including drinking fountains (however, cups have been installed) and bathhouses. No incidents have arisen as a result of these moves; however, company officials feel the bathhouses could be the most explosive area if desegregation is put to the test there. At present, Negroes and whites voluntarily segregate in the bathhouses.

The Union and the Contract

The union, a local of the United Steelworkers of America, has been in the company since the early 1940's. At the present time, it has approximately 500 members, of whom 50 percent are Negro. Negro members have served on committees for many years. At regular union meetings, Negro and white members generally sit on opposite sides of the hall, but Negroes feel free to participate in all discussions.

The local union has attempted to implement the company's

policies pertaining to desegregation. Its view has been consistent with the national union, which has strongly advocated nondiscrimination in employment.

Community Relations

The company's senior officer has served on committees for better race relations established by the Chamber of Commerce and by the city. His views reflect an interest in the betterment of Negro opportunities in all aspects of the city's life. He has worked quietly and effectively with Negro leaders to abolish discrimination from public places; a drive is now under way to provide equal treatment in such services as hospitals and taxicab operations.

Company II

Company II, a large company in the steel industry, has been an important employer in Birmingham for many years. Since the company is a subsidiary of a national firm, local management has been subject to change over the years. At the present time, officers in Birmingham represent a mixture of Southern and Northern backgrounds.

Employment-Manpower Utilization

WORK FORCE There are at present about 12,000 production and maintenance employees working in the plants. As of July 1964, approximately 30 percent of the total were Negroes, reflecting no significant change from the situation in July 1958, when records show that slightly less than 33 percent of all employees were Negro. Interviews and a study of company and union records revealed upgrading of Negroes in various positions.

FACTORS INFLUENCING CHANGE Executive Order 10925, management policy, and union cooperation have all been responsible for changes in the job opportunities for Negroes in the company over the past decade. Prior to 1962, separate lines of promotion for Negro and white employees existed. According to the company, several factors contributed to this situation: lack of training and education of Negroes for higher-grade positions; "informal" arrangements, wherein Negro workers were generally assigned to low-paying, menial jobs; and the lack of a nondiscrimination clause in the general union agreement.

Even though elimination of the double standard of promotion did not begin to occur generally until 1962, the company and union had given some attention to the matter several years before. However, the company states that "officials of Company II and the United Steelworkers had realized that ultimate success depended not only on their own skill but also on developments within the union locals and in the community." One necessary development was the signing of a new contract, on April 6, 1962, between the union and eleven major steel companies. This contract included the basis for broader lines of promotion to jobs above the pool level as well as a nondiscrimination clause. With the aid of this clause, company and union officials at the local level were able to work toward agreements providing for integrated lines of promotion.

The Employment Process

RECRUITING AND SELECTION The company has not hired many new employees in the past several years. Employees on layoff status are given preference whenever there are job openings. An examination of the company employment policy as far back as 1902 reveals little evidence of formal discriminatory hiring practices. The official company policy states that employment opportunities in the company will be made available without regard to race, color, creed, or national origin. It states further that the policy will be implemented by seeking to find the best qualified person for an existing vacancy without regard to race. Selection is made on the basis of the same tests given to both white and Negro candidates whenever a job requires specific skills.

PROMOTION POLICY Prior to 1962, separate lines of promotion for Negro and white employees existed in the company. Informal seniority rules and other arrangements used by the company and union operated to the disadvantage of qualified Negro employees. As a part of the nondiscriminatory program begun in 1962, each of the operating units in the company negotiated new agreements with the union in which lines of promotion were integrated.

The integration of promotion schedules gives Negroes new opportunities to move into jobs previously held only by white employees, but the nature of the seniority system precludes a rapid change. A company report states that at the present time Negroes hold a small percentage of skilled, clerical, technical, or supervisory jobs, about half of the semiskilled jobs, and the majority of the unskilled jobs. It is important to recognize that the average job held by Negroes is a higher-skill job than before, and that as Negroes acquire seniority, they will be eligible for still better jobs.

In 1962, new lines of promotion were established in all production and maintenance departments of the company. For example, in the Coke Department, before the change, Negroes could expect only to go up to the job of Larryman (Job Class 11). When the new scheme went into effect, a Negro served as an Oven Heater (Job Class 18) for the first time. Negroes will continue to share in promotional opportunities.

TRAINING AND EDUCATIONAL FACILITIES The company conducts an on-the-job informal training program for new workers and for those who are upgraded. The amount of time allotted for training depends on the individual and on the nature of the job he is being trained to perform. Negro and white workers are now given the same training in preparation for new jobs.

There are two formal training programs conducted by the company. One is given for operating and maintenance personnel when new equipment is installed, and is conducted by the equipment manufacturer with project engineering personnel. The other is an apprentice training program for journeyman craft jobs. Criteria for all apprentices include qualifying scores on written tests, high school graduation or equivalent, and certain age limitations. In addition to the training programs, there are advanced technical study evening programs dealing with various job operations. These programs are open to all employees who want them.

WAGE POLICY There is no difference in wages paid to Negro and white employees performing the same job. The highest rate paid to a Negro wage earner in July 1964 was $3.22 per hour, plus a cost-of-living adjustment of $0.185, and applicable incentive payments, for the job of Oven Heater at the coke plant. This is the top job level in its line of promotion and is currently held by several Negro employees. The lowest rate paid to any employee is $2.10 per hour, plus $.185 cost-of-living adjustment.

The Work Experience

PERFORMANCE ON THE JOB Company officials find no noticeable differences between the performances of Negro and white workers; however, the effectiveness of a Negro employee may be hampered in certain jobs by the unwillingness of a white employee to cooperate.

When asked if the attendance of Negro employees compared favorably to that of whites, a management spokesman said that such records were not kept by race. He added that it was his belief that absenteeism was a function of management control. He observed that generally when management takes a firm stand on absenteeism, Negro employees attend better than whites, but where management is lax, Negroes may do less well. In a sample survey of 100 employees, half white and half Negro, covering the first half of 1964, the absentee rate was relatively small for both groups, but somewhat higher for the Negro workers.

In general, the Negro worker represents a stable factor in the work force, and there are many who have been in the employ of the company for fifteen years or more. During 1964 the number of Negroes who quit their jobs was only one fourth the total for white workers.

RELATIONS BETWEEN WORKERS White and Negro employees generally get along well with each other, and both the company and the union are proud that there have been few incidents as the result of integrating work areas. Good relations exist, according to a company official, possibly because most of the employees come from rural areas, where there has been a long history of Negroes and whites working together on farms. Occasional trouble has been stirred up by "real fanatics in the plant—dyed-in-the-wool segregationists," but on the whole there has been an acceptance of the nondiscriminatory policies.

SERVICE AREAS One of the most difficult problems of integration has centered around the service areas. The water fountains in the plant have been desegregated by removing the "White" and "Colored" signs from them. No cups have been provided, but two water fountains are always located together. Generally, Negroes and whites continue to use their "own" fountains, as previously marked.

Rest rooms and bathhouses are situated near the main producing mills and auxiliary yard work areas. Some sanitation facilities are wholly for Negro personnel, and others, wholly for white personnel. Some combination units exist where Negro and white employees use opposite ends of the same building, separated by a wall in the middle. This arrangement follows the "separate but equal" doctrine, except that in some areas of the plant Negro facilities are more modern than those for the white personnel, while the reverse is true in other areas. The company explains that this disparity has come about as a natural result of replacing antiquated facilities with modern ones as the need arises. There is not much optimism about full integration of bathhouses and rest rooms. At the present time, at least, the company is not willing to force the issue and perhaps sabotage all of the progress that has been made. It is possible that when the men learn to respect each other on the job, the rest room and bathhouse issue will diminish.

The only eating facilities for production and maintenance personnel are coin-operated vending machines. The majority of employees bring their own lunches and eat at an opportune time during their 8-hour shift. No specific lunch hour is designated, since lunch is taken on company time. Lunch is eaten in the vicinity of the individual's work station.

The Union and the Contract

The company deals with approximately 14 locals of the United Steelworkers union. On the national level, the union has promoted nondiscrimination in employment and has recently signed a pact with 11 major steel firms stating the initiation of a serious effort to end discrimination. Representatives of the largest locals in the company were interviewed to determine what action is being taken by the unions and to assess the attitudes of local union leadership.

There are approximately 18,000 members in the 11 most important local unions with which the company deals. Of this number, approximately 7200 are Negro and 10,800 are white. The two locals studied have approximately 9000 members, of whom about 35 percent are Negro.

UNION LOCAL A This local was formed in 1944 and today is the largest union local in the South, with some 6000 members, approximately 65 percent white and 35 percent Negro. All members attend meetings in the union hall, where Negroes generally sit on one side of the room and whites on the other.

At present there are no Negro officers in the local, but several Negroes are on committees. A union official spoke of progress in his organization by noting that "I'm sending two colored men to Mobile to attend the Steelworkers' Legislative Council meeting. They will stay at the Battle House [a hotel] and be treated just as well as anyone there."

The union has cooperated with company efforts to revamp seniority provisions in the contract, which will do away with segregation. The president of the local gave several examples of Negroes being placed in jobs that have been held by whites in the past. "There have been few incidents. We're not having any trouble down here."

The local officers have had some difficulty implementing the nondiscrimination policy enunciated by the national union, but the future looks good to them. The president "will not permit discussion pertaining to race relations to be conducted at the open meetings." Apparently it would be difficult to control discussion of this type on the floor; therefore, racial matters are considered privately.

LOCAL UNION B This local was formed in 1937 and presently consists of approximately 3000 members, roughly 63 percent white and 37 percent Negro. No Negroes hold office in the union at present, but there are four Negroes on the twelve-man executive board.

The local has gone along with the national union policy on discrimination. An official of the union doubts, however, that there will be very much "mixing," since most of the employees are old-timers with years of seniority. The official spoke of a few "red necks" in the plant, but generally a good relationship exists between Negroes and whites, even when Negroes are placed in better jobs. There has been little or no hiring done by the company in ten years.

The union sponsors a Negro baseball team and a white bowling team, but mixed social functions are not held. In the attractive union headquarters, signs are still up designating white and colored rest rooms and water fountains. The official of the local said that the union has "not been forced to remove these yet," and if it did remove them, "nothing would change since Negroes and whites do not want to use the same facilities."

Community Matters

During the racial tension that existed in Birmingham in the spring and summer of 1963, the company was criticized for not taking an active role in promoting racial harmony. Critics thought that the company should apply economic pressure in the community in order to improve Negro job opportunities. This led to a controversy, with a leading official of the company at national headquarters maintaining that the concept that a company should "attempt to have its idea of what is right for the community enforced upon that community by some sort of economic means is repugnant to me personally and repugnant to my fellow officers—we have fulfilled our responsibility in the Birmingham area."

The responsibility had been discharged, according to the company official, in putting into effect a nondiscriminatory system of hiring and promoting, and in the efforts of local management, who, as private citizens, had worked to improve Negro job opportunities in the city. Major emphasis was placed on the belief that a company should not engage itself in establishing social standards in a community.

The president of the local company in Birmingham took an active role in groups working for the betterment of race relations during his term of office, 1946–1964. In 1949 he served on the board of trustees of the Jefferson County Coordinating Council of Social Forces, which coordinated the efforts of all major agencies working for civic and social improvement; in 1951 he served on an interracial committee formed within the Coordinating Council (the group brought a recommendation to the three-man city commission, of which "Bull" Connor was a member, to employ Negro policemen); he led a drive to build a nine-hole golf course for Negroes in the city and a new residential area that compares favorably with any middle-class development in the country; he used his influence to persuade Negro insurance companies and investors in the Birmingham area to make home mortgage money available to Negro home owners; from 1953–1961 he served on the board of trustees of Tuskegee Institute; and during the racial disturbances in 1963 he worked quietly behind the scenes with the Senior Citizens Committee of Birmingham to restore law and order.

During a recent reorganization of the company at the national level, the president of the Birmingham operations was transferred and a new position as Vice-President-South was created. The man who now fills the job agrees that the company should not use economic force in an effort to achieve certain social objectives, but he intends to work as a private citizen to promote good race relations in the city.

Company III

Company III has been in Birmingham since the early 1950's and has been an important source of employment during most of the past decade. It is locally owned and managed, and has operations in several states. The president of the company came to Birmingham from the West several years ago, but most of the other officers have lived in the city for many years. This company offers an interesting contrast to the others studied, since it performs most of its work under government contract, and it is in the aircraft industry.

Employment-Manpower Utilization

WORK FORCE The work force in May 1964 was approximately 2845, compared to 5648 in March 1963. This drop indicates the mercurial nature of employment characteristics in companies that work almost entirely under government contracts. Table 3 gives a breakdown of employment for the two periods cited.

In May 1964, Negroes occupied almost all of the unskilled positions, 30 percent of the semiskilled positions, and less than 0.7 percent of the skilled.

TABLE 3

Employment in Company III

	MARCH 1963					
	Total		**White**		**Negro**	
Classification	*Male*	*Female*	*Male*	*Female*	*Male*	*Female*
Officers & Managers	78	0	78	0	0	0
Professional	778	17	778	17	0	0
Technical	560	53	560	53	0	0
Sales	15	0	15	0	0	0
Office & Clerical	343	309	342	309	1	0
Skilled	2477	12	2463	12	14	0
Semiskilled	685	124	540	124	145	0
Unskilled	193	3	92	1	101	2
Service	1	0	1	0	0	0
TOTALS	5130	518	4869	516	261	2

	MAY 1964					
	Total		**White**		**Negro**	
Classification	*Male*	*Female*	*Male*	*Female*	*Male*	*Female*
Officers & Managers	106	0	106	0	0	0
Professional	461	22	461	22	0	0
Technical	244	24	244	24	0	0
Sales	14	0	14	0	0	0
Office & Clerical	162	190	161	190	1	0
Skilled	1260	7	1252	7	8	0
Semiskilled	260	52	182	52	78	0
Unskilled	40	2	1	0	39	2
Service	1	0	1	0	0	0
TOTALS	2548	297	2422	295	126	2

FACTORS INFLUENCING CHANGE Management policy, the union, and government pressure are all important elements in bringing about change. The company management and the union have taken a firm stand in their efforts to abolish discrimination in employment and to abide by President Kennedy's Executive Order 10925: ". . . it must be understood by all employees that they will abide by the program, or else . . ." Management instructed supervisory personnel to see that changes took place without any trouble. The union has taken a similar approach. There is little doubt that the government plays a major part in bringing about changes in employment practices, but the response of management and the union have been instrumental in enforcing change in a relatively peaceful way.

The Employment Process

RECRUITING AND SELECTION The recruitment of new personnel for the company is handled by the Alabama State Employment Office, which sends prospective employees to the company for selection. A high school education is not required for employment, and certain aptitude tests are administered by the company to all prospective employees, regardless of race.

PROMOTION POLICIES Promotion in the company is based on a combination of a man's ability to perform a job and his length of continuous service. Since all divisions within the company are now open, it is possible for Negroes to be promoted into jobs previously held only by white employees.

Work under union contract is broken down into approximately ten divisions. Within each division there are labor classifications, running from the lowest to the highest in skills. Seniority is held by an employee in the division in which he works, and promotion is made exclusively within the division. There is little or no exception made to the divisional bases of the promotional program, since the top jobs in all divisions are comparable.

Until the past few years, seniority divisions were segregated because of the "nature of the work." There were jobs within the plant designated as "Negro work," and divisions were maintained on a completely segregated basis. Company officials explained that this did not represent deliberate discrimination, but was the most efficient way to operate at the time. Negroes who had been hired to do "Negro work" were thought to be better off in all-Negro groups.

All divisions are now open to both Negro and white employees, and there are cases where Negroes have moved out of the all-Negro divisions to positions with white employees. Management speaks proudly of the fact that Negroes have crossed color lines and will continue to do so. The company operates a plant-wide layoff system based on seniority.

TRAINING AND EDUCATION The company operates an integrated training program for employees who wish to participate. There are approximately twenty-four courses available to employees, ranging in scope from blueprint reading to basic electronics. The classes are open to all who apply, subject to the approval of the applicant's immediate supervisor. Upon completion of a course, an employee is given a certificate, and the course is entered in his individual record of training. Several Negro employees have completed training programs in the past few years.

WAGES There is no differences in the wages paid to white and Negro workers in the same job classifications. Hourly wage rates range from approximately $2 an hour to $3 an hour.

The Work Experience

PERFORMANCE ON THE JOB Both union and management representatives agree that there are no noticeable differences between the performances of Negro and white workers, although sometimes Negroes were clearly better performers in certain jobs than whites, and vice versa. The thinking is unanimous that differences, if any, have to be analyzed on the basis of individual ability and not color.

RELATIONS BETWEEN WORKERS The general working climate in the plant is good. When work classifications were integrated, there were no serious disputes; and employees have tended to accept the situation. White workers have not objected to working with Negroes, and there are at least two cases where Negroes supervise white employees. One of these supervisors is responsible for an integrated work force now of twenty-five men (normally seventy-five) and he has said that he has had no trouble. He feels he is as much respected on the job as any of the white supervisors. He has been promoted regularly during his ten years of employment and has taken and passed several company training courses.

Shortly after the company integrated its work forces, supervisors were asked to submit reports on Negro workers. In all cases except one the reports were favorable to the employee. Such descriptions as "good work," "pleasant attitude," and "a good employee for the company," were found in numerous cases. These reports reflect optimism by supervisors over the relations between Negro and white workers in the plant.

SERVICE AREAS Water fountains, rest rooms, and eating facilities have all been integrated by the company, achieved largely by removing signs. The employees eat at picnic tables (soft drink machines are provided by the company), which are open to all, but Negroes generally segregate themselves at one or more tables, and whites do likewise. Custom, more than anything else, seems to dictate what is done here.

The Union and the Contract

UNIONS IN THE PLANT The company deals with locals of the International Association of Machinists, the Brotherhood of Carpenters, and the United Automobile Workers. The UAW, which has the largest unit, came into the company around 1952 and has had an active membership ranging from

900 to 8000 during the past decade. The present membership is low, approximately 1000, about 90 percent white and 10 percent Negro. There are no Negro officers in the union, even though there are Negroes who serve on the various committees. At the meetings, which are sparsely attended, Negroes sit anywhere they like and generally mix among white members. There are no integrated social functions conducted by the union, but it does sponsor both white and Negro bowling teams. An integrated team is not yet possible, since most bowling alleys in the city still operate on a segregated basis.

The acting president of the local and the international representative of the union seem anxious to eradicate discrimination in company employment practices, in accordance with goals set forth by the national union and the AFL-CIO.

The international representative of the union is a member of the Group Relations Subcommittee of the Community Activity Committee, a biracial group formed in 1963 to work with problems in race relations. He has been outspoken in defense of Negro rights on several occasions, one of these being the controversy over the proposed hiring of Negro policemen. On another occasion, when a member of the committee suggested that Governor Wallace be given an award for his role in civil rights, the union representative, among others, bitterly opposed it.

Community Relations

The company has played a role in community affairs through its senior officer, who participates in a group known as the Senior Citizens Committee. Generally, company management feels that "we run the company; our obligation is to the company, its employees, and not to the city." One company official made it clear that "we do not support any group to the left or to the right—including the NAACP, the Urban League, or the Ku Klux Klan—we run a business." Another official wanted it understood that "we don't need any advice or help—we can run our own business."

□ Summary

The research conducted for this essay leads to the following conclusions:

1. At present, peaceful race relations exist in Birmingham, and communication between the races holds much hope for the future. Machinery is in effect on the city level whereby racial problems can be discussed and suggestions made for their amelioration. A biracial committee, established by the mayor in May 1963, has gained experience; it provides an opportunity to promote good will in the community if those in command—namely the mayor—will act on recommendations of the group.

2. This article analyzed three companies in the basic steel and aircraft industries that have been important sources of employment in Birmingham. Any evaluation of the companies studied must take several significant factors into consideration: (a) even though the companies are vital to the economic life of the area, there has been a limited amount of hiring of new workers in the past decade; (b) changes toward eliminating discrimination at the workplace have taken place in a stable work force, where most workers have a long history of employment ranging from ten to thirty years; and (c) the companies studied depend on government contracts for a considerable portion of their business, which means that the government can use its influence, through such measures as Executive Order 10925, to bring about certain desired changes in employment.

3. In the companies studied, Negroes hold varying percentages of the jobs. Employment in two of the firms has not fluctuated over the past decade, but the job opportunities of Negroes have changed significantly in response to government pressure through Executive Order 10925 and the policies of employers and unions. The government seems to be the most important factor in bringing about change, but concerted management and union action has been essential in implementing new programs through which Negroes can progress on their jobs. Integrated lines of promotion in the steel companies occurred in 1962 after Executive Order 10925 was signed, and local management and union officials have cooperated to put the change into effect. Negroes are now being promoted into types of jobs they have never held before, such as millwright and oven heater in the steel plants.

4. The process of employment, including recruiting and selection, has been revamped by most companies studied so that all applicants are considered on an equal basis, regardless of race. In the moves to integrate lines of promotion and to eliminate segregated subdepartments, companies have abolished so-called "Negro" jobs and "Negro" work areas. In the past, Negroes were not required to establish qualifications at the time of hire. It was assumed that a Negro would never be promoted higher than some menial "Negro job," and therefore there was no need to require a high school education or a minimum grade on examinations. This has created a problem for some companies that would like to integrate departments but have no records to indicate qualifications of individual employees. Certain sacrifices will have to be made by employed Negroes in order to abolish segregation at the workplace. It is hoped that this will be a short-term phenomenon, but it depends, in large measure, on the effectiveness of equalizing educational opportunities in the public schools.

5. There were no cases reported of differences in wages paid to Negroes and whites performing the same jobs. Wages range from approximately $2 to $4 an hour.

6. In all cases, the companies indicate that there are no noticeable differences in the performances of Negro and white employees, and that any comparison would have to be made on an individual rather than on a color basis. Relations between white and Negro employees have been good in the plants, and transition under the new integrated promotion system has been orderly, with scarcely an incident. In cases where there have been some problems of adjustment, both employers and unions are optimistic about the future and believe there will be little difficulty in placing qualified Negroes in traditionally white jobs.

7. Service areas, including eating facilities, water fountains, rest rooms, and bathhouses, have been integrated in most of the plants to the extent of removing "White" and "Colored" signs. Varying approaches have been taken to this problem, and most company officials agree that bathhouses remain the crucial area for integration in those plants where they are found.

8. Negroes constitute a significant percentage of union membership in all cases studied, ranging from 10 percent in one to 50 percent in another. Even though there are no Negro officers serving in the unions studied, there are Negro members on the executive committees of most. Negroes attend meetings with white members and in some cases sit as an integrated group, whereas in others they sit together on one side of the union hall.

Nondiscrimination clauses have been written into the major agreements affecting workers in the basic steel industry. There is no nondiscrimination clause in the local contract for one of the companies studied, even though the national union has been a strong advocate of integration. However, company management has made significant strides in integrating its work forces and does not feel that a nondiscrimination clause in the local agreement is necessary.

9. The same approach to community matters has been taken by all companies studied. It is the unanimous feeling among them that a corporation can not and should not use its economic power in problems related to race relations in the city. In every case, officers of the companies have worked as private citizens to promote good will in the community. They have served on various committees, either by request or voluntarily, and they have been extremely effective in many cases.

NOTES

1. See the study by Langston T. Hawley, cited below.
2. For example, see: William H. Nicholls, *Southern Tradition and Regional Progress* (Chapel Hill: Univ. of North Carolina Press, 1960); Vivian W. Henderson, *The Economic Status of Negroes: In the Nation and in the South* (Atlanta: Southern Regional Council, updated *circa* 1961); Langston T. Hawley, "Negro Employment in the Birmingham Metropolitan Area," in *Selected Studies of Negro Employment in the South* (Washington: National Planning Association, 1955); Art Gallaher, Jr., *Houston* (Atlanta: Southern Regional Council, 1961); H. Ellsworth Steele, "Jobs for Negroes: Some North-South Plant Studies," *Social Forces,* XXXII, No. 2 (December 1953), 152–62; Herbert R. Northrup, *Organized Labor and the Negro* (New York: Harper, 1944); F. Ray Marshall, *The Negro and Organized Labor* (New York: Wiley, 1965); Robert H. Kinzer and Edward Sagarin, *The Negro in American Business* (New York: Greenberg, 1950); Harding B. Young and James M. Hund, "Negro Entrepreneurship in Southern Economic Development," in Melvin Greenhut and W. Tate Whitman, eds., *Essays on Southern Economic Development* (Chapel Hill: Univ. of North Carolina Press, 1964).
3. John C. Henley, *This is Birmingham: The Story of the Founding and Growth of an American City* (Birmingham: Birmingham Publishing Company, 1960), pp. 3–128.
4. Birmingham *News,* October 16, 1962.
5. *Ibid.,* April 6, 1963.
6. *Ibid.,* May 23, 1963, p. 54.
7. Interview with Mayor Albert Boutwell, August 13, 1964.
8. Birmingham *News,* May 1, 1964, p. 8.
9. U.S. Department of Commerce, Bureau of the Census, *1960 Census of the Population,* I, Part II, 49, 64; and *1950 Census of the Population,* II, Part II, 53.
10. *Ibid.,* I, Part II, 175, 199; II, Part II, 55, 59.
11. *Ibid.,* I, Part II, 159, 175; and *1950 Census,* II, Part II, 59.
12. All information presented in this section was obtained in interviews with company and union officials during the summer of 1964.

13 / Government and Equal Employment Opportunity

Samuel Krislov

I

In a welfare state, with one out of every eight employed persons receiving a government paycheck, state and Federal racial policies loom as major determinants of Negro employment. In a warfare state, with an estimated six million workers engaged in defense production, under Federal contracts, the economic leverage of the Federal Government is immense. And in a personal service economy, which is likely to be the eventual end product of industrial automation, governmental employment seems certain to become an even greater factor—one of the few potential areas of employment growth for a job-starved minority, since it is easier to create new patterns of employment in sectors of the economy where there are new jobs than to displace incumbent job holders. In the 1960's, nonwhite employment in all government services—national, state, and local, exclusive of military service—exceeded one million persons.

Traditionally, government has been regarded as a good employer for the Negro, but this is largely a reflection of the reputation of the Federal service. Nonwhites currently constitute about twelve percent of all government employees—a percentage equal to their share of the labor force generally, but slightly greater than the ratio of nonwhites to whites in the general population. But as is quite commonly known, nonwhites, until a few years ago, were relegated almost exclusively to the lower rungs of the bureaucracy—and this situation persists for the majority. Even in the higher status positions, nonwhites are concentrated in research or staff positions or in intergroup relations, rather than in decision-making line posts. It is to the improvement of status as well as to increase in numbers that recent efforts are addressed.

Should governmental structures contain within themselves a representative sampling of the total population? Will efficiency and capacity be sacrificed to the more political notions of consensus and social stability? American bureaucracies have generally included some representation of diverse social groups, thus reinforcing as well as mitigating the cleavages in our society. Even the operations of the Civil Service have not necessarily emphasized the positive recruitment of the best man for the job so much as the creation of barriers to keep out the obviously unfit. We have operated under a rule of reasonable qualification, within which there has been adequate room for the accommodation of political and ethnic considerations.

Negroes have suffered almost uniquely with regard to governmental representation—from lack of office holders to insist upon positions, from lack of voting power with which to bargain, and from the inability to turn out large numbers of applicants with the minimum qualifications for the medium range positions that are the usual stepping stones to decision posts. When overt discrimination is added to the picture, the present pattern of Negro governmental employment is the inevitable result.

Acceptance of segregation (or discrimination) by representatives of the public involves authoritative action and symbolic approval of such practices elsewhere. Conversely, the imposition of segregation in the Federal service during the Wilson administration dashed Negro hopes for general employment privileges throughout society, just as the current Equal Employment Program raises them. But though the showcase aspect of government employment is not the least significant one for the Negro and for other minority Americans, it is by no means the only one. Government employment is in itself a significant part of the economy, and a group denied or diluted in its potentials here suffers economically as well as psychologically.

II

It is beyond question that pervasive discrimination has existed in Federal service. Administrators admit this with exemplary candor. The traditional pattern of evasion had been continuously to ascribe such practices to the past, and claim complete eradication of such behavior today. Even this evasion has been dropped by most administrators in an attempt to do something about the problem.

Past practices have covered the spectrum of possible prejudicial action. A tacit policy of no hiring is the simplest form. More commonly, relegation of Negroes to subordinate clerical and menial tasks has been the effective policy, with occasional insignificant deviations. This Hamitic policy is perhaps less reprehensible than that of lower pay for equal work through differential classification for substantially the same position, or through differential rates of promotion or efficiency ranking.

The most thorough study of discrimination in the Federal service—unfortunately, one that was never published—remains a doctoral dissertation by William Bradbury of the University of Chicago. This survey of Federal practices in the era immediately after World War II is a valuable bench mark for measuring the efficiency of current programs.[1]

Bradbury had no trouble obtaining anecdotal material on discrimination from Negroes and whites alike. Supplementing quite explicit recollections, such as rebukes of white personnel officers by superiors for efforts to hire Negroes, and a survey of current employees—a one-man head count, as it were—were the experiences of wartime agencies in their efforts to relocate their staffs after the war. The OPA, under Chester Bowles, had been unusually open to Negro employment, particularly in the upper ranks, and the placement problems when the agency was dissolved were consequently the greatest of any of the temporary agencies. It was the considered opinion expressed in a long, careful memo, of the executive in charge of this process of placement that, "We have not found a single agency in which there has been no evidence of racial discrimination." [2] The degree of prejudice varied enormously, but obstacles were present everywhere.

Bradbury also essayed a more controlled study of whites and Negroes employed in a specific but unidentified operation, with close comparison of initial employment and rates of advancement. The study indicates pretty much what Herman Miller's gross comparisons of Negro-white income have shown: that Negro college graduates have expectations no greater than those of whites who have completed the eighth grade.[3] Bradbury found that Negroes with qualifications superior to those of incoming white employees were hired at lower levels and were promoted at a markedly slower rate. Even when eighty Negroes and whites educated at comparable Northern schools were matched—with superior qualifications for the Negro—the discrepancy remained.[4]

Why, then, did the Negroes stay in the agency? Bradbury concluded that the lower exit rate represented proof of a general pattern of discrimination. The normal way for a white of ability who was not promoted in one agency to advance was to transfer to another agency. Had as few as one-fifth of the Federal agencies in Washington practiced truly equal employment, he argued, the discrepancies in treatment of equally capable workers that he found could not have existed.[5]

As is indicated by common sense, as well as by Bradbury's necessarily elaborate design, the presence of discrimination is not ascertainable merely through total employment figures. The number of Negro priests represents operative conditions quite distinct from the attitudes of the Church. Availability of, training for, and aspirations toward, such positions are by no means uniformly distributed throughout the various population groups. The most receptive personnel officer will have little success where there are, and can be, no applications for open positions.

But availability is not a simple process in an industrial community. Roundabout development of human resources may be even more distinctive a characteristic of modern society than roundabout production of material goods. Recruitment is enmeshed in social relationships of various kinds—as simple a matter as a neighbor informing another of a vacancy in her office, or as complex a matter as a Civil Service recruiter visiting his own alma mater yearly, compared to a biennial trip to other colleges. But, in a larger sense, recruitment for executive, technical, and professional positions are processes in the development of conduits, complex patterns of education, acquaintanceship and apprenticeship that reach out, practically speaking, almost from birth.

An executive who attempts to implement the Equal Employment program, conscientiously examining its implications, is forced into an awareness of this long trail with its many possible detours. He can be quickly driven from objective evaluation of applicants to the less superficial examination of recruitment policies to be certain that they genuinely contribute to the quest for equality. Negro colleges in the South, once so infrequently visited by government recruiters, have had to build interviewing facilities in the wake of changed policies. Recruitment through office gossip can be supplemented by posting notices of vacancies. Publicity can be channeled into the Negro press.

Further soul-searching may result from a consideration of the proper definition of "qualifications" in terms of their actual application to performance on the job as well as to possible racial implications in the testing process. A truly sensitive administrator thus tackling the apparently simple problem of expanding opportunity can find himself driven to constant examination of the whole network of selection procedures and the entire philosophical problem of merit. In practice he must draw the line somewhere, deciding that ultimate total redress of social wrongs is beyond his efforts. The subjectivity of that line—and the human necessity of drawing it—constitutes the justification and rationalization for any given level of action on the part of the administrator, who can justify differing types of egalitarian behavior as he himself sees their desirability. The statistical employment result is quite logically defended at any of these levels as caused by forces other than those operating within the agency.

The obvious (and frequent) response to statistical evaluations of performance is that they cannot produce the answer to the problem of the existence of discrimination. Agencies vary so much in their requirements that statistics may be misleading. Thus, NASA's record in employing aeronautical engineers may look discriminatory, due to the scarcity of qualified Negroes, while the Post Office will make a better showing, since it requires relatively unskilled labor, for the most part. Conceding the force of this position, the President's Committee on Equal Employment Opportunity asserts that statistics do not give answers, but do provide the basis for asking questions.

At the present time, the committee requires an annual census, or "head count," of nonwhite employees. This unusual arrangement is itself a subject of some controversy. Such reports raise the fear that racial notations in personnel folders may contribute to discrimination, and suggest the possibility of systematic prejudice by supervisors.[6] As personnel officials sometimes complain in exasperation, the Equal Employment Program asks them to keep accurate figures on nonwhite employment, while at the same time insisting that no records be kept. This paradox is admitted and regretted by spokesmen for the committee. However, they point out the multiple objectives implicit in the program, noting that the tediousness and possible inaccuracies of regular head counts are less important than the possible evils of racial classification for personnel records.

Bearing in mind the possible small discrepancies inherent in the head count method (in at least one agency there has been a major disagreement over the accuracy of the count between the employment policy officer and the office of personnel) the data still can serve to pinpoint areas of Negro employment or lack of employment. Agencies that do not show improvement can be winnowed out from those that do. Sub-units of the same agency—particularly regional units—can be compared and assessed. The census can function as the beginning of an inquiry into the total pattern of employment in an agency. As statistics pile up, year after year, agency by agency, in gradually more refined form, that inquiry can become more informed.

The extent to which the committee inaugurates inquiry on the basis of such figures is problematic. No significant efforts were turned up during interviews with a wide variety of agencies and officers. Deliberately, the committee has directed its efforts to persuasion, in the frame of reference of its primary architect, President Johnson. Hobart Taylor, executive director of the committee, has been described by a national Negro leader as a "fixer" rather than a "confronter" of issues. Others close to him accept this label as essentially accurate. And John Hope II, in charge of the Program on Governmental Employment, has been described as one who believes that tenacity, rather than aggressiveness, is the primary attribute of a successful government reformer.[7]

The committee uses statistics in conjunction with other data when it is faced by controversy. The census is, in the main, a probe, a reminder, a call of responsibility to the agencies. Few quarrel with the general approach, though some critics believe that firmer reminders and more systematic follow-ups in the Kennedy manner, must supplement persuasion and reason.

The real force of the program comes from a conviction, now quite general throughout the bureaucracy, of its permanence. President Johnson's resolve that it is "the fixed, unalterable policy of the government" to achieve equal employment opportunity, is taken pretty much as a statement of intent, rather than as window dressing. If there has been a shade less intensity about the program—and there perhaps will be yet a further decline, as Johnson replaces the generally zealous "New Frontiersmen"—there has been a compensating note of permanence as a third administration continues the program. The President's own involvement and the parallel programs for women and older people suggest that something has been started that is in fact inevitable and enduring.

III

The importance of governmental employment for the Negro community is reflected in the overall statistics. From 1940 to 1962, 832,000 additional nonwhites found new employment in all levels of government—Federal, state and local. Of this total gain, approximately 200,000 positions were added at the Federal level and approximately 600,000 at the other levels of government. The early lag in the employment of Negroes at the local levels, and the closing of this gap, is evident in the fact that in 1940, when the national government was employing Negroes at a rate quite close to that of their ratio to the general populace, the employment of nonwhites by all government agencies was only 5.6 percent of total employment. In 1940, when only about one out of every four governmental employees was employed by the Federal government, about one half of all nonwhites in governmental service were at the Federal level. But by 1962 the ratio of nonwhites to total employment was almost the same at the Federal, state, and local levels.[8]

The drive for equal employment has shown that there is potential for growth even in the Federal Government at the present time. In a recent three-year period, 30,000 new positions were filled by Negroes. There is even improvement at local levels. From 1961 to 1962, 114,000 additional nonwhites were employed at all levels of government.[9] The fact that state and local governments have moved toward greater employment of nonwhites at rates commensurate with the Federal Government would indicate that more is operative here than sheer good will on the part of top Federal administrators. In short, a combination of economic and social forces has been moving toward equalization of employment. As better jobs are available and vacancies occur in state and local service, nonwhites move into the positions; as the political power of nonwhites increases, their ability to demand such job rights is equally augmented.

A pronounced lag exists in the case of Negro women who seek government employment. The very high proportion of blue-collar positions filled by Negro men at the Federal level has helped total Negro employment. Negro women have no such area of predominance, but compete principally in the lower clerical positions. As a consequence, Negro women in 1960 constituted about 11 percent of all employed women in the Federal bureaucracy, a percentage point or two below the male proportion. Similarly, Negroes constituted only 7 percent of all women employed in state and local public administration and 9 percent in educational services, at a time when nonwhites as a whole constituted nearly 11 percent of all government employees. On the other hand, the rate of increase of female employment has been extremely impressive. In the decade between 1950 and 1960, the number of Negro women engaged in state and local public administration at all levels more than doubled. In 1960, government service, including education, loomed as the source of employment for nearly 10 percent of all Negro women, compared to only 7 percent a decade before.[10] Besides various school positions, government service provides ample opportunity for clerical and stenographic help. "If it were not for the social security people [as a source of employment] I don't know what we would do," a counselor of a Negro high school in Baltimore is quoted as saying.[11] In such cities as Washington and Chicago, Negro women are quickly and easily employed as a result of the chronic clerical shortage. But the lower clerical positions share the limitations of the labor positions for men: they are dead-end jobs, with little opportunity for advancement and only nominal status and salary increases available as time goes on. These increases satisfy the need for minimal improvement but just begin to define the problem of overall advancement for 10 percent of our population. The problem of women in the Federal bureaucracy is special and complex as it is; the fact that a disproportionate number of Negro women go into the labor market adds to the general problem of status, advancement and morale.

In the Federal service, the intermingling of the racial problem with those of class and status brings about frustrations that are more clearly etched than in most aspects of our society. Class lines are rather neatly and decisively indicated for governmental purposes in the specification of different types of pay plans—Wage Board and Classification Services—trailing off into the "super-grades" and the higher political-managerial elite positions. Within these major categories, both class and status are carefully, even lovingly, demarcated.

It is likely that, in a bureaucracy, status is both more visible and more constantly in mind than in most comparable structures. In the first place, differentiation in an egalitarian society has to be artificially established: differences in rank establish authority rather than the reverse. Secondly, in such a structure the differences—including the distinctive privileges of each rank—are public knowledge. Not only is it true that all who inquire may learn; it is even necessary to broadcast and underline many differences in order to facilitate aspects of organization.

While classification and pigeonholing create an insecurity among those permanently consigned to the lower levels of the bureaucracy, they also provide the means for projecting doubts at the top. The Federal bureaucracy is nearly the perfect prototype of Riesman's "other-directed" American, with self-doubts easily aroused. The squeeze, however, is still greatest at the bottom of the pyramid, where the right to question superiors does not fully compensate for the doubts raised of individual worth, in the absence of non-universal criteria.

In short, status and class distinctions are manifest in a bureaucracy in titles and designations, carpeting on the floor, distribution of flags at specified levels of service, the right to use executive lunchrooms, and, not the least, in the size of paycheck. But the fact that these differentials are smaller than those of industry does not change the fact that they are more visible, less shielded from sight and consciousness, and more controversial in public sentiment.

Whether this condition leads to greater total dissatisfaction is doubtful. *The American Soldier* showed that the higher promotion rate of paratroopers in World War II resulted in a larger number of frustrations, but the job satisfaction, nonetheless, was greater than in the more rigid situation of the Military Police.[12] The merits of an open—and potentially climbable—hierarchy almost certainly offsets its psychic costs on a day-to-day basis.

The creation of jobs for the masses comes very close to Irving Kristol's concept of "the remittance man." That is, in our society, the poverty-stricken are hardly left alone to starve; rather, they are given some sort of compensation and then excluded from many aspects of meaningful existence. The feeling is widespread that this is closely approximated in a good deal of government employment. Oddly, this attitude prevails even in the upper regions of the bureaucracy. There is some feeling that "make-work" has been the pattern for a good many middle-level nonwhite positions throughout the Federal service. Even where job descriptions are precise and positions long established, a job in the Federal bureaucracy—as in most bureaucracies—is pretty much what you make of it. Negroes all too often find that their newly created posts have indefinite boundaries. Often the accouterments of office are obviously beyond the level of work demanded. By a sort of reverse compensation for the prevailing middle level pattern, the Negro bureaucrat at the upper levels is often given extra status —a fancier desk, a carpet, and a flag—when his position does not merit them. The suspicion that he is there to perform the function of Art Buchwald's Negro Ph.D. with engineering background (who speaks ten languages and whose job is merely to sit by the door) haunts virtually every major Negro bureaucrat.

The fact that some Negroes can concern themselves with this problem reflects the pronounced statistical success of the Equal Employment Program. On the whole, Negro leaders accept the Federal Government's attempts with restrained approval. The approval is tacit; the restraint is due to the limited nature of advances, coupled with a lack of real cumulative programming for the future.

Clearly, the Equal Employment Program has seen truly significant changes in the four years of its enforcement. Not only have Negroes garnered 20 percent of the new positions in the Federal service in this period, but they have significantly altered their pattern of employment. During those four years there has been a decline of fully 2½ percent in the number of Negroes under the Wage Board program and similar programs. This has been accomplished through a small decline in the Wage Board area and a heavy increase in the Classification Act and appointive type of position. Further, within the classification act categories, there has been only a slight increase—and therefore a relative decline—of Negroes at the GS 1–4 level and an increase of 9,000 at the GS 5–11 level. In the GS 12–18 level there has been a virtual doubling. It is in the last two categories that the most significant progress presumably has taken place.[13] If this is the pattern for future development, then we may expect to see significant numbers of Negroes in positions of decision-making responsibility in the next decade. If, on the other hand, this represents merely an immediate concession, with isolated, terminal advancement, then the rate of progress is clearly a dismal one. It is this uncertainty that accounts for part of the restraint in the approval of the Negro community.

But there is another important factor emerging from these same statistics, confirming the slow progress in the higher echelons of the bureaucracy. The improvements do not leave the Negro community precisely on a par with white bureaucrats in terms of distribution in positions of authority. Negroes still constitute only one percent of all those occupying a GS 12–18 position, and only 2.9 percent of those at the 9–11 level. They still constitute 19 percent of all Wage Board recipients and 27 percent of those who receive less than $5,000, but only 1.3 percent of those who receive $8,000.[14]

The change is thus relative to the initial differences. The improvement is in one sense significant; yet compared to the pattern of differences it may well warrant the description of tokenism. The spottiness of the record on a regional and agency basis also provides question marks for the effectiveness of the program. The prestige of many of the agencies that have had very modest improvements—such as the State and Justice Departments, as well as the Civil Service Commission itself—compared to agencies such as the Veterans Administration and the Postal Service, which have striven for great progress, has connotations of lower-grade achievement. Differential rates also suggest the possibility of slowing progress and declining zeal throughout the service. The greatest single obstacle to further advance at the present moment is undoubtedly the shortage of Negro talent for specific organizational positions. But the Negro community is skeptical as to whether as much ingenuity is being exercised in developing such talent as was exercised formerly in discrimination.

In 1948 Bradbury classified the agencies in terms of their attitudes on nonwhite employment and attempted to formulate propositions to account for the different patterns.

1. Old-line agencies, he suggested, were more likely to discriminate than newer ones.
2. Those with financial and business constituencies, including "liberal" regulatory agencies, were more likely to discriminate.
3. Mass organizations with routinized tasks are more likely to have large numbers of Negro employees and to maintain segregated units.[15]

Of these generalizations, the first two remain as valid today as when they were written. In most instances, the organizations appeared to maintain precisely the same order of acceptance or nonacceptance of Negroes as in 1948. But it is in the area of the third proposition that considerable progress has been made. Such organizations as the Veterans Administration, the General Services Administration, Social Security Administration, Postal Service, and even the Patent Office have been obvious points for administrative pressure. Encouraged by external forces, Negro employees have learned how to manipulate internal power to advantage. The Negro press has regularly—but not always wisely or even fairly—made such organizations targets of publicity. Administrators faced with their own internal moral problems and external recruiting difficulties find it desirable to improve racial conditions. In short, the agencies with the biggest problems in Washington are generally the easiest ones in which to begin reform. The Equal Employment Program thus becomes one of those general efforts where compliance is easiest where the situation is worst; this sets it off from such situations as school integration, where progress must be in the border or fringe areas first.

IV

The temptation is strong to think of the equality program in terms of the President's Committee on Equal Employment Opportunity and its actions, particularly in view of the accession of its former chairman to the Presidency. Yet there are numerous factors that make this focus misleading.

In the first place, the committee regards itself more as a catalyst than as an instigator of the program. Executive Order 10925 places the responsibility for implementation upon each agency. Following Lyndon Johnson's general political instincts, the committee has a small budget and staff that under no conditions could effectively police the bureaucracy. The emphasis in so limited an organization must be on persuasion, in accordance with Johnson's view of the operation, as well as his genuine enthusiasm for penny-pinching. Furthermore, the committee is almost immune from attack: failures must be assigned to the agency level where the operation, after all, takes place.

Departmental or agency activity, therefore, has been the key, and the achievements reflect the zeal of the top administrators and the degree of their control over their agencies. Some agencies—the Veterans Administration, and the Departments of Labor and Commerce—have their own procedures, at least as elaborate again as those of the committee. For example, monthly statistics are accumulated in the Commerce Department and used in constant reminders of the program. (Interestingly, sections of this department with above-average Negro employment have expanded their nonwhite rolls, while those sections with relatively few nonwhite employees continue to lag noticeably behind the average of the Federal structure.) The Federal Trade Commission, traditionally one of the agencies least receptive to Negro hiring, had a spurt of nonwhite employment, and now has settled down in the wake of overall employment cutbacks. Orville Freeman, engaged in many indifferent battles in trying to control the sprawling Department of Agriculture, has had little impact in this particular area. The department—called by one civil rights authority the "last rampart of the Confederacy"—has by and large successfully held Negro employment to administrators dealing with Negro clientele and problems, or to staff positions and symbolic roles. Indeed, the Civil Rights Commission was ready to criticize the department in 1964, and held off only until after the national elections. The rate of Negro employment at the GS 12–18 level was found in 1963 to be half the average for all agencies included in the committee census. The rate at the GS 5–8 level (3.1 percent) is even less favorable.

Congress has played an occasional role in supervising the program. For example, Senators Philip Hart and Jacob Javits have jointly and separately sent inquiries to agencies, posing both general and specific questions on progress in the equal employment area.[16]

The Civil Service Commission has also renewed its role in equal employment, consistent with its personnel responsibilities. Specification of promotion procedures, the rewriting of evaluation norms, and continuous emphasis on equal employment in personnel handbooks and directives have been supplemented by direct intervention in specific instances. The internalization of the program—personnel procedures, routine examinations and commonplace probing for irregularities—is increasingly a task absorbed by the commission.

Civil Service Commission employees have been able to influence many departments through the commission's responsibility for recruitment for many positions. The Civil Service Administrator, John Macy, himself a member of the President's Committee, has personally seen to it that the commission is active; on occasion, particularly in the early years, he personally intervened by letter, calling the attention of agency directors to specific problems. The Social Security situation, for example, which is regarded by Negro leaders as one of the worst in the whole Federal service, is said to have been called to Secretary of Health, Education, and Welfare Anthony Celebrezze's attention in this manner. Oddly, though, the commission's internal program for equal employment, as an employer of its own force rather than as overseer of other personnel policies, has no great reputation in the Negro community. Its statistical record for employees is admitted by its top administrators to lack impressiveness and certainly would seem to be one of those that could stand improvement.

While the President's Committee and the Civil Service Commission concentrate on the overall record and the total picture of minority employment, the dramatic and attention-getting appointments are made principally at the initiative of two other groups with acknowledged political power: the Democratic National Committee and the White House staff.

Louis Martin, the operative functionary for minority groups on the National Committee, and Lee White, his counterpart on the Presidential staff, are both Kennedy men who have had considerable seasoning and are politically aware of the complexity of their positions. "I can't sell statistics," Martin explains, as he pushes for Negroes in important positions. Individual breakthroughs for particular levels, regions and offices are sought and publicized, largely for political effect. "Hell, I even had a candidate for Secretary of State," Martin is reported to have said on one occasion. As in the appointment of district attorneys or assistant district attorneys, efforts may be made to help create local demand for a candidate, or pressure may be brought to bear upon an administrative unit to make a specific appointment. More commonly, the effort is directed to "loosening up" an agency in preparation for some specific appointments. In some instances, the Democratic Party and White House staff may in effect serve as recruiters for a position everyone hopes to fill with a minority group representative.

At the level at which Martin and White operate, GS 15 or so, race becomes merely an added factor on both sides of the ledger in an intense competition for what are regarded as desirable Federal openings. Martin indicates that his function is to be active solely in initial breakthrough efforts and that these are used for political advantage. The Democratic National Committee, for example, circulated a brochure listing Negro office-holders and emphasizing the President's role in equal employment. Lee White on one occasion asked all agencies to list all minority group members holding significant offices, and also to estimate the portion of their time devoted to minority group efforts—presumably striking a blow at one of the major Negro complaints that an inordinate number of minority group office-holders were solely involved in the Equal Employment Program itself.

The charge that fair employment has some of the aspects of a minority group WPA is not completely without justification. In agency after agency, a major portion of the increase in positions of GS 14 or above held by members of minority groups has been in intergroup relations. This has resulted in an influx of Negroes in higher positions, many of whom are organized in the National Association for Inter-Group Relations, an active group which has in turn recommended that intergroup specialists be hired throughout the government.

The use of employment policy officers separate from personnel officers is among the more interesting aspects of the program under the Eisenhower and Kennedy-Johnson administrations. The notion is that complaints should not be funneled through those persons responsible for employment policies. Such an arrangement would result in judges judging their own previous actions.

The President's Committee is authorized to make exceptions to this pattern, and some agencies do in fact designate the personnel office as their employment policy operation. The Postal Service, for example, has combined the personnel and the employment policy lines. In compensation, the Post Office has an elaborate hearing procedure, which involves the training of employment policy inspectors—whose normal duties run the gamut of departmental functions and who hear complaints at installations other than their own, so as to obviate the possibility of bias. In other agencies, the commanding officer or chief supervisor may be the official employment policy officer, while some staff member performs the *de facto* operations. The Navy follows this procedure, which in effect makes equal employment the command function. At least one prominent figure in the employment policy field—the former executive director of the committee—believes that this has been a successful procedure, reducing the exposure of the employment officer and shielding his agency from attack. In other agencies, particularly of middling size, the employment policy is assigned to a staff assistant or special assistant to the administrator as part of the residual or miscellaneous duties. In the State Department the employment policy officer is G. Mennen Williams, whose functions abroad take precedence over his internal function, while Richard T. Fox, designated neither as employment policy officer nor as a personnel employee, handles many of the functions that would normally be handled by the employment policy officer.

The level of the equal employment policy officer varies considerably. In some agencies he is directly under the chief administrative official of the agency; in others he reports to someone two or three levels below that height. The amount of time he may have to devote to this function also varies considerably, depending upon the establishment and the top administrators. Few agencies have full time employment officers. However, whatever the designation of the individual, many agencies have additional personnel involved in inter-group functions. Clearly leading them all is the Defense Department, with very complex intergroup problems, involving contracts, community relations, and military as well as civilian employees. Here a whole slew of highly specialized individuals are finding full-time employment. The Veterans Administration has a small central staff, with a large scale program using other employees on a less regularized basis, as does the Postal Service. These two agencies are generally credited with having the best developed programs in the government service. In other agencies the function is merely a very minute responsibility of a single individual with many diverse activities, who in effect relegates his function to a complaint service.

Regardless of the formal separation of employment policy from the personnel department, agencies vary in their actual day-to-day function. The employment policy officer may limit himself to complaints and view himself as a judge, as many do; if so, he is very likely to keep himself aloof from personnel so as not to be influenced by his relationship. If, on the other hand, he is particularly interested in recruitment or retraining, he may emphasize close liaison. Finally, the degree to which there is a need to develop relationships with personnel officers may depend upon the attitude toward compliance with executive orders. In the Veterans Administration, for example, the equal employment officers indicated little contact with personnel previously, because they had confidence in the programs and, indeed, in the accomplishments of personnel. They could then be free to look at the records of individual installations and to work at the local level. On the other hand, Internal Revenue, which historically has had a spotty record—very good in some regions, quite poor in others—and which has been faced with a prospect of a cutback in personnel in recent years, has seen fairly close relations with the hiring of at least one form of personnel man for full-time employment policy duties.

There is also considerable variation in what occupies an employment policy officer's time. In general, the President's Committee and most officers have downgraded the complaint function. This is in accordance with the recommendations of the Eisenhower committee and the wording of President Kennedy's Executive Order. Some officers emphasize strongly the recruitment function, and, particularly when they are Negroes, they may add considerable vigor to personnel and Civil Service recruitment drives. Other officers may very well limit their function to simple placement of a small number of individuals, rather than creating change in the total recruitment practice. Finally, the problem may be attacked in more long-range ways through supervisory education, examination of agency practices, and study of alternatives to these practices. The State Department, for example, has had under consideration programs for evaluation of the foreign service officers' examination and has aided a training program for potential foreign service officers held at Howard University. Similarly, the Social Security Administration has had a citizens committee to make recommendations for future development.

The committee is not limited to investigation of an agency on the basis of complaints, for it has authority to "scrutinize and study employment practices." Thus the head count is officially an instrument of approved policy. The independent role of the committee in auditing complaints, and its power to take jurisdiction encourages belief in the impartiality of its function. This has increased both the filing of complaints and the correction of abuses. The committee record is particularly impressive in the light of the past performance of similar operations.

V

The affirmative program has certainly been a success. There has been an effort to de-emphasize complaints as the principal focus of the program and to use them as a starting point for examining the pattern of agency behavior. The new policy implies preventative rather than corrective action.

The recruitment process has been given hard scrutiny in most agencies. The most valuable result has been the re-evaluation of the qualifications of workers already in the service, and the development of new skills. These aims are specifically charged to administrators under the program. The sensitivity exercised in the review of workers already in service has created better management relations throughout, and the results have been a source of pride to personnel officers and management. The Defense Department effected considerable saving through better utilization of its own personnel as against recruitment and training costs for outsiders, and the program was extended throughout the department. Many other agencies claim improved morale through opening up new opportunities for employees in what is, after all, a status-hungry bureaucracy. Some of these efforts perhaps represent standard Federal "grade-creep"—a tendency for superiors to seek friendlier relations with their subordinates by supporting higher grade classifications for the same work. Over the years there has been about one-tenth of a point of annual "grade-creep" for the bureaucracy as a whole. But some advancement clearly represents better utilization of available manpower.

The cry of "prejudice," in fact, often represents a vehicle for improved relations and the correction of bad managerial practices, born of many factors of which discrimination is an ingredient of only indeterminant nature. From its vantage point, the President's Committee believes that in many instances, when adjustments, coupled with a denial of race prejudice take place, the disclaimer is mostly window dressing, in which the committee acquiesces to make the agencies more receptive to a solution. From the departmental point of view, the committee happily takes the credit for successful corrective action in alleged cases of discrimination that are, in fact, often cases of poor communication or bad management.

In any event, the racial argument seems to result in remedies, whereas the cry of bad conditions would obviously be inadequate. The Patent Office, for example, made drastic changes in its stock depository—a large, unventilated basement that was dirty, louse-ridden, and even rat-infested—only when the Negroes complained and the agency was publicly attacked as "the most segregated unit in Washington." Similarly, another agency ignored complaints of file clerks for years and only discovered the existence of paper mites, the cause of the complaints, when the discrimination claim was raised. In a number of agencies, ratings, even on relatively objective matters such as accuracy, were left to the subjective evaluation of supervisors, though standards could have been drawn up. The remedy was effected only when Negroes complained about the practice, although it was really a case of bad administrative theory, rather than discrimination. Improved communications about possible job openings, more efficient employment practices and objective standards are among the other consequences of the Equal Employment Program in many different agencies of the Federal Government.

There seem to be limits of affirmative action with regard to racial mixing. Certainly there is room for considerable difference of opinion here. In the State Department, for example, some of the younger and more militant Negro professionals have circulated memoranda, insisting among other aims that recruitment of whites at the custodial and chauffeur level is a necessary step toward true equality. The almost complete Negro monopoly of such positions in Washington is a source of neither comfort nor pride to them. As a matter of fact, such monopoly tends quickly to establish an isomorphic identity between race and menial position, and precludes the likelihood that any whites will deign to take the same positions.

The pattern exists in a smaller and more tentative form in the various agencies' subdivisions and offices. A predominantly Negro office finds it hard to recruit and to retain whites. Some of the difficulty is identical with that of a white agency that suddenly throws its doors open to Negroes. Beyond this, there are the complex attitudes that even liberal whites hold about Negroes, and the overriding, simple fact that a greater range of alternatives is normally available to a white worker. Individual whites in predominantly Negro work situations are often uncomfortable and seek escape. Those agencies which have begun to think in terms of work force composition—and there are relatively few, since many think it inappropriate for a governmental agency to have any standard beyond individual merit—assume the desirability of a balance of races. Experience seems to show that, beyond a certain level, offices—like blocks in residential areas—can be "tipped," i.e., be more or less permanently identified as Negro work places or as lily-white establishments. This occurs and will occur increasingly at the lower clerical levels in the District of Columbia where hiring is done principally from a racially anonymous civil register that, because of the facts of labor supply, happens to be predominantly Negro in composition. The Civil Service Commission, for reasons of scarcity of supply, permits at least one other alternative—the hiring of clericals from outside Washington. Recruitment in carefully selected areas can, of course, result in whatever racial employment policy is desired. Most agencies have found this too much trouble; others are disturbed by the possibilities of overt discrimination creeping in through such recruitment.

The charge of prejudice may also be utilized as a weapon to gain special concessions, and there are evidences of "working the color line" throughout the Federal services. Sometimes prejudice is simply the last argument of an individual found wanting in ability or guilty of violating a regulation. At least some employment opportunity officers will review cases to see that the punishment inflicted is similar to that administered to whites under the same circumstances, even when there is an overt violation of regulations. The President's Committee, however, recognizes that some complaints are patently frivolous and do not require full-scale investigation. But where there is some degree of substance in a complaint, there is all too often a temptation to solve the matter by recommending corrective action, usually a promotion. The dangers, however, are recognized by all sides.

Indeed, the whole issue of so-called "reverse discrimination" has interesting ramifications for the Federal service, but the issue seems exaggerated. Most of the time the problem for an administrator will involve a choice between several individuals of approximately the same competence. The bureaucracy has learned to accommodate itself to external considerations, some overtly at odds with the Civil Service concept—political acceptability and Veterans' preference, for example—without serious damage to the merit system. The furor over a few irregular promotions in the Post Office died down rather quickly with the advent of a President skilled in the ways of Congress. But even these incidents merely illustrate the failure of the supervisors to meet prescribed regulations—and the promotability of the nonwhite individuals involved.

In many agencies, too, the pressure for equal employment has caused re-evaluation of artificial standards not truly related to better performance on the job. Many requirements have upon examination proved to be merely formal prerequisites of an unrealistic nature. The equal employment principles test the applicability of many of these requirements. If any group suffers from meaningless educational or experience requirements or irrelevant pen and pencil tests, it is, for sociological reasons, likely to be the Negro community that is hurt the most.

There is no evidence that there has been any significant deterioration of standards in any department as a consequence of the program. On the contrary, the principle of equal opportunity, intelligently applied, is consistent with the notion of merit and achievement. It is clear that some deviations from the principle of merit have begun to be eliminated from the Federal service; the suggestion that other obstacles have been created remains unproven.

Equal employment opportunity is, after all, a slogan and program that goes beyond racial matters, for practical political reasons, as well as idealistic considerations. Already the President's Committee's work on the status of women betokens the sincerest form of administrative flattery. Significantly, the program has engendered reforms not connected with race, and has produced a sensitivity on the part of higher administrators to all employees of the lower ranks, a state of mind formerly not always evident.

□ Conclusions

Equality of opportunity—which at first sight looks like a problem solved as simply as the stroke of a pen—is in truth as complex as the total race problem itself.

To date, all the major social groupings of our society—business, labor, agriculture, immigrant groups—have achieved social and political standing through governmental aid and intervention.[17] The Negro community appears to be no exception to that historical tendency. What is unique is the extent to which the government is involved in Negro self-development and to which it incorporates within itself the struggle for equal treatment on the basis of equal merit.

Governmental service has importance—and growing importance at that—in the American economy. But it is also a token, an earnest of behavior throughout the society. The most thorough study undertaken of images of public service held by the general population shows that Negroes have a pronouncedly more favorable view than whites of Federal employment. And well they might. Their preference is based upon the conviction that the government treats its employees more fairly and impartially than business and offers Negroes an opportunity to succeed.[18]

This gratifying response, however, masks a more fundamental attitude. Recent studies of Negro opinion also emphasize the disparity between the aspirations of the Negro and the small increments of opportunity that have so far been experienced by him in our society.[19] The expectations that have been

TABLE 1

Negro and Total Employment by Grade and Summary, All Agencies in President's Committee Salary Groups, June 1961 and June 1963, Census

Pay Category	JUNE 1961			1963			CHANGE FROM 1961			
	Total Employees	Negro Number	%	Total Employees	Negro Number	%	Total	%	Negro	%
Total all pay plans	2,197,360	282,616	12.9	2,298,808	301,889	13.1	+101,448	+ 4.6	+19,273	+ 6.8
Total Classification Act or similar	1,012,447	89,784	8.9	1,103,051	101,589	9.2	+ 90,604	+ 8.9	+11,805	+13.1
GS 1–4	355,446	64,242	18.1	355,329	66,169	18.6	− 117	(1)	+ 1,927	+ 3.0
GS 5–11	503,058	24,505	4.9	558,528	33,468	6.0	+ 55,470	+11.0	+ 8,963	+36.6
GS 5–8	—	—	—	315,203	26,452	8.4	—	—	—	—
GS 9–11	—	—	—	243,325	7,016	2.9	—	—	—	—
GS 12–18	153,943	1,037	0.7	189,194	1,952	1.0	+ 35,251	+22.9	+ 915	+88.2
Total Wage Board	568,835	106,853	18.8	560,211	106,665	19.0	− 8,624	− 1.5	− 188	− 0.2
Total Postal Field Service	566,151	83,187	14.7	582,475	89,323	15.3	+ 16,324	+ 2.9	+ 6,136	+ 7.4
Total other pay plans	49,927	2,792	5.6	53,071	4,312	8.1	+ 3,144	+ 6.3	+ 1,520	+54.4

(1) Less than 0.05 per cent.

Source: Adapted from *Report to the President,* the President's Committee on Equal Employment Opportunity, 1963, and *Annual Census* (mimeographed), 1961.

unleashed in the wake of desegregation are great, and
pronouncements are thundering. The future will measure
success, and the field of governmental service will likely prove
as good a yardstick as any.

MINNEAPOLIS, MINNESOTA
October, 1964

TABLE 2 *

Government Employment, Federal, State, and Local, Total and Nonwhite (1940–1962) (in thousands)

	1940	1956	1960	1961	1962
Government employees (total)	3,845	6,919	8,014	8,150	8,647
Nonwhite employees	214	670	855	932	1,046
Nonwhite as percent of total	5.6	9.7	10.7	11.4	12.1

Source: The Economic Situation of Negroes in the United States, Bulletin S-3, Revised 1962, U.S. Department of Labor.

NOTES

1. William Bradbury, Jr., "Racial Discrimination in the Federal Service: A Study in the Sociology of Administration" (Ph.D. dissertation, Columbia Univ., 1952, in Univ. Microfilms), n. 10.
2. *Ibid.*, p. 77.
3. Herman Miller, *Rich Man, Poor Man* (New York: Thomas Y. Crowell, 1964), p. 140.
4. Bradbury, *op. cit.*, p. 220.
5. *Ibid.*, p. 86.

6. These notations were common at one time, but were eliminated at the suggestion of the Civil Service Commission in the period after 1940. Some agencies continued to use them for sorting purposes, however. Thus, Social Security Administration has racially sorted employment figures through 1953, and, of course, since 1955.
7. These descriptions and other unreferenced material are based on interviews conducted during 1963 and 1964.
8. *The Economic Situations of Negroes in the United States,* Bulletin S-3, revised (U.S. Department of Labor, 1963), passim.
9. *Minority Group Study* (Annual reports of the Committee, mimeographed), 1961–1963.
10. *Negro Women Workers in 1960,* Bulletin 287 (U.S. Department of Labor, 1963), especially pp. 44–45. Negro women, it should be noted, average closer to the pay of white women than their male counterparts (Miller, *op. cit.*, pp. 91–93).
11. *Report of Social Security Administration Advisory Commission on Personnel Practices* (May 4, 1964), p. 18.
12. Samuel Stouffer, *et al., The American Soldier* (Princeton: Princeton Univ. Press, 1949), I, Ch. 6, chart 9.
13. *Minority Group Study.*
14. *Ibid.*
15. Bradbury, *op. cit.*, p. 106.
16. *Congressional Record,* December 5, 1963, pp. 22399–22408.
17. Kenneth Boulding, *The Organizational Revolution* (New York: Harper, 1953), *passim.*
18. Franklin P. Kilpatrick, Milton C. Cummings, and M. Kent Jennings, *The Image of the Federal Service* (Washington: Brookings, 1964), pp. 96, 159–60, 225.
19. Franklin P. Kilpatrick and Hadley Cantril, "Self-Anchoring Scaling," *Journal of Individual Psychology,* XVI (November, 1960), 7. It is interesting to note that this citation and the one above are by the same senior author.

14 / The Racial Practices of Organized Labor—the Age of Gompers and After

Herbert Hill

At the conclusion of the Civil War two significant developments made the establishment of a national trade union organization possible for the first time in the United States: the elimination of slavery as a labor system and the transformation of a rural and agricultural nation into an urban and industrial one.

From its inception as a national movement, organized labor found it necessary to deal with the prevailing attitudes of American society toward the Negro population. In 1866, the National Labor Union held its first convention, and was immediately confronted with the need to formulate a policy on racial practices. At its second convention in 1869 it requested Negro delegates to form their own all-Negro labor organization. Thus, a convention of Negro labor was held in 1869 in Washington, D.C., and the National Negro Labor Congress was formed with Issac Myers as president. The historian Rayford W. Logan has commented, "It is not without interest that the first large-scale exclusion of Negroes by private organizations in the post-bellum period was the handiwork of organized labor." [1]

The National Labor Union's exclusion of Negroes became a characteristic tradition of many major unions. The history of the American Federation of Labor (AFL), the most successful national labor organization, demonstrates that labor unions not only accepted racial distinctions but significantly contributed to the pattern of discrimination and segregation.

But another tradition may also be discerned in the history of the American labor movement. Some labor unions did struggle against society on racial matters, did act to protect the rights of Negroes, and did achieve equality of treatment for Negroes within labor organizations. This secondary tradition begins with the Knights of Labor in the period before they compromised on Negro rights under pressure from AFL officials, and includes the Industrial Workers of the World, which for a brief but significant time organized Negroes and whites, even in Louisiana and Mississippi, on an integrated basis.

In the early history of the AFL there were episodic but important realizations of working class interracial solidarity, especially in the New Orleans General Strike of 1892. Much later, the rise of the Congress of Industrial Organizations (CIO) gave great hope for the resurgence of the egalitarian tradition, especially in the mass-production industries where, historically, there has been a large concentration of Negro workers. The nondiscriminatory racial practices of the United Mine Workers, a major union in American labor history, further demonstrated that there were viable alternatives to the AFL tradition of exclusion and segregaion, and that this policy was not born of necessity. In certain unions today, such as the United Automobile Workers (UAW) and the United Packinghouse Workers (UPW), there is an ideological sensitivity to the "Negro question." However, Gunnar Myrdal's observation that "attempts to build a labor movement on the basis of workers' equality and solidarity . . . except in a few instances have proved futile" remains valid.[2]

Trade union racial practices have affected the status of Negro wage-earners and the welfare of the Negro community in every generation since the emancipation of the slaves. Thus, organized labor in the United States must be understood not only as a regulator of the relationship between worker and employer, but also as a significant social institution.

□ The American Federation of Labor

Early in its history, the AFL affirmed the principle that "working people must unite and organize, irrespective of creed, color, sex, nationality or politics." [3] The 1890 AFL convention passed a resolution declaring that the Federation "looks with disfavor upon trade unions having provisions which excludes from membership persons on account of race or color." [4] This question had arisen because the National Association of Machinists (later the International Association of Machinists) limited its membership to white persons only, and specifically made this racial qualification in its constitution. The convention requested that the Machinists union remove the discriminatory provision from their constitution, "so that all machinists shall be eligible for membership." [5] The union refused, and was not admitted to the AFL in 1890.

In this early period of his long career, Samuel Gompers, the first president of the Federation, believed that exclusion practices based on race were inimical to the best interests of labor. He urged working men to organize without regard to race and color, as a matter of both principle and common sense, because employers would continue to exploit them so long as they remained divided. "Wage-workers," he wrote, "like many others may not care to socially meet colored people, but as working men we are not justified in refusing them the right of the opportunity to organize for their common protection. Then again, if organizations do, we will only make enemies of them, and of necessity they will be antagonistic to our interests." [6]

At the eleventh AFL convention, in Birmingham, Alabama,

in December 1891, Gompers argued with delegates of the National Association of Machinists to persuade them to remove the union's ban on Negroes. The union insisted upon retaining the policy and practice of excluding Negroes from membership. Gompers presented his views in a letter to a friend.

If the colored man is not permitted to organize, if he is not given the opportunity to protect and defend his interests, if a chance is not given him by which he could uplift his condition, the inevitable result must follow, that he will sink down lower and lower in his economic scale. . . .

If our fellow white wage workers [*sic*] will not allow the colored workers to co-operate with him, he will necessarily cling to the other hand (that of the employer) who also smites him, but at least recognizes his right to work. If we do not make friends of the colored men they will of necessity be justified in proving themselves our enemies. . . . I wish the slogan would come forth among the toilers of the South, working men organize regardless of color.[7]

However, Gompers quite soon compromised his expressed desire to organize Negro labor by acquiescing in the discriminatory practices of many unions. In March 1895, James O'Connell, president of the National Association of Machinists, acting on Gompers' advice, reported that Gompers and other AFL leaders had suggested that the union shift the ban on Negro members from its constitution to the union ritual, and then apply to the AFL for membership. O'Connell was positive that rejection "would not stare us in the face." [8] O'Connell was correct. The color bar was removed from the union's constitution and placed in the ritual, where it performed the same function. When the union applied for membership to the AFL, it was accepted. For the next half century the Machinists union rigidly excluded Negroes from the craft and from union membership.

In 1902, when W. E. B. DuBois was writing a study of the Negro worker for Atlanta University, the secretary of the International Association of Machinists' Washington lodge wrote to DuBois that "the Negro is not admitted to the International Association of Machinists." Moreover, the secretary of the International refused to answer questions raised by DuBois as to the general membership eligibility of Negro workers. A labor leader, asked if he had ever worked with a Negro machinist, answered: "No sir: I never worked in a shop with a Negro as a machinist . . . I would not." [9]

Gompers attempted to bring the Brotherhood of Locomotive Firemen into the AFL on a similar basis. W. S. Carter, editor of the Firemen's journal, informed Gompers that a major reason for their hesitancy to affiliate with the AFL was that the union insisted upon excluding Negroes from membership. The union was willing, however, to eliminate the lily-white clause from its constitution on condition that it accomplish the same result by allowing each local to regulate membership qualifications.[10] Gompers gave the following answer:

> Does the AF of L compel its affiliated organizations to accept colored workmen? I answer no. Decidedly not. No more than it compels organizations to accept Americans, Frenchmen, Englishmen, Irishmen, or even Hottentots.
>
> What the American Federation of Labor declares by its policy [is] that organizations should not declare *against* accepting the colored man *because he is colored* . . . If a man or set of men array themselves for any cause against the interests of the workers their organizations have the right to say that their membership is barred. It should be at the wrong-doer against labor, it should not be a nationality or a race against whom the doors are barred.[11]

At the Brotherhood's convention in 1896, the union's Grand Master, F. P. Sargent, urged that in a forthcoming referendum the Firemen vote to affiliate with the AFL. Gompers, appearing before the convention, urged the union to admit Negro workers. Otherwise, he said, employers would hire Negroes at lower wage rates, thereby defeating organized labor.[12] To the Firemen's lodges he wrote:

> This question of race and color is more of a bugaboo urged among some workingmen to frighten them from performing their duties.

It is simply preposterous. What the AF of L has declared is that it is unwise for us to go forth emblazoned upon our banner our antagonism to a race . . . during the agitation for the abolition of slavery . . . unthinking people of the time could not understand that one could desire the abolition of slavery without falling absolutely in love with the slaves. This mistake seems to be repeated in our day only in another way.[13]

The referendum resulted in a majority vote for affiliation, but lacked the required two-thirds vote of the membership. According to W. S. Carter, many members believed the AFL's policy violated its constitutional provision guaranteeing the strict autonomy of affiliated organizations. Moreover, unlike the Machinists, they refused to transfer the Negro exclusion clause from their constitution and implement it in other ways, because "they do not care to belong to an organization that is not honest enough to make public its qualifications of membership." [14] The Brotherhood protested that it did not want its "honor" compromised by affiliation with a labor federation that pretended to oppose the exclusion of nonwhites but in reality would allow Negro exclusion to be practiced discreetly as a reward for new members. It should be noted that several important international unions openly excluded Negroes quite early in their history. Among these were the Cigar Makers National Union, which limited membership in 1868 to "white male" workers. In 1870 the International Typographical Union permitted its locals to exclude Negroes, as did the Bricklayers National Union in 1871, and the Carpenters and Joiners in 1870. In these and other unions exclusion of Negroes was the established pattern.

Segregated locals were originally conceived by the AFL as a temporary practice until a future time when racial exclusion was to be eliminated. But eventually, they became the preferred method of organizing Negro workers. Where Negroes were admitted into union membership AFL officials soon enforced segregated union locals as a matter of common practice, and this became the prevailing pattern within the Federation.

But, despite frequent vacillation and compromise, there

were notable examples of Negro-white labor solidarity in the AFL's early years. In St. Louis, George L. Norton's Marine Firemen's Union went on strike on March 10, 1892, when steamer owners refused to pay Negro workers equal wages. "As the men on strike are all Afro-Americans, thoroughly organized, and members of the American Federation of Labor," wrote the Cleveland *Gazette,* "it is believed that they will force the companies to accept their request." [15] White workers joined the strikers after the AFL issued a call for support. On April 3, thousands of Negro and white workers paraded together. One paper reported: "Numerous banners were carried by the men on parade, these being among them: 'Equal Rights for all! Fair wages and Union Men only' . . . After parading on the principal downtown streets . . . the men went to the Union Hall . . . where they were addressed for nearly two hours by labor agitators, white and colored." [16] The strike ended on April 6, 1892, with the employers refusing to grant union recognition, but making wage concessions.

The largely neglected story of the New Orleans General Strike of 1892 is even more significant. In this strike, "the first general strike in American history to enlist both skilled and unskilled labor, black and white, and to paralyze the life of a great city," 25,000 workers stopped all work for four days. They represented forty different AFL unions, united in the Workingman's Amalgamated Council, to which each union sent two delegates.[17]

The New Orleans General Strike, one of the most important in AFL history, demonstrated the viability of Negro-white labor unity. Here, skilled and unskilled workers, Negro and white, had united to defend common interests. Gompers stated:

To me the movement in New Orleans was a very bright ray of hope for the future of organized labor . . . Never in the history of the world was such an exhibition, where with all the prejudices existing against the black man, when the white wage-workers of New Orleans would sacrifice their means of livelihood to defend and protect their colored fellow workers. With one fell swoop the economic barrier of color was broken down. Under the circumstances I regard the movement as a very healthy sign of the times and one which speaks well for the future of organized labor in the "New South" . . .[18]

On certain public occasions Gompers would invoke the memory of the 1892 strike to demonstrate that the AFL supported Negro labor. But this only served to obscure the fact that by 1899 the policy had drastically changed. By then, Gompers was in effect justifying the already established discriminatory practices of many AFL affiliates, and his views now corresponded to the biased and restrictive policies of the craft unions that dominated the Federation.

At the end of the nineteenth century Negro workers in the North were concentrated in the ranks of the unskilled factory hands, and the AFL's refusal to organize industrial workers made union organization of mass-production and heavy industry impossible. Thus, the steady neglect of the Negro workers was in part the result of the Federation's policy of limiting union organization to skilled craft workers exclusively. Gompers had realized at the beginning of his career that competition with Negro workers could be eliminated only by bringing Negroes into labor unions, but the skilled white workers in the organized trades and their leaders had decided to end the competition by excluding Negroes from their unions and from the labor market. The president of the AFL adjusted his views and accepted that position.

With the admission of the Machinists in 1895, the Boiler Makers and Iron Ship Builders in 1896, and the International Brotherhood of Blacksmiths in 1897, all pretense of a nondiscriminatory policy of refusing affiliation to unions which overtly barred Negroes from membership was finally ended. These labor unions had provisions in their rituals banning Negroes from membership. A short time later, AFL officials no longer even requested that affiliated unions transfer constitutional racial bars to their union rituals, and the AFL admitted as affiliated groups international unions that openly excluded Negroes. In 1899 and 1900, Gompers welcomed the

Order of Railroad Telegraphers and the Brotherhood of Railway Trainmen to the AFL, although these unions restricted membership to whites as a matter of stated constitutional policy.

In 1897, Booker T. Washington, the most important Negro leader of the period, conducted an investigation of union racial practices. Upon completion of the study, he charged that labor unions were seriously hindering the economic advancement of the Negro workers by refusing to organize them and by preventing Negroes from entering into many desirable crafts and trades. The AFL was incensed by this attack and sharply criticized Washington's views at its 1897 convention. It also held a session on racial problems there. The convention reaffirmed the AFL's declaration that it "welcomes to its rank all labor, without regard to creed, color, sex, race or nationality" and that it favors organization of "white and black." The Federation denounced "as untrue, and without foundation in fact, the reported statement of Mr. Booker T. Washington . . . to the effect that the trade unions were placing obstacles in the way of the material advancement of the Negro."[19] But the pattern of exclusion and segregation was well established in the railroad unions and in many important AFL affiliates.

In 1902, the Stationary Engineers, a union that was already part of the AFL, changed its rules and instituted formal exclusion of Negro workers, without objection from Gompers. During this period, the AFL also had to decide what to do about its Negro locals, since in the past it had revoked charters of some central labor bodies that would not accept delegates from the Negro groups. However, in 1900, when unions of Negro workers in New Orleans were refused admission to the AFL central labor council, they formed a central council of their own and asked the AFL for a charter, promising to work with the white central labor council. The matter was left to Gompers' discretion, and he promptly approved this policy.[20]

At the next AFL convention, Gompers informed the delegates that "where there was a sufficient number of colored workers of one trade or calling, the suggestion was made that they be organized in separate unions," and that "this has generally been acquiesced in" and its "adoption has been recommended." Noting that some central labor bodies had refused to receive and give seats to delegates from Negro locals, Gompers claimed that to insist upon recognition of delegations of Negro workers would have meant "the dissolution of that organization." He thereupon suggested the formation of central labor bodies composed exclusively of Negro worker's unions. Gompers also suggested the approval of segregation as a matter of policy and the formation of separate trade councils for Negro workers. These did not, Gompers said, "necessarily proclaim that the social barriers existing between the whites and blacks could or should be felled with one stroke of the pen." [21]

The convention adopted the suggestion, amending the constitution to authorize the executive council to issue charters to separate central bodies when it was deemed advisable. It also accelerated the policy of placing Negroes into segregated Federal unions not affiliated with an international union but operating with a charter issued directly by the AFL. In reality these locals functioned under the same standards as the international unions that refused to admit Negro workers into membership.[22] Article 12, Section 6 of the AFL constitution, revised in 1900, reads: "Separate charters may be issued to central labor unions, local unions or federated labor unions, composed exclusively of colored workers, where in the judgment of the executive council it appears advisable." In 1909 the Brotherhood of Railway and Steamship Clerks and the Brotherhood of Railway Carmen, both of which openly barred Negroes, were admitted into the Federation.

□ Negro Exclusion and Its Consequences

Before the Civil War, Negroes comprised the traditional working class of the South. Slavery had the effect of demeaning work and cheapening the value of labor. After the end of slavery, the racial caste system continued to discourage whites from working, a serious problem in the rebuilding of the South. Labor tasks of a great variety were regarded by white men as "nigger work" even after 1865. The toilers were the Negroes, who performed every conceivable task—from picking cotton to constructing buildings and creating the much-admired ornamental ironwork on houses in and around New Orleans.

The eighteenth-century Irish traveler in the United States, Issac Weld, had observed that:

the principal planters in Virginia have nearly every thing they can want on their own estates. Amongst their slaves are found taylors, shoemakers, carpenters, smiths, turners, wheelwrights, weavers, tanners, and etc. I have seen patterns of excellent coarse woollen cloth made in the country by slaves, and a variety of cotton manufactures, amongst the rest good nankeen. . . . The work is done wholly by slaves, whose numbers are in this part of the country more than double that of white persons. . . .[23]

And according to Charles B. Rousseve:

Throughout the South "where the majority of white men were too lazy to work," by far the largest proportion of labor, skilled and unskilled, was performed by Negroes, both the freemen and the slaves. . . .[24]

Rousseve continues to state:

. . . the Negro, who in ante-bellum days performed all types of labor, skilled and unskilled, found himself gradually eliminated from the various trades.[25]

The poet and novelist James Weldon Johnson recalls in his autobiography Negro artisans in Jacksonville and elsewhere in the South during the 1880's:

All the most interesting things that came under my observation were being done by colored men. They drove the horse and mule teams, they built the houses, they laid the bricks, they painted the buildings and fences, they loaded and unloaded the ships. When I was a child, I did not know that there existed such a thing as a white carpenter or bricklayer or plasterer or tinner. The thought that white men might be able to load and unload the heavy drays or the big ships was too far removed from everyday life to enter my mind. . . .[26]

But by 1898, John Stephens Durham was describing, in the *Atlantic Monthly,* how the Negro's industrial advancement was "now checked by the interference of the labor organizations," which was a result of the "old guild idea of exclusiveness. . . ."[27] The Negro's "fate is involved in this struggle," stated Durham, who presented extensive data to prove that as trade union organization progressed Negro exclusion "became more and more prominent." Durham wrote that in the past ten years "there has been no racial utterance from any leader of authority [of unions] advocating equality of opportunity for the Negro," and that the labor movement "distinctly denies equality to the colored workman." According to Durham, the Negro was restricted to the lowest paying menial jobs as a result of trade union practices in many important crafts and industries, North and South. He cited Washington, D.C. as an example and wrote that:

at one period, some of the best buildings were constructed by colored workmen. Their employment in large numbers continued some time after the war. The British Legation, the Centre Market, the Freedmen's Bank, and at least four well-built school houses are monuments to the acceptability of their work under foremen of their own color. Today, apart from hod-carriers, not a colored workman is to be seen on new buildings, and a handful of jobbers and patchers, with possibly two carpenters who can undertake a large job, are all who remain of the body of colored carpenters and builders and stone cutters who were generally employed a quarter of a century ago.

Durham proceeded to give example after example of how AFL unions prevented Negro workers from working in a variety of occupations including those of baker, confectioner, printer, cooper, painter, and carpenter. Durham wrote: "A Negro working in the Government Printing Office can stay on as long as he is in government employment, but once out of public service he cannot secure work as a printer on a union newspaper or in a union office. The Negro, whatever his record, finds all doors closed against him. Thus, in our national capital may be observed the effects of the discrimination of labor organizations against the Negro."

Negro stevedores had worked on New Orleans wharves, according to Durham, but "the effective organization of white laborers was closely followed by the driving of Negroes from the levees at the muzzles of loaded rifles." In the iron industry, where the "union develops effective strength the black workmen must put down the trowel and take up the tray." Thus, ability to work, "the Negro's sole heritage from slavery and his only hope as a freedman, does not secure him opportunity."

Extending his inquiry into the North, Durham found the effects of the Negro exclusion policy to be even "more manifest." In Philadelphia in 1838, The Society of Friends had compiled a directory of occupations in which Negroes were employed. Significantly included were such skilled jobs as cabinet maker, plumber, printer, sail maker, ship's carpenter, stone cutter, and many others. By the end of the 1890's, Negroes had been forced out of most of these and other craft occupations.

In Philadelphia at the turn of the century work opportunities were growing, but not for the Negro, who experienced severe job curtailment and was increasingly limited to menial and service occupations. Durham observed that "today one may safely declare that practically all the trades enumerated . . . are closed against colored workmen. The large majority of the colored workmen of a half century ago and their descendants have come under the mansion house influence. . . ."

Durham concluded that in the past Negroes and whites formerly worked together in harmony in many skilled-craft occupations and industries and that given an equal chance, Negroes successfully took their place alongside white workmen. However, in the 1890's, because of labor union exclusion practices, the Negro artisan class was

> forced into work along menial lines . . . the colored man has come to be associated with this kind of work, and his effort to se-

cure the opportunity to do better is regarded with indifference or with a sense of helplessness. Thus, the Negro as a group is denied the work which it is capable of doing and detesting the work it is forced to do.

In the older seaboard cities of the South, Negroes had once been employed in a great variety of occupations, skilled and unskilled. However, in the last decades of the nineteenth century the process of Negro displacement had begun, and trade unions were a most important part of this development. Labor unions frequently were the instrument that forced Negro workers out of the jobs they had held for many years by replacing them with white workers after union organization.

George Sinclair Mitchell noted in 1936 that, "the Southern trade unionism of the last thirty odd years has been in good measure a protective device for the march of white artisans into places held by Negroes."[28] The white worker and his trade union displaced black labor on street railways, removed Negro firemen on railroads, took the jobs of Negro switchmen and shop workers, replaced Negroes in construction work and shipbuilding, and forced them out of hotel service and barbering. Mitchell wrote that the "typical city central labor body of Mobile or Savannah or Columbia or New Orleans or Richmond was a delegate meeting of white men drawn from white locals, jealous of every skilled place held by Negroes." The occasional Negro "Jim Crow" local received little or no help from its international union or the AFL. The result was that Negroes who through years of service had acquired the skill needed for craftsmen's work were denied membership in white unions and forced out of skilled jobs into service work at low wages. The Machinists, Boiler Makers, Car Repairmen and other AFL unions according to Mitchell "absolutely forbid Negro membership."

The evidence presented in 1902 by DuBois in the highly important Atlanta University study of the Negro worker is most relevant. DuBois investigated the racial practices of many unions throughout the country, and he found that forty-three national unions operating in both Northern and Southern states, including the railroad brotherhoods, had not a single Negro member. Twenty-seven others had very few Negro members, due in part to the refusal of these unions to permit Negro apprentices. DuBois concluded that only the United Mine Workers admitted Negroes on a nondiscriminatory basis. The Mine Workers, an industrial union with 20,000 Negro members, had more than half of the total Negro membership of the AFL in 1902. DuBois noted:

> . . . that it is manifest that the black mechanic is meeting strong resistance on the part of organized labor; that in both South and North the trade union opposes black labor wherever it can and admits it to fellowship only as a last resort.

In describing the principle of labor unity and interracial solidarity as practiced by the Knights of Labor, DuBois commented:

> This was high ground . . . to take—too high, in fact, for the . . . history of the labor movement from 1886 to 1902 so far as the Negro is concerned, has been a gradual receding from the righteous declaration of earlier years.[29]

DuBois credited Gompers with being a labor leader who had "to contend with narrow prejudice and selfish greed" but who had striven "to maintain high and just ideals" against the rapid degeneration of the AFL's racial practices. Negroes, DuBois wrote, "have met rebuff in their search for economic freedom." The industrial upbuilding of the South had brought to the labor market white persons who "from birth have regarded Negroes as inferior and can with the greatest difficulty be brought to regard them as brothers in his [*sic*] battle for better conditions of labor."

DuBois sent a critical estimate of the Federation's racial practices to Gompers and received the following reply from him:

> I should say that your statement is neither fair nor accurate. After careful perusal of the summing up of the attitude of the AF of L towards colored workmen, I should say that you are inclined, not

only to be pessimistic upon the subject, but you are even unwilling to give credit where credit is due.[30]

and then, parenthetically, Gompers added: "Let me say further, that I have more important work to attend to than correct 'copy' for your paper." The remainder of the DuBois report detailed the response of various labor leaders to the plight of the Negro workman. The study reported that ninety percent of unionized Negro carpenters in the South were organized in separate all-Negro union locals, while in the North very few Negroes were admitted into the Carpenters Union. In the large Northern cities "it is almost impossible for a Negro to be admitted to the unions, and there is no appeal from the decision." The same situation existed with the printers, the painters, and with other crafts. "Opposition on the part of Southern white workmen and the eagerness of union organizers to replace Negro by white laborers," commented DuBois, "explains the difficulty of extending the union movement and the justifiably suspicious attitude of Negroes toward it. . . ."

Documentation in the DuBois study describes how skilled Negro workers with "traveling cards" were refused admission to union jobs throughout the United States. In Cincinnati, one correspondent reported that Negro workers came from Chicago with white union members to perform a job. The white bricklayers received union cards and immediate work, while the Negro "was kept dancing attendance on the master of the local union and delayed upon one pretext and the other until he was driven from the city without being permitted to follow his trade because the local union did not give him his card." When one employer remodeled a building and gave this Negro a job as plasterer, "for the hod-carrier would not carry for him, and the Negro worker was compelled to work as a scab to get money enough to get out of town."

DuBois noted that Negroes feared to join the unions for seamen, firemen, or tobacco workers because they had learned from experience that, by demanding union wages, white workers would force them out of jobs. Bricklayers of equal skill in

South Carolina had a wage differential based on race. Negroes received $1.75 a day while unionized whites took home $2.50 for the same work.

Describing those unions which totally barred Negroes from membership by constitutional provision, DuBois cited the 1902 convention of the Stationary Engineers, which voted "to have the word 'white' placed before the word 'engineers' in one of the articles of their constitution." Mr. Grant, a union official who proposed the amendment, "said that if the Association granted 'the Negro this social equality he did not deserve,' it would lose all standing in the South, and that the Negro belonged in Africa." Of those unions which did not admit Negroes and offered the excuse that none were in the trade, DuBois singled out the plumbers as an example of a labor union that would "practically never admit a Negro."

In response to questions from DuBois, the secretary of the Boiler Makers Union wrote:

> There is not one man in this order that would present the application of a Negro for membership. This without laws forbidding him. Hence we have none. . . . I know that no Negro has worked at boiler making since the war.

The Wire Weavers' secretary added:

> Our laws, up to a few years ago, provided that only white males were eligible, but it at present makes no distinction but at the same time I am satisfied that our men would not work with a Negro. We work partner and coming in such contact with one another no white man would take a Negro for a partner. And I am frank enough to say that I don't think any of the men would allow a Negro to start at their trade.

The response of union leaders to the Atlanta University study contain frequent admission of how discrimination occurred in labor unions even without explicit clauses in union constitutions. In those early years, union leaders openly admitted to Negro exclusion. Thus the secretary of the Electrical Workers reported to DuBois: "I will state that we have no Negroes in our organization. We received an application from

Jacksonville, Florida, but it was thrown down by our locals."

When a Jacksonville local was granted a charter, it was soon revoked after the all-white central labor council discovered that the union was composed of Negroes. The Atlanta University study describes the events occurring in 1890 in Pittsburgh, where the Iron and Steel Workers Union had ordered four hundred workers to strike against the use of Negro labor.

DuBois documented the pattern of trade union discrimination that by 1902 had become the daily reality for the mass of Negro workers, North and South. Skilled Negroes were denied membership in those craft unions that controlled access to employment, and unskilled Negroes were prevented from learning a trade. Some Negro leaders responded to this dilemma by attempting to establish a system of Negro industrial and trade schools. But eventually they realized that this offered no solution. At a conference held at the Hampton (Virginia) Industrial School in 1898, Negro educators decided that "it was quite impossible for colored people to rise as long as the trades unions so generally excluded colored workmen. Some of the graduates at Hampton who had learned there, complained that they had not been able to work at their trades because [of being] excluded from the union." [31]

The pattern of union exclusion was also extended into manufacturing industries in the South. Negro workers were forced out of skilled jobs in the railroad industry, an important source of employment for Negroes in the South during the last two decades of the nineteenth century, as a result of the anti-Negro practices of the railroad unions. In the tobacco manufacturing plants of Virginia and North Carolina, the machine jobs were reserved for whites, and Negro workers were permitted to work at only the most unhealthy and least desirable occupations. During this period and even later, the AFL Tobacco Workers' International Union hardly reached Negroes in its efforts at organization.[32] DuBois noted that the textile workers clearly drew the color line, without acknowledging it:

The Negroes working at the trade have never been allowed to join the union, and the attempt to introduce Negro mill labor in Atlanta a few years ago so strengthened the Textile Union in the South that it is doubtful whether in the future a Southern cotton mill can employ any Negro labor unless it is ready to employ all Negro labor.[33]

DuBois concluded:

Here then, are the four great forces; the Northern laborer, the Southern laborer, the Negro and the employer. The Southern laborer, and the employer have united to disenfranchise the Negro and make color a caste; . . . the employer threatens that if they do raise labor troubles he will employ Negroes. The Northern laborer sees here the danger of a disenfranchised, degraded and yet skilled competition and raises the note of warning. Is not this a drama worth the watching?

Frequently, too, unionization meant the redesignation of "Negro jobs" as "white man's work" thus forcing Negroes out of jobs traditionally held by them. A 1913 report on the status of the Negro in Philadelphia concluded:

The Negroes in this section are practically shut out from all the skilled industries. . . . The great railway systems too, discriminate against the Negro, and here his opportunity is limited, no matter how high a degree of efficiency he may attain, to the menial and poorly paid tasks. He is excluded from practically all of the great industrial plants. . . . In brief, the Negro is denied the opportunity to earn an honest living in most of the big industries and commercial enterprises of this city.[34]

At this time there were less than two hundred Negro workers with skilled union status in the entire state of Pennsylvania, and their number was to diminish in the following years.[35]

An examination of the anti-Negro practices of the railroad unions (both Federation affiliated and nonaffiliated) is also revealing. The late Charles H. Houston, former Dean of the Howard University Law School, described how in 1909 the Brotherhood of Locomotive Firemen and Enginemen and the

Brotherhood of Railway Trainmen negotiated agreements with the Norfolk and Western Railway and other railroads to prevent the hiring of Negro firemen and brakemen. Houston wrote:

For the past fifty years the Big Four Brotherhoods have been using every means in their power to drive the Negro train and engine service worker out of employment and create a "racially closed shop" among the firemen, brakemen, switchmen, flagmen, and yardmen. They have just about succeeded on the Norfolk and Western and will soon succeed on all the other railroads in the South and Southwest unless they are checked by judicial decision and the force of public opinion.[36]

Houston, who as general counsel for the Association of Colored Railway Trainmen and Locomotive Firemen represented Negro workers in litigation against the lily-white railway brotherhoods, described other examples of how the powerful railway unions forced Negro workers out of employment:

Inch by inch, and yard by yard, down thru the years, the brotherhoods have been choking off the employment rights of Negro train and engine service employees. In 1890 the Trainmen, the Conductors, the Firemen and Switchmen's Mutual Aid Association demanded that all Negroes in the train, yard, and locomotive service of the Houston and Texas Central Railway System be removed and white men employed in their places. In 1898 the Trainmen tried to get all the Negro brakemen removed from the Missouri Pacific System. In 1899 the four Brotherhoods had all the colored porters on the Gulf, Colorado and Santa Fe Railway passenger trains removed and replaced by white brakemen. . . .

In 1909 the Firemen's Brotherhoods staged a bitter and violent strike against Negro firemen on the Georgia Railroad, demanding white supremacy and the replacement of Negro firemen by whites. In 1910 the Trainmen and the Conductors negotiated what is called the Washington Agreement with most of the Southeast railroads providing that no more Negroes were to be employed as baggageman, flagman, or yard foreman; they followed up in 1911 by negotiating a similar agreement with some of the railroads in the Mississippi Valley.[37]

A similar "history of aggression of the big four brotherhoods against the Negro firemen and brakemen . . ." occurred in many Northern states as well as in the South. Direct action was taken by the railway brotherhoods to force Negroes out of jobs on the Michigan Central as early as 1863 and on the New York, New Haven and Hartford Railway, the Baltimore and Ohio, and other lines, during World War I.

During World War II, the Brotherhood of Firemen and Enginemen distributed a strike ballot to prevent the hiring of Negro firemen on the Atlantic Coast Line Railroad. In 1943 the President's Committee on Fair Employment Practices initiated action against the four railroad brotherhoods because of the "Caucasian only" clauses in their Constitutions and because of their consistent record of discrimination against Negro railway workers. The unions remained firm in their anti-Negro practices and successfully defied the committee. Houston concluded that the operating railroad brotherhoods had established "the Nordic closed shop" on American railroads.[38]

In the last years of the nineteenth century and in the first decades of the twentieth, the harsh discriminatory racial practices of AFL-affiliated unions and the railroad brotherhoods were decisive factors in developing the pattern of Negro job limitation that was to continue for many generations.

Organized labor in the North and in the South directly forced Negroes out of jobs in the building and construction trades, in shipbuilding, on the railroads, and elsewhere, and refused to admit colored workers into union-controlled apprenticeship and other training programs in a variety of skilled-craft occupations.

At a later period, when Southern manufacturing plants were unionized, segregated white and Negro locals were established in most instances, and separate racial seniority lines of promotion were written into union contracts—with the result that Negro workers became even more rigidly limited to unskilled and menial job classifications.

Because of the AFL's craft orientation and discriminatory practices, most unions refused to organize Negro workers in the 1900's, thus denying them trade union protection during a period of intense labor exploitation. The consequences of the pattern of discriminatory racial practices by organized labor was an important and in some instances decisive factor in the barring of Negroes from full and equal participation in the economic life of the nation.

□ The Response of the AFL

The response of the AFL leaders, particularly Samuel Gompers, to the emerging pattern of discriminatory practices of affiliated unions, reveals the evolution of the Federation's policy toward Negro labor.

In the February 1898 issue of *The Federationist,* Gompers published an article by Will Winn, an AFL organizer in Georgia, entitled "The Negro: His Relation to Southern Industry." [39] This article serves as an illustration of the anti-Negro attitudes frequently expressed by AFL leaders at that period. Winn challenged the very idea that the Negro worker could be organized.

Wrote Winn:

> It was a fact patent to every observing man who has studied the Negro from contact that as a race, he does not give evidence of possession of those peculiarities of temperament, such as patriotism, sympathy, sacrifice, etc., which are peculiar to most of the Caucasian race, and which alone make an organization of the character and complicity of the modern trade union possible—sufficiently to warrant a hope that his condition might be improved by organization corresponding with the good results obtained through white organization.

Among "well-known traits" of the Negro which did not make him capable of unionization was "his distrust of his fellows in black and his deep-seated prejudice against the white workingman, the ignorance of the adults and his abandoned and reckless disposition." The Negro, according to Winn, had a decided advantage over the white worker because he could always find work in farms, and held a practical monopoly in carpentry, bricklaying and blacksmithing. He could work for whatever wages he received, as many hours as was required, and he was still "the happiest and most contented individual imaginable." Therefore, Winn explained, the Negro would not support trade unionism, which was a movement of the discontented.

The fact that Negroes were not organized was proof of their submissiveness, Winn claimed, ignoring the increasing opposition to unionization of Negroes by the all-white AFL unions. There were scores of Negroes, he claimed, ready to work at any price for the sake of education which the "state gratuitously offers their children."

Since Negroes could not be organized, Winn proposed that "colonization would be a practical and mutually agreeable solution of the Negro-labor problem." Those Negroes in favor of it were opposed only by capitalists while "Negroes themselves are friendly to the proposition." Winn suggested that Negroes emigrate to Cuba where they would "thrive and prosper as . . . nowhere else on earth." Once the Negro left, the white worker would be freed from "disorganizing competition," and would receive just compensation for his labor.

Winn's article is significant for two reasons. First, Samuel Gompers expressed his agreement with it and wrote a letter of praise to Winn stating that he had given the labor movement a good and fair statement of the subject.[40] Secondly, Winn, who opposed unionization of Negro workers, was chosen as one of the three organizers assigned to lead the AFL's Southern organizing campaign. None of the organizers chosen for the Southern campaign were Negro. One of them reported that he, a "full blooded Irishman," was "up against a hard proposition" in trying to organize "jews and niggers," for the "Nigras there is the most ignorant people in the world." [41] Gompers himself told Winn that "while it is desirable to organize them . . . yet the organization of the white workmen is of paramount importance and should not be hazarded." [42] When asked by a press representative why the

South had not been organized, Gompers gave three reasons, the first being "the fault of the Negroes." [43]

As editor of the *American Federationist,* Gompers published an article by John Roach that referred to the Negroes who had been brought to Chicago in 1904 to replace striking stockyard workers as "hordes of ignorant blacks," who possessed "but few of those attributes we have learned to revere and love" and who were but "huge, strapping fellows, ignorant and vicious, whose predominating trait was animalism." [44] At an earlier period Gompers had often stated that Negroes were forced into the role of strikebreakers because of the discriminatory practices of unions and had warned of the dire consequences of the anti-Negro policies of many affiliated organizations. But Gompers had rapidly retreated from that enlightened view.

In the early decades of the twentieth century the tradition of "accommodation" symbolized by Booker T. Washington was waning and a new, more militant, Negro leadership was emerging. This development was first expressed in the organization of the Niagara movement in 1905 and in the founding of the National Association for the Advancement of Colored People (NAACP) in 1909. From its inception the NAACP frequently protested against the AFL's anti-Negro practices, and in 1913 the Association presented a "minimum Program of Negro Advancement." A major point put forth was "the Right to Work: The End to Peonage; Equal Service and Equal Pay for the Negro." On behalf of the Association, W. E. B. DuBois wrote: "Whatever the tactics, the result is the same for the mass of white workingmen in America; beat or starve the Negro out of his job if you can by keeping him out of the union; or, if you must admit him, do the same thing inside union lines." When union labor "fights for humanity, its mission is divine," but when trade unions excluded Negroes from jobs and membership or practiced segregation and thereby forced competent Negro workers into starvation, "they deserve themselves the starvation which they plan for their darker and poorer fellows." [45]

☐ The AFL and Immigration: The Consequences of White Supremacy

The development of widespread anti-Negro practices within organized labor was accompanied by the AFL's frequent expressions of Anglo-Saxon superiority over European and Asian immigrants. Among the eight points cited in the AFL's program in 1906 entitled "Labor's Bill of Grievances," two strongly worded sections called for immigration restriction. The AFL asked for a law restricting all immigration and for a separate law aimed at preventing violations of the Chinese Exclusion Act. In calling for broad anti-immigration laws, the Federation believed, according to Gompers, that "maintenance of the nation depended upon maintenance of racial purity and strength," that the national interest would not be served by the arrival of "cheap labor that could not be Americanized and could not be taught to render the same intelligent efficient service as was supplied by American workers." [46]

In the first decades of the twentieth century the AFL openly invoked racial and noneconomic reasons for stressing the need to exclude immigrant labor. The Federation's attack upon immigrant groups impeded several major organizing efforts. During the steel industry campaign of 1909 and 1910, Slavic steelworkers were referred to as "foreign intruders" by John Mitchell, a high AFL official.[47] Ironically, in many instances European workers were ardent unionists and brought with them a sense of class struggle that made them more receptive to labor organization than American-born workers.

The attacks made upon the Chinese and Japanese were particularly vehement in their insistence on Caucasian superiority. Those who befriended the Chinese, Gompers stated in 1901, were either "dilettante sentimentalists," "profit hungry businessmen," or "degenerate politicians," scheming "to Chinese-ize the American people." At the 1901 AFL convention, the Resolutions Committee denounced the Chinese as "people of vice and sexual immorality who were incompatible with our moral concepts," and who were of "inferior social standards." [48]

Gompers had asked Congress to pass an Asiatic exclusion act in 1882, and he suggested total suspension of Chinese immigration for ten years. His most comprehensive statement on the subject appeared in a pamphlet of which he was coauthor, entitled, *Some Reasons for Chinese Exclusion: Meat Vs. Rice, American Manhood Against Coolieism—Which Shall Survive?* This work was first published by the AFL in 1902 and was brought out again in 1908, by the Asiatic Exclusion League. Gompers and his coauthor, Herman Gutstadt, the AFL representative in San Francisco, wrote that the racial differences between American whites and Asiatics would never be overcome. The superior whites had to exclude the inferior Asiatics by law or, if necessary, "by force of arms." The Chinese were congenitally immoral: "The Yellow Man found it natural to lie, cheat and murder and ninety nine out of every one hundred Chinese are gamblers." [49]

According to Gompers, the Asiatic peoples were lecherous, loved to live in filthy surroundings and damp cellars, and thus showed that the "instinct of the race remains unchanged." Although the Chinese servant worked faithfully in an "American household," explained Gompers, "he joyfully hastens back to his slum and his burrow to the grateful luxury of his normal surroundings—vice, filth, and an atmosphere of horror."

Gompers also attacked the Japanese. Typical of his comments was the abuse of the Japanese poet and socialist Sen Katayama, who was then visiting the United States. Gompers wrote in the May 1904 *Federationist* of ". . . this presumptuous Jap . . . and his 'leprous mouth' " and ". . . this mongrel's utterances." [50] At the 1904 AFL convention, delegates attacked "the 'Japanese' and all . . . Asiatics," and urged that the Exclusion Act be broadened to include Japanese and Korean workers.[51]

Gompers made it entirely clear that despite several examples of successful organization of Chinese workers he strongly opposed their unionization. He wrote:

I am inclined to believe that it would be unwise and impractical, to unionize a Chinese restaurant. Of course I realize the desirability of having every establishment possible unionized, and to organize our fellow workers, but you must take under consideration the further fact that the American labor movement has set its face against the Chinese coming to this country, and upon our demands the law has been passed for the exclusion of Chinese from the United States or from any of the territories or possessions of the United States. . . . In other words, the American labor movement stands committed against the Chinese coming to our country or any possession of our country.

It would be the height of inconsistency of our movement to unionize the Chinese against whom we have declared.[52]

It was during this period that the Federation also refused charters to agricultural workers' unions whose membership consisted mainly of Mexican and Japanese farm laborers in the sugar-beet fields of California.

In the September 1905 *American Federationist* Gompers wrote that the AFL desired no controversy with Negroes, "but if the colored man continued to lend himself to the work of tearing down what the white man has built up, a race hatred far worse than any ever known will result. Caucasian civilization will serve notice that its uplifting process is not to be interfered with in any way." [53]

At the turn of the century the AFL had fully capitulated to a policy of chauvinism and overt discrimination against Negroes, Orientals, and certain other ethnic groups. This development, together with the refusal to organize the unskilled and mass-production workers, further alienated Negroes from organized labor. The discriminatory pattern was now firmly established and would remain for many years. In discussing this period, Ginzberg and Eichner conclude ". . . the inescapable fact was that organized labor had turned its back on the Negro." [54]

□ Union Racial Practices after the Gompers Period

The craft unionism that dominated the AFL in the first decades of the twentieth century was characterized by a major concern with job control. Craft unions secured their power by achieving control of the labor supply in the various skilled-craft areas. A long list of restrictive practices together with separation of the skilled-craft occupations from other categories of labor enabled unions to maintain this control.

AFL unions and the railroad brotherhoods used their extensive powers to eliminate or limit Negroes as a group from competition in the labor market by a variety of methods. Among these were: (*1*) exclusion from membership by racial provisions in union constitutions or ritual by-laws; (*2*) exclusion of Negroes by tacit agreement in the absence of written provisions;[55] (*3*) segregated locals; (*4*)"auxiliary" locals; (*5*) agreements with employers not to hire colored workers and other forms of collusion; (*6*) separate racial seniority and promotional provisions in contracts, limiting Negro workers to menial or unskilled jobs;[56] (*7*) control of licensing boards to exclude Negro workers from craft occupations;[57] (*8*) refusal to admit Negroes into union-controlled apprenticeship training programs;[58] (*9*) negotiating wages and other terms of employment affecting Negroes while denying them admission into the collective bargaining unit; and (*10*) denial of access to union hiring halls, where such hiring halls are the exclusive source of labor supply.[59]

These and other discriminatory practices by major trade unions, in conjunction with the racial practices of employers, have had a cumulative effect in forming the occupational characteristics of the Negro labor force in the United States. The basic AFL attitude of excluding or limiting Negro participation in the labor force continued through World War I and after. The hostile attitude of labor unions toward Negroes led to tragic racial violence on several occasions, as in the East St. Louis, Illinois, race riots of 1917, where trade union provocation was a major factor.[60]

Negro workers had made their first significant gains in heavy industry during World War I and in the immediate postwar period, but most AFL unions practiced a rigidly exclusionist policy throughout the 1920's. In many instances Negro workers were able to enter industry only as strikebreakers. According to the Inter-Church Commission of Inquiry into the 1919 Steel Strike:

> It is evident that the great numbers of Negroes who flowed into the Chicago and Pittsburgh plants were conscious of strikebreaking. For this attitude, the steel strikers rightly blamed American organized labor. . . . Through many an experience Negroes came to believe that the only way they could break into a unionized industry was through strikebreaking.

Discriminatory practices by labor unions and the consequent strikebreaking by Negroes were also factors in the terrible Chicago race riots of 1919.[61]

The exclusionist practices of the AFL craft unions and the policy of limiting Negroes to segregated units continued under William Green, who succeeded Gompers as president of the AFL in 1924. The NAACP and other spokesmen for the Negro community frequently protested the racial practices of the Federation, but Green did nothing to curb discrimination in the AFL.

In 1934, the NAACP sent a delegation to meet with Green. The Association's general counsel, Charles H. Houston, presented signed statements of Negroes testifying to specific acts of racial discrimination by many AFL affiliates. As a result of widespread protests, the 1934 AFL convention adopted a resolution establishing a "Committee of Five to Investigate the Conditions of Negro Workers." After receiving documented complaints from NAACP branches throughout the country and hearing the Association's general counsel at its first meeting of the committee in Washington in 1935, Green announced that no further hearings would be held. John Brophy of the United Mine Workers' union, who was secretary of the "Committee of Five," publicly resigned in protest against the refusal of the AFL executive council to take action against racial discrimination.

During the 1930's, Negroes were concentrated as unskilled workers in the mass-production industries which the craft-proud AFL unions refused to organize. In the 1935 convention of the Federation a resolution calling for the organization of workers into industrial unions was defeated. But three weeks after the Atlantic City AFL convention, the Congress of Industrial Organizations (CIO) was formed, with John L. Lewis, president of the United Mine Workers, as Chairman.

In March 1937, the AFL expelled the CIO, which had grown to thirty-two international unions. Under the personal leadership of John L. Lewis, and with funds from the United Mine Workers, a great series of organizing campaigns and strikes took place in the auto, steel, and rubber industries; among packinghouse and textile workers; in mining, woodworking, shipbuilding, and communications; and among seamen, warehouse workers, and many others.

A major characteristic of these CIO organizing campaigns was that they represented a fundamental break with the traditional racial practices of the AFL. It had become evident that to organize the mass-production industries, in which great numbers of Negroes were concentrated, it was necessary for labor unions to reject racial discrimination and segregation. Even in the South, against great odds, several unions successfully brought Negro and white workers into the CIO. Although many AFL unions continued to discriminate against Negroes, in the early 1940's there was great hope for Negro wage earners with the new industrial unions of the CIO.

With the growth of the CIO in the mass-production sectors of the economy, with thousands of Negro workers organized for the first time in steel, auto, rubber, and packinghouse plants, hope existed that the AFL's craft-union tradition of racial exclusion and segregation would be thrust aside in the surge of industrial unionism.

Still, in 1940, and again in 1941, the AFL convention rejected resolutions introduced by A. Philip Randolph and Milton P. Webster of the Brotherhood of Sleeping Car Porters that called for the creation of a committee to investigate the discriminatory practices of AFL unions.[62]

In the debate during the 1941 convention, Randolph told the convention delegates:

> I want to cite a few of these cases [of discrimination]. . . .
>
> Negro painters in Omaha cannot get into the Painters' organization, nor can they secure a charter.

Plasterers and cement finishers in Kansas City, Missouri, cannot get into the organization nor can they get a charter.

The AF of L unions in the shipbuilding yards in New Orleans refuse membership to Negro workers, although the company has expressed a willingness to employ them.

Recently, Metal Trades Department unions have secured at some yards, through training formula [*sic*], a monopoly on trainees who will be upgraded in these yards.

Stabilization pacts between the OPM [Office of Production Management] and certain of the building trades have resulted in disqualifying qualified colored artisans from defense employment, and thereby retarding defense efforts.

In St. Louis, Negro artisans cannot get work, but white workers come from outside of St. Louis and are put to work.

The most conspicuous and consistent denial of employment of Negroes which can be attributed almost directly to union influence is found at the Boeing Aircraft Corporation in Seattle, Washington. From the very beginning of the National Defense Program, the Boeing Company has given as its excuse for not employing Negroes the fact that it had a contract with the Aeronautical Mechanics Union, Local 751, International Association of Machinists, AF of L, and that the union accepts white members only.

Randolph went on to relate the events in which the Boilermakers Union and the International Association of Machinists at the Tampa Shipbuilding Corporation in Florida forced 600 Negro workers out of jobs after securing a union contract in 1939. (The Boilermakers Union, the International Association of Machinists, and other unions forced Negroes out of their jobs at other shipyards and other defense installations during this period.)

The AFL convention of 1942 rejected another resolution offered by Randolph and Webster, similar to those they had offered in 1940 and 1941. It also rejected a resolution requesting "that workers who are now in Uncle Sam's uniform . . . be given the freedom and eligibility to join any union affiliated with the AFL at the end of the war without regard to race, color, religion or national origin. . . ." [63] Randolph continued to introduce resolutions against racial discrimination at AFL conventions, without success, until the merger with the CIO in 1955.

An examination of the proceedings of AFL conventions during the forties and early fifties confirms Gunnar Myrdal's statement that: "The fact that the American Federation of Labor as such is officially against racial discrimination does not mean much. The Federation has never done anything to check racial discrimination exercised by its member organizations." [64]

During the early 1950's, the traditional anti-Negro practices of many important international unions were continued. In 1953, when the International Brotherhood of Electrical Workers became the collective bargaining agent at the Bauer Electric Company in Hartford, Connecticut, it characteristically demanded that all Negro electricians be dismissed from their jobs, as Negroes would not be admitted into union membership. In this case the Supreme Court of Errors of Connecticut protected the job rights of Negro workers by issuing a cease and desist order against the IBEW.[65] The International Brotherhood of Electrical Workers (not to be confused with the International Union of Electrical Workers) has excluded Negroes from membership in the key local unions having jurisdictions in new construction installation and wiring.

Another important AFL affiliate, the Brotherhood of Railway and Steamship Clerks, continued to maintain many segregated local lodges, in Northern cities as well as in the South. In this union, as in the Brotherhood of Pulp, Sulphite and Paper Mill Workers and many others, the existence of segregated locals and separate seniority rosters frequently limited job mobility and violated the seniority rights of Negro union members.

After agreement was reached in 1955 to merge the AFL and the CIO, resolutions were adopted at the merger convention to eliminate racial discrimination and segregation within labor unions and to bring the benefits of trade unionism to millions of exploited Negroes. It was optimistically predicted that a new era for labor and for civil rights would ensue, and the NAACP and other Negro interest groups hailed the merger.

But now, a decade later, the reality is quite different from that anticipated at the time the merger took place. Progress in eliminating racial discrimination has been limited to minor isolated adjustments, and even these came only as a result of antidiscrimination laws, court orders, NLRB rulings, and public pressure from the Negro protest movement. The pattern of discrimination by the craft unions in several important areas, especially in the building and construction trades, remains intact, and with a few exceptions labor unions have resisted demands for a broad and significant alteration in their racial practices. Thus, organized labor has responded like other conservative institutions in American society to the demands of the contemporary Negro protest movement.

The tradition of racial discrimination within trade unions is the great historic failure of organized labor. In its early days, and for brief periods at a later time, American labor unions demonstrated that they could successfully organize without racial bias and resist the assumptions of white supremacy prevalent in society at large. But labor unions soon repudiated their original commitment to interracial working class solidarity and thus transformed themselves into restrictive institutions, representing the interests of a limited group, and devoted to maintaining the racial *status quo*. If the failure of organized labor to introduce the spirit of equality and democracy into the workplace has been a heavy burden for Negroes, it is also the tragedy of American labor as a social institution.

NOTES

1. Rayford W. Logan, *The Negro in American Life and Thought* (New York: Dial Press, 1954), p. 142.
2. Gunnar Myrdal, *An American Dilemma* (New York: Harper, 1944), p. 402.

3. *Proceedings of the 14th Annual Convention of the American Federation of Labor, 1894,* p. 25. (Hereafter proceedings shall be referred to as *AFL Convention,* with the year).
4. *AFL Convention,* 1890, p. 31.
5. *Ibid.,* pp. 20–29.
6. Letter to Frank D. Hamlin, April 30, 1890; letter to Charles W. Murphy, May 16, 1890; letter to Fred J. Carr, December 8, 1891; Samuel Gompers' letter-books, AFL Archives, Washington, D.C.
7. Letter to Jerome Jones, March 8, 1893.
8. James O'Connell, letter to John McBride, March 25, 1895; James O'Connell, letter to Samuel Gompers, February 26, 1896; James O'Connell, letter to Frank Morrison, March 20, 1903; AFL Incoming Correspondence. See also Frank E. Wolfe, *Admission to American Trade Unions* (Baltimore: Johns Hopkins Univ. Press, 1920), p. 120. (Material cited from archival correspondence is taken from: Bernard Mandel, "Samuel Gompers and the Negro Workers, 1886–1914," *The Journal of Negro History,* XL, No. 1 [January, 1955], 34–60, and Philip S. Foner, *History of the Labor Movement in the United States* (New York: International Publishers, 1955), II.
9. W. E. B. DuBois, ed., *The Negro Artisan, A Social Study,* Atlanta Univ. Publication No. 7, Seventh Atlanta Conference, Report of a Social Study made under the direction of Atlanta University, together with proceedings of the Seventh Annual Conference for Study of the Negro Problem, Atlanta University, May 27, 1902, pp. 151–88.
10. W. S. Carter, letter to Samuel Gompers, AFL Incoming Correspondence.
11. In *Locomotive Firemen's Magazine,* July 1896, p. 65.
12. Samuel Gompers, letter to F. P. Sargent, August 17, 1896; Samuel Gompers, letter to George W. Perkins, October 27, 1896; Report to the Sixteenth AFL Convention, 1896, p. 19.
13. Samuel Gompers, letter to W. D. Lewis, April 8, 1897.
14. W. S. Carter, letter to Frank Morrison, May 12, 1897.
15. Cleveland *Gazette,* April 9, 1892.
16. St. Louis *Globe-Democrat,* April 1, 2, 5, 1892.
17. Roger Shugg, "The New Orleans General Strike of 1892," *Louisiana Historical Quarterly,* XXI, April 1938, 547, 543.
18. Testimony before Industrial Commission, Washington, D.C., April 18, 1899. Quoted in Samuel Gompers, *Labor and the*

Employer, ed. Hayes Robbins (New York: E. P. Dutton, 1920), pp. 166–67.

19. *AFL Convention,* 1897, pp. 82–83.
20. Samuel Gompers, letter to James Leonard, March 9, 1900.
21. AFL Convention, 1900, pp. 12–13.
22. *Ibid.,* pp. 22–23, 117, 129.
23. Issac Weld, *Travels Through the States of North America and the Provinces of Upper and Lower Canada* (London: J. Stockdale, 1799), Vol. I, 145–52 (Letter XI).
24. Charles R. Rousseve, *The Negro in Louisiana, Aspects of His History and His Literature* (New Orleans: Xavier Univ. Press, 1937), p. 32.
25. *Ibid.,* pp. 135–36.
26. James Weldon Johnson, *Along This Way* (New York: Viking, 1933), p. 31.
27. John Stephens Durham, "The Labor Unions and the Negro," *Atlantic Monthly,* February 1898, 222–31.
28. George Sinclair Mitchell, "The Negro in Southern Trade Unionism," *The Southern Economic Journal,* II, No. 3 (January 1936), 27–38.
29. W. E. B. DuBois, *op. cit.,* pp. 151–88.
30. Samuel Gompers, letter to W. E. B. DuBois, January 5, 1903.
31. Andrew F. Hilyer, Chairman, Committee Hampton Conference, letter to Samuel Gompers, April 21, 1899.
32. Herbert R. Northrup, *Organized Labor and the Negro* (New York: Harper, 1944), pp. 103, 110.
33. W. E. B. DuBois, *op. cit.,* p. 168. (DuBois quotes from *Outlook,* LVI, 280.)
34. B. F. Lee, in the Philadelphia *Public Ledger,* April 13, 1913.
35. Richard B. Wright, Jr., *The Negro in Pennsylvania: A Study in Economic History* (Philadelphia, 1911), pp. 94–99.
36. Charles H. Houston, "Foul Employment Practice on the Rails" (based on a report to the Fortieth Annual Convention of the NAACP, Los Angeles, California, July, 1949), *The Crisis,* October 1949, p. 269. See also "The Elimination of Negro Firemen on American Railways—A Study of the Evidence Adduced at the Hearing Before the President's Committee on Fair Employment Practices," *Lawyer's Guild Review,* IV (1944), 32; Cayton and Mitchell, *Black Workers and the New Unions* (Chapel Hill, N.C.: Univ. of North Carolina Press, 1939), pp. 439–45.
37. Houston, *op. cit.,* p. 271.

38. *Ibid.*, p. 270. See C. Vann Woodward, *Origins of the New South* (Vol. IX of *A History of the South*) (Baton Rouge: Louisiana State Univ. Press, 1951), for an interesting summary of developments in Southern industry after 1877.
39. Will H. Winn, "The Negro: His Relation to Southern Industry," *The American Federationist,* IV, February 1898, 269–71.
40. Letter to Will H. Winn, January 19, 1898.
41. F. L. McGruder, letter to Samuel Gompers, May 26, October 4, 1899.
42. Letter to Will H. Winn, March 8, 1899.
43. *American Federationist,* May 1899, p. 57.
44. John Roach, "Packingtown Conditions," *American Federationist,* August 1906, p. 534.
45. W. E. B. DuBois, in *The Crisis,* May 1913, pp. 31–33.
46. Samuel Gompers, *Seventy Years of Life and Labor,* II, 160.
47. *American Federationist,* January 1911, pp. 6–8 (Jacob Tazelaar to John Mitchell).
48. *AFL Convention,* 1901, pp. 19–20.
49. Samuel Gompers and Herman Gutstadt. *Meat Vs. Rice: American Manhood Against Asiatic Coolieism—Which Shall Survive?* (San Francisco: Asiatic Exclusion League, 1908).
50. Samuel Gompers, "Three of the 'Others,'" *American Federationist,* May 1904, pp. 282–84.
51. *AFL Convention,* 1904, pp. 7–8.
52. Letter to D. L. Sullivan, June 24, 1904.
53. Gompers, *American Federationist,* September 1905, p. 636.
54. Eli Ginzberg and Alfred S. Eichner, *The Troublesome Presence* (New York: Free Press, 1964), p. 249.
55. According to Norgren, Hill, and Marshall, *Toward Fair Employment* (New York: Columbia Univ. Press, 1964), p. 43, "at least twenty-three national unions are known to have had segregated locals within their organizations in very recent years." (A list of international unions with segregated locals is included.)
56. Donald Dewey, "Negro Employment in Southern Industry," *Journal of Political Economy,* August 1952, pp. 279–93.
57. Stanley D. Spero and Abram L. Harris, *The Black Worker* (New York: Columbia Univ. Press, 1931), pp. 59–60.
58. Herbert Hill, *The Negro Wage Earner and Apprenticeship Training Programs* (New York: NAACP, 1960); also *Ap-*

prentices, Skilled Craftsmen and the Negro: An Analysis (New York State Commission Against Discrimination, 1960).

59. Donald F. Shaughnessy, "A Survey of Discrimination in the Building Trades Industry, New York City" (April 1963). Dr. Shaughnessy's study was the basis for the *Report of the New York Advisory Committee to the U.S. Commission on Civil Rights* (August 1963).
60. Elliott M. Rudwick, *Race Riot at East St. Louis* (Carbondale, Ill.: Southern Illinois Univ. Press, 1964); and accounts in the St. Louis *Star,* July 3, 1917, and St. Louis *Globe-Democrat,* July 8, 1917. Also Herbert Hill, "Labor Unions and the Negro," *Commentary,* December 1959, pp. 479–88.
61. The Chicago Commission on Race Relations, *The Negro in Chicago* (Chicago: Univ. of Chicago Press, 1922), pp. 357–435.
62. *AFL Convention,* 1941, p. 250.
63. *AFL Convention,* 1942, p. 580.
64. Myrdal, *op. cit.,* p. 402.
65. *International Brotherhood of Electrical Workers* vs. *Commission on Civil Rights,* 140 Conn. 537, 102 A2D 366 (1953).

BIBLIOGRAPHY

For further data on the contemporary racial practices of organized labor and on the economic status of Negroes see:

HENDERSON, VIVIAN. *The Economic Status of Negroes: In the Nation and in the South.* Atlanta: Southern Regional Council, 1963.

HILL, HERBERT. "Racial Inequality in Employment: The Patterns of Discrimination," *The Annals of the American Academy of Political and Social Science,* CCCLVII, January 1965, 30–47.

———. "Twenty Years of State Fair Employment Practice Commissions: A Critical Analysis with Recommendations," *Buffalo Law Review,* XIV, Fall 1964, 22–69.

———. "Has Organized Labor Failed the Negro Worker?" *The Negro Digest,* XI, May 1962, 41.

———. Testimony before the Special Subcommittee on Labor, January 15, 1962, in *Equal Employment Opportunity,* Hearings Before the Special Subcommittee on Labor of the Committee on

Education and Labor, House of Representatives, 87th Congress, 2nd Session, Part 2. Washington, D.C., Government Printing Office, 1962, pp. 25, 718–44.

———. "Racism within Organized Labor," *The Journal of Negro Education,* 1961, No. 2, pp. 109–18.

———. "Labor Unions and the Negro," *Commentary,* XXVIII, December 1959, 479–88.

———. *The Negro Wage-Earner and Apprenticeship Training Programs.* New York: The National Association for the Advancement of Colored People, 1960.

MILLER, HERMAN P. Testimony on S. 773, S. 1210 (Bills Relating to Equal Employment Opportunity) Before the Subcommittee on Employment and Manpower of the Senate Committee on Labor and Public Welfare, 88th Congress, 1st Session (1963). Washington, D.C., Government Printing Office, 1963, pp. 321–88.

Congressional Record—House, January 31, 1963, pp. 1496–499 (Testimony of Herbert Hill on Racial Practices of International Ladies Garment Workers Union). Also HILL, HERBERT. "The ILGWU—Fact and Fiction," *New Politics,* 1962, No. 2, pp. 7–27.

For an analysis of legal development in preventing employment discrimination, through the courts and through administrative agencies, see:

HILL, HERBERT. "The Role of Law in Securing Equal Employment Opportunity: Legal Power and Social Change," *Boston College Law Review,* Spring 1966.

15 / The AFL–CIO and the Negro

John E. Hutchinson[1]

"I believe," Walter Reuther told the founding convention of the AFL-CIO in 1955, "that this labor movement of ours will make a great contribution in the field of civil liberties and civil rights." [2]

There was some cause for optimism. The unification of the AFL and CIO came at a time of increasing trade union sensitivity to the claims of the Negro. There was now among the affiliates of the AFL at least a protocol of equality: gone were the color bars in all AFL union constitutions but one; racial equality was the official aim of virtually all affiliates and an emerging fact in some; discrimination was what George Meany later called a "bootleg product," [3] contrary to policy and rarely confessed. The CIO had given a warmer home to the Negro, and brought to the merger a better record than the AFL and a stronger disposition to improve. The architects of labor unity wrote an egalitarian stand into the constitution of the new federation.

One of the primary purposes of the AFL-CIO, the document said, was "to encourage all workers without regard to race, creed, color, national origin or ancestry to share equally in the benefits of union organization." [4] The constitution authorized the establishment of a Committee on Civil Rights "vested with the duty and the responsibility to assist the Executive Council [of the federation] to bring about at the earliest possible date the effective implementation of the principle stated in this constitution of non-discrimination in accordance with the provisions of this constitution." [5] The committee was to be aided by a Department of Civil Rights. The founding convention also passed resolutions calling for the creation of internal machinery for the settlement of civil rights complaints; for the enactment on union initiative of antidiscrimination clauses in all collective bargaining agreements; for the amendment of Senate Rule 22; and for legislation that would set up a Federal fair employment practices system, abolish the poll tax, and make lynching a Federal crime.

Skeptics might have pointed to the restrained language of the constitutional pledges, to the absence of disciplinary provisions, and to the undisturbed tradition of individual union autonomy; but for the moment all seemed well. Said the then special counsel of the NAACP, Thurgood Marshall:

> We in the NAACP salute the merged AFL and CIO. . . . A large measure of the success in the fight for human dignity that has come about has resulted from the recognition by organized labor [of the necessity] of extending labor's fight from inside the plant to the community in general. So, those of us in the fight for Negro justice can now depend upon an even stronger support from this new consolidated arm of organized labor.[6]

He spoke particularly of the South:

> The whole vicious program against Negroes in the South will without doubt lead to further violence and pressure against organized labor. . . . Organized labor must insist not only on organizing in the South, but must insist that it be done on a completely integrated basis without any compromise in the slightest detail to the segre-

gated policies prevalent in the South. . . . Organized labor has a more important task then ever before in seeing to it that the plants involved are not only organized on a completely non-racial basis, but that the communities surrounding those plants are run in a democratic fashion.[7]

This was a large order even for a reigning monarch. "We have had striking evidence in the last few days," AFL-CIO president George Meany said, ". . . that the Constitution and the Bill of Rights and the civil liberties we all like to boast of do not prevail in certain parts of our country for those people whose skin is a little different color from that of ourselves. . . . This Constitution does not prevail in the Southland." [8]

Nor, of course, did it wholly prevail in the federation. The admission of Negroes into the old AFL skilled-craft unions in the building, metal, and printing trades was minimal. The CIO, built on the principle of one union to an industry, had organized many more Negro workers, but custom kept most of them in the dirtier jobs; in the South particularly, there was widespread segregation in jobs, union meetings, and in the more fraternal aspects of union life. On the subject of racial equality, there was among too many AFL-CIO affiliates a protestation without will; where there was a will to move, there was often insufficient authority; where there was internal progress, there was in many places an external hostility, with formidable means; and in almost all unions there was a tension on race between anxious leaders and prejudiced followers. The AFL-CIO's policy was clear, but federation control was greatly limited. The affiliates gave their votes for equality, but their credentials were mixed. The vocal were usually sincere, but the silent were many, and not of one mind. It was a long way from federation policy to local fact, and the civil rights movement was restless. Criticism was bound to come.

*

"From the outset," the AFL-CIO executive council reported to the 1957 convention, "the AFL-CIO assigned top priority to its civil rights policy. In accordance with its constitutional mandate, the federation took firm and decisive steps. . . ."[9] James B. Carey, the president of the International Union of Electrical Workers (IUE), from the CIO, and a strong advocate of civil rights, had become chairman of the federation's Committee on Civil Rights. This committee met several times during 1956, criticizing the formation of White Citizens Councils in the South and noting the failure of a move to set up a Southern Confederation of Labor in protest against the AFL-CIO's stand on civil rights. Meany had also appointed a Subcommittee on Civil Rights to process complaints against affiliates. The executive council reported the admission of the first Negroes into Local 38 of the International Brotherhood of Electrical Workers (IBEW) in Cleveland and into Local 8 of the Bricklayers in Milwaukee;[10] the negotiation by the Oil Workers and the Communication Workers—both former CIO industrial unions—of antidiscrimination clauses in their agreements with Southern employers; and the removal by the Switchmen of the color bar from their constitution and the subsequent employment and unionization of forty Negro switchmen on the Georgia railroads.

The convention recommended that all affiliates set up their own internal civil rights committees, negotiate civil rights clauses in their agreements, and work for equality of opportunity in all apprentice training programs. It also urged that the President's Committee on Government Contracts refuse business to all employers consistently guilty of discrimination in hiring and promotion, and that the National Labor Relations Board (NLRB) designate the use of race-hate propaganda in representation elections as an unfair labor practice. It supported the Supreme Court decision on the public schools, and renewed its backing of strong executive and legislative action in the field of civil rights.

In December 1957, however, Carey resigned from his chairmanship of the Committee on Civil Rights. He felt, according to the New York *Times,* "that he had not been given enough power or freedom to do an effective job of stamping out racial bias in unions . . . he felt he was being hamstrung. . . ."[11]

There was impatience elsewhere. The following year the NAACP submitted to the AFL-CIO a list of charges of specific discrimination filed by Negro workers against the Railway Clerks, the Hod Carriers and Common Laborers, the Plasterers, the Plumbers, the Papermakers, the Pulp and Sulphite Workers, the Operating Engineers, and the Communication Workers; it also charged that the Railroad Telegraphers, the International Brotherhood of Electrical Workers (IBEW), the Painters, the Railway Carmen, the Boilermakers, the Sheet Metal Workers, and the Carpenters excluded Negroes "by tacit consent" or limited Negro membership to segregated or auxiliary locals.[12] "What we need here," said the New York *Amsterdam News,* a Negro newspaper, "is action on the part of the AFL-CIO. . . . All of us know what is wrong. What we are asking is that the AFL-CIO do something about it. And it goes without saying that we expect the NAACP not to swallow Mr. Meany's platitudes hook, line and sinker." [13]

"It should be recognized," the AFL-CIO executive council reported to the 1959 convention, "that on the industrial scene, the trade union is the most important single institution in the drive for equal employment opportunities." [14] The council stated that a major portion of industry was covered by collective bargaining agreements containing antidiscrimination clauses; that in nine out of ten cases the complaints processed internally by the federation met with prompt and helpful response on the part of affiliates; that many state and local central labor bodies now had their own civil rights or fair employment practices committees; that the federation planned to launch a number of local community-wide surveys of union racial practices; and that the AFL-CIO had recently set up a Southern Advisory Committee composed of the executive officers of the state central bodies of thirteen Southern states. The federation's Civil Rights Department, the council said, had assisted affiliates in negotiating fair employment clauses in contracts and in setting up machinery for them but had been severely handicapped by the lack of cooperation from most employers and all the national employer organizations. There was, nevertheless, a "clear and urgent need for greater and more effective participation in our civil rights program on the part of our affiliates, national, state and local." [15]

A. Philip Randolph, president of the Brotherhood of Sleeping Car Porters and the leading Negro trade union spokesman was unhappy. He conceded that some progress had been made, but declared that the federation had failed to support the Civil Rights Committee and the Civil Rights Department as it had supported programs to eliminate communism and corruption. In particular, he called for the expulsion of the Railroad Firemen and the Railroad Trainmen if they did not expunge the color bar from their constitutions in six months. "Who the hell appointed you guardian of all the Negroes in America?" Meany asked Randolph from the podium.[16] He noted that when he became secretary of the AFL in 1940 there were twenty affiliated unions with constitutional color bars, and argued that the expulsion of the two remaining offenders would remove them from the influence of the AFL-CIO and merely institutionalize their internal prejudices. "I wonder," asked Joseph Collis, president of the American Newspaper Guild, "what would be the attitude of most of the delegates here if this were an issue of religious discrimination." [17]

The following year the NAACP published a detailed criticism of the AFL-CIO's record on civil rights.[18] The report charged that the federation's effort had been uncoordinated and ineffective; that it had repeatedly refused to take action against discriminatory unions on its own initiative; that the removal of color bars was often only a public relations gesture; and that, in particular, the Committee on Civil Rights, relying as it did on persuasion and pronouncements, was as often as not ineffective. It also alleged that White Citizens Councils and the Ku Klux Klan had taken advantage of the timidity of national unions and moved into positions of influence in many Southern locals; that Negroes in the South were voting in increasing numbers against AFL-CIO unions; that most of the building trades unions had continued their traditional exclusionary practices; and that with the exception of the industrial unions—such as the United Automobile Workers (UAW), the United Steel Workers of America (USWA), and the Oil Workers—major affiliates of the AFL-CIO had persisted in negotiating discriminatory arrangements into their collective bargaining agreements.

The NAACP issued a separate report on apprenticeship.[19] This report claimed that no important inroads had been made by Negroes into the traditionally discriminatory craft-union apprenticeship programs; that Negro participation, such as it was, declined as skill and wages increased; and that not even enough Negroes were being recruited to replace those Negro craftsmen who left the trades for one reason or another.

A 1961 report by the U.S. Commission on Civil Rights—based largely on a study of conditions in Atlanta, Baltimore, and Detroit—lent support to the charges.[20] "Negro participation is, and always has been," the commission said, "minimal." [21] In St. Louis, there were only seven Negro apprentices out of 1667 in craft programs in the building, metal, and printing trades. In Atlanta, there were 20 Negroes among 700 registered apprentices in the construction industry, and all of them were in the dirtier trowel trades—bricklaying, plastering, lathing, and cement finishing. In Baltimore, out of 750 building-trades apprentices, only 20 were Negroes. In neither Atlanta nor Baltimore were there any Negro apprentices at all in the Iron Workers, the Plumbers, the IBEW, the Sheet Metal Workers, and the Painters. Even in Detroit, less than 2 percent of all craft-union apprentices were Negroes. Particularly in the building trades, union membership or referral was a virtual necessity for employment; and while the participation of Negroes in the industry as a whole had increased 50 percent in the last decade, in some local unions it had declined or was nonexistent. Some building-trades international unions maintained segregated locals in the same city; the result was a competition for jobs in which Negroes came off second-best. There was some token use of Negro craftsmen on government projects, but in private construction it was a common practice to bring in white craftsmen from other areas rather than employ local Negroes from the same union. Nevertheless, there was substantial resistance to the desegregation of locals among Negro members, who feared they might lose what influence they had in union affairs.

Union membership, the commission said, was readily available to Negroes in industrial plants. Negroes had always been there, and collective bargaining in industrial plants usually started after the work force was established, not the other way around, as in construction. The situation was more egalitarian, but by no means perfect. Some industrial unions in Atlanta had Negro officers but separate drinking and toilet facilities, as well as integrated meetings with segregated seating; separate eating places and even separate time clocks were customary. In Baltimore, segregated facilities were rare, and integrated social and recreational functions were frequent. Large numbers of Negroes were employed in industrial plants in all three cities, but Negroes were most often found in the unskilled and semiskilled jobs. Some unions in Detroit and Baltimore did nothing about discrimination in employment; others tried to persuade their employers to integrate their hiring and promotion procedures; but while a few of the contracts studied had provisions in them directed against discrimination on the job, none dealt with discrimination in hiring. There was no disparity in wage rates for similar work in Baltimore and Detroit, and contract enforcement was nondiscriminatory; but in Atlanta there were some complaints of Negroes being laid off in violation of seniority rights, and of different wages for equal work.

Negroes fared no better in industrial apprenticeship programs than in those of the crafts. One Detroit manufacturing company employed 40,000 workers, 23 percent of whom were Negroes; the company had 289 apprentices, one of whom was a Negro; there were 10 Negroes among 750 trainees in other training programs conducted by the same company. The Automotive Tool and Die Makers Association in Detroit administered an apprenticeship program jointly with the UAW in which all 370 students were white; only one Negro had ever participated in the course. The Detroit industrial apprenticeship programs, however, were typically controlled by the employers; unlike the crafts, the industrial unions had little influence in the selection of apprentices. Discrimination was the rule, but this was generally not the fault of the unions. Indeed, the commission noted, a strong stand on equality by employers often received the support of union leaders, even in the face of strong dissent by their members. "Management," the commission said of discriminatory practices, "is primarily responsible." [22]

The problem was national, the responsibility diffuse, the remedies meager. Only the courts, the commission said, had acted with any force against discrimination in employment, but litigation was slow and expensive. The NLRB had been ineffective. Congress had refused to interfere with the right of unions to determine the conditions of membership. The Bureau of Apprenticeship and Training of the United States Department of Labor depended upon the voluntary cooperation of unions and employers in developing standards for apprenticeship programs registered with it, and it had never required equality of treatment as a condition of the benefits—such as draft deferment for students, financial aid, and permission to pay wages below statutory rates—that are available under Federal law to registered programs. "The currently federally approved programs," the commission said, "rather than decreasing the industrial handicaps of Negro workers, are actually perpetuating and enlarging them. . . ." [23] Federal judicial and administrative remedies against external discrimination were limited; against internal discrimination they were nonexistent. "The only machinery," the commission said, "relating to such internal matters has been established within the labor movement itself." [24]

But it was not, the commission said, very effective. The AFL-CIO had no enforcement powers. Affiliated unions were autonomous, and in the main not very interested in civil rights. " 'Laissez-faire,' " the commission said, "seems to be the policy of the bulk of international unions toward the racial practices of their subordinate locals. . . ." [25] Discipline was rare, and usually a response to Negro votes. "Clearly," the commission said, "there is an institutional disability within the labor movement that may well forestall the translating of enlightened parent resolutions into local action. This disability is in large measure the same that is suffered by any democratic institution bound by the will of its electorate." [26]

Meanwhile, Randolph had taken the lead in forming the Negro-American Labor Council (NALC), the explicit purpose of which was to work for equality within the framework of the AFL-CIO rather than attempt to set up a separate Negro federation. Speaking for the Council, Randolph again attacked the AFL-CIO.[27] The charges were familiar, but strongly phrased and wounding. Meany replied that the NALC was making cooperation impossible by issuing unfounded broadsides against the AFL-CIO; the NALC should, he said, work with the federation rather than pursue a policy of "criticism, slander and accepting every complaint as true just on the basis that it was made." [28] He had no objection to the NALC, he added, "provided they keep out of our business and attend to their own." [29]

Jurisdiction was not conceded. Randolph, on behalf of the NALC, proposed at two successive meetings of the AFL-CIO executive council the adoption of a code of fair trade-union racial practices that would call for the abolition of segregated locals, for full equality in apprenticeship programs, for the expulsion of discriminatory unions after six months' notice, and for the adoption of more effective policing procedures. The council was unreceptive; several of its members, the New York *Times* reported, had made "little secret of their irritation at the vehemence with which the Randolph group had been attacking labor's record. . . ." [30] The council appointed a subcommittee to study Randolph's recommendations.

The result was a censure. In a report employing the strongest language against an associate since the federation's condemnation of James Hoffa in 1957, the subcommittee accused Randolph of "incredible assertions . . . false and gratuitous statements . . . unfair and untrue allegations." [31] It held him responsible for the gap that had developed between organized labor and the Negro community, and charged him with reverse discrimination in that the Sleeping Car Porters had no Caucasians as members or staff, nor any antidiscrimination provisions in its contracts. The report was adopted by the executive council, with Randolph the only dissenter.

Randolph found the report "distressing, innocuous, sterile and barren. . . ." [32] He resented, he said, the tendency to equate opposition to trade union policies with opposition to the trade union movement. He rejected the charges against the Sleeping Car Porters, saying that they had a white lawyer, a white economist, a white accountant, and would welcome white members. The AFL-CIO, he said, was beset by "moral paralysis, pessimism, defeatism, cynicism," and was trying to brainwash the public into an acceptance of "a whitewash of labor's do-little civil rights record." [33] Meany, he said, had done "some creditable things against the evil of Jim Crow. . . . Our only complaint is that he hasn't done enough and has taken too long to do what he has done." [34]

*

"In the past two years," the executive council told the 1961 convention, "organized labor has been in the forefront of a nation-wide drive to eliminate these unfair and immoral practices of racial discrimination. . . . Through compliance procedures, area and regional conferences, and through expanding civil rights machinery among AFL-CIO affiliates, labor has stepped up the pace of [the] civil rights drive in its own ranks." [35] Twenty-four affiliates now had civil rights committees of their own. Fourteen others reported the administration of fair employment programs by their own staff. Twenty state federations and "many" local central bodies were conducting civil rights programs.[36] Labor schools and conferences had put an increasing emphasis on civil rights in their curricula. The Southern Advisory Committee had met several times, and a Midwestern Advisory Committee had been organized. The Civil Rights Department had successfully intervened to obtain membership and proper seniority rights for Negroes in the Baltimore Fire Fighters and the Louisville Distillery Workers.[37] The Bricklayers and the IBEW had negotiated antidiscrimination clauses in their national apprenticeship agreements. The Railroad Trainmen had dropped the color bar from their constitution. Nine out of ten complaints received by the Civil Rights Department had resulted in "firm and determined" steps toward compliance by affiliates.[38]

Randolph took the floor. His previous charges, he said, "were no reflection on the sincerity and good faith of the leadership. But it has been my opinion that our unions have not grasped the significance and the depth and the magnitude of the civil rights revolution. . . . My proposals were rejected. I was condemned and denounced . . . [but] I am willing to go through the fires in order to abolish second-class status for black people in this country." [39] He asked for the expulsion of the Railroad Firemen if they did not drop the color bar from their constitution within six months, for the suspension of affiliates who did not abolish Jim Crow practices, and for an order to affiliates to end "nepotism and cronyism" in apprenticeship programs.[40] None of his suggestions was accepted, the federation repeating its former stands on internal civil rights machinery, segregated locals, the negotiation of antidiscrimination clauses in contracts, open apprenticeshp and seniority systems, decisive action by the Federal Government against discriminatory contractors, and more effective civil rights legislation.

Meany commented at the time on the resignation of the ILGWU vice-president Charles Zimmerman from the chairmanship of the Committee on Civil Rights. "No one," he said, "is volunteering for the job these days. We lost our last chairman—as good a friend of minorities as ever lived—because he got tired of being hit over the head." [41]

*

The NAACP reiterated its charges in 1962. Hard-core discrimination, it alleged, persisted in the building trades. The Hod Carriers, for example, barred Negroes from desirable jobs in Chicago, and their white locals in other cities refused to recognize the traveling cards of Negro members. The Railway Clerks still had 150 segregated locals. Negro workers in Texas had filed suit against the United Steel Workers to abolish separate seniority lines in their contract. The Metal Trades Department of the AFL-CIO was "directly responsible" for the negotiation of separate promotion clauses in contracts with several major oil companies in Louisiana; similar clauses were found in "virtually every plant" organized in the South by the Papermakers and the Pulp and Sulphite Workers.[42] The Railroad Trainmen, according to a complaint filed by Negro workers in Florida with the President's Committee on Equal Employment Opportunity, had conspired with the Atlantic Coast Line Railroad and other companies to have Negro brakemen classified as porters so as to deny them equality of treatment in wages and seniority. In the South, particularly in Alabama and Georgia, White Citizens Councils and the Ku Klux Klan had recruited substantial numbers of white union members. In Montgomery and Savannah, the Klan advertised its meetings in the local halls of the Carpenters. In Lithonia, Georgia, the Stonecutters and the Klan shared the same meeting hall. In the Montgomery bus boycott, the local building trades council and the bus drivers' union had allegedly led repeated attacks on Negroes and were sometimes identified with Klan activities. In many Southern cities, Negro children attended integrated schools while their parents, if admitted to union membership at all, met in segregated halls. But NAACP Labor Secretary Herbert Hill was hopeful. "The protest against racism within organized labor," he said, "may become the rallying point for the regeneration of the American labor movement." [43]

At the 1963 AFL-CIO convention, Meany made these comments:

In our search for the answers, we have been favored in recent years with a stream of free advice and opinion graciously extended to us by a new school of critics—sometimes termed the "disenchanted liberals" or "disillusioned friends of labor." . . . While the membership of this group appears to be small—its productivity is amazing. . . . For authority and support they simply rely upon one another. . . . In this way myths and fallacies are born, planted in the public mind and in the editorial pages of the daily press. . . . They say we neglect our responsibilities in the field of civil rights. . . . As the saying goes, they must publish or perish. It's just unfortunate that they chose the wrong alternative.[44]

AFL-CIO secretary-treasurer William F. Schnitzler reported on events since the last convention.[45] Meany had directed all state and local central bodies to hold their meetings in non-segregated facilities, had been responsible for the appointment of minority group specialists to the Federal Bureau of Apprenticeship and Training, and had recommended that the Department of Labor set up a nation-wide network of job information centers for minority groups. He had also appointed a special task force—composed of Walter Reuther, Randolph, Schnitzler, C. J. Haggerty, president of the Building Trades Department, and himself—to assist local central bodies in establishing community-wide civil rights committees. Meanwhile, thirty-eight state central and forty-five major local central bodies now had standing civil rights committees. Integrated state body conventions had been held in eight Southern states since the last AFL-CIO convention—in one case, at least, in violation of state law. The Locomotive Firemen, the last holdout, had removed the Caucasian-only clause from their constitution.[46] One hundred and eighteen AFL-CIO unions had signed an agreement with the President's Committee on Equal Opportunity committing themselves to speeding the process of integration within their own ranks.[47]

Of 55,000 unions locals in the AFL-CIO, only 172, in 19 affiliates, were segregated. Five unions often accused of discrimination—the IBEW, the Bricklayers, the Plasterers, the Machinists, and the Painters—had negotiated a number of collective bargaining agreements with antidiscrimination clauses. The Retail, Wholesale and Department Store Union had eliminated departmental segregation and racial seniority lines in Charleston, South Carolina. Seven printing trades unions had signed nondiscriminatory agreements with their employers in Philadelphia. The Tobacco Workers had integrated their locals in a number of Southern towns. Progress in nondiscriminatory hiring, seniority, and promotion procedures had been made in the South by the UAW, the Retail Clerks, the Carpenters, the American Federation of Government Employees, the Rubber Workers, the Aluminum Workers, the Pulp and Sulphite Workers, the Steel Workers, the Laundry Workers, the Oil Workers, and the American Federation of State, County and Municipal Employees. A number of building trade locals in the South had admitted Negroes for the first time.

The Building Trades Department made its own report on civil rights:

> The unions affiliated with this department, unlike some others, have never had constitutional bars against the admission of Negroes into membership. . . . [Any sidewalk superintendent] will have to concede that he has seen Negroes working side by side with whites. This has been generally true in every area of the nation. . . . However, a wave of complaints against non-employment of Negroes in the building trades was set in motion by certain organizations early in 1963. No evidence was submitted to prove these allegations. Yet they were accepted at face value even in official circles.[48]

The general presidents of all affiliates in the building trades had therefore issued a statement stating, among other things, that the acceptance of apprentices was "based on many factors most of which are totally unrelated to any form of discrimination. . . ." [49] Building trades unions had "of necessity avoided training excessive numbers of young men"; entry into the trade was "geared primarily to job opportunities based upon past experience." [50] Apprenticeship programs had little impact on the general problem of unemployed youth. The statement continued:

> It is the firm view of the General Presidents that the elimination of problems real or imaginary with respect to job opportunities is to

take steps to create more jobs. . . . Applicants for entrance into the industry must possess qualifications that will indicate they can be taught these skills. Accordingly, we do not intend to delegate to outsiders the qualifications for entrance into the industry and union membership. The skills of our craftsmen are our main stock in trade and represent a bulwark of strength to our Nation. They cannot be diluted or fragmentized without destroying economic conditions in the industry and the ability of our employers to perform effectively.[51]

The statement recommended the adoption by all local unions of a four-point program. Local unions were urged to recruit members regardless of race. Where a local union operated an exclusive hiring hall or job referral system, applicants should not be identified by race and should be referred to jobs without discrimination "if their qualifications meet those required by the employer." [52] Local unions operating a referral system but not an exclusive hiring hall should refer all applicants regardless of race. Finally, all locals should accept and refer applicants for apprenticeship training without discrimination.

Randolph supported the convention's resolution on civil rights. "[T]he resolution before us," he said, "is the strongest statement on civil rights ever to come before a convention of the AFL-CIO. . . . It firmly commits organized labor to a front-line role in the civil rights revolution." [53] But he offered an admonition. "The labor movement," he said, "cannot afford to measure its achievements in the field of racial justice by the standards of other institutions. . . . It is not enough to compare ourselves favorably with government or management." [54]

Randolph proposed the formation of a joint committee of Negro trade unionists and AFL-CIO leaders, and the holding of periodic meetings between labor and civil rights leaders. He also suggested that Meany, Reuther, and other AFL-CIO spokesmen go into areas of racial crisis and speak to the rank and file. "The leadership of organized labor," he said, "seems to be in advance of the membership. . . ." [55]

Meany spoke favorably of Randolph's statement and proposals, and also of lonelier times. "I recall," he said, "when we didn't have such an active interest in this field. . . . I recall when Phil Randolph, Milton Webster [vice-president of the Sleeping Car Porters] and two or three of us would sit down during a convention and see how far we could go. We had Matt Woll, Dave Dubinsky, and Bill Green. . . . I know that Phil Randolph came here year after year after year, and made his speech, made his plea. He didn't have too much help. . . ." [56]

*

What should be the verdict? How do we measure the contribution of the AFL-CIO to racial equality?

A trade union is an organization devoted primarily to the workaday benefits of its members. It often adopts other purposes, usually of high repute and service, depending upon the accidents of environment and leadership. Both alone and in concert with others, it tends to clothe its endeavors with a high philosophy, quite often, and genuinely, claiming the human condition as its natural jurisdiction. The tradition is admirable, but should not obscure the priorities. The American labor movement, of all its counterparts, has hewn closest to job-conscious unionism—to the primary pursuit of economic gain and to the protection of those already its own. Its horizon is broad, but less pretentious than others. Racial equality is one of its established goals, but for some leaders and many followers the matter is less than urgent.

A union is a polity. Its leaders are elected, and are moved in most matters of importance by the immediate preferences of their members. However apostolic the leadership or all-embracing the union creed, union members also are ordinary citizens—limited in their expectations, but insistent on results; conditional in their loyalty to private institutions; fearful of their security; and very often quite prejudiced. Armed with voting power, more now than ever before, they restrain both good and evil. In the field of civil rights, like most of their compatriots, they are a conservative force.

Most union leaders are unexceptional men, and their behavior is in some fashion predictable. They are agents of protest and protection; but grievances have priorities, and racial discrimination is not high on the Caucasian list. They often enter office with the heat of youth, but spend most of their days at a lower temperature. They grow with leadership, but they are seldom crusaders. They are proud of their movement, but usually expect less of it than the yearning critic. They are not noticeably lacking in courage, but they like their security. They are mostly men of reasonable conscience, but the interests of their members come first. The majority of their members do not like to be disturbed. Race questions disturb.

The spectrum of opinion on civil rights among union leaders is wide. The open bigot is rare, at least in the North. The covert bigot is more numerous, both North and South: restrained in public by official policy and political caution, he is ready with the racial barb among good friends or on long evenings. Much more plentiful are the limited egalitarians, strong on public resolutions and private misgivings, ardent for caution, angry at criticism but sparing in risk: their commitment to equality can be as much formal as felt, their attempts at interracial fraternization a clumsy affair. There are also the confined egalitarians, substantial in number but weak in voice, victims of unhappy traditions, fearful of lost votes, and hopeful of rescue by the law from the prejudices of their members.

There remain the true believers, unassessable in number but hardly a majority, strong in faith but varying in adventure and effect, custodians of a simple faith but members of a complex tribe. They join the Negro in union debates, and sometimes feel the wrath of their constituents. Their behavior is usually a compound of courage and calculation, a respectable contest between principle and self-preservation not always impressive to those on safer ground. Their road is hard.

The AFL came to maturity in an age when discrimination was popular and nearly universal. White men ran the nation and the crafts; the crafts dominated the AFL. The federation was in fact a confederacy, a creature of delegated and very limited powers, almost impotent on racial questions. Both

Gompers and Green, according to contemporaries, were unprejudiced in private, and did their best for the Negro in thankless times. "In my younger years," John L. Lewis has written of his close personal relationship with Gompers, "I worked with the American Federation of Labor doing legislative and organizational work under the direction of Mr. Samuel Gompers. . . . I saw Mr. Gompers often. . . . During all of that period, Mr. Gompers never uttered one syllable derogatory to any ethnic group and it does his memory a grave injustice for anyone, high or low, to suggest or imply otherwise." [57] Green, according to Meany, "carried the ball" on civil rights before indifferent AFL audiences "for many, many years, convention after convention." [58] But both Gompers and Green were permissive presidents: they governed only by mild persuasion; to them federation politics and peace came first. Some unions—notably the United Mine Workers of America—admitted Negroes on an equal basis with whites, but these were few. The white crafts were the great majority, virtually immune to federation reprisal, jealous of intervention, faithful to the mores, and not at all amused by Negro claims. Randolph, in his annual prayers for justice from the AFL, always had courtesy from the chair, but received little from the floor either in grace or votes. Race was an inconvenience.

The CIO overshadowed the AFL in both the litany and fact of tolerance. The decade of its birth had a spirit of equality. The leadership of the new movement was ideologically committed to racial justice. Its industrial structure necessarily brought membership to Negroes in large numbers and greater disciplinary power to national offices. Best of all, the system and the payroll brought new strength to Southern men of generous mind. Integrated meetings were an early feature of the CIO in the South. In Texas and elsewhere, the CIO brought Negroes into state and local political organizations and helped them win their right to vote. Interracial social affairs began to take place in the 1940's. During the 1950's, the CIO was perhaps the largest institutional contributor to civil rights campaign funds in the South. In 1955, long before any federation mandate, the Texas CIO instructed its officers to hold integrated conventions, and other Southern state bodies followed suit. Organizational power was a factor in conversion, but so were the effects of example. Young racists became mature egalitarians in the ranks. Adolescents who had sought out "red-boned niggers" to molest for sport turned into advocates of racial justice, often at the cost of bodily harm to themselves. The record was by no means perfect: not all CIO leaders were virtuous and there were great injustices in the plants, but the institution as a whole had an effect. There are those who argue that the CIO was the vanguard of the civil rights movement in the South.

In the AFL, Meany was a new breed of president, blunt in manner, a gatherer of unusual majorities, just on race questions and strong in their advocacy, and both critical and defensive of his wards. His influence for racial equality was buttressed by the merger with the CIO, which brought with it a good record and an established policy. Various affiliates of the AFL in later years and in mounting numbers had also shown greater hospitality to the Negro. The unification of the two organizations created an aggregation strongly committed to laudable ends.

The presidency of Meany produced from 1955 a degree of federation authority unknown to the AFL or even the CIO. In particular, the supervision by the federation of the affairs of unions accused of corrupt practices is without any real parallel in American trade union history.[59] Its authority was less spectacular in racial matters, but still there was improvement over the past. There was a swifter pace, a new awareness, and stronger pledges; a better hearing for the Negro, a deeper probing of internal union affairs, and an attack from the top on the formidable barriers of autonomy and tradition. There can be little quarrel with the formal policies of the AFL-CIO on race; on virtually every issue it has taken an earlier and stronger stand than have its contemporary institutions. If advocacy is evidence enough, Meany and at least some of his associates are truly bent on equality, willing to strain the authority and good will they enjoy in the pursuit of needed change.

But the fight is uphill. The mistrust of federation discipline remains. Autonomy is still the basic principle of federations, mutable only in extreme situations. On civil rights, there are few votes for revolution.

There will be no expulsions as there were in the drive against corruption. Corruption and racial discrimination are not comparable save in their undesirability. "I agree," Meany told a gathering of the NALC, "that discrimination is just as bad as corruption . . . But it is a different kind of disease. Corruption begins at the top. The rank and file are seldom aware of it. . . . Discrimination is opposed at the top, but it is carried out below. . . . Do we cure this disease by expelling the parent union, whose leaders—and a majority of whose members—are on the side of equal opportunity? I think not." [60]

The argument is decisive; the nuances of the analysis do not alter its essence. Discrimination, unlike corruption, occurs in some degree in virtually every trade union in the United States. In a few organizations it is endemic; in most it is opposed in policy but at some level practiced in fact; and nearly everywhere it is a mirror of the community outside. The expulsion of all affected unions, whether they are seen as real offenders or as products of the culture, would destroy the federation. Expulsion or other punishment on a selective basis would ignore the partial blame of history and environment, straining the sense of justice and perhaps bursting the bonds of federation. There is neither mood nor justification for Draconian measures. The roots are too deep, the blame too large, the price too high.

There are other barriers to effective action. Apprehension, based on prejudice or not, is real. Unemployment is substantial, and men fear for their jobs. Fear increases with uncertainty; particularly in the building trades, where the vagaries of weather and investment make for a special uncertainty of income, newcomers are not always welcome. Openings for apprentices are limited in any event: the restriction of numbers is still a prime source of union power for the crafts. Ironically, whether from lack of education, information, or motivation, qualified Negro applicants for admission to apprenticeship programs appear to be in short supply. Since competence is a major issue with craftsmen, the case against racial quotas or the dilution of standards seems ironclad to them.[61] Fear and pride of craft are strong allies.

Other arguments are less persuasive. Sponsorship as a condition of union membership, an old and perhaps, in less sensitive times, a harmless tradition is today an effective bar to the recruitment of Negroes into the crafts.

Filial succession, by now a proud tradition in union presidencies,[62] is hard to take at lower levels. Meany has said: "It is . . . understandable that a man who has spent years learning a trade, who is proud of his skills, wants to pass it on to his son—just as a merchant wants to pass on the business he has built to his son." [63] This argument undermines the craft case for standards of competence and ignores the veto that exclusion from union membership often has on employment. It has little appeal for Negroes in search of their first economic opportunity.

Individual union authority is a problem. It depends largely on bargaining patterns and the control of union funds. In the crafts, with more localized bargaining than in the industrial unions, constitutions and customs are often a strong brake on the ability of parent organizations to alter the ways of their local affiliates. A few times, locals have been placed in receivership to speed the process of integration—but affiliates have votes and prejudices, *de facto* local practice is difficult to change even with the firmest contractual language and national instructions, and the government gives uncertain support to international unions.

Protocol and prejudice remain. "There are unions," the United States Commission on Civil Rights stated, "which use antidiscrimination as a bargaining tool only as a device which can be surrendered at the bargaining table. . . ." [64] The lack of enthusiasm for civil rights is only too evident among some union officials: the defensive speech in convention, the balder comments in the corridors, the poor joke after hours, are too much a part of the dialogue. Protocol is a cover for inertia; autonomy is a convenient excuse for indifference; union democracy and the culture seal the trap.

The verdict on union actions should be based on proper expectations. The average critic expects too much of the federation. No doubt there is prejudice and indifference; but the essential fact is inability. No doubt the AFL-CIO could have done more to justify the higher hopes, but not much more. Neither employers nor churches nor most other private and public institutions can surpass its record of protestation or performance when all factors are considered. It is hard to foresee more than marginal improvement. The will for great change, in some quarters at least, is there; the power is not. The pace of voluntary advance will be slow.

*

Before the House Judiciary Committee, Meany stated:

> I think it is fair to say that we are the only one, among the civil rights forces, which has openly called for legislation for the correction of shortcomings in its own ranks. . . . Some segments of the labor movement have ignored the established policies. . . . We have said so to ourselves, before Congress and elsewhere. We have pleaded for legislative help to translate principle into practice. But until very recently there has been very little disposition on the part of Congress, or the country as a whole, to provide that help. . . . When it comes to legislation, it has been the labor movement that has asked for equal employment opportunity laws, applicable to unions as well as to management; while it has been the employers and their associates which, at every level—local, state and Federal—have been in bitter opposition.[65]

The law has been weak. Few cases on fair employment have reached the courts; the disposition of them has been generally favorable to Negroes, but the cost of judicial relief is high and the process slow.[66] The NLRB has offered little protection to

Negroes suffering from discrimination on the job, and none at all to Negroes barred from employment or union membership because of race.[67] The President's Committee on Government Contracts could only withdraw business, and its successor, the President's Committee on Equal Employment Opportunity, has no additional sanctions to impose. The Department of Labor makes rules on apprenticeship selection, but its only disciplinary power is the hardly fatal one of withdrawing recognition.[68] Existing fair employment laws in Northern and Western states, according to the most recent major study of them, "have up to now resulted in only a very modest and spotty decrease in discriminatory employment practices. . . . Only a comprehensive Federal statute, effectively enforced, could substantially affect the prospects for Negroes in the skilled and semiskilled trades." [69]

Now there is a new Federal Civil Rights Act.[70] The AFL-CIO joined with civil rights groups in founding a lobbying organization, the Leadership Conference on Civil Rights, and fought hard in Congress for the law. The Act prohibits discrimination on grounds of race by both unions and employers; in particular, it prohibits discriminatory exclusion or expulsion from unions, discrimination in job referrals, classification by race in union membership or structure, and efforts by unions to force employers to discriminate. On the other hand, it specifically rejects the idea of quota systems and preferential treatment, leaving the problem of standards for administrators and the courts. It relies on conciliatory moves at first, but authorizes individual appeals to the courts and legal action by the Attorney General to enjoin patterns of discrimination he believes to exist. It is not retroactive, and awaits the fortunes of politics for its enforcement. It is not an especially strong law, but at least it is new. It should have an effect.

Meanwhile, the AFL-CIO has announced the launching of a "vast drive" for equality in support of the Civil Rights Act.[71] The federation has said it will conduct a nation-wide education campaign on civil rights among its members, encourage political alliances with Negro organizations, participate increasingly in community integration programs, provide assistance to non-union workers in filing complaints under the Act, lobby for sufficient funds to administer the law, and watch its progress with amendments in mind. It has recommended that its 139 affiliates use economic pressure against discriminatory employers, assign one full-time official each to the federation for civil-rights activities at local central bodies, and place a national staff officer in charge of internal civil rights affairs. All of the approximately 800 local central bodies have been instructed to establish civil rights committees and to conduct education and action programs among their affiliates and in their communities. The new law seems to have created new energies.

*

"I know the Negro is impatient," Meany said in 1963. "He has a right to say he wants these things, and he wants them now. He has waited a long time." [72] The atmosphere is quiet at present, and Roy Wilkins has referred amiably to "family disputes" between the NAACP and the AFL-CIO.[73] But the peace might be short. The NAACP has assigned a new priority to fair employment, and was ready to levy charges against discriminatory unions and employers when fair employment provisions of the Civil Rights Act went into effect in 1965. Criticism of the AFL-CIO from one source or another will surely continue, and perhaps increase, straining needed friendships but hastening change. Embarrassment is a prod, and custom does yield to adverse publicity. The AFL-CIO should not expect drawing-room manners or scholarly calm from the Negro and his allies —the injustice is too great, the impatience too strong. Nor should the Negro expect the federation to enjoy the barrage, or to perform miracles with earthly means. Understanding is possible. The best men of both movements know the factors, and appreciate the mutual dependence that exists; the partnership might be more durable than the tempers. "Together," Martin Luther King told the 1961 AFL-CIO convention, "we can be the architects of democracy. . . . Some of us will have to get scarred up, but we shall overcome. . . . Some more of us will have to go to jail. . . . But we shall overcome . . . The arc of the universe is long, but it bends towards justice. . . ." [74]

Fraternity might prevail if risk is shared. Who will pay the price?

NOTES

1. I am grateful to Jack Barbash, Herbert Hill, Herbert Perry, Fred Schmidt, and Philip Taft for their advice on this chapter.
2. *Proceedings,* AFL-CIO Convention, 1955, p. 6.
3. *American Federationist,* March 1964, p. 4.
4. *Ibid.,* Article II, Section 4, p. xxix. There are between 1½ million and 2 million Negroes in the AFL-CIO out of a total membership of some 13 million.
5. *Ibid.,* Article XIII, Section 1(b), p. xlviii.
6. *Ibid.,* pp. 107-109.
7. *Ibid.,* p. 109.
8. *Ibid.,* p. 26.
9. *Proceedings,* AFL-CIO Convention, 1957, II, 221.
10. The admissions took place after action against the locals by the state fair employment commissions involved, and after the NAACP indicated that litigation against the locals was being considered. Meany intervened personally with both locals.
11. New York *Times,* April 12, 1957.
12. Memorandum from Herbert Hill to Boris Shiskin, then Director of the AFL-CIO Civil Rights Department, December 4, 1958. See also a letter from Hill to Charles S. Zimmerman, then the Chairman of the AFL-CIO Civil Rights Committee, February 10, 1959 (NAACP, 1959, both letters).
13. Quoted in Paul Jacobs, *The State of the Union* (New York: Atheneum, 1963), p. 65.
14. *Proceedings,* AFL-CIO Convention, 1959, II, 186.
15. *Ibid.,* I, 607.
16. New York *Times,* September 24, 1959. The sally does not appear to have been recorded in the proceedings of the convention.
17. *Proceedings,* AFL-CIO Convention, I, 497.

18. *Racism Within Organized Labor—A Report of Five Years of the AFL-CIO, 1955-1960* (New York: NAACP, 1961).
19. *The Negro Wage-Earner and Apprenticeship Training Programs* (New York: NAACP, 1961).
20. *Employment,* Report of the U.S. Commission on Civil Rights, Part III (Washington: U.S. Government Printing Office, 1961).
21. *Ibid.,* p. 104.
22. *Ibid.,* p. 63.
23. *Ibid.,* p. 139.
24. *Ibid.,* pp. 141-42.
25. *Idem.*
26. *Idem.*
27. New York *Times,* March 1, 1961.
28. *Idem.*
29. *Idem.*
30. *Ibid.,* February 27, 1961.
31. *Ibid.,* October 13, 1961.
32. *Idem.*
33. *Ibid.,* November 12, 1961.
34. *Idem.*
35. *Proceedings,* AFL-CIO Convention, 1961, II, 64.
36. *Ibid.,* II, 167.
37. Job integration is a particularly sensitive issue with fire fighters, since it involves sharing sleeping quarters. Similar problems exist in railroading, seafaring, and cross-country trucking.
38. *Proceedings,* 1961, II, 169.
39. *Ibid.,* I, 467.
40. *Idem.*
41. New York *Times,* October 13, 1961.
42. Herbert Hill, "Has Organized Labor Failed the Negro Worker?" *Negro Digest,* May 1962, p. 10.
43. *Ibid.,* p. 15.
44. *Proceedings,* AFL-CIO Convention, 1963, I, 21-24.
45. *Ibid.,* pp. 214-22, 228.
46. It was on their second attempt. The first ended in defeat by a convention vote.
47. Among the AFL-CIO unions evidently not signatory to the agreement were the Locomotive Firemen, the IBEW, the Machinists, and the International Typographical Union. See "Un-

ion Program for Eliminating Discrimination," *Monthly Labor Review,* January 1963, p. 58–59.
48. *Proceedings,* AFL-CIO Convention, 1963, II, 299.
49. *Ibid.,* II, 300.
50. *Idem.*
51. *Idem.*
52. *Ibid.,* II, 301.
53. *Ibid.,* I, 212.
54. *Ibid.,* I, 207.
55. *Ibid.,* I, 211.
56. *Ibid.,* I, 239-40.
57. Letter to the author, December 18, 1964.
58. *Proceedings,* AFL-CIO Convention, 1963, I, 239.
59. See John Hutchinson, "The Constitution and Government of the AFL-CIO," *California Law Review,* December 1958.
60. *News from the AFL-CIO,* November 9, 1962.
61. Federal statistics, the AFL-CIO Building Trades Department claims, show that in forty-seven cities in 1963, Negro journeymen and apprentices amounted to 5.3 percent of the whole, while the comparable ratio in sixty-five mainly industrial companies participating in the "Plans for Progress" program of the President's Committee on Equal Employment Opportunity was only 2.6 percent in December 1962 (Building Trades Department Memorandum, August 20, 1963). Randolph has argued for preferential treatment of Negroes in apprenticeship and other training programs (*Proceedings,* AFL-CIO Convention, 1963, pp. 210-11). Meany opposes it. "No individual white workers should be penalized for past practices in which he may have had no voice. Furthermore, these demands reject equality of opportunity; they merely replace one kind of discrimination for another" (*News from the AFL-CIO,* July 25, 1963).
62. Maurice Hutcheson succeeded his father, William Hutcheson, as president of the Carpenters in 1952. John Lyons succeeded his father, John Lyons, as president of the Iron Workers in 1961. In 1963, S. Frank Raftery was elected to succeed his father, Lawrence M. Raftery, as president of the Painters.
63. *News from the AFL-CIO,* August 1, 1962.
64. U.S. Commission on Civil Rights, *The Fifty States Report* (Washington: U.S. Government Printing Office, 1961), p. 145.
65. New York *Times,* July 17, 1962.

66. See Michael I. Sovern, "The National Labor Relations Act and Racial Discrimination," *Columbia Law Review,* VI, April 1962, 563-632.
67. The NLRB has recently decertified a small independent union for refusing to process the grievances of Negro members in a segregated local (147 NLRB 166; *Wall Street Journal,* July 3, 1964, p. 1). Both Roy Wilkins and Herbert Hill have urged the general adoption of decertification as a sanction against discriminatory unions. The measure is drastic, and if widely applied, might be chaotic in result. Of course, a real threat of such action might swiftly alter ancient ways.
68. 28 *Fed. Reg.* 13775 (1963).
69. Paul H. Norgren and Samuel E. Hill, *Toward Fair Employment* (New York: Columbia Univ. Press, 1964), pp. 230, 278. See also Herbert Hill, "Twenty Years of State Fair Employment Practice Commissions: A Critical Analysis with Recommendations," *Buffalo Law Review,* XIV, Fall 1964, 1. The New York State Commission for Human Rights recently handed down an unprecedented ruling in which it ordered Local 28 of the Sheet Metal Workers in New York City to end its discriminatory practices, scrap its current waiting list, and recruit members on a nondiscriminatory basis (Lefkowitz *vs.* Farrell, C-9287-63, New York State Commission for Human Rights, 1964). According to Norgren and Hill, most public and private agencies discriminate in one degree or another against racial minorities (*op. cit.,* p. 36).
70. Public Law 352 (1964), Title VII.
71. New York *Times,* August 5, 1964; September 3, 1964.
72. *Proceedings,* AFL-CIO Convention, 1963, I, 240.
73. New York *Times,* September 3, 1964.
74. *Proceedings,* AFL-CIO Convention, 1961, I, 288–89.

V

Education and Training of the Negro

16 / The Guidance of Negro Youth

Eli Ginzberg and Dale L. Hiestand

This chapter will seek to determine how Negro youth can be helped to find and take advantage of better employment opportunities. First we will consider the conditions and circumstances in which Negro youngsters grow up in terms of family background, income, education, location, and occupational trends. After these have been delineated as realistically as possible, we will consider the kinds of assistance which are likely to prove most effective.

□ Population Trends

Negroes constitute a relatively small minority of the population—in 1964, Negroes accounted for approximately 21.5 million persons in a total population of 194 million, or little more than 11 percent. These totals hide, however, some striking developments. Between 1950 and 1964, the Negro population increased at a rate two-thirds again as fast as the white population. In recent years, the Negro-white population ratio has been 1 to 9; the ratio of Negro births to white births has been about 1 to 6.

This rapid growth in the Negro population has two implications. In the first place, there is a large discrepancy between the dependency ratios of the Negro and white communities. For every 100 whites of working age, there are 84 whites above or below working age; for the Negro population the figure is 102—about 25 percent higher. Even if there were no other differences, the Negro community faces a more difficult task in raising its children because it has relatively more children to raise.

Secondly, the higher birth rate among Negroes in recent years means that they have constituted and will continue to constitute a relatively high proportion of the young people about whom educators and guidance personnel are concerned. In 1960 Negroes constituted 10.5 percent of the total population, but 11.3 percent of the high school age population, 12.9 percent of the elementary school age population, and 13.4 percent of the preschool age population were Negro. The percentages have been increasing, and will continue to increase in the future, as the elementary school age group reaches high school age, and the preschoolers reach elementary and then high school age.

□ Family Structure

We have slowly come to appreciate that the public school system operates on a built-in assumption in preparing young people for work and life: that before they enter school, youngsters live in a family environment in which their parents help them to acquire basic habits and social values. The social disorganization characteristic of many neighborhoods in large cities, and the resulting difficulty that many schools in these neighborhoods face in seeking to instruct children, has drawn attention to the crucial role of the family in child development, and the frequency with which the family fails to perform its function.

Table 1 presents data on the family structures within which

TABLE 1

Percentage Distribution of White and Nonwhite Children Aged 6 to 13 Years, by Type of Family Situation, 1960

	Aged 6 to 9		Aged 10 to 13	
	White	*Nonwhite*	*White*	*Nonwhite*
TOTAL NUMBER	12,669,543	2,034,908	12,277,777	1,784,083
Percent	*100.0*	*100.0*	*100.0*	*100.0*
Living with both parents	91.8	67.4	89.5	65.4
Living with father only	0.9	1.9	1.2	2.4
Living with mother only	5.6	20.3	6.9	20.8
Living with neither parent	1.3	9.6	1.8	10.3
In group quarters	0.4	0.8	0.6	1.1

Source: U.S. Bureau of the Census.

white and Negro children grow up ("Negro" is used interchangeably with "nonwhite" throughout this chapter except where distinctions can readily be made). Several important findings emerge: Practically all of the younger white children (over 98 percent) live with at least one of their parents. The overwhelming majority live with both parents. At least 1 young Negro child in 10 lives with neither parent and only about two thirds live with both parents. The majority of the Negro children who do not live with either parent live with a grandparent. Over 1 in every 5 Negro children lives with his

TABLE 2

Percentage Distribution of White and Nonwhite Children Aged 17 and Under by Family Income and by Family Situation, 1960

		Husband-Wife Families		Other Families with Male Head	Families with Female Head	
Income of Family	*Total*	*Child of head*	*Other relative*	*Child or relative of head*	*Child of head*	*Other relative of head*
WHITE CHILDREN						
TOTAL NUMBER	*54,850,316*					
Percent	*100.0*	*90.3*	*2.5*	*1.2*	*5.1*	*0.9*
Under $2000	8.0	5.2	0.2	0.2	2.2	0.2
$2000 to $3999	15.0	12.6	0.4	0.2	1.6	0.2
$4000 to $5999	26.3	24.5	0.5	0.3	0.8	0.2
$6000 to $7999	23.0	21.9	0.5	0.2	0.3	0.1
$8000 and over	27.7	26.9	0.9	0.3	0.2	0.2
NONWHITE CHILDREN						
TOTAL NUMBER	*8,536,444*					
Percent	*100.0*	*65.9*	*9.0*	*2.7*	*16.4*	*6.0*
Under $2000	33.3	16.1	2.6	1.0	10.6	3.0
$2000 to $3999	30.8	21.6	2.5	0.8	4.3	1.6
$4000 to $5999	19.8	15.9	1.7	0.5	1.0	0.7
$6000 to $7999	8.6	6.8	1.0	0.2	0.3	0.3
$8000 and over	7.5	5.5	1.2	0.2	0.2	0.4

Source: U.S. Bureau of the Census.

mother while only 1 in 20 white children lives with his mother. Thus, about one third of all Negro children, but only about one tenth of all white children, are growing up in family structures that are *per se* handicapping.

Even these figures understate the degree of family disorganization in which Negro children grow up. The table presents a cross-sectional analysis at only one point in time. When allowance is made for prior and subsequent disorganization, and for the fact that many parents may in fact be stepparents (the Census does not differentiate) the probability is strong that only 1 Negro child in 2 grows up in what could be defined as a normal family—one in which he lives with both parents throughout his childhood and adolescence.

□ Economic Status of Families

To have both parents at home is one desideratum for normal development. An adequate family income is another. In 1960, one third of all Negro children under the age of seventeen were in families with less than $2000 annual income; and almost the same proportion were in families with annual incomes of between $2000 and $4000. The comparable figures for white children were 8 percent and 15 percent, respectively (Table 2). This means that almost two thirds of all Negro children, in comparison to less than one quarter of all white children, were growing up under adverse economic circumstances.

We can look at the matter from another point of view—in terms of the proportion of children in families whose economic circumstances are satisfactory or good. Fifty percent of the white children, as compared with only about 16 percent of the Negro children, were members of families that had incomes of over $6000, and were thus able to provide them with the full range of essentials and even some luxuries during their formative years. In general, it is the family's income that determines in large measure whether a child will have enough to eat, a balanced diet, adequate room in which to

TABLE 3

Percentage Distribution of White and Nonwhite Children Aged 17 and Under By Family Situation and by Family Income, 1960

Family Situation	Total	Under $2000	$2000 to $3999	$4000 to $5999	$6000 to $7999	$8000 and over
WHITE CHILDREN						
TOTAL NUMBER	54,850,316	4,405,734	8,249,902	14,423,304	12,598,513	15,172,863
Percent	*100.0*	*100.0*	*100.0*	*100.0*	*100.0*	*100.0*
Husband-wife families	92.8	67.8	86.4	95.3	97.3	97.5
Other families with male head	1.2	2.0	1.5	1.1	0.9	1.1
Families with female head	6.0	30.2	12.1	3.6	1.8	1.4
NONWHITE CHILDREN						
TOTAL NUMBER	8,536,444	2,846,226	2,624,279	1,691,071	735,778	639,090
Percent	*100.0*	*100.0*	*100.0*	*100.0*	*100.0*	*100.0*
Husband-wife families	74.9	56.3	78.2	88.8	89.9	89.9
Other families with male head	2.7	2.9	2.6	2.6	2.7	2.6
Families with female head	22.4	40.8	19.2	8.6	7.4	7.5

Source: U.S. Bureau of the Census.

sleep and study, proper clothing, suitable medical and dental attention, and access to other services that can contribute to his development.

The hardships under which many Negro children grow up is indicated again by Table 3, which shows that for the one third of the children in families who received less than $2000 income only slightly more than half were living with both their parents. The table makes another point: the number of white children in broken families with very low incomes approximately equaled the number of Negro children in similar circumstances. Moreover, even among the Negro children growing up in more affluent households, about 1 out of every 10 lived in a broken family. Together, these data indicate multiple pathological factors, a high degree of disorganization, and widespread poverty or near-poverty among Negro families.

□ More About the Negro Family

Students of social problems have long known that a much higher proportion of Negroes than of whites is found among most institutionalized populations, particularly in corrective institutions. Table 4 shows that the rates for Negroes are 2 to 4 times as high as those for whites, especially in the young adult groups. This is an important reason why a substantial number of Negro families are disrupted for shorter or longer periods of time: one parent, and occasionally even both parents, are institutionalized. Between the ages of twenty and forty, young people should be establishing themselves in their work and making a place for themselves in the community. The high percentage of Negroes who are institutionalized at some time during these years contributes to the proportion who do not succeed in establishing themselves. They are handicapped themselves, and this adversely affects their children.

In 1961 there were almost 4.3 million births, of which 240,000, or 6 percent of the total, were illegitimate. Here again striking differences can be found between the races. Of

TABLE 4

Institutionalized Population as a Percentage of Total Population, White and Nonwhite Males by Age, 1960

Age	White Males	Nonwhite Males
20–24	1.7	4.9
25–29	1.5	5.6
30–34	1.5	5.8
35–39	1.5	5.1
40–44	1.7	4.2
45–49	1.9	3.8

Source: U.S. Bureau of the Census.

667,000 Negro births, 149,000, or roughly 22 percent, were illegitimate. The corresponding figure for whites was under 2 percent. While it can be contended that illegitimacy has a different significance in Negro and white communities, in that Negro children born out of wedlock (and their mothers) are less likely to be criticized by their families or ostracized by their communities, the fact remains that such children carry an extra burden.

The high rate of illegitimacy among Negroes is related to a surprising fact: on the average, Negroes tend to marry somewhat later than do whites. As Table 5 indicates, the average age for marriage for both men and women is about six months higher for nonwhites than for whites.

This brings us to the last dimension of family structure that we will discuss. Table 6 shows that among 14- to 17-year-olds, less than 6 percent of all unmarried whites but more than 18 percent of unmarried Negroes are living without either parent. In the age group 18–24, the striking fact is that about 26 percent of all unmarried white males and about 20 percent of all unmarried white females are living in "group quarters"—

TABLE 5

Median Age in Years at First Marriage, White and Nonwhite Men and Women, 1960

	White	Nonwhite
Male	22.6	23.1
Female	20.2	20.6

Source: U.S. Bureau of the Census.

primarily on college campuses or in the Armed Forces. Significantly, the proportion of young Negroes in group quarters is about 10 percentage points less for each sex. Much learning and socialization is derived from living with one's peers; the data show that more whites have the advantage of group living.

□ Family Pathology: An Overview

We have seen that a very high proportion of Negro youth are born into and grow up in broken families, in many of which the economic resources required for maintaining a reasonable standard of living are lacking. Different attitudes and living patterns probably compensate in part for some of these limitations—Negro grandmothers more readily assume the responsibility for raising their daughters' children, and the Negro group enjoys a more tolerant attitude toward illegitimacy; nevertheless, at least half and probably as many as three quarters of all Negro children are growing up under handicapping family conditions and circumstances. The comparable proportion of handicapped white children is more nearly between one quarter and one third.

TABLE 6

Percentage Distribution of Single Adolescents and Young Adults by Family Situation, 1960

	ADOLESCENTS (14–17 YEARS)				YOUNG ADULTS (18–24 YEARS)			
	Male		**Female**		**Male**		**Female**	
	White	*Nonwhite*	*White*	*Nonwhite*	*White*	*Nonwhite*	*White*	*Nonwhite*
TOTAL NUMBER	4,984,245	686,389	4,575,840	650,521	4,337,776	606,722	2,755,316	455,284
Percent	*100.0*	*100.0*	*100.0*	*100.0*	*100.0*	*100.0*	*100.0*	*100.0*
IN HOUSEHOLDS	97.6	96.3	98.8	98.1	73.7	82.5	80.5	91.5
In primary families	*96.8*	*94.7*	*97.9*	*96.6*	*65.7*	*74.1*	*69.0*	*81.9*
Head of family	a	0.1	a	0.1	0.6	0.9	0.7	3.7
Child of head	93.0	80.6	94.2	82.5	59.9	57.9	63.0	60.7
Grandchild of head	1.9	7.7	1.8	7.2	1.2	4.3	1.1	4.2
Other relative of head	1.9	6.3	1.9	6.8	3.9	11.0	4.2	13.3
Other (secondary families, primary and secondary individuals)	0.8	1.6	0.9	1.5	8.0	8.4	11.5	9.6
IN GROUP QUARTERS	2.4	3.7	1.2	1.9	26.3	17.5	19.5	8.5

a = less than 0.05 percent.
Source: U.S. Bureau of the Census.

□ Residence and Migration

The ease or difficulty with which children and young people are prepared for adulthood is affected not only by their families but also by the type of communities in which they grow up. One important factor in this regard is whether they move, and how often, during the period when they are of school age, or while they are young adults. We know that people move in order to improve their economic circumstances. But we have not recognized so easily the special difficulties that many experience as a result of being uprooted from their accustomed surroundings and having to sink new roots in a strange environment.

In 1960 there were approximately 9.5 million Negroes below the age of twenty-one, of whom 6.5 million lived in urban areas, 2.1 million were in rural areas but not on farms, and 900,000 were living on farms. Nearly all of those on farms and in small rural communities were in the South. This means that nearly 1 out of every 3 Negro youngsters was growing up where the prospects of receiving a good education were bleak, and the prospects of adult employment even bleaker.

An even more important finding is that the vast majority of young Negroes are being born and are growing up in urban areas. As Table 7 shows, outside of the South Negroes are almost exclusively in urban areas; even in the South about half of the adolescents are growing up in urban communities.

Table 7 also shows that fewer young Negro women than young Negro men are in rural areas, a reflection of the fact that many of the girls find jobs as domestics, while the men find jobs in agriculture. There are also relatively fewer young Negro women than young Negro men in the South, for the Negro girls who become domestics often find their jobs in other regions.

As young people who grow up on farms and in rural nonfarm communities reach adulthood, a considerable proportion of them move into urban areas. Table 8 shows the percentage

ABLE 7

Percentage Distribution of Young Negroes: Region, Urban, and Rural, 1960

Region	Male 14 to 19	Male 20 to 24	Female 14 to 19	Female 20 to 24
TOTAL NUMBER	903,712	569,398	918,336	642,315
Percent	*100.0*	*100.0*	*100.0*	*100.0*
Urban	62.9	70.1	67.3	78.0
Rural non-farm	24.6	22.5	21.4	16.1
Rural farm	12.5	7.4	11.3	5.9
NORTHEAST—total	*13.0*	*16.5*	*13.8*	*18.6*
Urban	12.0	15.4	13.2	18.0
Rural non-farm	1.0	1.1	0.6	0.6
Rural farm	0.0	0.0	0.0	0.0
NORTH CENTRAL—total	*14.8*	*16.8*	*15.6*	*18.5*
Urban	13.7	15.3	14.9	17.9
Rural non-farm	0.9	1.4	0.6	0.5
Rural farm	0.2	0.1	0.1	0.1
SOUTH—total	*67.3*	*59.3*	*65.9*	*56.9*
Urban	32.9	33.6	34.7	36.4
Rural non-farm	22.1	18.4	20.0	14.7
Rural farm	12.3	7.3	11.2	5.8
WEST—total	*4.9*	*7.4*	*4.7*	*6.0*
Urban	4.3	5.8	4.5	5.7
Rural non-farm	0.6	1.6	0.2	0.3
Rural farm	0.0	0.0	0.0	0.0

Source: U.S. Bureau of the Census.

of the 1960 population that had moved within the previous five years to and from states in which there was a substantial Negro population. More than 10 percent of the Negro population in seven states and the District of Columbia had entered the states within the previous five years. This was true also of the white populations of ten states and the District of Columbia. The out-migration data reveal that four scattered

TABLE 8

Migration Rates: Selected States, 1960*

	White			Nonwhite		
	In-migrants	*Out-migrants*	*Net migration rate*	*In-migrants*	*Out-migrants*	*Net migration rates*
Massachusetts	5.9	7.5	−1.6	13.1	6.9	+6.2
Connecticut	9.0	7.7	+1.3	15.4	5.2	+10.1
New York	3.6	6.9	−3.3	7.7	4.2	+3.5
New Jersey	9.2	7.5	+1.7	11.0	4.8	+6.2
Pennsylvania	3.9	7.0	−3.1	5.2	4.3	+0.9
Ohio	6.7	7.8	−1.1	7.5	4.4	+3.1
Indiana	7.8	9.3	−1.5	8.6	6.0	+2.6
Illinois	6.9	8.8	−1.9	8.4	5.2	+3.2
Michigan	4.9	7.6	−2.7	6.0	5.4	+0.5
Wisconsin	5.5	6.7	−1.1	16.3	5.4	+10.9
Iowa	6.1	10.1	−4.0	12.9	11.2	+1.7
Missouri	8.7	10.7	−2.0	7.7	6.7	+1.0
Kansas	11.5	15.9	−4.4	15.1	15.4	−0.3
Delaware	16.3	11.7	+4.6	9.7	6.2	+3.5
Maryland	14.1	10.7	+3.4	6.7	4.5	+2.2
District of Columbia	24.0	54.9	−30.9	10.7	6.8	+3.9
Virginia	15.4	13.3	+2.2	4.5	6.9	−2.4
West Virginia	5.7	13.9	−8.2	4.4	15.2	−10.8
North Carolina	8.0	9.2	−1.1	3.1	7.5	−4.4
South Carolina	11.2	11.0	+0.2	2.1	8.9	−6.8
Georgia	10.9	11.0	−0.1	2.6	6.9	−4.3
Florida	30.5	9.7	+20.8	8.9	4.4	+4.4
Kentucky	7.2	11.3	−4.1	5.1	8.0	−3.0
Tennessee	8.8	11.3	−2.6	4.5	7.2	−2.6
Alabama	9.5	10.1	−0.6	2.2	7.0	−4.7
Mississippi	11.1	12.0	−0.9	1.9	9.7	−7.8
Arkansas	11.3	14.6	−3.3	3.4	10.9	−7.6
Louisiana	9.2	8.4	+0.8	2.3	4.8	−2.5
Texas	8.8	9.1	−0.3	4.1	5.0	−0.8
California	14.2	6.4	+8.0	14.1	3.4	+10.7

* Migrant status is based on 1960 vs. 1955 residence; rates are per hundred population in 1960.

Source: U.S. Bureau of the Census.

states lost 10 percent or more of their Negro population in the same period and that fourteen states and the District of Columbia lost 10 percent or more of their white populations.

The extent to which the white population is shifting about is revealed by the fact that every state, except Florida and California, that gained 10 percent or more through in-migration lost at least 10 percent during the same period. The net population changes due to in- and out-migration were quite small in comparison to the gross turnover of the population.

Against this background of the general movements of population, the mobility of Negro youth can be seen more clearly. Table 9 reveals that, of the approximately 1.8 million young Negroes between the ages of 14 and 19 in 1960 only about half had not moved in the previous five years, although most of those who did move were still living in the same county. Still, over 200,000 had moved to another county in the same state or to a different state.

Mobility was much higher among the young adults. Only about 28 percent of those between the ages of 20 and 24 were living in the same house at the end of these five years. The largest group had moved to another location within the same county. However, about 25 percent had moved away from the county, most of them to another state. More detailed examination of such data by states reveals that in 1960 about 20 percent of the young Negroes between the ages of twenty to twenty-four in the Northeast and North Central regions had arrived there within the preceding five years. In the West the corresponding figure was between 35 and 40 percent. Even in the South, 10 percent of the Negroes in this age group in 1960 had moved from a different state since 1955.

These high rates of mobility have implications for educational planning. First, most school systems must be geared to accepting a large number of students newly settled in the neighborhood. Moreover, in the Northern and Western states characterized by heavy Negro in-migration, the school systems must be prepared to cope with a large number of children who received their early schooling in the segregated

TABLE 9

Mobility of Young Negroes, 1955–1960

Residence	NUMBER				PERCENT			
	Aged 14–19		Aged 20–24		Aged 14–19		Aged 20–24	
	Male	*Female*	*Male*	*Female*	*Male*	*Female*	*Male*	*Female*
TOTAL	*903,712*	*918,336*	*569,398*	*642,315*	*100.0*	*100.0*	*100.0*	*100.0*
Same house in both years	463,657	440,023	169,927	169,591	51.3	47.9	29.8	26.4
Different house in U.S.	419,546	459,328	359,758	449,263	46.4	50.0	63.2	70.0
Same county	312,365	350,714	219,026	304,580	34.6	38.2	38.5	47.5
Different county	107,181	108,614	140,732	144,683	11.8	11.8	24.7	22.5
Same state	50,369	51,063	45,633	52,904	5.6	5.6	8.0	8.2
Different state	56,812	57,551	95,099	91,779	6.2	6.2	16.7	14.3
Abroad	1,787	1,972	8,325	2,752	0.2	0.2	1.5	0.4
Moved, residence in 1955 not reported	18,722	17,013	31,388	20,709	2.1	1.9	5.5	3.2

Source: U.S. Bureau of the Census.

schools of the South. Since many Negro youngsters who grow up in the South end their schooling in the communities where they were born and only then move to another locale in or out of the state, their teachers should recognize their potential mobility and help them prepare for it. This applies particularly to teachers of young people who grow up on farms or in rural nonfarm communities and are statistically likely to move to an urban center.

The earlier finding of high mobility among the white population points up the fact that many Negroes who remain in the South will be increasingly exposed to persons not native to their communities. Many white in-migrants will be from other parts of the South, but many will be Northerners, with different attitudes and values, particularly with respect to race relations.

□ Preparation for Work

This brings us to the last body of data that we will review—the educational and occupational experience of young Negroes. Table 10 reveals that in 1960 there was still a disturbingly large percentage of young Negro men in the South, about 1 in 14, who were functionally illiterate when they reached adulthood—that is, that they had less than a fifth-grade education. Although a small number of whites and Negroes are unable to learn because of mental and emotional disorders, this 7 percent is far above the normal incidence of "learning blocks" and reflects educational deprivation.

As a rule of thumb, high school graduation is becoming a requirement for most jobs. Only slightly more than one fifth of the Negro males and about one fourth of the Negro females in the South in 1960 met this criterion; the corresponding proportion in regions outside of the South is roughly one third of all Negro youth. Clearly, an alarmingly large proportion of Negroes are not receiving adequate education. In contrast, almost 3 of every 4 white men achieve at least the minimum educational preparation for the world of work (high school

TABLE 10

Percentage of Young Nonwhites by Level of Education Completed, 1960

	South		Other Regions	
	Male	*Female*	*Male*	*Female*
TOTAL	*74.6*	*66.8*	*72.2*	*64.9*
Less than 5 years of schooling completed*	7.2	4.3	3.1	3.2
No more than elementary schooling*	33.8	23.8	17.5	13.9
At least high school graduation†	22.6	26.5	33.6	32.7
At least some college‡	6.9	7.4	11.0	10.4
College graduation§	4.1	4.8	7.0	4.7

Source: U.S. Bureau of the Census.

* 18–19 year olds
† 20–24 year olds
‡ 22–24 year olds
§ 30–34 year olds

graduation). But access to the best jobs requires college graduation and more; here white men have an advantage of 7 to 1.

Other data, comparing the education of young men with that of their fathers, reveal that while both white and Negro men have acquired on the average considerably more education than their fathers, the gains at the upper end of the scale—high school and completion of college—were considerably greater for whites than for Negroes.

Another dimension of the difference between the educational achievements of whites and of Negroes is illuminated by a consideration of acceleration and retardation. What percentage of each age group is in advance of or behind its appropriate grade level? These data are found in Table 11. At age ten, when boys are ordinarily in the fourth or fifth grade if they entered school at age six and progressed normally, in each region of the country a considerably higher proportion of Negroes than of white youngsters are already retarded. At

TABLE 11

Level of School Enrollment at Selected Ages, Males, by Region, in Percent, 1960

Age and grade	White *North-east*	 *North Central*	 *South*	Nonwhite *North-east*	 *North Central*	 *South*
AGE 10	*100.0*	*100.0*	*100.0*	*100.0*	*100.0*	*100.0*
6th grade or above	5.5	3.2	2.9	9.4	6.6	5.2
5th grade	57.4	53.2	44.7	45.0	40.6	33.2
4th grade	30.8	37.1	39.5	34.4	38.5	37.2
3rd grade or below	6.3	6.5	12.9	11.2	14.3	24.4
AGE 16	*100.0*	*100.0*	*100.0*	*100.0*	*100.0*	*100.0*
12th grade or above	7.1	3.4	3.3	8.8	5.9	4.3
11th grade	51.9	49.9	39.0	35.1	30.2	22.8
10th grade	26.7	33.6	33.9	28.3	33.1	27.1
9th grade	8.9	8.6	13.3	16.9	18.8	19.2
8th grade or below	5.4	4.5	10.5	10.9	12.0	26.6
AGE 20	*100.0*	*100.0*	*100.0*	*100.0*	*100.0*	*100.0*
College senior or above	8.9	4.9	4.7	5.6	3.0	3.0
College junior	39.7	38.7	29.6	15.3	16.0	11.9
College sophomore	25.4	31.7	31.6	17.7	18.5	17.4
College freshman	10.1	11.0	12.6	9.3	14.7	12.2
High school senior	8.4	7.7	11.6	21.9	24.6	23.7
High school junior or below	7.5	6.0	9.9	30.2	23.2	31.8

Source: U.S. Bureau of the Census.

sixteen, relatively twice as many Negroes as whites are likely to be retarded one or two years, particularly in the South. In both age groups, however, it is noteworthy that a higher proportion of Negro than white youngsters have been accelerated.

At age twenty the story changes. At this age there are considerably more young white men than Negroes who are in their junior or senior year in college or who have already graduated. In each region of the country almost half of all the Negro men still in school are in high school, while the comparable figures for whites are of the order of 15 to 20 percent. The data for Negro women substantially parallel those for Negro men.

Education is the key to personal development, and it also provides the foundation for the adult's occupational life. The fact that Negroes tend to be less well educated than whites helps to explain two important aspects of the recent experiences of young Negro men. The ratio of Negroes to the total number of men inducted into and enlisted in the Armed Forces has been consistently lower than their proportion of the population. With a large pool from which to select, the Armed Forces have tended to accept the better-educated young men, and Negroes account for a higher than average proportion of the less-educated.

As was pointed out in the report of the U.S. Commission on Civil Rights in 1963, service in the Armed Forces enables many men to broaden and deepen their knowledge and skills and eases their later occupational and social adjustment. The Negroes who are rejected for military service miss out on this help in their later adjustment.

□ Occupational Situation

Another result of the lower average level of education of Negroes is reflected in the much higher unemployment rates that have come to characterize the Negro labor force. The national unemployment rate, which fluctuated between 5 and 6 percent from 1958 to 1964, was more recently reduced to 4 percent or less. Then and now the rate for Negroes has been roughly twice than for whites. To make matters worse, the unemployment rate for young people has been roughly twice that of the entire population. Unemployment rates of 20 percent for young Negro males and of 30 percent and more for young Negro women have been common. While inferior education does not explain all of this differentially high rate, it accounts for a significant part.

The occupational progress of Negroes is suggested by their level of accomplishment relative to that of the white population. Table 12 sets forth the occupational status of high school graduates age twenty-five to thirty-four in 1960. It should be noted in passing that a high school diploma does not reveal the quality of the education. The presumptive evidence is that the Negroes receive a considerably inferior education because in general their teachers are less capable and their facilities less desirable.

Of the males, Negro high school graduates were three times more likely than whites to enter service or unskilled work and somewhat more likely to become operatives and farm laborers. Almost equal proportions of white and Negro young men were in clerical occupations. On the other hand, whites were four times as likely as Negroes to become farm or nonfarm managers or proprietors; three times as likely to be salesmen; and twice as likely to become professional workers, technicians, or craftsmen and foremen.

The occupational distribution of women also reveals strong differentials: while 56 percent of the white women became clerical workers, only 22 percent of the Negro women obtained clerical work. The same general proportions held in the other white-collar fields. Stated in another way, only about 1 in 4 of the white girls, but over 4 out of 10 Negro girls, became service workers. Differentials just as striking existed for those with other levels of educational achievement.

In summary, Negroes with the same level of formal schooling reached a noticeably lower level of occupational achievement than did whites: because on the average their education was relatively inferior; because relatively more of them are in the South where opportunities are generally not so good; and because racial discrimination continues to exist in the North and the South.

TABLE 12

Occupational Distribution of High School and Elementary School Graduates Aged 25 to 34, by Sex and Color, 1960

	Males		Females	
	White	*Nonwhite*	*White*	*Nonwhite*
High School Graduation				
TOTAL	*100.0*	*100.0*	*100.0*	*100.0*
Professionals	7.3	2.9	6.5	5.1
Managers	9.2	2.2	2.8	1.1
Clerical	9.9	11.7	55.9	22.2
Sales	7.5	2.2	6.6	2.6
Craftsmen and Foremen	26.4	13.1	1.1	1.1
Operatives	21.1	26.7	11.7	17.0
Service	4.7	14.7	9.7	41.0
Laborers, exc. farm and mine	4.0	13.4	0.3	1.0
Farmers	4.7	1.1	0.3	0.2
Farm Laborers	1.0	1.4	0.7	0.7
Occupation not reported	4.2	10.6	4.3	8.0
Elementary School Completion (8 years)				
TOTAL	*100.0*	*100.0*	*100.0*	*100.0*
Professionals	1.1	0.4	1.2	0.7
Managers	3.5	1.0	1.5	0.4
Clerical	3.2	2.7	8.8	1.8
Sales	2.4	0.7	6.3	1.0
Craftsmen and foremen	24.7	10.8	1.9	0.5
Operatives	37.2	32.3	44.7	18.7
Service	3.9	12.1	24.9	62.3
Laborers, exc. farm and mine	10.5	23.8	1.2	1.0
Farmers	6.1	1.7	0.5	0.3
Farm Laborers	3.1	5.1	2.2	3.5
Occupations not reported	4.1	9.4	6.8	9.9

Source: U.S. Bureau of the Census.

□ Implications for Guidance

Our aim has been to place into perspective the current situation regarding Negro youth—the families into which they are born and reared, the communities in which they grow up, the communities into which they relocate, the extent and quality of their schooling, their opportunities to serve in the Armed Forces, and selected information about their occupational achievement. In this concluding section we will present the principal policy recommendations implicit in these findings.

1. A serious guidance effort must consider the Negro family. Unless steps are taken to help compensate for the disorganization and poverty that are characteristic of such a high proportion of all Negro families, there is little likelihood that the educational and vocational performance of many Negroes will prove satisfactory. Help must be offered to give the Negro child a better start in life.

2. There is no prospect that schools can provide equal opportunity for all children unless those that must train large numbers of Negroes are more strongly staffed and provide special services. The Negro child is much more likely than the white child to have a background that provides inadequate preparation and stimulation.

3. There is urgent need to restructure the curricula of many schools, especially those in the rural South, so that young Negroes as well as whites growing up in these communities will have an opportunity to acquire at least some of the broader knowledge and skills that will help them to adjust to the urban communities to which so many of them will migrate.

4. In turn, it is important that the schools in the urban communities of the South and North to which large numbers of Negroes who have not completed their education are likely to migrate provide special supporting services to ease the adjustment of these youngsters.

5. Special efforts are required to improve the education of Negroes who enter and complete college. Otherwise, there is a distinct likelihood that the occupational gap between whites and Negroes will widen at the upper end of the scale.

6. The retardation of Negroes throughout the school system suggests that special factors are at work within the educational structure and in the Negro family and community that warrant study and correction. A two-year loss of time in fourteen years of schooling is a serious handicap.

7. The fact that a smaller-than-proportional number of Negroes are accepted for military service leads to a further handicapping of the Negro group. Experimentation is called for to see what might be done to increase the acceptance of Negroes for military service so that they might have this advantage.

8. Discrimination in employment at the present time and in the recent past has left an indelible mark upon many Negro parents, teachers, and others in a position to influence the young. However, the accelerated efforts to remove this and other forms of discrimination are now under way, using the full power of the Federal Government as well as the power and influence of many state and local governments, trade unions, employer groups, and other public and private agencies. This points to the desirability of advising young Negroes not to make their plans in terms of past experience. More Negroes should take the calculated gamble that they will soon be able to get any position for which they are qualified in almost any region of the country.

9. Finally, the large number of young Negroes who end their education without graduating from high school, and the very small proportion who complete college, points to the desirability of expanding and broadening adult educational opportunities, and that those in a position to guide young Negroes persuade them to make use of these broadened opportunities.

□ Concluding Observations

The thrust of this analysis underlines the disabilities under which many young Negroes prepare for work and life. But it is not a completely depressing picture. A significant minority of Negroes are not severely handicapped; in fact many are only slightly handicapped. It is very important that all who deal with Negroes or make policy affecting them realize that Negroes are not a homogeneous group of socially disorganized, poorly educated people with low incomes. Many fit this description, but a significant proportion do not.

Closely related is the finding that, while on most scales of social disability relatively more Negroes tend to show poorer ratings than whites, the fact remains that Negroes account for only slightly more than 10 percent of the population and about 15 percent of recent births. This means that the absolute number of disadvantaged whites is greater, often considerably greater, than the number of disadvantaged Negroes. Hence, public policies that aim to provide preventive and remedial services should attempt to include all who require them, white and Negro alike.

Many important factors involved in the formation of attitudes and values—the availability of models, intergroup relations, and other subtle factors operating to condition the development of Negro youth—have been passed over in this presentation. It is important for the reader to appreciate that this is a partial, not a conclusive, treatment of the subject. We sought to develop our material in terms of the hard facts of objective reality and to leave to one side the equally important facts relating to psychological determinants.

Aside from considerations of time and space, there was a reason for our emphasis. We sought to delineate those areas where government might make a significant contribution. Not that government alone can do the whole job. But government remains the most potent instrument in our society for equalizing the opportunities of young people.

SELECTED BIBLIOGRAPHY

The Conservation of Human Resources Project at Columbia University has dealt with related facets of this subject in a series of investigations published during the past fifteen years, noted below. All of the books have Eli Ginzberg as the senior author and were published by the Columbia University Press, New York City.

The Optimistic Tradition and American Youth. 1961.
The Ineffective Soldier: Lessons for Management and the Nation. 3 vols. 1959.
The Negro Potential. 1956.
The Uneducated. 1953.
Occupational Choice: An Approach to a General Theory. 1951.

The following books by Ginzberg also deal with these subjects:

The Negro Challenge to the Business Community. New York: McGraw-Hill, 1964.
The Troublesome Presence: American Democracy and the Negro. New York: Free Press, 1964.
Human Resources: The Wealth of a Nation. New York: Simon & Schuster, 1958.

Also:

Hiestand, Dale L. *Economic Growth and Employment Opportunities for Minorities.* New York: Columbia Univ. Press, 1964.

17 / Job Training Through Adult Education: A Second Chance for the Negro and the Community

Albert A. Blum and
Charles T. Schmidt, Jr.[1]

A truly circular process helps to make many Negroes members of a disadvantaged class. The Supreme Court's 1954 school-segregation decision, if it did nothing else, pointed up the inferiority of the education available to the Negro, an education that left him less qualified for employment than the average white.

Now the sons of these disadvantaged Negroes are taking their seats in school. Educators are concerned with giving them a chance in life by providing a good primary and secondary education. But this first chance for the children may only raise false hopes if their parents are not given a second chance to gain the skills they need to secure worthwhile jobs in our society. Otherwise the adults may stay in the lost generation of the disadvantaged, thus making it more likely that their children will be unable to break free of the old pattern.

This chapter deals with the role of adult education in giving the Negro his second chance. We will examine the role of human relations commissions, school systems, Negro leaders, and community action programs in providing job training for the Negro. We will focus on Detroit, but will also look at what is going on elsewhere.

None of these groups, except in isolated cases, has provided the programs necessary to achieve an upgrading of the adult Negro labor force. Yet job training has been successful under certain conditions. It has to be based in the community and result from the pressure and aspirations of the Negro and his protest movements. The training must also be related to the needs felt by the Negro poor, and not be based on the opinions of well-to-do whites and Negroes on the problems of the hard-core unemployed. Moreover, it is necessary that trainees reap recognizable benefits in the form of jobs.

□ Human Relations Commissions

The need for job training is generally recognized in many cities throughout this country. To see what community-wide organizations concerned with the problems of minority groups were doing to satisfy this need, we surveyed human relations commissions.

One of the consistent demands in local civil rights disputes is that the city government set up a human relations commission, and more than five hundred localities have done so, with varied results. Some criticize these commissions as fostering talk or research instead of action. This charge is surely true regarding job-training programs, for little indeed is done. It is true that many of these local organizations gather statistics about Negro unemployment—mainly gross totals of the number of Negroes in the local work force and the numbers employed and unemployed. But rarely do they find out the number of jobs presently and potentially available, the kinds of skills they require, and the skills the local unemployed or underemployed Negroes possess. Consequently, they are unable to formulate realistic training requirements, particularly since they even more rarely relate local labor market conditions to the needs of the national labor market.

Why is it that these commissions are so inactive in the field of adult education? For one thing, many of them interpret their authority too narrowly. Detroit's commission, for example, has the authority to develop programs to increase understanding, to promote good will, and to cultivate responsibility for the common welfare. It is supposed to try to "correct situations which it finds to be endangering the peace and welfare of the community, or to be unjust and discriminatory, through negotiation and education." With such a vague mandate, any type of program could be initiated. If job-training courses are not initiated, it is because a commission has failed to assess the Negro's major needs in terms of the actual situation. Inactivity also often results from a commission's interpretation of its proper role as only an advisory one. Moreover, because such commissions are political bodies, their members frequently do not wish to antagonize anyone; therefore, they are willing to preach the need for action but not to go further. As a result, commissions are too often places where problems are discussed but never resolved.

Another important reason for the failure of human rights commissions to engage in job-training programs is that a majority of these organizations feel their main purpose is to ease group tensions. To many, tension appears to be synonymous with explosion. Since the dramatically explosive issues have been overt discrimination in housing, in public accommodations, in public school education, and in employment, these issues have attracted the most attention, often in response to individual complaints. When commissions do present any adult education programs, these tend to deal with means of achieving better human relations in the community.

□ Educational Institutions

For about ninety years, Detroit's Board of Education has provided adult education courses. During the 1963–1964 school year, it offered 325 courses in academic subjects, arts and crafts, avocations, business and commerce, Americanization, home and family, and trades and vocational subjects. At a time when the Federal Government was making financial assistance available to programs designed to train adults (and a fair share of this assistance went to the Detroit school system, as we shall see), the Detroit Board of Education nevertheless felt forced to raise the tuition fees for the 1963–1964 school year because of a shortage of funds. This move reduced the number of students taking such courses from 23,000 to 9000 in one year. Consequently, the Board decided to lower tuition for the 1964–1965 academic year, and to do away with it altogether for those working toward an eighth-grade certificate or a high school diploma.

While teachers and administrators in the elementary and secondary school systems are concerned about the failure of Negro children to work up to their potentials and are consequently developing a host of enrichment programs to attempt to involve parents in their children's education and to prevent dropouts, the adult education program in Detroit remains basically a one-man operation with insufficient research, evaluation, experimentation, or consultation with interested groups. Little that is new in the way of motivating adults and strengthening the courses seems to be forthcoming. The job market is supposedly taken into account, and special classes can be organized in any approved subject upon request from a sufficiently large group. But courses are normally developed on "the basis of ninety years of experience," or after discussion with the administrators of the schools in which they are offered. There is rarely any consultation with the Negro block clubs, fraternal organizations, or community leaders. The programs are announced almost exclusively through the distribution of printed brochures, although some television and radio spot announcements have been used.

Of the approximately 325 subjects offered during the 1963–1964 academic year, about 150, or approximately 46 percent, have job training or skill improvement as their purpose. There is a serious question as to whether many of the unemployed or unskilled Negroes attend these courses. A 1956 study concluded that "definitely, the low income group in the City was not reached" by the city's adult education program. It listed those whom Detroit adult education failed to serve: older adults; young adults; those unable to afford class fees and accompanying costs; those handicapped physically, emotionally, or mentally; the illiterate; those not able to participate in programs in the evening; the unemployed; those in need of training and retraining opportunities; those new in the community; and those whom the community had failed to motivate. Therefore, the programs obviously attracted and served middle-class or upper-class whites who were long-term residents of Detroit.[2]

Less isolated from the Negro community is the work being done by the Detroit Board of Education in youth and adult education job-training programs Federally sponsored under the Manpower Development and Training Act (MDTA). To house this extensive and expanding program, the Board of Education in 1964 purchased a large surplus U.S. Government building to serve as a Youth and Adult Skill Training Center, with a capacity of approximately 3000 students per year. Programs may also be held at other localities as demand requires.

As of June 30, 1964, there were 46 MDTA programs within the city of Detroit proper, with 86 classes, enrolling a total of 1765 trainees. Of these, 265 had dropped out before the training was completed, 644 completed the training and 956 were still enrolled in training. Of the 644 who completed training, 503 obtained employment in jobs related to their training, 67 obtained unrelated jobs, 42 were unemployed, and 32 were unavailable for work. None were considered unqualified for work.

The school administrators of the MDTA programs are troubled because they do not know enough about the people who need training, nor how they should be attracted into the programs. The Michigan Employment Security Commission (MESC) is responsible for choosing the trainees and eventually placing them in jobs, but its selection techniques have been criticized. Although the MESC has conducted a young-worker registration drive, it usually has been able to secure enough students for the programs from existing lists of job applicants or from among those who possess the motivation to come into the MESC office of their own accord. It is doubtful that these are the people who need training most desperately. The MESC, or any other agency or organization trying to attract prospective trainees, must somehow use its resources to improve its image, at least among the poor and Negroes, so that it can appeal to the thousands who through ignorance, fear, lack of motivation, difficulty with application forms and bureaucracy, or dissatisfaction with past contacts will not apply to the agency.

The school system has a graver responsibility than most other groups to provide sound job training for the adult Negro. One reason for this major responsibility is that it was the school system (and the society of which it is a part) that failed to provide the Negroes who are now adults with the skills needed in our industrial society when they were young. But more important, the school system must be concerned with job-training programs because these adult, untrained, undereducated Negroes have children now in school.

Educators have been groping and searching for methods by which to motivate the Negro child toward higher achievement. They argue that he must gain a better image of himself and that his parents can help him toward this desired end. Recent educational research has emphasized the value of "significant others," particularly parents, in raising achievement levels. Schools have been attempting to involve the Negro parents in their work, for example, through soliciting their help in reading programs. But what better way is there of involving the parents and showing that education is of value than through an adult education program that can train the adult Negro to hold the job he so desperately needs? The Negro child soon learns from his culture that it does not pay to set his sights too high, and that he cannot improve his situation by working hard in school: the proof is that his parents lack skill and work. To break this cycle, training is necessary not only for the child but also for the adult Negro—and the training must result in jobs. The "significant other" with whom the child identifies must be a working father, male relative, or friend whose education, even if delayed, has resulted in employment, and who is, therefore, more willing to believe that education will pay off for the child as well.

□ Programs Organized by Negroes

The branches of national civil rights organizations in Detroit seem to be relatively uninterested in job training, the "dull part of desegregation." That this is a tragic omission can be seen when one examines what a Negro protest organization can do in this field. An example, in Detroit, is the Trade Union Leadership Council (TULC), which has the best and most active training program sponsored by a volunteer organization in all of Detroit. It is a program that, without Federal assistance and mainly through local contributions and energy, has within two years trained approximately 600 individuals, over 90 percent of whom were Negroes.

The TULC, founded in 1957 by union members and officials to combat discrimination within labor and elsewhere, eventually broadened its horizons. It recognized that the "problem of job discrimination and discrimination within the unions were problems that should be dealt with within the community as well as within labor." As a result, it expanded its membership to include nonunion people and its program to include the establishment of the TULC Educational Center in 1962–1963.

The school is in an old hardware store. "We started out with four blank walls . . . and all the work has been done by the members. The architect was a member, the plumber was a member, the carpenter was a member—everything was volunteer work. We came around every night, shooting the breeze, grabbing a mouthful of nails and a hammer, and wham, wham, back and forth," and the school was built. Now another building has been added. Other contributions of money and energy have come from individuals in the community, labor organizations, community services, schools, and churches.[3]

The TULC's students have learned a variety of skills. At first, the training emphasized secretarial and clerical skills (the number of students was often limited by the number of typewriters available), but more recently it has been expanded to include business English, remedial reading, speed reading, business math, power sewing, leadership training, and preapprenticeship electrical training. Students can also take "cosmetic" courses on proper appearance, as well as cultural ones in piano, modern dance, and art. The teachers are unpaid volunteers, some of whom are secretaries at union offices in the city. Classes are usually held in the evening, and there are no registration fees. No applicant is refused admission, although some may be encouraged to take remedial training before enrolling in the more advanced courses.

The students range in age from sixteen to sixty and include the employed as well as the unemployed. The TULC makes an active effort to secure students mainly through personal contacts. The program boasts a high rate of placement of its graduates and a low dropout rate. The TULC has further hopes. If funds become available, it plans to hire a full-time educational director "to organize a full schedule of day and night classes in a wide range of business, technical and academic fields." It believes that "fulfillment of these goals will give to our city an education center unparalleled in the country and will set an example of community cooperation never before attained." [4]

The TULC's success is due not only to its devoted leadership but also to its use of the Negro community as the source both of students and of funds, ideas, staff, and leaders. Its members (particularly those who are union officials) have been able to insure, directly or indirectly, that its trainees are placed in jobs. The students know this, and stick with the courses, despite the simple facilities and the lack of professional teachers. The TULC has made its center, with its bars and cabarets, a community meeting place for Negroes, but has also created a place where Negroes can be trained for jobs.

What the TULC has done for Detroit, the Opportunities Industrialization Center (OIC) has done for Philadelphia. Both organizations have their roots in the Negro community, but the base of the OIC is not in the labor movement. In Philadelphia a few years ago, disturbed by the fact that so many firms were not hiring Negroes, a group of Negro ministers sponsored a "selective patronage" boycott against these companies. When the companies argued that they would hire Negroes if they had the skills, these ministers began to push for a training program. They asked the business firms to donate money and equipment. The companies gave $250,000; the Ford Foundation contributed another $200,000; and the Negro community dug into its pockets to give another $102,000. Housed in a former police station, renovated for training purposes, the OIC seems more successful in attracting Philadelphia Negroes (the programs are not limited to Negroes) to its courses than are the Federally sponsored MDTA programs in the area. More people applied for enrollment than there were spaces. A vast majority of those who have graduated from OIC have been placed in jobs. Convinced of the value of OIC's approach, the Labor Department gave it a grant of almost $500,000 in December 1964.[5]

Much of the OIC's success springs from the involvement of the Negro in the program, the pride the Negroes feel in its success, and from the opportunity for self-help it provides. The organization sprang from a need felt by the Negroes; it was started by Negro leaders; it has been supported financially, in some measure, by the Negro community and by fees paid by those students who can afford them; and it permits communication to take place between the Negro leadership and the white power structure. The Negro can now negotiate more forcefully with industrial leaders, for the Negroes who are now peacefully trying to provide executives with trained personnel were earlier involved in more direct action against them. The OIC's philosophy is to take the struggle off the streets and into the classroom.

The TULC and OIC programs indicate that an important ingredient in the success of any job training program for Negroes is the involvement of Negroes in agitating for it, developing it, and criticizing it. One of the difficulties of most training programs is that the people with the least skill and education and those who have been out of work the longest are the ones who hesitate the longest before entering such programs, and are the first to drop out. Those hard-core unemployed who do graduate benefit markedly. One reason for the failure of these people to enter programs has been a failure of communication. The Negro community and its leadership, once involved in these programs, can promote them better through private talks than other programs are promoted by the brochures and announcements so frequently used and so rarely read—particularly when the prospective trainees are semiliterate. Just as young students in school need pressure and support from "significant others," such as their parents and peers, if they are to do well in school and remain committed to education, so do adult Negroes need such support and pressure if they are to participate in and gain from job-training programs. If their peers in the Negro community and the leaders of the national and local civil rights organizations are committed to job-training programs, the adult Negro will be more likely to be committed as well.

The families of the Negroes involved also have a role to play in job-training programs. To reinforce the change in attitude needed for the long-unemployed and disheartened adult to become a student, his wife and other members of his family also ought to be involved in adult education through group discussions and other activities.[6] The failure to make use of such "significant others" helps explain why there is such a large dropout rate among adults taking training programs and why those with the least education tend not even to enter these programs. The success of future programs rests in large part on how much of this lesson is learned.

☐ Job Training in a Coordinated Attack on Poverty

Job-training ought to be part of a community's coordinated antipoverty and antidiscrimination program. One such program has been developed in Detroit—the Total Action Against Poverty, or TAP.[7]

TAP grew out of a realization of the possibilities of assistance that would be available after the eventual passage of the antipoverty act by Congress. Aware of the problems faced by the poor, Detroit's mayor appointed a committee in 1964 to plan a constructive and coordinated assault against unemployment and poverty. TAP's goals are "to develop responsible citizens, generate greater participation in community life and the problems of others, and build into the lives of the impoverished the skills and aspirations for useful and rewarding lives." Having learned of some of the weaknesses of existing training programs, TAP's program recognizes that three factors are essential to its success:

> First, the attack against poverty must be comprehensive and coordinated. A host of services of high quality must be concentrated in priority areas in order to meet the problem.
>
> Second, these services must be offered where the disadvantaged are—in their own neighborhoods. Maximum help cannot come from downtown or from some centralized agency to which the poor cannot relate themselves.
>
> Third, that unless new jobs are opened so that work becomes available to the poor, the program will be unsuccessful.

Within a number of target areas, small community centers are to be set up in which community action will be mobilized. "The staff will enlist the cooperation of institutions and facilities in the surrounding neighborhood: the churches, union halls, lodges and fraternal organizations, the schools. Even vacant store fronts should be pressed into service. It is into these locations, where the local population feels at home, that the programs should flow."

Community action will focus on six types of programs. Job-related adult education is one of these, but it is not a priority program, and the details of its implementation are not spelled out. However, job training could be tied in with a priority item, such as the community school concept. This program, worked out in the Great Cities Project in Detroit, is based on the idea of relating the schools in poor neighborhoods to the total community, and includes the provision that school buildings will "be kept open in the evenings for programs which range from unstructured meetings to short term courses and recreational activities." Job training for young adults between the ages of sixteen and twenty-one will take place in residential centers so that they can "participate in organized educational and training programs while living in a supportive environment."

In approaching unemployment, TAP's goal is to "prepare low income people for the world of work, this includes literacy, academic and vocational training and, where necessary, helping people overcome the psychological blocks which inhibit or prevent them from taking advantage of training and/or job resources." All of this is important and essential, but the only specific recommendation for immediate adult training is designed to produce various types of assistants to work in the target projects. Very few detailed, immediate projects in the area of adult job-training programs are specified—however, there is a long-term commitment in this field. TAP does propose that a job-opportunity inventory be started and maintained in order to provide "a more efficient system of matching jobs, training and people."

TAP learned much from the successes and failures of other attempts at fighting poverty: its use of a community center in the area where the disadvantaged live as the focus of activities; its recognition that such people need, and should plan, their own special programs and services of many different kinds; its desire to train those who live in the community and suffer from its endemic hardships to work with their fellow residents; and its awareness of the need to coordinate activities and its willingness to bring all interested organizations, such as schools and churches, together—all of these are major steps in the right direction.

And yet, perhaps because of the immensity of its task, if it does not take certain additional steps, the Total Action Against Poverty may in fact become only a Partial Action Against Poverty.

It is hard, for example, to discover exactly what TAP will do to help unemployed adults to gain the job skills now needed to secure employment. This vagueness in goals is partly intentional, since the TAP planners argue that the specific programs should be developed by the poor themselves. But some aspects are spelled out specifically, while others are not. TAP's community centers "may provide space for training sessions and meetings." There may be some training as a by-product of Great Cities School. There will be training for the sixteen- to twenty-one-year-olds. And although TAP's long-term goals include adult education for jobs, only the training of workers for community centers or community-related projects (such as day-care centers or neighborhood conservation projects) is specified in the priority section where this training is discussed, and even there the emphasis is on the sixteen- to twenty-one-year-old group.

TAP may eventually reach the unemployed worker who is over twenty-one, but it appears that this may take a long while—a serious shortcoming for many reasons. The first is that it obviously condemns a part of the population to poverty and joblessness through lack of training. True, various community services, such as medical and mental health programs, will be made available to members of this group. But their main problem is not that they are sick; it is that they are unskilled and unemployed.

Second, some of the projects given priority would achieve more rapid and lasting success if they were coordinated with an adult job-training program. Let us, for example, examine

TAP's programs for education, a priority item. It suggests a host of worthwhile activities that will enrich the life of the children, including the community school concept, where the goal is to get the parent interested and involved in school activities so that he will help his child improve in school work. But, as we mentioned earlier, a deeper involvement would result from effective adult job training and placement taking place within the school, for, as one educator put it, "a father who feels defeated by the world is not in a good position to give his son a sense of optimism and a feeling that he can achieve anything himself." [8]

Under the Economic Opportunity Act of 1964, a community action program is eligible for grants if it:

> (*a*) mobilizes and utilizes resources, public or private . . . in an attack on poverty; (*b*) provides services, assistance, and other activities of sufficient scope and size to give promise of progress toward elimination of poverty or a cause or causes of poverty . . . ; (*c*) is developed, conducted, and administered with the maximum feasible participation of residents of the areas . . . ; (*d*) is conducted, administered, or coordinated by a public or non-profit private agency, or combination thereof.[9]

Though the Federal aid Detroit seeks (as do other cities) will be most helpful to its program, much of what is proposed in TAP is possible without Federal assistance. A community that wants to provide the adult Negro with a second chance can develop a program by itself.[10]

Such a program should include the following elements: (*1*) the civic leadership committed to job-training activities as part of a coordinated program; (*2*) the Negro community involved in planning, execution, and administration; (*3*) the school system active in developing the job-training courses; (*4*) business firms and unions using their influence in support of such programs, and helping to insure placements; (*5*) educators both in the public schools and in the universities conducting research on how to educate the adult poor most effectively; (*6*) adult students receiving financial assistance or being able to work part-time; (7) the skills taught being usable on more than one job so that the trainee can be more flexible in his job search; and (*8*) the community developing a growing economy to provide jobs for the trainees.

The community must of course recognize that its activities alone may not be able to solve the problem of securing enough jobs for its residents, since national policies and activities elsewhere will affect the local job market. Still, such a community program might break the vicious cycle that poor education has imposed upon the Negro by stunting his skills both as a child and as an adult. To some, this may indeed appear to be the "dull side" of the Civil Rights Revolution; it can, however, be its most exciting and rewarding side.

NOTES

1. The authors would like to thank Daniel H. Kruger, Michael Borus, and Janet West of Michigan State University and Peter E. Siegle of the Center for the Study of Liberal Education for Adults for their cooperation in this study.
2. United Community Services of Metropolitan Detroit, *Adult Education,* March 1960, pp. 24, 26, and *passim.*
3. "Trade Union Leadership Council: Experiment in Community Action." Reprinted by TULC from *New University Thought,* September-October 1963.
4. *TULC Youth and Educational Center,* undated pamphlet.
5. *Wall Street Journal,* August 4, 1964, p. 1.
6. U.S. Department of Health, Education and Welfare, *Training the Hard-Core Unemployed,* Cooperative Research Monograph No. 13 (Washington: U.S. Government Printing Office, 1964), pp. 19, 69.
7. See *Total Action Against Poverty,* Proposed Community Action Program for Detroit, Michigan (Detroit, June 1964). All quotations concerning TAP come from this booklet.
8. Jean D. Gambs, "The Self-Concept: Basis for Re-Education of

Negro Youth," in William C. Kvaraceus, ed., *Negro Self-Concept: Implications for School and Citizenship* (Medford, Mass.: Tufts Univ. Press, 1964), p. 15.

9. Deborah P. Wolfe, "Section B: What the Economic Opportunity Act Means to the Negro," *The Journal of Negro Education,* XXXIV (Winter 1965), 90.
10. This study was completed late in 1964 and does not report on the many events that have taken place in Detroit and elsewhere since that date—particularly as a result of the impetus of the passage of the Economic Opportunity Act.

VII

Discrimination and the Law

18 / The Law and Racial Discrimination in Employment

Sanford Jay Rosen[1]

Employment discrimination is a major factor contributing to the disadvantaged economic and social status of Negroes in America. The purpose of this chapter is to review the legal responses to employment discrimination and to indicate the scope and character of remedial techniques presently or potentially available.

As a background to consideration of the role of law in this area, the initial section briefly outlines the major modes of employment discrimination. Next, consideration is given to the primary constitutional foundations for legal responses and to the Civil Rights Act of 1964, which promises to make its impact felt throughout this realm of the law. At each subsequent stage in the study, in fact, the question will be asked, "What bearing has the Civil Rights Act on this legal remedy?" Examination is then made of the judicially enforced duty of fair representation—its origins, development, weaknesses, and potentials. Theories of "state action," and the utility of full-blown constitutional approaches, are then detailed. Next, consideration is given to potential legal support for union and employer activities designed to eliminate internal discrimination, and to legal responses to the direct-action techniques of the civil rights movement. Judicial enforcement of the orders of Fair Employment Practices Commissions (FEPC), Federal, state and local, is then examined, and inquiry made into the appropriate interplay between judicial and administrative activity in this field. A canvass is then made of the antidiscrimination techniques that may be available to, and are now being used by, the National Labor Relations Board (NLRB). Finally, the conclusion attempts to comment broadly on what may be expected in the way of future development.

□ Modes of Employment Discrimination

Initially, discrimination may follow forms or practices developed by employers who may, for example, fail or refuse to hire Negroes. Even when Negroes find employment, they are often more subject to layoff than whites; they are likely to be relegated to, and frozen in, so-called "Negro jobs," *i.e.*, the physically difficult, poorest paid, and most unpleasant positions in the shop, such unskilled or semi-skilled jobs as those involving custodial and maintenance work; particularly in the South, they may be paid at lower scales than white workers for equivalent work or consistently receive less favorable work assignments than white workers in equivalent positions.

Employment agencies, both public and private, often abet employer practices of discrimination by accepting and filling orders on a "white only" basis, by referring applicants differently according to race, or even by entirely refusing to cater to Negro job applicants.

Discrimination is also often enhanced, extended, or even required by labor unions with whom employers must generally share control over workers' conditions of employment. There are four basic ways in which labor unions limit Negro and nonwhite access to jobs and exercise general discriminatory control over work conditions. First, there are various ways in which union membership, and therefore effective representation, is denied to Negroes. Second, some unions have segregated Negroes into separate or auxiliary local unions. Third, craft unions often restrict Negro entrance into apprenticeship training programs. Finally, unions may engage in discrimination when negotiating and administering collective bargaining agreements.

In the past, exclusion of Negroes from membership was often achieved pursuant to "Caucasians only" clauses in union constitutions. Today, discriminatory exclusion is rarely an admitted union policy, but it is still practiced. In some skilled trades, where Negroes have been traditionally excluded from membership, priority in admission is still given to sons or close relatives of present members, all of whom are white. Some unions also exercise discriminatory control by means of skills admissions tests administered by them, particularly in implementing permissible closed shop arrangements. Negroes excluded from the union are often entirely excluded from the industry, or they are denied equal opportunities within the industry, and they have no hand in the determination of their conditions of labor.

A decreasing number of unions maintain segregated locals. Notoriously, this practice leads to the formation of ghettos in employment, and is exceedingly disadvantageous to the Negro worker. In the craft union context, Negroes are often restricted to poorer locations and their jobs are subject to jurisdictional raids by white locals. In the industrial union context, the Negro local is often prejudicially excluded from playing an effective role in negotiating and administering collective bargaining agreements.

Apprenticeship training is a significant means of entrance into many skilled trades. Training programs are often supported and supervised by government agencies, and they are theoretically subject to joint union-management control. However, unions, particularly craft unions, are often able to exercise veto-like control over admissions, thereby excluding Negroes who are vastly underrepresented in such programs.

Industrial unions do not often exclude Negroes from membership, and they normally do not have control over the hiring and apprenticeship processes, but they do have significant leverage over employment conditions in that they negotiate and enforce collective agreements with seniority provisions controlling layoffs, recall rights, promotional opportunities, and other interests of the workers. When Negroes are placed in segregated departments and promotional sequences, they can be effectively imprisoned in the unskilled and menial jobs.

There are, of course, variations on and some additions to the major modes of employment discrimination; there is, in fact, a full continuum of devices that may be used separately or in combination by discriminating agencies. As it may bear upon employment, discrimination can range in impact from the quiet indignity of separate toilet facilities to the total trauma of job exclusion; it can range in subtlety from the making of tacit agreements controlling both access to employment and working conditions to the providing of facilities and good offices to the local Ku Klux Klan and White Citizens' Council. Legal responses may therefore appear to be uneven, for they will tend to depend in part upon the nature of the interest to be protected, the subtlety of discrimination and the ability with which it may, according to the techniques of law, be brought into the light.

□ The Civil Rights Act of 1964: The New Point for Departure

At common law, employers and trade unions, considered to be private and voluntary bodies, were free to discriminate against and generally deal with workers as they chose. The last few decades, however, have witnessed the advent of far-reaching statutes, based on Congress's constitutional power over interstate commerce and the police power of the states, which extensively regulate employer-employee and internal union relations.[2] In an earlier period, moreover, amendments were added to the Federal Constitution that ultimately had the effect of modifying or even superseding the common law at least so far as racial discrimination is concerned. The first such amendment was the Thirteenth, which prohibits slavery and involuntary servitude. This basic prohibition actually has had little direct bearing on the specific legal responses to the subtle, multifaceted and variant problems of employment discrimination other than to the extent that it has promoted a general climate of constitutional law and policy. In the past, formulation and development of legal responses to employment discrimination has been colored primarily by the existence of the Fourteenth Amendment and its "equal protection" clause. By itself, and as related back into the "due process" clause of the Fifth Amendment, this clause prohibits government-executed, -sponsored or -supported racial discrimination.

The coloration of the Fourteenth Amendment will, of course, continue in the future, but it will be supplemented and rivaled now by the existence of the Civil Rights Act of 1964, which statutorily carries forward the philosophy of the Civil War Amendments.[3] Two titles of the new Federal act have direct relevance in the area of employment discrimination. First, Title VI, which is based upon Congress's power to choose when and how it will disburse funds, provides machinery to assure that Federal funds will not be used to support racially discriminatory practices.[4] It is expressly provided, however, that the machinery for cutting off Federal benefits is not to be used against employment discrimination "except where a primary objective of the Federal financial assistance is to provide employment." The portion of the Civil Rights Act most significant as an immediate and direct legal response to employment discrimination is, consequently, Title VII.[5] This title, which is based upon Congress's plenary power over interstate commerce, establishes elaborate Federal administrative and judicial machinery to enforce statutory equal employment opportunity requirements.

Title VII is to go into full effect in stages over five years. Ultimately, employers of twenty-five or more employees are to be prohibited from discriminating or segregating in employment or hiring practices; labor unions operating hiring halls or having twenty-five or more members will not be permitted to discriminate or segregate in membership or representation; employers, labor unions, and joint labor-management committees will be prohibited from discriminating in apprenticeship or other training programs; and employment agencies will not be permitted to discriminate in classification of applicants and in job referrals. There are several important qualifications that clarify the scope of the prohibitions. Bona fide seniority or merit systems, and systems by which employment conditions are differentiated from locale to locale, are not abrogated by the statute. In addition, professionally developed ability tests are permissible means, under the statute, by which to make differentiations. Finally, a provision states that the title is *not* to be interpreted to require that an employer hire, or an employment agency refer, or a labor union accept for membership, quotas of employees from particular minority groups.

The enforcement machinery under Title VII constitutes a mixture of various components: Federal and state, administrative and judicial. Provision is made for a five-man bipartisan Equal Employment Opportunity Commission, the function of which is to administer the provisions of the title, investigate "unlawful employment charges," and attempt to resolve disputes through "informal methods of conference, conciliation, and persuasion." The commission is to take such action when it finds "reasonable cause to believe that the charge is true."

When coercive enforcement of the title is required, however, the commission plays only a subsidiary role. It is not empowered to adjudicate unlawful employment practice charges or to issue binding orders, and it cannot bring suit to enforce the provisions of the title. Generally, only persons filing charges with the commission or, if a charge was filed by a commissioner, only persons said in the charge to be aggrieved by the alleged unlawful employment practice, may bring civil action in the appropriate Federal district court.

Although the brunt of enforcement initiative is thus thrown upon private parties, the available remedies are otherwise flexible. The courts are empowered to grant such affirmative relief as may be appropriate, and the enforcement burden on the individual is eased somewhat in that further provision is made for public assistance. In the first place, the trial court is empowered, upon application of the claimant, to appoint counsel for him and "may authorize the commencement of the action without the payment of fees, costs, or security. [In addition] Upon timely application, the court may, in its discretion, permit the Attorney General to intervene in such civil action if he certifies that the case is of general public importance." Moreover, although the Attorney General is not empowered to bring court action on individual complaints, he may bring civil suit when he "has reasonable cause to believe that any person or group of persons is engaged in a pattern or practice of resistance to the full enjoyment of any of the rights secured by this title, and that the pattern or practice is of such a nature and is intended to deny the full exercise of the rights" described in the title. Finally, while the commission is not initially permitted to bring suit in its own right to remedy an unlawful employment practice, it may recommend to the Attorney General that he intervene in a claimant's civil action or that he bring an action under the "pattern or practice" provision. The commission is also empowered to "commence proceedings to compel compliance with" court orders issued in civil actions brought by individuals.

On the face of it, the title appears to say that individuals cannot invoke court action without first proceeding before the Equal Employment Opportunity Commission. There is, however, some legislative history to the effect that "the individual may proceed in his own right at any time. He may take his complaint to the Commission, he may bypass the Commission, or he may go directly to court." [6] It is clear, on the other hand, that resort cannot be made to the Federal Commission's processes until an opportunity has been given for available state remedies to be exhausted.[7] In addition, in any judicial proceeding brought by an individual "upon request, the court may, in its discretion, stay further proceedings for not more than sixty days pending the termination of State or local proceedings . . . or the efforts of the Commission to obtain voluntary compliance."

Because of the recent advent of the Civil Rights Act, particularly of Title VII, it might mistakenly be assumed that future development of legal responses will be all but preempted by this specific congressional program. But, even after 1969, when Title VII goes into full effect, its coverage will not encompass the nation's many small commercial operations involving companies with twenty-five or fewer employees or labor unions with twenty-five or fewer members. Furthermore, there will undoubtedly be other circumstances, not covered by or contemplated in Title VII, in which the law will be called upon to confront problems in the area of employment discrimination. In addition, Title VII explicitly reserves to aggrieved individuals the right to resort to any remedy existing under state law, and it is likely that other Federal remedies will not be preempted or entirely supplanted by it.[8] It is clear, on the other hand, that civil rights organizations that have a great deal to do with the promotion or sponsorship of legal challenges to employment discrimination do not intend to give up resort to other potential Federal remedies willingly.[9]

For a complete understanding of the proper context for effective operation of the new FEPC apparatus, it is appropriate and relevant to study other possible alternative or supplemental legal devices that may be available to assist the racially discriminated worker. In undertaking this study, however, it will be important always to keep before us the fact of the new Civil Rights Act's existence and the specific content of its provisions. Its potential bearing on the future form of other lawful antidiscrimination tools cannot be overly stressed. At one extreme, courts and other adjudicative agencies might be discouraged from experimenting with new and additional legal responses, and some of its provisions may make it exceedingly difficult to secure legal support for particular programs that are designed to remedy and redress racial discrimination. On the other hand, when attempts are made to use administrative and judicial institutions affirmatively, in requesting more far-reaching assaults on discrimination and, more passively, in requesting official sanction or legitimization for more extensive direct-action programs, the possibility that strength can be drawn from its specific provisions and from its spirit will be continuously worth considering. It will, in essence, be useful to promote the view that this statute, which has been called the "most important legislation enacted in recent decades" and "one of the half dozen most important laws . . . enacted in the last century," [10] contains in its spirit and principle a kind of general amendment of the entire body of American law.

□ The Judicially Enforced Duty of Fair Representation[11]

The first major judicial response to employment discrimination came with the Supreme Court's announcement, in *Steele vs. Louisville & N.R.R.*, 323 U.S. 192 (1944) of the duty of fair representation. At issue in the case was the power of a union, the Brotherhood of Locomotive Firemen and Enginemen, to negotiate with employers a collective agreement that had as its conspicuous purpose and consequence first the limitation and then the destruction of the employment opportunities of the Negroes it represented. To avoid the question of whether a union, certified by the government as an exclusive bargaining representative, could constitutionally discriminate, the Court discovered and announced a statutory duty of fair representation, holding that:

> . . . the Railway Labor Act imposes upon the statutory representative of a craft at least as exacting a duty to protect equally the interests of the members of the craft as the Constitution imposes upon a legislature to give equal protection to the interests of those for whom it legislates. Congress has seen fit to clothe the bargaining

representative with powers comparable to those possessed by a legislative body both to create and restrict the rights of those whom it represents . . . but it has also imposed on the representative a corresponding duty . . . to exercise fairly the power conferred upon it in behalf of all those for whom it acts, without hostile discrimination against them.[12]

From the very first it was clear that suits for damages and injunctive relief would lie to enforce the duty, and that companies that were parties to union discrimination could be joined as defendants. As initially formulated, however, the duty only covered workers subject to the Railway Labor Act; racial discrimination was prohibited only in the negotiation and drafting of formal collective bargaining agreements; and protection was available only against unions actually representing the plaintiffs. By the time the Civil Rights Act of 1964 was passed, the duty had been greatly extended. Workers subject to the National Labor Relations Act (NLRA) were also protected. The duty had to be met not only when the collective agreement was negotiated and written but also when it was administered in the grievance process. And a union was also prohibited from making agreements that discriminatorily invaded the employment rights of workers that it did not actually represent.

Although the fair representation duty has been put to some fruitful use in particular cases, its total impact on employment discrimination has been minimized as a result of weaknesses inherent in its judicial character and limitations of its scope.[13]

The basic weaknesses of the judicially nurtured and enforced duty are interrelated. First, courts are essentially neutral agencies that do not customarily engage in prosecutional activities; they merely adjudicate claims that are brought before them on a case-by-case basis. Such adjudications are exceedingly time consuming, for extensive inquiry into the facts is necessary, and there are endless procedural ways in which proceedings can be lengthened. Moreover, attempted suits may fail without decision on the merits, for it is within the power of unfriendly judges to impose procedural and technical impediments. Second, there is no government apparatus to prosecute fair representation claims in the courts; consequently, there is no centralized enforcement of the duty. Third, lacking government prosecution, the individual Negro worker and such civil rights or other organizations as are willing to support him bear the burden of initiating and prosecuting claims and stand the risk of paying for enforcement. Because these adjudications are expensive, time consuming and precarious, suit is undertaken only by the most outraged of individuals and only in critical circumstances.[14]

As presently refined, the judicially enforced duty of fair representation is subject to four major limitations. First, the duty is imposed only on unions. An employer is subject to legal sanction only if he is involved with a union in discriminatory action. When there is no union functioning or seeking to function as collective bargaining agent, as is often the case in the South, or when employers discriminate unilaterally, workers are not protected.

Second, even when unions are present, it does not appear that they are obliged to resist employer discrimination or to make reasonable efforts to overcome the effects of past discrimination.

Third, since only invidious discrimination, *i.e.* discrimination not based on relevant differences, is prohibited, it has generally been held that a plaintiff must prove that the defendants were, in fact, motivated by race in drawing a challenged distinction. Situations often arise, however, in which the union and the employer are able to argue that distinctions were based upon other valid criteria. In such circumstances, most courts have required that the plaintiff prove that these criteria were a pretext. Under these conditions, it is exceedingly difficult to reach and remedy the more subtle discriminatory devices. In addition, although job applicants appear to be protected by the duty, difficulties of proof limit its usefulness almost exclusively to the protection of persons already employed. Two recent decisions, however, indicate a new judicial tendency toward requiring union and employer to bear the burden of demonstrating that their allegedly legitimate reasons for discriminating were, in fact, the criteria that motivated them. It is also possible that the courts could adopt a salutary rule that upon a *prima facie* demonstration of racial discrimination or of circumstances that give rise to a strong inference of such discrimination, *e.g.* in the absence or extreme underrepresentation of Negro employees or union members, the burden of proof permanently shifts and union and employer must not only go forward with the proof, but must also bear the burden of persuasion.

Fourth, probably because of the clear congressional purpose not to "impair the right of a labor organization to prescribe its own rules with respect to the acquisition or retention of membership therein," the courts have been loath to extend the statutory duty of fair representation to proscribe racial exclusion from union membership.[15] But, unless Negroes are guaranteed equality of opportunity to become union members, there can be no such thing as fair representation, if this is to mean representation that is not differentiated according to race.[16] Union decisional processes are political; the offices and bureaucrats respond to votes and to other political stimuli. It cannot be expected that Negroes, excluded from membership and participation in the union, will be represented equally with whites who are members and who are therefore able to participate. And, not only does exclusion adversely affect conditions of employment for Negroes, but it also renders them incapable of sharing in fringe benefits that are available within the union, *e.g.* death benefits, legal services and advice, and group insurance programs, and further augments their "badges of inferiority." Requirement of nondiscrimination in union membership policies will not be a full solution to union racial discrimination or apathy, but once in the union the Negro at least begins to have a fighting chance. His vote can be counted! He is also in a better position to apply to superior union councils for responsible action against discrimination by his local union, and he may also be able to obtain judicial and administrative protection, under the Labor-Management Reporting and Disclosure Act of 1959, for his political rights within the union.

Were it not for the fact that the new membership requirements of Title VII of the Civil Rights Act probably renders it unnecessary, it is highly likely that the Supreme Court, to avoid a constitutional determination, would have found it necessary to extend the duty of fair representation to include nondiscrimination in union membership. The Court may yet have to face the issue, for Title VII does not go into full effect until 1969, and even then it does not purport to cover all unions. Furthermore, the NAACP intends, in the meantime, to press the issue in the courts,[17] while the National Labor Relations Board has held that it cannot constitutionally assist unions that exclude Negroes in becoming or remaining statutory collective bargaining agents.

Despite these developments, all that can now safely be said about the vitality and probable form of the judicially enforced duty of fair representation is that prediction is made difficult by the advent of Title VII. Once the title becomes viable, it is not clear that anyone challenging alleged discrimination will want to employ the cumbersome judicial procedures and vague rules of the Steele case and its progeny. Certain significant advantages accrue under Title VII; unilateral discrimination by employers can be remedied, the courts are expressly invited to relieve plantiffs of prosecutional expenses, and provision is made for government support of private litigation. If fair representation actions are brought, there may nevertheless be a tendency on the part of courts, because of the legal climate created by the Civil Rights Act, to give wider scope and more effective protection under the Steele doctrine, but the result may be just the opposite. The courts may be reluctant to provide remedies under this doctrine precisely because more specifically tailored remedies are available under the Civil Rights Act, which also offers courts the opportunity of avoiding decision by requiring exhaustion of available state remedies and possibly, as well, invocation of Federal administrative proceedings. It is not too much to hope, on the other hand, that in conducting judicial proceedings under Title VII the courts will import whatever good can be found in the orthodox fair representation cases while also avoiding their unfortunate pitfalls.

There is one way in which the policy of fair representation may be judicially refined to complement the new Title VII remedies. The Supreme Court has recently held that individual workers who allege that they have not been given their due under a collective bargaining agreement have a Federal right to sue for breach of the agreement and of the duty of fair representation.[18] Possibly recognizing a more satisfactory approach to such problems than external judicial review, the Court further indicated that interested individuals might have a right to intervene and participate in grievance and arbitration proceedings whereby collective agreements are administered and the individual's rights under them are determined. Other high tribunals, moreover, have held not only that individuals possess the right to intervene and participate, but that they may also invoke the grievance and arbitral processes if their collective bargaining agents refuse to do so. There is no reason why an individual who is aggrieved because of alleged racial discrimination in the the administration of a collective agreement should not be able to avail himself of such judicial or internal actions. Furthermore, the growing practice of incorporating nondiscrimination clauses into collective agreements and the demonstrated willingness of arbitrators to enforce such clauses augurs well for the usefulness, in the racial context, of techniques of individual participation in the internal administrative processes of collective bargaining.[19]

□ The Constitution, State Action, and Employment Discrimination

Arguments that employment discrimination violates the Constitution are primarily based on the equal protection clause of the Fourteenth Amendment, which provides that "No State shall . . . deny to any person within its jurisdiction the equal protection of the laws." [20] As interpreted in the controlling decisions of the Supreme Court, only discriminatory governmental or "state action" is prohibited.[21] But the state need not directly undertake discriminatory action for such to be "state action" in the constitutional sense. State requirement, involvement, sanction or ratification, support or enforcement, has been held sufficient to convert otherwise private discrimination into that of the state. Furthermore, private agencies performing the functions of the state have been held to fall within the prohibitory edicts of the Constitution, as have private agencies that appear for all intents and purposes to be the state.

Using the various state action concepts that have been refined so far by the Supreme Court, it is possible to argue that in many circumstances ostensibly private employment discrimination violates the Constitution. Labor unions, sanctioned, supported, and protected by government in their collective bargaining capacities might generally be held subject to constitutional standards.[22] Employers who fill government contracts or who perform government projects are arguably performing government functions. Government can be said to be involved in otherwise private action when it subsidizes, supports, and supervises employment training programs or employment agencies or employers. Going beyond the doctrines thus far refined in court decisions, it can be argued that general permission, license, or regulation by government is sufficient government action or involvement to warrant the imposition of constitutional requirements. Such a position, or even a more extended one, might be justified by the fact that, in our contemporary mass society, the power exercised by labor unions and corporate and other employers, and indeed by many other such "voluntary private associations," is very like the political power of government, insofar as the exercise of such associational power greatly affects important interests of the subject individuals.[23] Starting from such a view of organizations and society, it has been recommended that significant private centers of power, as petite governments, should be subjected to constitutional requirements that protect individual rights.[24]

No Supreme Court decision has yet held that a union or an employer is constitutionally required not to discriminate. The Steele doctrine, however, was formulated in recognition that the favored statutory status of labor unions might be sufficient to constitute their collective bargaining conduct as government action. And, Justice Murphy, concurring in the Steele case, did reach the constitutional issue and would have held that labor unions were prohibited from discriminating in membership. A similar holding was actually made by the Supreme Court of Kansas in 1946. And the California Supreme Court also held that, in the light of constitutional implications, it was unlawful for a racially closed union to be tied to a union shop. There have, in addition, been a number of very recent decisions applying constitutional standards to employment discrimination. The NLRB has held that, under the Constitution, it cannot continue the certification as a statutory bargaining agent of a union that discriminates in membership. A Federal appellate court has held that the rule of *Brown vs. Board of Education,* 347 U.S. 483 (1954), prohibiting segregation in public schools, is fully applicable to vocational and technical schools. A Federal district court has held that an apprenticeship training program, operated by union and management but supported, regulated and supervised by state and Federal government agencies and specifically called upon to supply apprentices to work on the construction of a United States courthouse and office building, was subject to constitutional requirements of nondiscrimination. Finally, a state court in New York held that a union's filial preference system in its apprenticeship program rendered it impossible for Negroes to gain admission and consequently violated both the state fair employment law and the Fourteenth Amendment.

Even with the passage of the Civil Rights Act of 1964, it can be expected, for a number of reasons, that attempts will continue to be made to establish constitutional prohibitions against employment discrimination. First, impatience with other antidiscrimination machinery is likely to give birth to renewed attempts to apply the standard doctrines, and to breed pressure to seek court acceptance and application of the more far-reaching concepts of state action. Second, constitutional argument is also likely to remain tempting, for there is at least a psychological advantage to be gained by having an antidiscrimination program that is founded directly on constitutional or fundamental, rather than mere statutory, requirement. Third, under a full-blown constitutional approach it might be contended, with enhanced hope of general success, that unions and employers must affirmatively resist discrimination by other parties. Fourth, it might also be pressed that the Constitution imposes an affirmative obligation to overcome and compensate for the effects of past discriminatory practices—for example, that there would be an obligation not only to abolish dual seniority lists but also to prepare and train Negroes so that they could bid on the better jobs to which their accrued seniority would entitle them.[25] Finally, even in cases in which constitutional theories are not adopted, they might have ancillary usefulness. Courts faced with well-constructed constitutional arguments that they would prefer not to resolve are often capable of finding other ways to give the plaintiff what he seeks. The Steele doctrine, for example, was formulated in part to avoid constitutional decision, as was undoubtedly the Supreme Court's decision that Title II of the Civil Rights Act interdicted state prosecutions of participants in peaceful sit-in demonstrations (*Hamm vs. City of Rock Hill,* 379 U.S. 306 [1964]).

Although initially tempting, constitutional arguments are likely to prove to be ill-suited to the task of remedying employment discrimination, particularly as the more crass forms of discrimination fall by the wayside, and it becomes more clear that problems of employment discrimination are very much tied to broader problems of automation, underemployment, and unemployment.[26] If justifiable and fruitful use are to be made of constitutional arguments, it is acutely necessary that the arguments be exceedingly well constructed and that the possible consequences of both victory and defeat be carefully considered. The prospect that a constitutional argument might be held to be invalid increases in a number of circumstances: when progressively subtle discrimination is challenged, when very advanced theories of state action are prompted, and when the Constitution is used more as an offensive weapon (for example, to require special compensatory treatment of Negroes) than as a defense against continued active discrimination. Other than loss of the particular case or point, which may itself be significant, the most important consequence of losing a constitutional argument is that it may appear that more has been lost than in fact was. At its extreme, the danger is that it will appear to many that the end sought to be achieved by the rejected constitutional argument is itself prohibited by the Constitution—consequently, lower level political and legal attempts to achieve the desired end will become more difficult.

Even a successful constitutional argument may not be an unmixed blessing. The proponent of such an argument, particularly one that is premised on an expansive view of state action, might find that he has won more than he bargained for or even desired. A victory might result in the wholesale introduction of constitutional standards and guarantees into union and employer activity. And, while it might be appropriate for courts to impose a constitutional prohibition against racial discrimination on an organization generally thought to be in the private sector, it does not necessarily follow that it would be wise for them to hold such organizations subject to such constitutional standards as religious freedom, free speech, and fair trial.[27] Although it might be possible to limit constitutional penetration to prohibition of racial discrimination and attendant improprieties, it is likely that the courts would prefer not to face the problem at all. Before the passage of the Civil Rights Act, the courts, because of social necessity, may have been comparatively willing to take the risks involved in applying and extending the doctrine of state action, but with the availability of statutory remedies, and the consequent decrease in necessity, the court will most likely avoid the constitutional issues whenever possible.[28]

☐ Self-Help and the Law

Basically there are two kinds of self-help activities, directed toward remedy of employment discrimination, that warrant consideration here: first, there is self-corrective action undertaken by agencies of employment that formerly discriminated, particularly unions and employers; second, there is self-help or direct action, as resorted to by representatives and allies of the class that has been subjected to discrimination.

Legal Protection for Good-Faith Union Antidiscrimination Activities

Initially, it might appear that the most fruitful place to look for union action would be in the AFL-CIO. Good work can certainly be accomplished by the federation, but it is generally work of an educational, persuasive, or conciliatory nature. Although the AFL-CIO has a functioning civil rights apparatus, it unfortunately has no real coercive power by which to force its will upon constituent international members that engage in or tolerate racial discrimination.

Actually, it is in the international and national unions that the best potential for legally supported remedial activity can be found. Although the local union is generally the seedbed of racial discrimination, the international is "more conspicuous and it is relatively easy to bring moral pressure to bear on it." [29] And, unlike the AFL-CIO, when moved to act the international is not limited to education and persuasion; it can apply broad control powers over members and locals. For example, it is within the power of an international union to certify and decertify local unions; place locals under trusteeship; merge locals; discipline local officers; discipline local members, who are automatically members of the international; and adjudicate appeals of local disciplinary action. Such international action must conform to the requirements of the union constitution and to such state law as regulates internal union relations and discipline.[30] International action must also be in accord with the Federal Government's Labor Management Reporting and Disclosure Act, the provisions of which constitute a bill of substantive and procedural rights for union members and govern the imposition of trusteeships and the conduct of elections.

Before the passage of the Civil Rights Act of 1964, many international unions established civil rights machinery and forceful steps were taken by some unions to eliminate or oppose local discrimination.[31] For example, trusteeships have been imposed to eliminate discrimination, segregated locals have been merged to create biracial locals, and the charters of segregated locals have been revoked and reissued to new integrated ones. Now that the Civil Rights Act imposes statutory requirements of nondiscrimination on unions, it is to be expected that there will be a sharp increase in self-corrective activities. It is also likely that courts and administrative agencies will hold that in many circumstances good-faith implementation of antidiscrimination policies constitutes proper grounds for an international to invoke discipline, place a local under trusteeship, set aside a local election or perhaps even disqualify a candidate.

The United States Labor Department has already indicated its willingness to ratify antidiscrimination action by an international. Thus far the question has arisen only in relation to the Department's enforcement of Title III of the Labor Management Reporting and Disclosure Act, which governs the imposition and conduct of trusteeships. In the one case in which a ruling was required, the Department declined to find that there was probable cause to believe a violation of Title III resulted when a trusteeship was imposed to eliminate segregation in the facilities of a local union hall.

Two court decisions subsequent to the passage of the Civil Rights Act indicate that there is likely to be a judicial willingness to sanction good faith attempts to end discrimination, and to assure that alleged antidiscrimination steps do not in fact exacerbate the effects of the old discriminations. Both cases involved actions brought to forestall attempts by international unions to achieve ostensibly antidiscriminatory ends by merging formerly segregated locals.

In the first of these cases, merger was opposed by the white local. The case involved an attempt by the American Federation of Musicians to merge Chicago Local 208, a Negro local having approximately 1100 members, with Chicago Local 10, a white local having approximately 12,000 members. Local 10 had originally recommended merger, but voluntary negotiations over the arrangements had broken down. The International Executive Board then recommended a merger guaranteeing to the members of Local 208 the exclusive right, over a period of six years, to elect certain officers in the merged local. The membership of Local 10 rejected the proposal, and when the international attempted to place the local under trusteeship, suit was brought in Federal district court. After a hearing, preliminary and permanent injunctions were denied, for the court held that the local and its members had failed to exhaust available internal union remedies. The court, however, also went on to approve the purpose of the trusteeship and merger plan. It stated that no provision of the Labor Management Reporting and Disclosure Act had been violated, and it declared that, despite the temporary establishment of different racial classes, since the purpose of the plan conformed to that of Title VII of the Civil Rights Act, the title would not have been breached had it been in effect.

The second merger case involved the Tobacco Workers' International Union. Local 208, a Negro local in Durham, North Carolina, brought suit in Federal district court against the international, alleging a violation of Title III of the Labor Management Reporting and Disclosure Act. Local 208 opposed the international's action in taking control of the local and transferring its membership to the previously all-white Local 176. Upon transfer into Local 176, all former members of Local 208 were to be placed behind the members of Local

176 for seniority and other purposes, regardless of whether their accrued seniority was actually greater than that of any or all of Local 176's members. Local 208, attempting to challenge the merger plan before the NLRB and the President's Committee on Equal Employment Opportunity, sought to continue the *status quo* pending such proceedings. To assure proper adjudication of the claim, the district court enjoined the international from imposing a trusteeship on the plaintiff local or revoking its charter or depriving it or its members of any lawful rights until the NLRB takes jurisdiction.

Examination of the few inconclusive or incomplete court and administrative actions does not yet reveal a clear pattern of legal response to union self-help actions. Sufficient data should appear in the next few years so that observers will be able to ascertain the extent to which the law will permit unions a free hand in cleaning house. It is likely that unions will be allowed broad discretion in devising means of voluntary compliance, and more, with national and state antidiscrimination law. While this response would be useful, it is axiomatic that governmental agencies should not permit or ratify programs that give the appearance of progress without assuring real protection for Negroes, particularly for rights that may already have accrued even within systems of segregation.

Legal Support for Stockholder Activities to Compel or Promote Nondiscriminatory Employment Practices by Corporate Employers[32]

Acting on their own initiatives, a number of employers have adopted rather advanced positions in seeking to eliminate employment discrimination; some, in fact, have gone so far as to endorse and carry out concepts of compensatory justice by actively recruiting and cultivating Negroes as employees, even to the extent of favoring them over whites with substantially equivalent qualifications. Employer actions to eliminate racial discrimination do not raise the legal problems brought about by similar activities of labor unions. Unlike the case of labor unions, there is no legal provision for direct supervision of the internal means by which high-level corporate officials choose to exercise control over the functional components of their corporations, the lower levels of management, or the corporate bureaucracy in general, in order to assure fulfillment of fair employment policies. Legislative, judicial, and administrative rulings prohibiting employment discrimination can, of course, be expected to promote a general legal atmosphere that may further induce management to eliminate racial discrimination. However, the law has direct relevance in promoting self-help activities not by corporate management but by the corporate owners. Even on this level, it is possible only to speculate about somewhat unlikely future legal responses that may be of dubious utility.

In the past, a few attempts have been made by stockholders in publicly held corporations to compel management to include nondiscrimination and other social proposals in materials sent to all stockholders for consideration in proxy votes. Each such attempt has failed in the courts and before the Security and Exchange Commission (SEC). The SEC, in fact, has adopted and applied an administrative rule that "general economic, political, racial, religious, social, or similar causes" are not proper subjects for stockholder action. But, since the public policy of a great many states, and now of the nation, unequivocally requires nondiscrimination in hiring and employment practices, it might be possible to argue to the courts or to the SEC that, in order to assure conformity to law and to avoid disruption of corporate business and economic loss as a result of legal or other actions to promote conformity to law, appropriate materials on this subject may now be submitted by stockholders for consideration in proxy votes.[33] It might also be possible to argue that stockholder action, most likely in the form of stockholders' derivative suits, to remove directors who wilfully violate the law by discriminating or by permitting discrimination, should be entertained. In addition, it might be possible to use the process of electing directors as a means of bringing management hiring practices into the open for consideration by stockholders and others. A stockholder could run, or put someone up for office in the corporation, and thereby solicit the other stockholders for their proxies. In his solicitation, such a stockholder would make statements revealing his platform; by judicious formulation of his views on employment discrimination, he could make it necessary for management also to reveal its position on that matter.

Direct Action and the Law

Self-help by members and allies of the class subject to discrimination takes various forms, many of which are characterized under the general label of "direct-action techniques." Direct action covers a broad continuum of activities that ranges, for example, from boycotts of the products and services of employers or others who discriminate, to picketing and to measures that are more physically disruptive, such as sit-ins, lie-ins and chain-ins. Generally, the underlying purpose of such activities is to bring direct economic, moral, and political pressure to bear on the discriminating agency or to bring about publicity that will indirectly have the same effect. Potential customers, suppliers, investors, employees, or employers are exhorted not to deal with an organization that allegedly discriminates; the government is cajoled to act; general public support and indignation is invited, as is the attention of higher level officials and components of the target organization; operations may be actively disrupted by the demonstrators. The consequences of direct action are so immediate that often the contested practices and issues are remedied and resolved before the legality of the particular tactic that has been employed can be tested judicially. Sometimes a discriminating organization is particularly vulnerable—for example, when a business or product has a significant Negro clientele and cannot afford to maintain formal resistance to Negro demands. Such organizations prefer to negotiate and resolve differences privately, rather than prolong injury by resorting to the courts. Upon resolution of a dispute, an organization that has been the target of direct action is likely, often as a demonstration of good faith, to withdraw or refuse to prosecute such complaints as it may earlier have filed, and pressure may be brought to bear on state prosecutors to quash any outstanding public complaints. Sometimes, however, direct action is tested in the courts; this has been particularly true when tactics involving picketing or other physical movement or placement of persons at or about the discriminating agency's place of operation are used. The rules evolved in these cases are likely, however, to be applied in cases testing other such activity as well.[34]

The first of the picketing cases took place in the mid-1930's. After declaring that picketing in support of requests that an employer hire a particular percentage of Negroes did not involve a "labor dispute," and hence was not protected from injunction by state little Norris-LaGuardia Acts, two state courts readily enjoined such activities. One court explicitly held that the purpose of the picketing was illegal in that it involved an attempt to secure discharges of members of one race in order to arrange employment for members of another race. Without disagreeing, the United States Supreme Court later held that such peaceful picketing, at least where the purpose was to induce an employer to hire Negroes in the ordinary course of personnel changes and where there was no suggestion of percentage quotas, involved a "labor dispute" within the meaning of the Federal Norris-LaGuardia Act, and, consequently, could not be enjoined by a Federal court (*New Negro Alliance vs. Sanitary Grocery Co.,* 303 U.S. 552 [1938]).

In a subsequent case, *Hughes vs. Superior Court,* on the other hand, peaceful picketing had been undertaken to compel an employer to hire Negroes in proportion to Negro customers. The Supreme Court, affirming the decision of the California Supreme Court, held that the fourteenth and first amendments did not bar a state from effecting its public policy against quota hiring by enjoining picketing that was conducted for such a purpose. The Court stressed in Hughes that picketing is not speech alone, but speech plus patrolling and possible coercion, disorder, and intrusion upon private property. Picketing was held "not beyond the control of the state if the manner in which . . . [it] is conducted or the purpose which it seeks to effectuate gives ground for its disallowance." [35]

Under the Constitution, it appears that states are, for the present at least, free to interdict picketing and other direct action tactics that are conducted in a nonpeaceful or disruptive fashion or that fall within the Hughes "illegal purpose" doctrine. Thus states may refuse to permit picketing or other activities that, for example, prevent work at construction sites or block the entrances to a business; and apparently the state can still prohibit actions that seek to accomplish the hiring of Negroes at the expense of present white employees or that seek to compel establishment of racial quotas. The decisions of the Supreme Court and of state and lower Federal courts indicate, on the other hand, that peaceful picketing, for the purpose of ending racially discriminatory practices of employers or unions or employment agencies, is constitutionally and statutorily, as a result of anti-injunction laws and perhaps now of the Civil Rights Act, protected as long as the purpose of the activity is not to promote solutions that are themselves discriminatory or illegal.

The law in this area is developing, however. First, "illegal purpose" has been defined by some courts to mean that the sole purpose must be illegal before total prohibition is permissible. If legal and illegal purposes are not part of a single, incommutable course of action, a court must be selective in its prohibition.

Second, "quota hiring" is to be distinguished from "reasonable racial balance." A demand for the latter may be protected by the first amendment while a demand for the former is not. Third, to the extent that quota hiring is designed to create racial classifications designed to redress the effects of past discrimination, it may be a permissible, and perhaps required, state objective. For example, the California Supreme Court has said that a school district is under an affirmative duty to integrate its schools when segregation is caused by housing patterns unrelated to any official action. This affirmative duty finds an analog in demands for quota or preferential hiring of Negroes. To the extent that there is an affirmative duty to redress past discrimination, picketing to demand that private individuals do their part is constitutionally protected.

Fourth, an illegal purpose, justifying state interference with direct action, obviously may not be merely any purpose upon which a state's incumbent officers happen to frown. Southern governors, courts and legislators may disapprove of integration and have public policies in opposition to it. Yet, since such policies are constitutionally interdicted, picketing in opposition to them, even when that picketing is of private enterprises which carry on discriminatory practices, is permissible. Similarly, picketing to dramatize a demand for new legislation is protected, even when the proposed legislation is counter to current public policy.

Since American values about racial matters are in a process of flux, as is reflected by the debate over "compensatory justice" or "preferential treatment," it is arguable that picketing not brigaded with disorderliness or direct coercion should be placed on the same footing as all other forms of speech. The years since Hughes have pointed up the important role of the informational picket line in the "uninhibited, robust, and wide-open" debate that the Supreme Court has recently held to be guaranteed by the first amendment.

Legal Responses to Alliances Between Unions and Civil Rights Activists

One other kind of direct-action program, involving situations in which unions and civil rights activists unite to engage in combined activity against employers, is beginning to come under the scrutiny of legal agencies.[36] Although a clear pattern of response has not yet developed, a couple of interesting incidents have already occurred. First, the NLRB held, and was sustained by an appellate court, that "employees' concerted activities to protest of racially discriminatory hiring policies and practices are protected" by the NLRA. An employee who had picketed his employer in an attempt to have a racially discriminatory hiring practice eliminated was ordered reinstated with back pay.

The second incident concerned the other side of the labor-civil rights coin, for it involved the recent action of a Baltimore civil rights organization in helping the AFL-CIO, with that organization's blessing and support, to organize workers into unions. This particular alliance has shown some success in that the Laundry and Dry Cleaning International Union recently won a representation election, apparently at least in part as a result of the civil rights group's activities. The successful election was contested by the employer on the grounds that the union, and others subject to its control, *i.e.* the civil rights activists, had "engaged in a deliberate and sustained campaign of inflammatory and intemperate appeals to racial emotions and prejudices of employees of The . . . Company, thereby creating an atmosphere surrounding the election which prevented a free and fair expression of employee choice." [37] The NLRB's Regional Director recommended that the employer's objections be overruled and that the union be certified as the bargaining representative of the employees involved. In so recommending, the Regional Director first distinguished a recent NLRB decision that prohibited irrelevant, intemperate, and inflammatory appeals to racial prejudice by concluding that:

The civil rights drive has for its aim the achievement of equality for the Negro in all areas of American society, including the economic sphere. It is the opinion of the undersigned that such a connection is not proscribed. Therefore, the civil rights issue, where it is not invoked solely to stir up anti-white sentiment and is invoked for the purpose of telling employees that "freedom" and "equality" has been and will be achieved by concerted [union] action, is germane to a union election campaign.

A union election is often an emotional proceeding. Campaign literature usually appeals to some type of emotion.

. . . .

. . . [A]n appeal to racial self-consciousness may produce a variety of emotions, depending upon the context. In some cases, such appeals may result in vicious race hatred. In other circumstance, such appeals may promote reasoned and admirable ambition in an unfortunate race of people.[38]

It is important to note that the Regional Director did not rule that action of a civil rights organization could not void an election, rather he ruled that the particular election was free and fair.

These two incidents justify expectations that some legal support will be available for cooperation between unions and civil rights groups. It is possible as well, however, that if a civil rights organization, seeking to aid a union, were to engage in conduct violating the Federal labor statutes, for example, a secondary boycott, legal sanctions might be imposed —against the union, if it is vulnerable under the labor statute in question, or against the civil rights organization.

□ Judicial Enforcement of Fair Employment Practices, Statutes, and Executive Orders

Over the past three decades, considerable energy has been expended in creating and managing administrative machinery specifically designed to supervise employment relations in order to promote fair employment practices. Such governmental machinery, which has been established and operated on Federal, state, and local levels, can provide particularly flexible and advantageous means of promoting nondiscrimination in employment. Broad and continuing supervision of employment activities can be undertaken. Coercive sanctions, readily fashioned according to need, can be intermixed with education and conciliation. The expense of investigating and proceeding is borne by the government. When particular cases are adjudicated, the administrative tribunal is not limited by the strict evidential and technical requirements incidental to judicial proceedings.[39]

The emphasis of this section is primarily on resort to courts in implementing general Fair Employment Practices (FEP) programs. Chapter 19 examines in greater depth the actual functioning of Fair Employment Practices Commissions (FEPC), the administrative machinery generally charged with primary implementation of statutory directives.

Federal Fair Employment Practices Programs

Various FEP programs have been established by the Federal Government. The latest such program was established by Congress under Title VII of the Civil Rights Act of 1964, and has been detailed earlier in this chapter. Although administrative machinery is created under Title VII, adjudication of claims and enforcement in general is placed in the courts rather than the administrative body. There is, however, another Federal FEP program that is oriented more toward administrative rather than judicial enforcement. In 1941, without specific congressional authorization, President Roosevelt created the first of a series of presidential FEPC's. The last of these committees, the President's Committee on Equal Employment Opportunity, was established by President Kennedy in Executive Order 10925, which prohibited discriminatory employment practices by Federal Government agencies, by private companies contracting with the Federal Government and by labor unions representing employees of such contracting companies. Pursuant to the Executive Order, nondiscrimination clauses are written into all government contracts over a certain value, and compliance reports and other actions are required of companies and unions that are covered. This current program has been extended by Executive Order 11114 to prohibit employment discrimination on Federally assisted construction projects. Most recently the President's Committee was dissolved by Executive Order 11246. Its authority over government contract employment has been vested in the Labor Department's Office of Federal Contract Compliance.[40]

Before the passage of the Civil Rights Act, inquiry into the

President's authority raised difficult questions of constitutional law involving the separation of executive and legislative functions. Since Congress expressly recognized the President's Committee, in Title VII, the constitutionality of the executive program would appear to be well founded and the subject need not be pursued here.

The ultimate sanction under the present program is termination of the discriminating company's government contracts and/or disqualification from further government contracts. The program, however, does provide a number of other means by which compliance with its requirements may be sought. The Office of Federal Contract Compliance may publish or cause to be published the names of noncomplying companies and unions. Publicity can also be used affirmatively, through the issuance of certificates of merit in recognition of compliance. In addition, the office is authorized to recommend to the Equal Employment Opportunity Commission or to the Department of Justice that proceedings be brought under Title VII. The office may also recommend to the Department of Justice that judicial action be undertaken to enjoin attempts to avoid or to prevent compliance, or that criminal proceedings be commenced to punish the furnishing of false information to the office.

Although occasional resort had been made to available coercive sanctions by the old President's Committee, by far the major portion of the committee's energies were directed to securing voluntary compliance; the same is likely to be true of the Office of Federal Contract Compliance. Its primary methods of achieving voluntary compliance are conciliating individual complaints, securing nondiscrimination pledges from employers and unions, and conducting conferences and seminars on employment discrimination and the means by which it can be eliminated. These noncoercive means of compliance are essentially the only weapons that the office itself has available to use against labor unions, for the obligation under a government contract really runs only from the contractor to the government. Of course, the office may bring union discrimination to the attention of the Justice Department or the Equal Employment Opportunity Commission, both of which administer Title VII.

The President's Committee neither brought nor instigated the bringing of judicial proceedings against any company or union, and no such organization appears to have sued the Committee. Recently, however, the Attorney General filed suit against the Building and Construction Trades Council of St. Louis and five of its member locals under a nondiscrimination clause in a Federal construction contract and under the pattern and practice provision of Title VII. Moreover, at an earlier time, suit was brought, on a third party beneficiary theory, by an individual who claimed to have been discriminated against in violation of contractual nondiscrimination provisions that had been negotiated in response to the President's program. The Federal district court first hearing the case held that the Executive Order had not created a private right of action against contractors; consequently, it was held that the plaintiff had no standing to sue. On appeal, it was observed that there was no express provision for a private judicial remedy. The court, however, concluded that the order contemplated that court action would be invoked only as a last resort; consequently, it was held that the question of Federal court jurisdiction over a suit by an individual did not have to be faced until the plaintiff had exhausted available administrative remedies. Since individuals are now empowered to bring suit under Title VII of the Civil Rights Act, the courts may never have to face the issue whether an individual's suit can be premised exclusively on the President's Executive Order. However, the courts may have to decide the question whether, when the President's Executive Order is applicable, an individual may sue pursuant to Title VII before proceeding before the Office of Federal Contract Compliance. Although Title VII does not address the precise question, it appears to embody a general congressional policy to follow the usual rule of administrative law that, when primary jurisdiction over the subject matter of a dispute has been given to an administrative agency, courts will rarely exercise jurisdiction until available administrative remedies have been exhausted and the courts may rule accordingly.

State and Local Fair Employment Practices Programs

Since 1945, when New York passed the first full-blown state Fair Employment Practices Act (FEPA), twenty-five states and Puerto Rico have enacted some kind of mandatory law prohibiting racial discrimination in private employment. Many of these acts are executed by FEPC's or more general Civil Rights Commissions or other administrative agencies, whose formal decisions are specifically enforceable through the invocation of judicial proceedings. In addition to the activity on the state level, a growing number of municipalities have enacted Fair Employment Practices Ordinances or Provisions of their own.

Very early in the development of state FEPA's, the Supreme Court indicated that such statutes, enacted to enforce the spirit of the Fourteenth Amendment, are not themselves prohibited by the Fourteenth Amendment but are permissible and laudable exercises of state police power. More recently, the Court upheld application of the Colorado FEPA against a commercial airline company operating in interstate commerce. The Court ruled that, as applied, the state statute did not impose an undue burden on interstate commerce and that regulation of racial discrimination in the interstate operations of carriers was not preempted by the Railway Labor Act, the Civil Aeronautics Act and its successor, the Federal Aviation Act, nor by the Presidential Executive Orders requiring government contractors to agree not to discriminate against employees or applicants for employment. It is clear, moreover, that under Title VII of the Civil Rights Act of 1964 it was not the purpose of Congress to preempt the field of FEP regulation, and also that it was expressly contemplated that state FEP programs would play a significant role within the Federal program. In the light of these constitutional and legislative decisions, the continued vitality of state and local programs seems assured and an understanding of their operations is vital for any meaningful prognostication about the new comprehensive Federal program.

State FEPA's are enforceable through procedures that vary somewhat from state to state, but, although differing in detail, the procedures generally conform to a broad administrative pattern. Initial complaints are usually brought by aggrieved individuals, but some commissions may entertain complaints brought by other parties, including civil rights organizations. In addition, many commissions are empowered to act on their own motion and provision is often made for the state's Attorney General or some other public official to file complaints. When a complaint is filed, a preliminary investigation is conducted by a trial examiner and, if probable cause is shown, that is, if it appears that there is a reasonable *prima facie* case of discrimination, a commissioner or the commission attempts to arrange an amicable settlement by conciliation and negotiation. If such a settlement cannot be arranged, the commission may conduct a formal administrative hearing. Uniformly, however, state and local FEPC's have relied heavily on conciliation and voluntary compliance through informal proceedings; as on the Federal level, formal action has been a last resort. But as civil rights pressure continues to mount, there are indications that greater use is being made of formal proceedings and coercion.

Once a hearing has been conducted, the commission can generally issue a formal order requiring a variety of corrective actions or exonerating the charged party. Any party who is adversely affected by such a final order may then seek judicial review. If a commission order is disobeyed, enforcement must also be sought in a judicial proceeding, for commissions generally have no direct power to enforce their own orders. With the exception of Wisconsin, however, where a judicial ruling that the state FEPA did not give rise to judicially enforceable obligations was immediately overruled by the legislature, courts have been generous in lending their assistance to embattled commissions. Under many state statutes, specific enforcement is available; consequently, courts may issue injunctions and contempt citations will lie to punish disobedience. Provision is sometimes also made for fines and other criminal sanctions to be assessed for violations of FEP requirements. Invocation of such sanctions may be strictly judicial or, if administrative proceedings are conducted, a full-scale judicial trial *de novo,* where all issues including the facts are completely adjudicated anew, often before a jury, is usually required. When an FEPC seeks injunctive or other specific enforcement of its orders, on the other hand, judicial proceedings are in the form of review, and the court's factual inquiry is limited to determining whether there is "substantial evidence" to support the agency's findings; the court does not decide whether a violation has, in its opinion, in fact been proven. Reviewing courts, however, are empowered to modify agency orders that are arbitrary or capricious or founded upon an error of law, or are beyond the agency's power under the statute.

Until recently, most FEPC's rarely pursued their mandates with sufficient aggressiveness to precipitate formal agency proceedings; invocation of judicial proceedings, either for review or for enforcement, was even more seldom. It is impossible that the small number of formal administrative and judicial proceedings resulted because the commissions' informal methods were optimumly effective, and it cannot have resulted entirely from the failure of aggrieved individuals to file charges. Such justifications do not begin to explain why many commissions empowered to investigate and proceed on their own motions failed to do so; or how it happened that the discrimination in the New York building trades continued unabated almost up to the present time, although the state had the pioneer FEP law; or how it happened that, although the first case brought under the first New York statute involved discriminatory exclusion from union membership, for almost twenty years thereafter no effective steps were taken to eliminate discrimination in admission to other unions. Unfortunately, the paucity of formal proceedings was related to a lack of forcefulness and effectiveness and both were related to problems of insufficient funds, insufficient and inadequate staff, and lack of sustained and meaningful political support and pressure. As the civil rights movement or revolution accelerates, however, a substantial body of formal agency and judicial actions is being built. Recent notable successes of FEPC's, working with ample resort to or threat of judicial coercion, indicate that this administrative-judicial combination may yet make good on its initial promise of becoming the most consistently effective legal means to oppose and eliminate employment discrimination. Those who are charged with implementing Title VII and other relevant Federal programs will do well to remember that, although voluntary action and conciliation are preferable, decisiveness and coercion must be visible and readily available to assure success. In addition, broad-based attacks, founded on the Attorney General's power to proceed against patterns of resistance, will undoubtedly be essential. Rapid and widespread compliance is not likely to result if the government relies for enforcement almost exclusively on the adjudication of such individual complaints as may be brought by aggrieved parties.

□ The National Labor Relations Board— FEPC by Surprise?

Of all the recent legal developments concerning employment discrimination, perhaps the most arresting are those involving the decisions of the NLRB enforcing the duty of fair representation.[41] The NLRB, which is charged with the administration of the major Federal statute governing general labor-management relations, has at its command two instruments that can be directed against union (and employer) discrimination: jurisdiction to adjudicate claims of both employer and union unfair labor practices prohibited under the NLRA, and authority to remedy such wrongs when they are proven. It is also empowered to aid unions in becoming and remaining exclusive bargaining representatives and, in this capacity, to conduct and supervise representation elections.

Unfair Labor Practices

The NLRB's modern enforcement of the duty of fair representation began with the nonracial Miranda Fuel Company case.[42] Applying the approach developed in that case, a majority of the NLRB subsequently ruled that racial discrimination might result in three kinds of unfair labor practices: restraint or coercion of employees in the exercise of their rights of self-organization; unlawful encouragement of employees to join unions; and the failure of a union and an employer to fulfill their concomitant obligations to bargain together in good faith.

In Miranda Fuel the NLRB first concluded that a violation of Section 7 of the NLRA results when a union, in processing a grievance, violates its duty of fair representation arising under Section 9(*a*) of the Act.[43] Section 7 provides that:

> Employees shall have the right to self-organization, to form, join, or assist labor organizations, to bargain collectively through representatives of their own choosing, and to engage in other concerted activities for the purpose of collective bargaining or other mutual aid or protection, and shall also have the right to refrain from any or all of such activities. . . .

The majority of the NLRB was of the opinion that this provision guaranteed employees freedom from "unfair or irrelevant or invidious treatment by their exclusive bargaining agent in matters affecting their employment." It was held that remedy against such treatment by a union is available under Section 8(*b*)(*1*)(*A*), which provides that it is an unfair labor practice for a union "to restrain or coerce employees in the exercise of the rights guaranteed in section 7. . . ." It was further held that, pursuant to Section 8(*a*)(*1*), which provides that it is an unfair labor practice for an employer "to interfere with, restrain, or coerce employees in the exercise of the rights guaranteed in section 7," remedy is also available against employers who accede to prohibited union conduct. Although a divided panel of the Second Circuit refused to enforce the NLRB order in Miranda Fuel, only one of the judges expressly rejected the Sections 7–8(*b*)(*1*)(*A*)–8(*a*)(*1*) theory, and the NLRB has applied this theory in subsequent cases. In the Hughes Tool Company case, the NLRB announced, almost simultaneously with the signing of the Civil Rights Act, that regardless of whether Negroes are discriminated against in membership, a union's failure to process grievances of Negro employees for racial reasons violates its duty of fair representation and is remediable under Section 8(*b*)(*1*)(*A*).[44] Moreover, shortly after the Hughes Tool decision, the NLRB also expressly ruled that the maintenance and enforcement of a collective bargaining agreement that racially discriminated in job allocation gave rise to an unfair labor practice under Section 8(*b*)(*1*)(*A*).[45]

In the Miranda Fuel case, the NLRB brought an additional pair of unfair labor practice provisions to bear upon problems of fair representation. Specifically, use was made of Sections 8(*a*)(*3*) and 8(*b*)(*2*), which impose parallel duties on employers and unions not to discriminate or to promote discrimination in employment "to encourage or discourage membership in any labor organization." [46] The NLRB concluded that "a statutory bargaining representative and an employer also respectively violate Sections 8(*b*)(*2*) and 8(*a*)(*3*) when, for arbitrary or irrelevant reasons or upon the basis of an unfair classification, the union attempts to cause or does cause an employer to derogate the employment status of an employee." Although, in refusing enforcement of Miranda Fuel, two judges of the Second Circuit Court rejected the application of the Sections 8(*b*)(*2*)–8(*a*)(*3*) theory, the NLRB has continued to apply this theory. In the Hughes Tool case it was held, in a context of segregated local unions, that by withholding treatment from a Negro applicant (*i.e.* the processing of his grievance), which would have been available to him had he been eligible for membership in the white local, the white local violated Section 8(*b*)(*2*); and in the Local 1367, ILA case, again in a context of segregated local unions, it was held that maintenance and enforcement of a racially discriminatory collective bargaining agreement violated Sections 8(*a*)(*3*) and 8(*b*)(*2*).

Before the Miranda Fuel decision, it seemed highly unlikely that the NLRB would make use of either the Sections 8(*a*)(*3*)–8(*b*)(*2*) theory or the Sections 7–8(*b*)(*1*)(*A*)–8(*a*)(*1*) theory to combat discrimination and unfair treatment against Negroes or others who had actually been permitted to join the allegedly discriminating union. Under the first theory, it was clear that discrimination against nonmembers violated the express terms of the NLRA. And it was comparatively easy to develop arguments under the second theory that when a union discriminated against Negroes or others who could not become members, union members and those who could become such were given cause to fear that they should remain or become members in order to avoid discrimination. Discrimination against Negroes could, consequently, be said to encourage whites to become members and thereby to coerce or restrain them as well from exercising their rights under Section 7. It is obvious that the doctrines formulated in Miranda Fuel and the other cases go well beyond this, for protection does not depend upon lack of membership or eligibility for membership. If these doctrines are ultimately upheld in the courts, they should prove to be significant devices for administrative remedy of employment discrimination.

There is one other unfair labor practice provision, not employed by the NLRB in Miranda Fuel, that has bearing on the enforcement of the duty of fair representation. Under Section 8(*b*)(*3*), it is an unfair labor practice for a union "to refuse to bargain collectively with an employer, provided it is the representative of his employees subject to the provisions of section 9(*a*)." Section 8(*d*) defines "to bargain collectively" as "the performance of the mutual obligation of the employer and the representative of the employees to meet at reasonable times and confer in good faith with respect to wages, hours, and other terms and conditions of employment. . . ." Comparatively early in the judicial development of the duty of fair representation, Professor (then Solicitor General) Archibald Cox suggested that the duty of fair representation could be broadly read into the union's duty to bargain collectively in good faith so that §8(*b*)(*3*) would thereby provide a basis for individuals to bring unfair labor practice claims.[47] Professor Michael Sovern challenged the Cox position by submitting that the obligation arising under Section 8(*b*)(*3*) was intended merely to parallel the employer's obligation under Section 8(*a*)(*5*) and, since there is no direct duty of fair representation on the employer, "the duty to bargain collectively, then, probably does not include the duty to represent fairly." Judge Medina, in his opinion in the Miranda Fuel case, appears to have adopted the Sovern position. In its recent Hughes Tool decision, however, a majority of the NLRB adopted the Cox approach and held that the white local's refusal to process Negro claimants' grievances violated Section 8(*b*)(*3*). It was reasoned that since the processing of grievances is a part of the continuing collective bargaining process "[a] refusal to process a grievance is, therefore, a refusal to bargain," and "since, as is well settled, the majority union has a statutory obligation to represent all employees in the unit fairly in collective bargaining . . . a breach of that duty is a breach of the duty to bargain." [48] In the Local 1367 decision, the Board further explicated its underlying reasoning:

> We hold that under the National Labor Relations Act a labor organization's duty to bargain collectively includes the duty to represent fairly . . . Section 8(*d*) speaks, *inter alia,* of a mutual obligation of employers and unions "to confer in good faith" and to sign "any agreement reached." These quoted phrases contemplate, in our opinion, only lawful bargaining and agreements, for the statute does not sanction the execution of agreements which are unlawful. *Because collective bargaining agreements which discriminate invidiously are not lawful under the Act, the good-faith requirements of Section 8* (d) *necessarily protect employees from infringement of their rights; and both unions and employers are en-*

joined by the Act from entering into contractual terms which offend such rights. Contrary to the Trial Examiner, Section 8(*d*) cannot mean that a union can be exercising good faith toward an employer while simultaneously acting in bad faith toward employees in regard to the same matters. Section 8(*d*), as all other provisions of the Act, was written in the public interest, not just in the interest of employers and unions, and it is not in the public interest for patently invalid provisions to be included in collective labor agreements. We conclude that when a statutory representative negotiates a contract in breach of the duty which it owes to employees to represent all of them fairly and without invidious discrimination, the representative cannot be said to have negotiated the sort of agreement envisioned by Section 8(*d*) nor to have bargained in good faith as to the employees whom it represents or toward the employer.[49]

Although the NLRB did not take this position in the Local 1367 case, a majority soon took the short step from the thought embodied in the italicized portion of that opinion and held, in the Local 12, Rubber Workers, case, that unions are under affirmative obligation to oppose discrimination by employers in terms and conditions of employment.

The Power to Aid Unions in Becoming and Remaining Exclusive Bargaining Representatives

Through its powers to conduct and regulate representational elections, to certify unions as exclusive statutory bargaining representatives, and to compel employers to bargain with unions, the NLRB has additional weapons that may be used to great advantage against racial discrimination. A number of unions, particularly in the skilled building trades, have sufficient economic strength to establish themselves as exclusive bargaining representatives without the aid of the NLRB, but for less fortunate unions NLRB action in this area could prove to be effective, at least as a stimulus to other activities in curbing racial discrimination.

From its beginning, the NLRB has refused to consider race

a valid criterion for the determination of the appropriate bargaining unit to be represented by a union that is seeking statutory certification. Until very recently, on the other hand, the NLRB declared that it had no power to remedy undemocratic practices within the structure of union organizations. It consistently held that "neither exclusion from membership nor segregated membership *per se* represents evasion on the part of a labor organization of its statutory duty to afford 'equal representation' "; rather that:

> in each case where the issue [of discrimination] is presented the Board will scrutinize the contract and the conduct of a representative organization and withhold or withdraw its certification if it finds that the organization has discriminated against employees in the bargaining units through its membership requirements or otherwise.[50]

Although the Board repeatedly admonished unions that, upon a showing of a denial of equal representation, it would consider rescission of certification, certification was never actually rescinded because of racial discrimination, and, moreover, allegations of past discrimination never moved the NLRB to deny certification. Of late, however, it has begun to exercise its powers in this area in order to promote nondiscrimination in union representation.

In 1962, in the Pioneer Bus Company case, the NLRB once again threatened to rescind the certification of a union that engaged in racial discrimination. The case involved an election petition filed by the Transport Workers Union, AFL-CIO, which was resisted by an already certified independent union on the ground that it had executed collective bargaining agreements that barred a representation election at that time. The Transport Workers Union argued, and the Board held without dissent, that the agreements in question, which divided the employees into two bargaining units based solely upon race, did not bar a representation election.

Concerned with constitutional considerations, the NLRB stated that:

Consistent with clear court decision in other contexts which condemn governmental sanctioning of racially separate groupings as inherently discriminatory, the Board will not permit its contract-bar rules to be utilized to shield contracts such as those here involved from the challenge of otherwise appropriate election petitions. We therefore hold that, where the bargaining representative of employees in an appropriate unit executes separate contracts, or even a single contract, discriminating between Negro and white employees on racial lines, the Board will not deem such contracts as a bar to an election.

Although the NLRB further expressed the view that "the execution of such [separate] contracts [executed on the basis of race] is in patent derogation of the certification," decertification was not ordered because it had not been requested and because "we deem it unnecessary to take such action at this time in view of the impending election which we here direct." [51] Subsequently, in the Hughes Tool Company case, however, the NLRB unanimously held that "the Pioneer Bus doctrine requires that the certification issued jointly to . . . [the segregated local unions], be rescinded because the certified organizations executed contracts based on race and administered the contracts so as to perpetuate racial discrimination in employment." [52]

Having thus decided that racially discriminating unions may not receive the imprimatur of certification and the protection of the contract bar doctrine, the NLRB is likely to take the necessary further steps to maximize its sanction by refusing to entertain unfair labor practice complaints that seek to compel employers to bargain collectively with such derelict unions, and by holding that an employer who bargains with such a union deprives employees of their freedom to choose an appropriate union.

Although there is strong medicine in the powers available to the NLRB pertaining to the status of unions as exclusive bargaining representatives, these powers by no means supply complete or universal remedies. As already noted, there are many unions that can do very nicely without NLRB support. In addition, in some circumstances exercise of the NLRB's powers in this area could prove more harmful to Negro, as well as white, workers, than representation by a discriminatory union. If unions that discriminate are denied NLRB support as exclusive bargaining representatives, workers might sometimes have to do without union representation, for there may be no other union available. Negro workers, no longer at the mercy of a discriminating union and a discriminating employer, will find themselves at the tender mercies of only a discriminating employer who is not even subject to a duty of fair representation. For decertification and other such sanctions to be meaningful, it may be necessary for there to be another nondiscriminating union available to challenge the discriminating union or fill the void if the discriminating union is unable to hold on without challenge. On the other hand, it is possible that a meaningful threat to a local union's representational status, aided by the pressure of publicity, or more effective pressure from the parent international union, may be just what is needed to compel a discriminating local to end its illegal practices. But, even if this were the consequence in many situations, some unions, particularly in hard-to-organize Southern regions,[53] might find it difficult to cease discriminating even when threatened with decertification, for they are likely to be faced with racially oriented campaigns by employers and others to persuade workers not to elect them as collective bargaining agents.[54]

If unions are to be able freely to renounce racial discrimination, the NLRB should attempt to afford them adequate protection against appeals to race hatred in representation campaigns.[55] The search for a reasonable standard of protection that takes into account constitutional and statutory guarantees of free speech may prove to be difficult, but the old NLRB policy, which required misrepresentation, fraud, violence, or coercion before voiding a representation election or otherwise acting to assure a fair election was somewhat unrealistic. It would be particularly unrealistic now that a union may not, without being subject to harsh NLRB sanctions and other legal prohibitions, demonstrate that the employer's claims are wrong, that is, demonstrate that it is in fact racist. Fortunately, as a part of its general new attitude of affirmative opposition to racial discrimination, the NLRB has taken more positive steps in the representational election campaign area as well. Although holding that racial matter, presented by an employer, that is "temperate in tone . . . [and] related to the choice before the voters," is permissible,[56] it has, on the other hand, also recently held that "inflammatory" propaganda that renders "a reasoned basis for choosing or rejecting a bargaining representative" impossible is not permissible.[57] To delineate permissible resort to racial matter from that which is not permissible, the NLRB proceeded to articulate the following test:

> So long, therefore, as a party limits itself to *truthfully* setting forth another party's position on matters of racial interest and does not deliberately seek to overstress and exacerbate racial feelings by irrelevant, inflammatory appeals, we shall not set aside an election on this ground. However, the burden will be on the party making use of a racial message to establish that it was truthful and germane, and where there is doubt as to whether the total conduct of such party is within the described bounds, the doubt will be resolved against him.[58]

The line between that which is permissible and that which is not is a difficult one to draw in the abstract under the NLRB's new test. As with many such tests, it should not prove to be so difficult in application. Should this not be so, it would not necessarily follow that a clearer or more stringent line should be drawn. There may be constitutional and perhaps also statutory guarantees of free speech that must be considered. In addition, representation elections are not sterile affairs conducted under laboratory conditions; it is impossible to withdraw racial considerations from such campaigns, and it is by no means clear that this would be desirable or is desired. It is, for example, quite likely that racial considerations will increasingly be interjected into election campaigns, not by employers seeking to defeat unions, but by unions, backed by civil rights organizations, seeking election. Any clear and fast rule prohibiting all employer interjection or discussion of racial matters might, at least before the Civil Rights Act, have had to cut both ways and exclude such civil rights campaigning.

The NLRB: Its Advantages and Its Relation to Title VII of the Civil Rights Act

As yet, the Supreme Court has not passed upon the new NLRB antidiscrimination doctrines. If upheld, however, this kind of NLRB enforcement of the duty of fair representation is likely to provide a useful administrative alternative and adjunct to the essentially court-based remedies of Title VII of the Civil Rights Act, to the judicially enforced duty of fair representation, to state administrative and judicial programs and to the activities of the Office of Federal Contract Compliance. To the extent that the NLRB can be employed in an antidiscrimination capacity, it has several advantages over many other modes of enforcement. In the first place, charged with general supervision of labor-management relations, the NLRB is in an excellent position to relate fair employment policies to broader contexts of employment and industrial regulation. Second, since the NLRB and its agents conduct their proceedings within the structure of the administrative process, rather than according to stringent judicial standards of procedure, it provides a somewhat more flexible agency for treatment of these problems. Third, and related to the last:

> The concomitants of administration—the power to investigate, to urge informal settlement and to provide an expeditious hearing, and the expertise of the personnel involved—all suggest that the NLRB is equipped to handle these problems more speedily and more fairly than are the courts. This is even true in the light of the great difficulties which the Board has faced in keeping its dockets anywhere near current. With all of its overload and backlog, it provides a more effective forum for solution of these problems than the courts.[59]

A fourth advantage is that "[t]he Board has broad latitude in fashioning remedies, including cease-and-desist orders and backpay awards, to those who are victims of illegal discrimination." [60] Fifth, "[t]he statute gives the General Counsel the sole and independent responsibility for investigating charges of unfair labor practices, issuing complaints and prosecuting cases where his investigators find evidence of violation of the act." [61] Aggrieved individuals are, consequently, generally relieved of the heavy financial burden of vindicating their rights. Last, although the NLRB insists that it may not act to prevent or remedy an unfair labor practice until a charge has been filed with it, "[s]uch charges may be filed by an employer, an employee, a labor organization, *or other private party*." [62] It might, therefore, be possible to persuade the NLRB to entertain complaints brought by civil rights organizations, thereby facilitating concerted campaigns against discrimination.

Discussion of the NLRB cannot end here, for complete assessment of its potentialities requires consideration of the effect of Title VII of the Civil Rights Act. It is not enough that a majority of the NLRB is willing to implement policies of antidiscrimination, and that no explicit preemptive effect should be ascribed to Title VII. There remains the difficult question of whether the NLRB can or should continue to enforce these policies through its own procedures, particularly those dealing with certification, now that policies of nondiscrimination are embodied in the explicit rules and provisions of Title VII. While it may be argued that the NLRB should use all its powers to vindicate the now-clear national policy, there are dangers to be considered. It is, for example, quite possible that the NLRB might make a finding that a union is in fact excluding Negroes when proceedings under the Civil Rights Act might result in opposite findings. Furthermore, it may be that the advantages of NLRB proceedings do not justify pursuing remedies for decertification now that more direct and appropriate remedies, affirmatively requiring desegregation and nondiscrimination, are available under Title VII. Title VII's rules against employer and union discrimination could thus eclipse or even preempt the new NLRB decertification decisions. On the other hand, NLRB enforcement of nondiscrimination, particularly through the remedying of unfair labor practices, involves no greater risk of conflict between such NLRB proceedings and court proceedings under Title VII than already exists between NLRB unfair labor practice proceedings and court actions to enforce collective bargaining agreements under Section 301 of the Labor Management Relations Act. In the Section 301 situation, however, both forums are generally available; it may not be inappropriate for this to be true in the Title VII context as well. The existence of Title VII might, on the other hand, actually require additional NLRB action, at least by way of modification of the rules regarding interjection of racial matter into representation campaigns. After all, it is one thing to say that an employer can use the fact that the union believes in equality of membership and equality of employment in his propaganda at a time when the union has a choice. It is quite another thing for the employer to use this argument when the union has no choice, and indeed when the law prohibits the employer from discriminating whether or not a union exists. The test of "truthfulness" is significantly changed when the legal context is changed, and the responsibility for protecting the parties from injuries inflicted because they obey the law becomes less a matter of administrative policy and more a matter of compelling rule.

□ Conclusion

To date, the law has refined a number of highly flexible and useful responses to employment discrimination; it is in the process of refining still more; and, particularly when the relation of unemployment and underemployment to employment discrimination becomes more apparent to the society at large, it undoubtedly will refine and develop responses that are not even contemplated at present. Whether formally amended or not, it is clear that future development of the law in this area will be greatly influenced by the Civil Rights Act of 1964, and particularly by Title VII of that act. At present, it can be speculated that because of Title VII the judicially enforced duty of fair representation will rarely be employed in independent proceedings involving racial discrimination and that the likelihood that constitutional concepts of state action will be expanded and given direct application has been minimized. On the other hand, it is to be expected that aggressive FEPC activity will be stimulated on all levels of government, and it appears that the NLRB is intent on playing a major role in this field regardless of Title VII. In addition, legal support for good faith self-help of all kinds can be expected to increase and become more sophisticated.

Some of the present and developing legal approaches are more ubiquitous than others, but none is so comprehensive and efficient as to exclude automatically consideration or use of the others, and none can supply easy solutions to the variant and difficult problems of employment discrimination. Often circumstances will promote a single-minded approach or tactic, but circumstances may also increasingly require or suggest a multilevel approach. No firm rules or recommendations can be made for the edification of those persons and institutions directly engaged in this process of extending and ramifying law, but one general principle can appropriately be drawn. Each situation should be gauged and necessary action taken with consideration made of what is being sought, not only in the short but also in the long run, and with healthy awareness of all reasonably probable consequences and ramifications. Now that a significant catalogue of legal devices is available, increased attention can be paid to the creation of a stable but viable system of law in this area.

NOTES

1. I am indebted to Clyde W. Summers, Professor of Law, Yale University Law School, Melvin J. Sykes of the Maryland and Baltimore Bars, and R. Wayne Walker, Assistant Professor of

Law, University of Maryland School of Law, for reading and criticizing the manuscript of this chapter. Miss Barbara Ann Spicer of the Maryland School of Law, class of 1965, conducted research that instructed me as to a number of the points covered and also checked my citations for fidelity to source. Miss Mary Ann Tuur of the Maryland School of Law, class of 1965, put the citations into the proper form. I thank Dean William P. Cunningham of the Maryland School of Law for making available funds to support this research. A final debt is owed Miss Margery Hackerman, Miss Loraine Hazman, and Mrs. Barbara Pasarew, who, with good humor, performed the difficult task of typing the various drafts of the study.

A completely documented version of this chapter appeared as an article in the August, 1965, issue of the California Law Review (53 Calif. L. Rev. 729).

2. The most important general Federal labor statutes, each of which will be touched upon from time to time, are: The National Labor Relations Act (Wagner Act), 49 Stat. 449 (1935), as amended, 29 U.S.C. §§151–67 (1958), as amended, 29 U.S.C. §§153, 158–60 (Supp. V, 1964), hereafter cited as N.L.R.A. The Labor Management Relations Act (Taft-Hartley Act), 61 Stat. 136 (1947), as amended, 29 U.S.C. §§141–87 (1958), as amended, 29 U.S.C. §§153, 158–60, 186–87 (Supp. V, 1964), hereafter cited as L.M.R.A. The Railway Labor Act, 44 Stat. 577 (1926), as amended, 45 U.S.C. §§151–63, 181–87 (1958). The Labor-Management Reporting and Disclosure Act (Landrum-Griffin Act), 73 Stat. 519 (1959), 29 U.S.C. §§401–531 (Supp. V, 1964), hereafter cited as L.M.R.D.A.
3. 78 Stat. 241 (1964). See Recent Statute, The Civil Rights Act of 1964, 78 Harv. L. Rev. 684 (1965).
4. 78 Stat. 252 (1964). See The Civil Rights Act 1964: Text, Analysis, Legislative History 91–102 (BNA 1964), for an analysis of Title VI.
5. 78 Stat. 253 (1964). See generally, Berg, Equal Employment Opportunity Under the Civil Rights Act of 1964, 31 Brooklyn L. Rev. 62 (1964); Comment, Enforcement of Fair Employment Under the Civil Rights Act of 1964, 32 U. Chi. L. Rev. 430 (1965); Hall v. Werthan Bag Corp., 61 L.R.R.M. 2458 (M.D. Tenn. Mar. 3, 1966).

6. 110 Cong. Rec. 13694 (daily ed. June 17, 1964) (remarks of Senator Humphrey); accord, The Civil Rights Act of 1964: Text, Analysis, Legislative History 45–46 (BNA 1964); cf. Gaynor v. Rockefeller, 21 App. Div. 2d 92, 248 N.Y.S. 2d 792, 56 L.R.R.M. 2210 (1964) (state judicial action entertained although resort had not been made to available state administrative remedies), aff'd on other grounds, 58 L.R.R.M. 2260 (N.Y.C.A. Jan. 14, 1965). The complaint was dismissed, one of the grounds being that adequate remedy was available before the State Commission for Human Rights.
7. Sec. 706(*a*)–(*e*), 78 Stat. 259–60 (1964); sec. 709 (*a*)–(*b*), 78 Stat. 262–63 (1964). Under sec. 709(*b*), the commission is empowered to enter into agreements with state and local agencies that effectively enforce their own antidiscrimination laws. The effect of such agreements will be virtually to suspend the operation of Title VII within the agreeing state or locale. An agreement may be rescinded when it no longer serves the interest of effective enforcement of Title VII.
8. On June 12, 1964, the Senate, by a vote of 59 to 29, decisively rejected an amendment, proposed by Senator Tower, to give significant preemptive effect to Title VII. See also Local 12, United Rubber Workers of America, 150 N.L.R.B. No. 18, 57 L.R.R.M. 1535, 1539–40 (Dec. 16, 1964) (the National Labor Relations Board held that its jurisdiction was not limited by Title VII); Berg, supra note 5 at 92–96; Report of the Committee on State Labor Relations, ABA Section of Labor Relations Law, 56 L.R.R. 394 (1964); cf. Smith v. Holiday Inns of America, Inc., 336 F. 2d 630 (6th Cir. 1964); Gaynor v. Rockefeller, supra note 6.
9. See New York Times, p. 1, col. 6 (July 3, 1964), for a statement of Robert Carter, General Counsel for the NAACP, expressing his intention to use the NLRB, where its machinery is available, rather than the procedures of Title VII.
10. 33 U.S.L. Week 3110 (Oct. 13, 1964).
11. See generally Aaron, Some Aspects of the Union's Duty of Fair Representation, 22 Ohio St. L. J. 39 (1961); Blumrosen, Legal Protection Against Exclusion From Union Activities, 22 Ohio St. L. J. 21 (1961); Cox, The Duty of Fair Representation, 2 Vill. L. Rev. 151 (1957); Herring, The "Fair Representation" Doctrine: An Effective Weapon Against Un-

ion Racial Discrimination?, 24 Md. L. Rev. 113 (1964); Rosen, Fair Representation, Contract Breach and Fiduciary Obligations: Unions, Union Officials and the Worker in Collective Bargaining, 15 Hastings L. J. 391 (1964); Sovern, The National Labor Relations Act and Racial Discrimination, 62 Colum. L. Rev. 563 (1962); Weiss, Federal Remedies for Racial Discrimination by Labor Unions, 50 Geo. L. J. 457 (1962); Wellington, Union Democracy and Fair Representation: Federal Responsibility in a Federal System, 67 Yale L. J. 1327 (1958).

12. 323 U.S. 192, 202–03 (1944).
13. See generally Herring, supra note 11, at 113–48. Herring engaged in careful and intense analysis of the racial fair representation cases, and he communicated with the attorneys in these cases. In an unpublished version of his article ("The Doctrine of Fair Representation in the Hands of the Courts and The National Labor Relations Board" [unpublished divisional paper, Yale Law School, 1963, on file at the Yale Law Library]), he reported that:

> In theory, the doctrine of fair representation assures Negroes that their jobs cannot be affected by unfairness on the part of their collective bargaining representatives. In fact, Negro workers have made extremely limited use of judicial coercion under the *Steele* standard; and when they have tried to take advantage of its apparent protection, they have secured only a slight practical amelioration of their position.

Nowhere are the weaknesses and limitations of the judicially enforced duty of fair representation more dramatically manifested than in its use to oppose harmful racial discrimination on the part of the Railroad Brotherhoods. Of particular note, the Brotherhood of Locomotive Firemen, defendant in the Steele case, has been an unsuccessful respondent in the Supreme Court in two other such cases. Until recently, nevertheless, it continued to maintain a "Caucasians only" clause in its constitution and, it is clear, it has used its lily-white policy to the extreme detriment of those Negroes who have been unfortunate enough to come within the ambit of its collective bargaining powers. As to cases that the Brotherhood of Locomotive Firemen has defended in the Supreme Court, see Steele v.

Louisville & N.R.R., 323 U.S. 192 (1944); Tunstall v. Brotherhood of Locomotive Firemen, 323 U.S. 210 (1944); Graham v. Brotherhood of Locomotive Firemen, 338 U.S. 232 (1949); see also Oliphant v. Brotherhood of Locomotive Firemen, 262 F. 2d 359 (6th Cir. 1958), cert. denied, 359 U.S. 935 (1959).

14. Sometimes, on the other hand, these difficulties have been to the advantage of plaintiffs. Instances have been reported in which allegedly discriminating parties have settled suits out of court, fearing great pecuniary expense should they lose in court.
15. §8(*b*)(*1*), 61 Stat. 141 (1947), 29 U.S.C. §158(*b*)(*1*) (1958).
16. See Greenberg, Race Relations and American Law 185 (1959); 3 U.S. Commission on Civil Rights Report, Employment 146 (1961); Aaron & Komaroff, Statutory Regulation of Internal Union Affairs, 44 Ill. L. Rev. 425, 436 (1949); Givens, Enfranchisement of Employees Arbitrarily Rejected for Union Membership, 11 Lab. L. J. 809, 812 (1960); Hewitt, The Right to Membership in a Labor Union, 99 U. Pa. L. Rev. 919, 936–39 (1951); Rauh, Civil Rights and Liberties and Labor Unions, 8 Lab. L. J. 874, 875 (1957); Summers, The Right to Join a Union, 47 Colum. L. Rev. 33, 49–51 (1947); Wellington, The Constitution, the Labor Union, and "Governmental Action," 70 Yale L. J. 345, 373–74 (1961); Comment, Discrimination in Union Membership: Denial of Due Process Under Federal Collective Bargaining Legislation, 12 Rutgers L. Rev. 543, 544–45 (1958).
17. Letter from Barbara A. Morris, Associate Counsel of the NAACP to the author, August 27, 1964.
18. Humphrey v. Moore, 375 U.S. 335 (1964). See Barbash, Due Process and Individual Rights in Arbitration, 17 N.Y.U. Ann. Conf. Lab. (1964 as yet unpublished); Ratner, Some Contemporary Observations on Section 301, 52 Geo. L. J. 260, 290–95 (1964); Rosen, Fair Representation, Contract Breach and Fiduciary Obligations: Unions, Union Officials and the Worker in Collective Bargaining, 15 Hastings L. J. 391, 409–27 (1964); ———, The Individual Worker in Grievance Arbitration: Still Another Look at the Problem, 24 Md. L. Rev. 233, 271–81 (1964); Report of the Committee on Labor Arbitration, Individual Rights in Grievances and Arbitration,

ABA Section of Labor Relations Law, 56 L.R.R. 418, 423–25 (1964); Note, 5 B.C. Ind. & Comm. L. Rev. 848 (1964).

19. As to the advantages and desirability of individual participation, see generally, e.g. Givens, supra note 16, at 296–301; Rosen, The Individual Worker in Grievance Arbitration: Still Another Look at the Problem, 24 Md. L. Rev. 233 (1964); Summers, Individual Rights in Collective Agreements and Arbitration, 37 N.Y.U.L. Rev. 362 (1962). See also Local 12, Rubber Workers, 150 N.L.R.B. No. 18, 57 N.L.R.B. No. 18, 57 L.R.R.M. 3515 (1964).
20. The Fourteenth Amendment requirement, imposed on states, is also imposed on the Federal Government under the Fifth Amendment. See e.g. Bolling v. Sharpe, 347 U.S. 497 (1954).
21. See e.g. Burton v. Wilmington Parking Authority, 365 U.S. 715, 721–22 (1961); Shelley v. Kraemer, 334 U.S. 1 (1948); The Civil Rights Cases, 109 U.S. 3, 11–14 (1883).

    On the meaning of "state action," see generally Abernathy, Expansion of the State Action Concept Under the Fourteenth Amendment, 43 Cornell L. Q. 375 (1958); Van Alstyne & Karst, State Action, 14 Stan. L. Rev. 3 (1961); Haber, Notes on the Limits of Shelly v. Kraemer, 18 Rutgers L. Rev. 811 (1964); Henkin, Shelley v. Kraemer: Notes for a Revised Opinion, 110 U. Pa. L. Rev. 473 (1962); Horowitz, The Misleading Search for "State Action" Under The Fourteenth Amendment, 30 So. Cal. L. Rev. 208 (1957); Karst & Van Alstyne, Comment: Sit-Ins and State Action—Mr. Justice Douglas Concurring, 14 Stan. L. Rev. 762 (1962); Lewis, The Meaning of State Action, 60 Colum. L. Rev. 1083 (1960); McKenny, An Argument in Favor of Strict Adherence to the "State Action" Requirement, 5 William & Mary L. Rev. 213 (1964); Peters, Civil Rights and State Non-Action, 34 Notre Dame Law. 303 (1959); St. Antonine, Color Blindness but Not Myopia: A New Look at State Action, Equal Protection, and "Private" Racial Discrimination, 59 Mich. L. Rev. 993 (1961); Schwelb, The Sit-In Demonstration: Criminal Trespass or Constitutional Right?, 36 N.Y.U. L. Rev. 779 (1961); Williams, The Twilight of State Action, 41 Texas L. Rev. 347 (1963).
22. See Hewitt, The Right to Membership in a Labor Union, 99 U. Pa. L. Rev. 919, 939–42 (1951); Summers, The Right to

Join a Union, 47 Colum. L. Rev. 33, 56 (1947); Wellington, The Constitution . . . , supra note 16, at 360; Comment, Discrimination in Union Membership . . . , supra note 16, at 543; note, 42 Minn. L. Rev. 942 (1958). But see Cox, The Role of Law in Preserving Union Democracy, 72 Harv. L. Rev. 609, 619–20 (1959); Ellis, Constitutional Right to Membership in a Labor Union—5th and 14th Amendments, 8 J. Pub. L. 580, 594–95 (1959).

23. See e.g. Friedmann, Corporate Power, Government by Private Groups, and the Law, 57 Colum. L. Rev. 155 (1957); Jaffe, Law Making by Private Groups, 51 Harv. L. Rev. 201 (1937); Summers, Union Powers and Workers' Rights, 49 Mich. L. Rev. 805, 815–16 (1951); Wirtz, Government by Private Groups, 13 La. L. Rev.

24. See Berle, The Twentieth Century Capitalist Revolution 75–115 (1954); Gellhorn, American Rights 163–95 (1960); Miller, Private Governments and the Constitution (1959); Berle, Constitutional Limitations on Corporate Activity—Protection of Personal Rights From Invasion Through Economic Power, 100 U. Pa. L. Rev. 933 (1952); ———, Legal Problems of Economic Power, 60 Colum. L. Rev. 4 (1960); Countryman, The Constitution and Job Discrimination, 39 Wash. L. Rev. 74 (1964); Horowitz, supra note 21; Howe, Forward: Political Theory and the Nature of Liberty, 67 Harv. L. Rev. 91, 95 (1953); Miller, The Constitutional Law of the "Security State," 10 Stan. L. Rev. 620 (1958). But see, e.g. Van Alystyne & Karst, supra note 21, at 36–44; Karst & Van Alstyne, supra note 21; McKenney, supra note 21.

25. See generally Lichtman, The Ethics of Compensatory Justice, Law in Transition 76 (1964); but cf. note 70 Yale L. J. 126 (1960), in which benign quotas in housing are criticized.

26. See Countryman, supra note 24, at 89; Ming, Critique on "The Constitution and Job Discrimination," 39 Wash. L. Rev. 104 (1964).

27. Compare the fears of Blumrosen, Legal Protection Against Exclusion From Union Activities, 22 Ohio St. L. J. 21, 31–33 (1961); Cox, supra note 22, at 619–20; Ellis, supra note 22, at 594–95; Wellington, supra note 22, 372, with the willingness of Miller, Private Governments and the Constitution (1959); Berle, Constitutional Limitations on Corporate Activity . . . ,

supra note 24; ———, Legal Problems of Economic Power, supra note 24; Howe, supra note 24, at 95; Miller, The Constitutional Law of the "Security State," supra note 24.

28. Before the passage of the Civil Rights Act it might also have been possible to press the courts to use the Federal antitrust laws to oppose employment discrimination. See The Sherman Act, 26 Stat. 209 (1890), as amended, 15 U.S.C. §§1–7 (1958); Marcus, Civil Rights and the Anti-Trust Laws, 18 U. Chi. L. Rev. 171 (1951); Robison, Giving Reality to the Promise of Job Equality, 1 Law in Transition Q. 104, 107 (1964). Such actions would, when involving labor unions, have had to overcome the exemption that labor unions generally enjoy from the coverage of the antitrust laws. United States v. Hutcheson, 312 U.S. 219 (1941); see Winter, Collective Bargaining and Competition: The Application of Antitrust Standards to Union Activities, 73 Yale L. J. 14 (1963). Unions are not exempt, however, when they participate with nonlabor groups, particularly management, in activities illicit under the antitrust laws. UMW v. Pennington, 381 U.S. 657 (1965); Local 189, Amalgamated Meat Cutters v. Jewell Tea Co., 381 U.S. 676 (1965). And there has been one successful private action involving collusion to discriminatorily monopolize a labor market: Menifee v. Local 74, Lathers Int'l Union, 3 Race Rel. L. Rep. 507 (N.D. Ill. March 3, 1958) (consent decree); see Greenberg, Race Relations and American Law 185–86 (1958). But see Waters v. Paschen Contractors, Inc., 227 F. Supp. 659 (N.D. Ill. 1964); but cf. Apex Hosiery v. Leader, 310 U.S. 469 (1940). Aside from the difficulties of framing proper issues under existing antitrust law, the major drawback but also the chief advantage of the antitrust device is that litigation of such cases is exceedingly difficult, time consuming, and expensive. See Herring, supra note 11, for a comment of the counsel for Local 74 of the Lathers as to why the Menifee case was settled; id. at 145 n. 163 (comment of the counsel for the plaintiff Negroes as to why they agreed to settle the case).

29. Marshall, Union Racial Practices and the Labor Market, 85 Monthly Lab. Rev. 269, 270 (1962).

30. See generally e.g. Summers, The Law of Union Discipline: What The Courts Do in Fact, 70 Yale L. J. 175 (1960);

———, Judicial Regulation of Union Elections, 70 Yale L. J. 1221 (1961).

31. An increasing number of international unions are establishing more effective civil rights apparatus. See Roster of Civil Rights Committees of National and International Unions Affiliated with the AFL-CIO (Oct., 1961 AFL-CIO mimeo); 3 U.S. Commission on Civil Rights, Employment 142 (1961); see also AFL-CIO, Policy Resolutions Adopted November 1963 by the Fifth Constitutional Convention 91–92 (1964).

    Particularly effective programs have been established by the United Automobile Workers and the United Packinghouse Workers, two unions with large Negro minorities. See e.g. Hope, Equality of Opportunity: A Union Approach to Fair Employment 109–35 (1956); UAW Fair Practices and Anti-Discrimination Department, Handbook for Local Union Fair Practices Committees (1961 rev.); Norgren, Employing the Negro in American Industry 146 (1959).
32. The following discussion is based largely on a memorandum prepared in 1964 by the Rutgers Law School Branch of the Law Students Civil Rights Research Council, a national organization. The memorandum was made available to the author by Miss Shirley Fingerhood, a New York City attorney who acts as the research director for the national group.
33. It seems likely that it is only a question of time before the SEC will be called upon to allow or disallow such a proposal. Although the proposal could be interpreted to violate Rule 14*a*-8(*c*)(*2*), if it is carefully drafted to give the SEC room to maneuver, it is not impossible that in the light of the Civil Rights Act of 1964 and mounting pressures, the SEC would find it politically inauspicious to disallow the proposal. If a number of such proposals were submitted for a number of companies, the SEC might find it all the more difficult to disallow, cf. Calore v. Powell-Savory Corp., 57 L.R.R.M. 2928 (N.Y. App. Div. July 2, 1964), where the court held that "In view of the temper of the times and the current of contemporary public opinion, we deem such a charge [of racial discrimination], when falsely made against a labor union, to be libelous *per se*. . . ."
34. See generally annot., Nonlabor Picketing or Boycott, 93 A.L.R. 2d 1284, especially 1301–07 (1964); Note, Racial Picketing

Protesting Discriminatory Employment Practices, 18 U. Miami L. Rev. 488 (1963); Note, 18 Rutgers L. Rev. 677 (1964).

35. 339 U.S. at 465–66; compare Thornhill v. Alabama, 310 U.S. 88 (1940) with International Bd. of Teamsters, Local 695 v. Vogt, 354 U.S. 284 (1957); Giboney v. Empire Storage & Ice Co., 336 U.S. 490 (1949). See Farmer v. Moses, 232 F. Supp. 154 (S.D. N.Y. 1964).
36. On "Labor-Civil Rights" relations generally see e.g. Lipset, Kahn, Gomberg, & Hill, An Exchange: Negroes and the Labor Movement, 1 New Politics 135 (Spring, 1962); Marshall, Unions and the Negro Community, 17 Ind. & Lab. Rel. Rev. 179 (1964); Raskin, Civil Rights: The Law and the Unions, The Reporter 23 (Sept. 19, 1964).
37. The Archer Laundry Co., No. 5-RC-4522, Sept. 9, 1964 (Regional Director, NLRB, mimeo.), p. 1.
38. Ibid., p. 10. The NLRB has adopted the recommendations of its Regional Director. Archer Laundry Co., 150 N.L.R.B. No. 139, 58 L.R.R.M. 1212 (Jan. 29, 1965).
39. Bonfield, State Civil Rights Statutes: Some Proposals, 49 Iowa L. Rev. 1067, 1117 (1964). See also Bamberger and Lewin, The Right to Equal Treatment: Administrative Enforcement of Antidiscrimination Legislation, 74 Harv. L. Rev. 526 (1961); Girard and Jaffee, Some General Observations on Administration of State Fair Employment Practice Laws, 14 Buffalo L. Rev. 114 (1964); Rabkin, Enforcement of Laws Against Discrimination in Employment, 14 Buffalo L. Rev. 100 (1964); Spitz, Tailoring the Techniques to Eliminate and Prevent Employment Discrimination, 14 Buffalo L. Rev. 79 (1964).
40. Executive Order 11246, 30 Fed. Reg. 12319 (Sept. 18, 1965), was issued after this chapter appeared in the California Law Review. The jurisdiction of the President's Committee over discrimination in Federal Government employment was vested in the Civil Service Commission.

    For the history and development of the various Presidential FEP programs see e.g. Norgren and Hill, Toward Fair Employment 149–79 (1964); Ross, All Manner of Men (1948); Ruchames, Race, Jobs and Politics: The Story of FEPC (1953); 3 U.S. Commission on Civil Rights, op. cit. supra note

31, at 6–17 passim (1961); Kovarsky, Racial Discrimination in Employment and the Federal Law, 38 Ore. L. Rev. 54 (1958); Maslow, FEPC—A Case History in Parliamentary Maneuver, 13 U. Chi. L. Rev. 407 (1946); Norgren, Government Contracts and Fair Employment Practices, 29 Law & Contemp. Prob. 225 (1964).

As to coverage and operations under the last presidential program, see The President's Committee on Equal Employment Opportunity, Report to the President (Nov. 26, 1963); The President's Committee on Equal Employment Opportunity, the First Nine Months (Jan. 15, 1962); Birnbaum, Equal Employment Opportunity and Executive Order 10925, 11 Kan. L. Rev. 17 (1962); Ginsberg, Non-Discrimination in Employment: Executive Order 10925, 14 Milit. L. Rev. 141 (Oct., 1961); Holleman, The Job Ahead for the President's Committee on Equal Employment Opportunity, 12 Lab. L. J. 618 (1961); Norgren, supra; Powers, Federal Procurement and Equal Employment Opportunity, 29 Law & Contemp. Prob. 468 (1964); Taylor, Jr., The President's Committee on Equal Employment Opportunity, 16 Sw. L. J. 101 (1962); ———, Equal Employment Opportunity, 15 N.Y.U. Ann. Conf. Lab. 35 (1962).

41. Until recently most discussion of NLRB action on this level was speculative. See Greenberg, Race Relations and American Law 178–83 (1959); Cox, The Duty of Fair Representation, 2 Vill. L. Rev. 151 (1957); Maloney, Racial and Religious Discrimination In Employment and the Role of the NLRB, 21 Md. L. Rev. 219 (1961); Sovern, The National Labor Relations Act and Racial Discrimination, 62 Colum. L. Rev. 563 (1962); Weiss, Federal Remedies for Racial Discrimination by Labor Unions, 50 Geo. L. J. 457, 471–77 (1962). Present scholarly commentary is made on actual and directly relevant Board decisions. See Albert, NLRB-FEPC?, 16 Vand. L. Rev. 547 (1963); Herring, The "Fair Representation" Doctrine; An Effective Weapon Against Union Racial Discrimination?, 24 Md. L. Rev. 113, 148–62 (1964); Sovern, Racial Discrimination and the National Labor Relations Act: The Brave New World of Miranda, 16 N.Y.U. Ann. Conf. Lab. 3 (1963); Comment, Discrimination of the NLRB: The Scope of Board Power Under Sections 8(*a*)(*3*) and 8(*b*)(*2*), 32 U. Chi. L.

Rev. 124 (1964); Comment, Racial Discrimination and the NLRB; The Hughes Tool Case, 50 Va. L. Rev. 1221 (1965). See also e.g. Blumrosen, The Worker and Three Phases of Unionism: Administrative and Judicial Control of the Worker-Union Relationship, 61 Mich. L. Rev. 1435, 1504–23 (1963); Note, Administrative Enforcement of the Right to Fair Representation: The Miranda Case, 112 U.PA. L. Rev. 711 (1964).

42. Miranda Fuel Co., 140 N.L.R.B. 181 (1962), enforcement denied, 326 F. 2d 172 (2d Cir. 1963).
43. The relevant portion of section 9(*a*) provides that:

> Representatives designated or selected for the purposes of collective bargaining by the majority of the employees in a unit appropriate for such purposes, shall be the exclusive representatives of all the employees in such unit for the purposes of collective bargaining in respect to rates of pay, wages, hours of employment, or other conditions of employment. . . .

44. 147 N.L.R.B. No. 166, 56 L.R.R.M. 1289 (July 1, 1964). As to the long history of the Hughes Tool Co. Cases, see Herring, supra note 41, at 151 n. 185.
45. Local 1367, ILA, 148 N.L.R.B. No. 44, 57 L.R.R.M. 1083 (Sept. 11, 1964). See also Local 453, UAW, 149 N.L.R.B. No. 48, 57 L.R.R.M. 1298 (Nov. 6, 1964), where racial discrimination in seniority reduction was held to violate these sections; Local 12, Rubber Workers, 150 N.L.R.B. No. 18, 57 L.R.R.M. 1535 (Dec. 16, 1964), where discriminatory refusal of union to process, through arbitration, Negro members' grievances concerning back pay claim resulting from challenge to dual seniority system and refusal to process Negro members' grievances calling for desegregation of plant facilities was held to violate §8(*b*)(*1*)(*A*); cf. Tanner Motor Livery, Ltd., 148 N.L.R.B. No. 137, 57 L.R.R.M. 1170 (Sept. 29, 1964), where employer was found to violate §8(*a*)(*1*) by discharging employee who picketed to protest employer's failure and refusal to hire Negroes.
46. Under Section 8(*a*)(*3*) it is an unfair labor practice for an employer

> by discrimination in regard to hire or tenure of employment or any term or condition of employment to encourage or discourage

membership in any labor organization . . . [except as to specific classes of union shop agreements].

Section 8(*b*)(2) provides that it is an unfair labor practice for a labor organization

to cause or attempt to cause an employer to discriminate against an employee in violation of subsection (a)(3) of this section or to discriminate against an employee with respect to whom membership in such organization has been denied or terminated on some ground other than his failure to tender the periodic dues and the initiation fees uniformly required as a condition of acquiring or retaining membership.

47. Cox, supra note 41, at 172–73.
48. Hughes Tool Co., 147 N.L.R.B. No. 166, 56 L.R.R.M. 1289, 1291, 1292 (July 1, 1964).
49. Local 1367, ILA, 148 N.L.R.B. No. 44, 57 L.R.R.M. 1083, 1085–86 (Sept. 11, 1964). Italics added by the author for emphasis.
50. N.L.R.B., 10th Annual Report 18 (1945).
51. 140 N.L.R.B. at 55.
52. 147 N.L.R.B. No. 166, 56 L.R.R.M. 1289 (July 1, 1964).
53. See Marshall, Some Factors Influencing the Growth of Unions in the South, 13 Ind. Rel. Research Ass'n, Proceedings of the 13th Annual Meeting 166 (1960).
54. See Peters, The Southern Temper 234–40 (1958); Segal, Racism Stymies Unions in the South, The New Leader (Nov. 11, 1957); Wheeler, The Impact of Race Relations on Industrial Relations in the South, 15 Lab. L. J. 474 (1964); Comment, Employee Choice and Some Problems of Race and Remedies in Representation Campaigns, 72 Yale L. J. 1243 (1963). But cf. Marshall, Union Racial Problems in the South, 1 Ind. Rel., A Journal of Economy and Society 117 (May, 1962).
55. See Sachs, The Racial Issue as an Antiunion Tool and the National Labor Relations Board, 14 LAB. L. J. 849 (1963); but see comment, Employee Choice and Some Problems of Race and Remedies in Representation Campaigns, 72 Yale L. J. 1243 (1963); Bok, The Regulation of Campaign Tactics in Representation Elections Under the National Labor Relations Act, 78 Harv. L. Rev. 38, 67–74 (1964).

56. Allen Morrison Sign Co., 138 N.L.R.B. 73, 75 (1962).
57. Sewell Mfg. Co., 138 N.L.R.B. 72 (1962).
58. Idem at 71–72. Office of the General Counsel of the NLRB, Summary of Operations, Calendar Year 1962, 8 Race Rel. L. Rep. 313, 314 (1963). Shortly after the Sewell ruling, the General Counsel of the NLRB announced that:

    Because of the substantial importance of this problem in the administration of law, the Office of the General Counsel would consider it necessary if appropriate charges were filed in a given case involving appeals to racial prejudice to issue an unfair labor practice complaint. This would permit a Board determination whether in certain circumstances appeals to racial prejudice do not merely interfere with free choice in an election but whether such appeals may not also constitute an unfair labor practice against which a remedial order should be obtained.

    Evidently the General Council's invitation was quickly accepted. See Borg-Warner Corp., 148 N.L.R.B. No. 98, 57 L.R.R.M. 1097 (1964).
59. Blumrosen, supra note 41, at 1514.
60. Employment, note 16, at 145–46.
61. N.L.R.B., 26th Annual Report 18 (1962).
62. N.L.R.B., 26th Annual Report 76 (1962). Italics added for emphasis.

19 / Fair Employment Practice Laws—Experience, Effects, Prospects

Paul H. Norgren

□ Introduction

The passage of the Federal Civil Rights Act of 1964 marked the completion of a comprehensive Federal policy outlawing racial discrimination that extends to virtually every phase of our national life.[1] Indeed, the Act does considerably more than round out the coverage of the policy: it also prescribes ways and means of implementing and enforcing the legal guarantees of equal treatment for racial and other minorities. It does this for the previously established bans on discrimination in voting rights and on segregation in public schools and other publicly owned facilities as well as for the newly established prohibitions against discrimination in employment, in places of public accommodation, and in Federally assisted programs. The Act also broadens and strengthens the powers of the United States Commission on Civil Rights, established by the Civil Rights Act of 1957. And, finally, it establishes a Community Relations Service, to provide assistance to communities "in resolving disputes . . . based on race, color or national origin."

The section of the 1964 Act that merits closest attention in the context of the present volume is Title VII, which bears the heading "Equal Employment Opportunity." In essence, this section prohibits discrimination in employment affected by interstate commerce because of race, color, creed, sex, or national origin, and provides for the administration of voluntary compliance by an appointive commission and for enforcement in the Federal courts. It became effective on July 2, 1965—one year after the date of its enactment.

The statutory ban on job discrimination in Title VII is, of course, not in itself an innovation. Twenty states[2] and seven major cities[3] already had enforceable fair employment practice laws in effect before the Civil Rights Act of 1964 was passed; three additional states had laws that were for all practical purposes nonenforceable.[4] Moreover, discrimination in the Federal Civil Service had been proscribed by law since 1940.[5] That Title VII is a *Federal* measure, however, is a fact of considerable significance—especially for the nation's Negro minority. Job discrimination is already prohibited by existing laws in every industrial state in the North, and in most of the nonindustrial states as well. On the other hand, with the recent exception of Kentucky, no Southern state has yet enacted fair employment legislation of any kind and only two Southern cities have Fair Employment Practices (FEP) ordinances.[6] Since the existing FEP laws continue in effect, the main proximate result of Title VII will therefore be to bring the Southern states for the first time under a legislative ban on discrimination in the job market and the workplace.[7]

A Typical State FEP Law—Content and Administration

The first enforceable fair employment legislation covering private employment was adopted by New York State early in 1945. With a few substantial exceptions, to be noted presently, all of the later state and local FEP laws have been modeled on the New York statute. Hence, it is possible to outline the salient features of a typical state (or municipal) law. It is also possible to describe the typical procedure in securing compliance with the nondiscrimination mandate—although, as we shall see, the procedure developed in New York State is significantly nontypical.

The typical FEP law first defines the discriminatory practices based on race, creed, color, or national origin that are declared unlawful. They include actions of employers, such as refusal to hire or discriminatory discharge; of employment agencies, such as refusal to refer for employment; and of labor organizations, such as exclusion from membership or segregation of members by race. The typical statute also establishes an appointive commission with responsibility for obtaining compliance with the antidiscrimination mandate. Thirdly, it instructs the commission to receive complaints of discriminatory treatment from aggrieved individuals and to secure redress for these persons from the employers, employment agencies, or unions committing the unlawful acts.

When a typical FEP commission (FEPC) receives a complaint, it first conducts an investigation to determine the truth of the allegation. If sufficient supporting evidence is found, a commission official confers privately with the employer, employment agency, or union involved, and through "conciliation and persuasion" endeavors to bring about voluntary correction of the discriminatory act—for example, the hiring or reinstatement of the complainant. If this effort succeeds, the case is concluded. If it fails, the commission may convene a hearing, at which the entire case is reviewed in public and the respondent subjected to questioning by the commission. If the original finding of probable cause is sustained, the commission may issue an order requiring the respondent to take corrective action. Such orders are enforceable in the courts, and refusal to comply makes the respondent liable to contempt action. In practice, however, the great bulk of complaints are either adjusted during the conciliation stage or remain unadjusted. FEPC's rarely invoke the public hearing and order-issuance procedures.

Title VII of the Civil Rights Act of 1964

The Federal FEP title, like the state and local laws, forbids discrimination by employment agencies and labor organizations as well as by employers. Unlike most of the state and local laws, however, Title VII includes within the definition of "unlawful employment practices" discriminatory *general* rules and practices as well as specific discriminatory acts against individuals.[8] It also creates a five-member Equal Employment Opportunity Commission, and authorizes it to receive and deal with complaints of alleged discriminatory acts—from aggrieved individuals, from organizations, or from individual members of the commission itself. It directs the commission to investigate such complaints, and, if it finds there is reasonable cause to believe they are true, to "endeavor to eliminate [the] . . . unlawful employment practice by informal methods of conference, conciliation and persuasion." However, the commission is not empowered to hold public hearings or issue cease-and-desist orders in cases where conciliation fails. Instead, the title provides that when the commission fails to obtain voluntary compliance within thirty days, the *complainant* (or, in cases initiated by commission members, the allegedly aggrieved person) may bring court action against the respondent, and the court may issue an order requiring compliance.

In cases where the alleged discriminatory action occurs in a state or locality that has its own FEP law, the aggrieved person is required to file his complaint under the state or local law first, and may only complain to the Federal commission after sixty days have expired. Similarly, when a complaint is initiated in such a state or locality by a member of the Federal commission, the commission must first notify the appropriate state or local officials, allowing them at least sixty days to eliminate the discriminatory practice before commencing Federal action.

Section 709(*b*) authorizes the Federal commission to conclude cooperative agreements with state and local commissions under which it may agree to cede its residual jurisdiction over compliance administration to the state or local agencies, in order to give them final jurisdiction in all compliance cases. The Federal commission may "reimburse such (state and local) agencies for services rendered to assist the Commission in carrying out this title." However, the commission is empowered to rescind any such agreement "whenever it determines that the agreement no longer serves the interest of effective enforcement of this title."

It is apparent from these provisions that the existing state and local laws and commissions are to continue functioning and that any state or local laws adopted in the future will also have active functioning status. It is, moreover, the apparent intent of the Federal law that the state and local commissions shall have final power to administer compliance within their areas, provided they meet the Federal commission's standards of effective administration. Thus, Title VII in effect establishes a coordinate system of Federal, state, and local FEP legislation, under which the Federal government has full administrative jurisdiction in areas where state or local laws are lacking, and residual or "watchdog" authority where such laws are in effect.

However, the title also provides for Federal compliance action by another route, independent of the priority accorded state and local commissions. Section 707 authorizes the U.S. Attorney General, "whenever [he] has reasonable cause to believe that any person or group of persons is engaged in a *pattern* or *practice*" (italics added) of proscribed discrimination, to bring civil court action requesting injunctions against the violators. This provision appears to be designed primarily for dealing with pervasive noncompliance transcending state lines, such as discriminatory policies of firms with multistate operations.

□ State and Municipal FEP Commissions—Compliance Approaches and Procedures

One explicitly stated purpose common to all fair employment laws is to provide redress for individuals subjected to discriminatory actions by firms, employment agencies, or unions. A broader and more basic purpose, however—clearly indicated in the Federal FEP title and in several state and local laws, and implied in the rest—is to eliminate discriminatory general rules and practices followed by such organizations. For the most part, employment discrimination stems not from isolated actions by management and union officials, but from long-established policies and practices that apply to entire firms or establishments, with resultant large-scale discriminatory treatment of minority groups. The paramount question concerning Title VII, therefore, is whether the coordinated system of Federal, state, and local FEP legislation that it establishes will further this basic purpose. However, owing to the crucial importance of administration and enforcement in determining the effectiveness of this type of legislation, a more useful formulation of the question is whether the system of laws can be administered in a manner that will bring about substantial and progressive elimination of discriminatory employment policies and practices.

A recently completed study of past experience under state and local FEP laws has yielded significant evidence bearing on this question.[9] The study revealed that notable progress in abating racial job discrimination has occurred in a few jurisdictions, as compared with generally very minor gains in states and cities with FEP laws. It also revealed, however, that the substantial progress in these few jurisdictions was not attributable to any differences in legislative substance, but rather to certain distinctive approaches and procedural techniques followed by the commissions in these areas in administering and enforcing compliance. Analysis of these findings indicated that appropriate extensions or modifications of the successful approaches and techniques, if adopted by state and local FEP commissions generally, would substantially increase their effectiveness. The application of this conclusion for greater progress toward eliminating employment discrimination is apparent, since the state and local laws continue in effect under Title VII. Moreover, utilization of the proposed approaches by the Federal commission will also enhance its effectiveness in administering compliance with the equal opportunity mandate at the national level.

The findings and conclusion of the study are summarized in the following pages. The discussion of experience is confined to FEP laws enacted during the period 1945–1955. While more than half of the existing state and local laws fall outside this category, most of these have been operative for such a brief period that no useful appraisal of their effectiveness is possible. In addition, the laws of Alaska and New Mexico, although passed during the period under consideration, are omitted in view of the nearly negligible Negro populations in these states. The discussion is therefore limited to the laws of ten states—New York, New Jersey, Massachusetts, Connecticut, Pennsylvania, Michigan, Minnesota, Oregon, Washington, and Rhode Island—and the city of Philadelphia.

The analysis of the effects of FEP laws on minority groups is confined to their impact on Negro workers. While a number of other "color" minorities, including Mexican-Americans, Puerto Ricans, and Indians, are subject to employment discrimination, the Negro group is by far the largest such minority. It is, moreover, the only minority for which relevant factual information is obtainable on a significant scale.

As we have noted, most of the currently operative FEP laws are modeled on the pioneering New York State law, and hence are closely similar in content. There are, however, substantial differences among the commissions responsible for administering the laws—differences in financial resources, in size and caliber of the commissions and their supporting staffs, and in the approaches and methods utilized in securing compliance with the nondiscrimination laws. In the commissions covered by the present analysis the significant differences are between the New York State and Philadelphia agencies on the one hand, and the Massachusetts, Connecticut, Pennsylvania, Michigan, Minnesota, Oregon, and Washington commissions on the other. Since the seven agencies in the second group are closely similar, both in financial resources and in compliance approach and procedures, we shall refer to them collectively in the ensuing discussion as the "normative" commissions.[10] Nearly all of the commissions established since 1955 also fall in this category.

Throughout the period since its inception in 1945, the New York State Commission on Human Rights has had the largest annual budget and operating staff of any state or municipal FEP agency. In 1960, for example, it had a budget of nearly $1 million, and a professional staff of 80. By contrast, the Michigan commission, the best financed of the normative agencies, had a budget of only $150,000 and a professional staff of 10. Even when account is taken of its larger compliance work load, the budgets and staffs of the normative commissions are woefully small compared with those of the New York agency.[11] The only agency that approached equality with the New York commission in this respect was the Philadelphia Commission on Human Relations, which had a budget of $144,000 and a staff of 19.[12] Since Philadelphia has a Negro labor force only one-third that of New York State—and a correspondingly smaller compliance work load—the Philadelphia commission was thus fairly close to parity with the New York State commission.

Under nearly all of the state and local laws studied, the only approach to enforcement explicitly specified is the processing and adjustment of complaints filed by aggrieved individuals. True, the agencies are empowered to deal with general discriminatory practices revealed in the course of investigating complaints. However, the normative commissions have been forced by their extremely limited budgets to confine their efforts largely to correcting individual grievances.

On the other hand, the New York State and Philadelphia commissions have given increasing attention to eliminating discriminatory policies and general practices, while continuing to perform their complaint-redressing function. The New York commission has, in fact, been conducting such "pattern-centered" compliance efforts since early in its career. It approaches this function in two principal ways: through compliance agreements negotiated with employers in the course of processing individual complaints; and through "informal investigations" of charges filed by civil rights and other organizations. The New York commission has also conducted pattern compliance efforts on its own initiative, in a number of industries, although it lacks enforceable jurisdiction in such cases. The Philadelphia commission possesses the broadest power to take pattern-based compliance action of any FEP agency. Under the Philadelphia ordinance, the commission is authorized to conduct investigations of discriminatory general practices and issue verified complaints on its own initiative; to hold public hearings in such cases in lieu of private conciliation efforts; and to issue cease-and-desist orders and have them enforced in the courts. The commission has made increasing use of this power in recent years. It has enabled the agency to direct its major efforts toward entire local industries characterized by pervasive discrimination, and has proved highly effective in such situations.

In negotiating compliance agreements with noncomplying employers, both the New York State and Philadelphia commissions have in recent years increasingly pressed for inclusion of "affirmative compliance" provisions. Under such a provision the respondent management agrees not only to abandon its discriminatory rules and practices, but to make an affirmative effort to employ Negroes in nontraditional jobs. The intent of such provisions is not that employers hire Negroes who are less qualified than white applicants, but rather that they broaden their recruitment efforts in order to attract qualified Negro applicants.

Following the completion of conciliation agreements with noncomplying employers, the New York State commission conducts periodic surveys of racial employment patterns in the affected plants as a check on the manner and extent of compliance. The Philadelphia commission also conducts such surveys, although less regularly. The experience of both commissions shows that this practice is effective in spurring managements to meet their compliance commitments.

Many employment agencies, both private and public, discriminate against Negroes and other color minorities—most commonly by complying with employer requests for workers that specify "whites only." While this practice is most prevalent in the South, it is also quite common in most states with FEP laws, despite the fact that it is prohibited under all existing fair employment statutes. The persistence of discriminatory job transactions is particularly anomalous in *public* employment offices in states where discrimination is prohibited by law. It is attributable, in the main, to the failure of the United States Employment Service (USES)—the policy-setting Federal agency—to establish a mandatory policy forbidding the state-operated offices to honor discriminatory job orders, and to the USES's practice of allocating operating funds to these offices on the basis of their record of total placements, which actually encourages the acceptance and filling of discriminatory orders. A further contributing factor is the state employment services' refusal, in the great majority of states with FEP laws, to co-operate with the FEPC's by reporting discriminatory employer requests. Even in the states where such reporting arrangements are in effect, however, the practice has by no means been eliminated.

Racial discrimination by labor organizations in the North is confined mainly to certain craft unions, chiefly in building construction, printing, and railroad transportation; hence the union compliance problem confronting state and local FEP commissions is limited in its industrial and occupational scope. On the other hand, the commissions have found it much more difficult to obtain compliance from discriminatory unions than from discriminatory managements. Exclusion of Negroes from membership, and discrimination in job referrals—the most prevalent forms of craft-union discriminatory practice—stem not only from racial prejudice but, to an even greater extent, from deep-rooted restrictionist attitudes prevailing among craft-union members. Consequently most such unions strongly resist all efforts to make them relinquish these practices. The difficulty is compounded by the fact that union discriminatory practices involve, in virtually all cases, explicit agreements with or tacit acquiescence by employers. Hence the union discrimination problem cannot be dealt with effectively unless compliance commitments are obtained from both unions and managements.

Largely because of these obstacles and complexities, the state and local FEPC's without exception have displayed a marked reluctance to take action against discriminatory unions. Moreover, their efforts have been almost exclusively confined to processing complaints by individuals or small groups of Negro workers and have seldom resulted in more than token compliance.

In the past, the New York State and Philadelphia agencies have been just as reluctant as other FEP agencies to take action against discriminatory labor organizations. It is only within the last five years that the Philadelphia agency has begun serious efforts to halt discriminatory practices by the city's craft unions. The New York State Commission has been even more tardy in this respect: its first successful action against an exclusionist craft union was begun late in 1963 and concluded in mid-1964.[13]

□ FEPC Compliance Activities—Experience and Effects

Despite their unimpressive records in combating union racial practices, the overall performances of the New York State and Philadelphia commissions makes them unique among existing state and local FEP agencies. The distinctive feature of their performances is the strong emphasis both commissions have given to securing broad-based and affirmative compliance by refractory managements. Moreover, Negroes have made significant employment gains in both jurisdictions, and as we shall see, the evidence indicates that these gains have occurred largely as a result of the commissions' compliance efforts.

The most direct evidence of this progress is found in the commissions' post-settlement surveys of respondent firms' employment patterns. Analysis of these surveys shows that in a large proportion of cases substantial numbers of Negroes have obtained employment, often in lines of work formerly closed to them, following the consummation of compliance agreements. The surveys made in traditionally Negro-excluding industries are especially noteworthy. In 1958 the New York commission made analyses of all follow-up reviews conducted since its establishment in banks, insurance companies, and department stores. A case-by-case comparison of post-settlement with pre-settlement employment patterns revealed that in the great majority of cases substantial improvements occurred in both the numerical representation and the occupational status of Negroes. For example, none of the thirteen banking concerns reviewed had more than a handful of Negro employees at the time of the original investigation. When the recheck surveys were conducted in the middle 1950's, seven of these banks each had more than 100 Negro employees in a variety of white-collar occupations—and almost equally large increases had occurred in three others. The analyses of insurance companies also showed consistent, marked increases in the number and occupational status of Negro employees. One large insurance company, which in 1945 had no racial minority employees, by 1956 was employing 750 Negroes in a wide variety of occupations, including many supervisory positions. The review of department store experience revealed equally impressive gains. While only one of the fifteen stores surveyed had Negro employees in jobs above the menial level in 1945, by 1958 fourteen of these stores were employing substantial numbers of Negroes in sales, office, and other nontraditional positions. And in communications-utilities firms, employment of Negroes rose from 2.2 percent of total employment in 1950 to 5.0 percent in 1960, with an accompanying marked upgrading of their occupational level.

Further evidence of the efficacy of the pattern-centered approach is provided by developments in Philadelphia. Although the Philadelphia Commission on Human Relations did not utilize its power to initiate broad-based compliance action until the late 1950's, it has already made substantial headway. In 1958, it conducted a detailed investigation of racial employment practices in the city's hotel and restaurant industry, followed by a series of public hearings involving both management and union officials. Subsequently the commission published a report of its findings, showing that racial discrimination by both employers and unions was widespread. This action, and the ensuing negotiations with individual managements and union officials, resulted in a notable improvement in both the number and level of job assignments for Negroes in Philadelphia's restaurants and hotels. By 1962, sizeable numbers of Negroes were employed in most of the occupations from which they had formerly been excluded, holding jobs as waiters, bartenders, cashiers, desk clerks, and in clerical positions.[14]

Subsequently the commissions conducted a similar investigation of employment practices in the city's banks. The commission did not hold public hearings in this instance. Prior to issuing its report, however, it made a recheck of the industry's racial employment pattern. The survey showed that the number of Negroes employed in the banks had increased by forty percent in the interim, indicating that the investigation itself had spurred the bank managements to better compliance.[15]

As we have noted, the New York and Philadelphia commissions' compliance achievement record has been conspicuously weak in industries organized by discriminatory craft unions. With the exception of the Philadelphia commission's hotel and restaurant action in 1958, neither commission took any meaningful steps against any such unions until 1963, following a wave of Negro group demonstrations directed specifically against the plumbers, electricians, and other exclusionist building-trades organizations. In the spring of that year, the Philadelphia commission held a series of public hearings to investigate allegations that racial discrimination was practiced by unions and employers in the city's building trades. It subsequently cited six local craft unions[16] and four contractors for policies and practices that effectively excluded Negroes from union membership and employment opportunity. The unions later committed themselves to admit qualified Negroes to membership and to apprentice training programs, and the employers made similar commitments with respect to employing Negro journeymen and apprentices. Following these commitments, the commission conducted a publicity campaign aimed at inducing Negro building craftsmen to seek membership in these unions and Negro youths to seek admittance to their apprenticeship programs. As a result, five of the six unions admitted Negro craftsmen and apprentices for the first time. While the numbers admitted were small, owing to a shortage of qualified candidates, this episode constituted a major step toward eliminating discriminatory racial practices by unions in Philadelphia.[17] In August 1963, the commission took initial steps toward similar action to halt racial discrimination by craft unions and employers in the city's printing industry. In this instance, however, the commission did not find it necessary to conduct public hearings. Following brief negotiations, both the unions and the employers' organizations agreed to discontinue the discriminatory practices.[18]

Two other major FEP agencies also instituted pattern-based compliance actions against discriminatory craft unions at this time. In July 1963, the Pennsylvania Human Relations Commission issued an order citing seven Pittsburgh building-trades locals,[19] and directing them "to accept for immediate membership any qualified nonwhite craftsmen" and "to accept an appropriate number of qualified nonwhite applicants . . . in all future apprenticeship programs." The case had been referred to the state commission by the Pittsburgh municipal commission, following a finding of discriminatory exclusion of Negroes and lengthy compliance efforts by that body. The unions agreed to abide by the order.[20] Later in 1963, the New York State commission, following the filing of a complaint by the state's Attorney General, took compliance action against the New York City unit of the Sheet Metal Workers Union, Local 28, on similar grounds. When efforts to obtain voluntary compliance proved fruitless, the commission ordered the local to end its traditional father-son apprenticeship selection practice, which "automatically excluded" Negroes, and to accept members solely on the basis of their qualifications.[21] The commission subsequently sought enforcement of its order in the courts, and in August 1964, a State Supreme Court judge issued a decision upholding the commission. The decision, which followed extended meetings with representatives of the union, the employers, and the commission, included a commitment by the union to obey the commission's order.[22]

These actions by the Philadelphia, New York State, and Pennsylvania commissions were initiated shortly after Negro groups in both the states had picketed and conducted other mass demonstrations protesting racial discrimination by construction craft unions.[23] In view of the commissions' failure to take meaningful compliance action against such unions in the past, it is apparent that the protest demonstrations were a major factor in their decision to institute such action at this time.

Little direct evidence of the effects of compliance efforts was obtainable from the other FEPC's studied, since none of these agencies conduct follow-up reviews of racial employment patterns. However, some indication of the relative effectiveness of the several commissions surveyed can be obtained by making a comparison of Census figures on Negro employment in their respective jurisdictions. The following table makes such a comparison among five jurisdictions for 1950 and 1960 in three industry classifications: general merchandise and variety stores, banking and other finance, and public utilities (except transportation). These classifications are comparable with three of the traditionally Negro-excluding activities referred to earlier in discussing the New York and Philadelphia commissions' experience: department stores, banks, and communications utilities. The jurisdictions included in the comparison, in addition to New York State and Philadelphia, are Pennsylvania (excluding Philadelphia), Michigan, and Connecticut—three states with normative commission states and relatively large Negro populations.

Negro Employment as Percentage of Total Employment in Selected Industries and FEP Law Jurisdictions, 1950 and 1960

State or City	**General Merchandise & Variety Stores**		**Banking & Other Finance**		**Public Utilities (except transportation)**	
	1950	*1960*	*1950*	*1960*	*1950*	*1960*
New York State	3.2	7.4	0.9	2.1	2.8	5.1
Philadelphia	6.8	10.8	1.7	2.7	6.3	11.0
Pennsylvania (except Philadelphia)	1.7	1.4	1.2	0.8	1.7	1.9
Michigan	3.0	3.8	1.3	1.6	4.6	5.7
Connecticut	2.4	3.2	0.9	1.1	1.5	2.2

Source: U.S. Census of Population, 1950: Vol. II, *Characteristics of the Population,* Parts 7, 22, 32, 37. *U.S. Census of Population, 1960: Detailed Characteristics,* Final Report PC (1), 8D, 24D, 34D, 40D.

It will be noted that the Negro proportion of total employment rose between 1950 and 1960 in all three industries in New York State and Philadelphia. It also rose throughout in Connecticut and Michigan, and in one classification in Pennsylvania. However, the gains in New York State and Philadelphia were consistently larger than those in the states with normative commissions. The changes in the former two areas ranged from a gain of 60 percent in Philadelphia department stores and banks to one of 133 percent in New York banks, while in the three latter states they ranged from a loss of 33 percent in Pennsylvania banks to a gain of 47 percent in Connecticut public utilities.

The improvements in Negro job status in the states with

normative commissions revealed by the foregoing analysis are not sufficiently large or consistent to indicate any major positive effect of the commissions' efforts to secure compliance with the FEP mandate. The much larger rise in the figures for New York State and Philadelphia, however, are clearly in line with the gains shown by the follow-up survey data. These figures, therefore, strengthen the earlier, tentative conclusion that the pattern-based compliance activities of the New York and Philadelphia commissions have brought about a significant abatement of discriminatory employment practices in these jurisdictions.

□ How FEP-Law Administration Can Be Improved

As noted earlier, the existing state and municipal laws continue in effect under the Federal FEP title. However, the foregoing review of experience has revealed that, with two notable exceptions, the impact of these laws in reducing pervasive employment discrimination has been small.

The effectiveness of FEP legislation depends chiefly on the approach and conduct of the administering commissions. Accordingly, the proposals and suggestions outlined below are aimed primarily at improving administration of the laws and are based largely, though by no means entirely, on the relatively successful approach followed by the New York State and Philadelphia commissions.

First of all, commissions should direct their main compliance effort toward eliminating plant-wide and organization-wide discriminatory policies and practices. Since it would not be politically feasible to discontinue processing and adjusting individual grievances, the two functions must be carried on simultaneously. However, the primary emphasis should be given to ending pervasive practices, for only through this approach can significant progress toward racial equality in the labor market be achieved.

In pursuing this objective, commissions should program their pattern-centered compliance activities in advance for periods of at least a year, and preferably longer. This will enable them to administer the law on a coordinated basis—for example, by including all establishments in an industry characterized by widespread noncompliance in a single compliance action. It will also enable them to establish meaningful time priorities, giving attention to those situations in which discrimination is most prevalent. It will probably be necessary in most instances for the commissions themselves to initiate such compliance actions, since most complaints filed with them are confined to actions against individual organizations. However, complaints filed by civil rights organizations will undoubtedly provide a justifiable basis for programmed compliance actions in some instances. In this context it is important to note that only six of the existing FEP laws empower the commissions to take enforceable compliance action on their own initiative.[24] It will therefore be necessary to amend the remaining state and municipal laws, investing commissions with the power to initiate action to end pervasive discrimination by employers, employment agencies, and unions.

In negotiating conciliation agreements with noncomplying employers, commissions should give primary attention to securing provisions for affirmative compliance—that is, provisions committing the management to make an active effort to employ Negroes in nontraditional jobs. Owing to the severely handicapped job market status of most Negro workers, such provisions are necessary if FEP laws are to have any significant effect. The affirmative compliance commitment should not, however, prescribe "quotas" of Negroes to be employed, either *in toto* or in particular occupational categories. Indeed, many state and local FEP laws, as well as Title VII of the Federal Civil Rights Act, explicitly prohibit commissions from requiring employers to hire or promote personnel on any kind of quota basis. Moreover, experience has shown that adequacy of compliance is best determined by later informal surveys, assessed in the light of attendant circumstances and results achieved, without reference to any predetermined goal.

Acceptance of the affirmative compliance principle by an

employer does not mean he will be expected to hire Negroes who are less qualified than white applicants. However, other measures that will help in meeting this commitment are open to many employers. One way is to broaden the scope of recruitment efforts in order to attract larger numbers of qualified Negro applicants. Another way is to modify the formal educational requirements for job eligibility where, as is often the case, they are unnecessarily high.

Following conciliation agreements with noncomplying managements, commissions should conduct periodic surveys of employment patterns in their establishments. Experience in New York State and Philadelphia shows that this practice not only provides a means of assessing the manner and extent of compliance but also spurs managements to meet their commitments. The customary method of conducting post-settlement surveys in New York State is to have commission investigators make physical inspections of respondent employers' plants. Racial employment patterns are now ascertained through visual "head counts" of Negro employees—a cumbersome and time-consuming procedure. The survey process would obviously be greatly facilitated if employers included racial identifications in their employment records, since racial employment patterns could then be obtained directly from recorded information. However, none of the state or local FEP laws require employers to keep such records, and few are willing to do so of their own volition. Thus, there is an evident need to amend existing laws by adding such a requirement, and a corresponding provision requiring unions to maintain racial identifications in their membership rosters.

Fortunately, the Federal FEP title furnishes a prototype for amending the state and local laws in this respect. The Federal Act provides that:

> . . . every employer, employment agency and labor organization subject to this title shall (*1*) keep such records relevant to the determination of whether unlawful employment practices have been or are being committed, (*2*) preserve such records for such periods, and (*3*) make such reports therefrom, as the commission

shall prescribe by regulation or order, after public hearing, as reasonable, necessary, or appropriate for the enforcement of this title or the regulation or orders thereunder.

The Act exempts from this requirement persons who are subject to existing state and local FEP laws, but adds the proviso that the Federal commission "may require such notations on such records which such employer, employment agency, labor organization or joint labor-management committee keeps or is required to keep as are necessary because of differences in coverage methods of enforcement between the state or local law and the provisions of this title." Thus it is apparent that employers and unions are required to keep records in substantial conformity with the standards established by the Federal commission, even when they are subject to state or local FEP laws. And it is equally apparent that the implementation of this record-keeping and reporting requirement would be simplified and expedited if the state and local laws were amended to conform to the provisions of the Federal title.

Owing to the meager achievements of FEPC's in dealing with unions in the past, there is little direct experience on which to base suggestions for improving their performance in this area. However, the successful experience of the New York State and Philadelphia commissions, while primarily oriented toward promoting compliance by employers, can also be used as a basis for dealing with discriminatory unions, if the distinctive causal factors underlying the racial practices of many unions are taken into account.

To begin with, it is obviously just as essential for commissions to adopt a pattern-centered approach in seeking compliance by discriminatory unions as it is in dealing with discriminatory managements. It is clear from earlier commission experience that adjusting individual complaints of union discrimination will almost invariably result in mere token compliance.

In conducting compliance negotiations with local craft unions, commissions will in many instances undoubtedly encounter strong resistance from local leaders as well as rank-

and-file members. However, there are several ways in which commissions can reduce such resistance. One way is to institute simultaneous negotiations with the employers directly affected. If the employers can be committed to accepting Negro journeymen and apprentices as employees, the union leaders will be put under pressure to admit them to union membership. Union resistance is also likely to be reduced if the commission includes unions in several distinct but related crafts—for example, unions within the building or printing trades—in the same compliance proceeding. This approach has two obvious advantages, from the unions' point of view, over proceeding against a single local: it distributes the attendant unfavorable publicity among several unions; and it distributes the influx of Negro youths seeking admission to apprenticeship rolls. Commissions may also be able to soften local union resistance by involving the heads of national unions in the compliance negotiations. The presidents of nearly all of the national unions, craft and industrial, are committed by their organizations to the racial equality mandate; and, moreover, they are usually in a position to exert pressure on recalcitrant leaders of affiliated locals.

In the comparatively few actions taken against discriminatory craft unions, nearly all of the commissions surveyed have tended to continue the conciliation efforts for unduly long periods, even when there was no longer any prospect of obtaining compliance through this approach. However, the Philadelphia Commission on Human Relations has been able to avoid this tendency, primarily because the Philadelphia ordinance alone among FEP laws empowers the administering agency to proceed directly to public hearings, without the necessity of first engaging in "conference, conciliation, and persuasion." The commission has conducted such hearings in a number of instances involving exceptionally resistant unions and has found them effective in getting at the facts of the situation and expediting compliance agreements. Its experience in this area suggests that FEPC's, when dealing with recalcitrant unions or recalcitrant managements, should discontinue their conciliation efforts as soon as determined resistance manifests itself and should proceed to the public hearing stage.

In view of the deep-rooted restrictionism prevailing among craft workers, it would probably be unrealistic for FEPC's to attempt to obtain strong commitments from craft unions—or, at any rate, to expect them to make very determined efforts to fulfill such commitments. Nevertheless, commissions could make a good case for including affirmative compliance provisions in conciliation agreements with unions—especially with regard to admission to apprentice training programs. As a result of decades of rigid exclusion from apprenticeship, there are virtually no qualified Negro electricians, plumbers, or sheet metal workers in many localities. It could therefore hardly be called discrimination in reverse if some preference were given to Negro apprenticeship applicants in these trades over the next few years. In cases where it is not possible to obtain meaningful commitments, the task of recruiting Negro workers to implement compliance might well be undertaken by the commission itself. In the Philadelphia building trades case, the commission conducted an extensive publicity campaign aimed at obtaining qualified Negro journeymen and apprenticeship applicants for referral to the six formerly exclusionist unions. Unfortunately, very few of the more than three hundred applicants who appeared proved to be qualified.[25]

It is equally important that provision be made for post-settlement surveys of developments under union conciliation agreements, to check on the manner and extent of compliance. It may also be desirable, in cases where continued resistance to compliance is manifestly widespread, to provide for policing of the compliance process. Thus, in the Philadelphia building trades case, the agreements included a provision that commission representatives be present at membership and apprenticeship qualification examinations given by the unions to insure fair and impartial testing.[26]

The most important single requisite for making FEP laws effective is that the administering commissions be supplied with adequate operating funds. Budgets must be sufficient to afford salaries that will attract commissioners of high caliber and to permit employing a sufficiently large supporting staff.

Nearly all of the commissioners and other officials of the normative commissions surveyed stated that if budgets were adequate, and if the legislation were amended to give them the necessary powers, they would lose no time in instituting pattern-centered compliance programs based on affirmative compliance; and there is reason to believe that most of the more recently established commissions would do the same. Thus, it is primarily the state legislatures, through low budget appropriations, that are responsible for the inadequate administration of most of the state and local laws.

As we have noted, only the New York State and Philadelphia commissions have approached budget adequacy. The New York commission's budget for the 1963 fiscal year, exclusive of the amounts allocated to enforcing nondiscrimination in housing and public accommodations, was approximately $1.1 million. Assuming this figure to be adequate for New York State—and probably it is not—the budgets of the normative commissions studied would have to be raised from the current range of $150,000–$250,000 to a range of $600,000–$900,000, and comparable increases would be required in other states with FEP laws. If FEP laws are enacted in the Southern states, the agencies created to administer them would undoubtedly require budgets of this magnitude, owing to the large Negro populations and the pervasive discrimination patterns that characterize these states, which would lead to heavy work loads for their commissions.

□ Prospects for Fairer Employment Practices Under Title VII

The Federal FEP Title became operative on July 2, 1965. Since the existing state and municipal commissions are to continue functioning actively, and have priority of jurisdiction, the main administrative task of the Federal commission will be to administer Title VII in the Southern states, and in the ten rural states in the North that still lack state or local FEP laws. However, it will also play an indirect role in the administration of existing FEP statutes. In line with Section 709(*b*), it may be expected that the Federal commission will seek to conclude agreements with the state and municipal commissions, whereby the latter will be given exclusive power to administer compliance rulings within their respective jurisdictions in return for commitments to meet standards of compliance policy and procedure prescribed by the Federal body. Title VII, therefore, poses two major questions concerning the future administration of FEP laws in this country: whether the Federal commission operating under the provisions of Title VII can bring about significant compliance in the South with the antidiscrimination mandate; and whether, through its residual, or watchdog, function in relation to existing state and local FEP agencies, it can speed up the present slow pace of progress toward racial job equality in the North.

Racial job discrimination is patently both more prevalent and more intensive in the South than elsewhere. The restrictions on referral, hiring, placement, and promotion of Negroes commonly found in the North are even more common in the Southern region, and are usually also applied further down on the occupational scale. In addition, a variety of other discriminatory arrangements seldom found in Northern workplaces, such as separate seniority rosters, segregation in such facilities as cafeterias, drinking fountains, and toilets, and Jim Crow union locals, are widely established in the South.

It is commonly believed that, owing to more deep-rooted racial antipathies among Southern white workers, racial employment practices are more firmly entrenched and more difficult to alter in the South than in the North. This belief largely explains why most Southern managements are strongly opposed to FEP legislation. Apart from their own racial predilections, they fear that abolition of the existing racial practices and arrangements would be strongly resented and resisted by white employees and would result in work stoppages, racial clashes, and other disruptive incidents. However, significant modifications of the traditional racial employment patterns have been instituted in a variety of establishments throughout the South in recent years. These instances of successful employment integration, while they affect only a small fraction of all Southern workplaces, are nonetheless sufficiently numerous and widely dispersed to indicate that the prevalent pattern of racial practices is not as deeply implanted as has been generally assumed. Some of the earliest of these developments occurred in Federal Government establishments. Racial discrimination in Federal civilian employment has been prohibited by law since 1940; serious efforts to enforce the ban date from the middle 1950's. Since that time, Negroes have made considerable progress in gaining Federal jobs in Atlanta, Birmingham, and other major Southern cities. In Atlanta post offices, for example, Negroes comprised nearly 50 percent of the work force in 1962, and were employed in a number of clerical, public-contact, and supervisory positions.[27] Over approximately the same period, discriminatory practices have been modified and substantial racial integration effected in the Southern plants of a number of national manufacturing concerns, including DuPont, Goodyear, International Harvester, Lockheed Aircraft, United States Steel, Western Electric, and others. In the earlier instances, integration was instituted by the order of the high company managements, with little if any overt pressure from government agencies. The integration programs effected since 1961, however, have been undertaken largely as a result of pressure exerted by the President's Committee on Equal Employment Opportunity, the agency established by President Kennedy in 1961 to enforce the nondiscrimination provision in Federal contracts. Finally, within the past two years, locally-owned enterprises have also begun employing Negroes in nontraditional jobs in various Southern communities, including Atlanta, Augusta, Memphis, Nashville, New Orleans, Dallas, and Houston. For the first time, Negroes are employed in retail-sales positions in these and other cities. In most instances the breakthroughs have occurred as a direct result of boycotts or mass protest demonstrations.[28]

All of these instances have had two features in common. In the first place, the decision to institute integrated employment was not voluntary on the part of local management, but was imposed from without in every case—by Federal law or administrative agencies, by the national management of the company, or by pressure from organized Negro groups. Second, in virtually all instances the transition from discrimination and segregation to equal opportunity and integrated employment took place smoothly and without any manifest resistance on the part of white workers.

Thus, despite the strong views to the contrary of many Southern businessmen and most Southern political leaders, the conclusion seems warranted that racial equality in employment can be promoted through FEP legislation in the South as well as in the rest of the nation. In order to be effective, however, it is evident that any such legislation must be administered on the basis of eliminating discriminatory general practices and employment patterns, and must be vigorously enforced in all cases of persistent noncompliance. With specific regard to Title VII, it is evident that the Federal commission, if it is to make significant headway in promoting racial equality in employment in the South, must follow essentially the same compliance policies and approaches as those already outlined for state and municipal commissions. We may therefore conclude this chapter by recapitulating the proposals for improving the administration of FEP laws that were set forth in the preceding section.

FEP commissions—whether Federal, state or local—should direct their main compliance efforts toward eliminating discriminatory policies and general discriminatory practices by employers, employment agencies, and unions, while giving necessary attention to complaints by aggrieved individuals. They should plan and program these efforts in advance over a period of one or more years, giving priority of attention to industries, occupations, or geographic areas in which discriminatory treatment of racial minorities is most prevalent. In negotiating compliance agreements, they should obtain affirmative commitments from employers to employ nonwhites in traditionally white jobs, and from white unions to enroll nonwhite members. In dealing with recalcitrant employers, employment agencies, or unions, they should abridge their conciliation efforts and institute direct enforcement measures at an early stage. And they should conduct periodic follow-up surveys of racial employment patterns in all establishments and organizations involved in compliance actions.

Finally, if the commissions are to undertake effective compliance measures, they must be assured of adequate budgets. Congress, the state legislatures, and the municipal councils must provide their commissions with the operating funds necessary to establish salaries for commissioners commensurate with the talent required, and to employ sufficient supporting staffs to implement the above policies and approaches. At the state and local levels this will require, in nearly all instances, appropriations ranging from double to more than triple the amounts currently being allocated.

In addition to administering compliance with the fair employment mandate in the South, the Federal commission may be able to bring about, or at least expedite, the adoption of effective administrative policies and procedures by existing state and local commissions. By virtue of its power to conclude agreements with these agencies, granting them final jurisdiction over the enforcement of compliance, the Federal commission will be in a position to obtain commitments from them to follow its recommendations. Provided the necessary funds are forthcoming, the Federal commission will be able to strengthen its position by offering to reimburse the agencies for a portion of the additional costs entailed in meeting these commitments.

In negotiating such agreements, therefore, the Federal commission should seek to obtain commitments by the state and local agencies to focus their major efforts on eliminating discriminatory employment policies and general practices, and on securing affirmative compliance agreements from noncomplying employers and unions. It should also seek to have state and local commissions agree to deal with diehard noncompliers by invoking enforcement sanctions at a reasonably early stage, rather than engaging in unduly prolonged conciliation efforts. To facilitate appraisal of commission effectiveness under these agreements, provision should be made for submission of periodic reports by the state and local agencies to the Federal commission, recounting in detail the extent and results of their compliance activities.

If compliance policies and methods along the lines indicated by the analysis of the experience of existing FEPC's are adopted by the new national commission as well as by the existing state and local fair employment agencies, and if the respective legislative bodies provide the funds required for their effective implementation, equality of job opportunity for Negroes and other "color minorities" will be a realizable goal in all sections of the country.

NOTES

1. Public Law 88–352, 88th Congress, H. R. 7152, July 2, 1964.
2. The twenty states, and the years in which their laws were enacted are: New Jersey and New York (1945), Massachusetts (1946), Connecticut (1947), New Mexico, Oregon, Rhode Island, and Washington (1949), Alaska (1953), Michigan, Minnesota, and Pennsylvania (1955), Colorado and Wisconsin (1957), California and Ohio (1959), Delaware (1960), and Illinois, Kansas, and Missouri (1961).
3. Baltimore, Cleveland, Minneapolis, Philadelphia, Pittsburgh, St. Paul, and Toledo. Through special understandings with their state governments, most of the discrimination cases originating within these cities are handled by the municipal agencies.
4. Idaho (1961), and Iowa and Vermont (1963). Three additional states—Arizona, Nebraska, and Nevada—have laws that apply only to employment under state-government contracts.

5. Ramspeck Act, Title II, 54 Stat. 1211 (1940); superseded by Title I, 5 U.S.C. sec. 631a (1958).
6. In 1962, Richmond, Virginia, and El Paso, Texas, adopted FEP ordinances. In both instances, however, the ban on job discrimination is limited to municipal government employment. Two border areas—Baltimore and Delaware—have had enforceable FEP statutes since 1960.
7. Since 1941, a provision forbidding discrimination in employment has been included in most Federal procurement contracts, and five successive Presidential committees charged with administering the ban have functioned during this period. This stricture, of course, applies to Federal contract employment over the whole country. However, the various President's Committees have failed to effect a significant improvement in the racial practices of Federal contractors; and they have been especially ineffective in the South. While the currently functioning committee, established by President Kennedy in 1961, has a better record of effectiveness than its predecessors, its positive achievements in the South during the first two years of its existence were limited to a small number of plants in scattered locations, mainly branch operations of Northern-based manufacturing concerns. See President's Committee on Equal Employment Opportunity, *Report to the President, November 26, 1963* (Washington: U.S. Government Printing Office, 1964), pp. 10–13; P. H. Norgren and S. E. Hill, *Toward Fair Employment* (New York: Columbia Univ. Press, 1964), Chapter 7.
8. Section 703, subsections a(*2*) and c(*2*).
9. Norgren and Hill, *op. cit.*
10. The New Jersey Division Against Discrimination, while similar to the New York and Philadelphia commissions in some respects, closely resembles the seven normative commissions in other respects; hence it is omitted from the discussion.
11. It is worth noting that the members of the New York Commission serve on a full-time basis and receive annual salaries of $19,500, whereas the commissioners in six of the seven normative commissions serve only part-time and receive small *per diem* allowances. In the seventh state, Massachusetts, they receive salaries of $5000 a year.

12. Increased to 32 persons in 1963, with a corresponding increase in appropriation. *Annual Report,* 1963, p. 3.
13. See below, pp. 554–55.
14. Philadelphia Commission on Human Relations, *Report of Progress in the Integration of Hotel and Restaurant Employment,* June 1962, *passim.*
15. Philadelphia Commission on Human Relations, *Report of 1961–1962 Survey of Philadelphia Banks,* June 1962, p. 33; *Annual Report for 1963,* March 1964, p. 3.
16. Representing plumbers, steamfitters, sheet metal workers, roofers, and electricians (two locals).
17. Philadelphia Commission on Human Relations, *City Contract Compliance: Progress in 1963,* April 1964, *passim.*
18. Letter to the author from Terry C. Chisholm, Acting Director, Philadelphia Commission on Human Relations, June 22, 1964.
19. One local each of painters, electricians, structural iron workers, elevator constructors, and heat insulation workers, and two plumbers' locals.
20. Pennsylvania Human Relations Commission, Final Order, July 10, 1963.
21. *Lefkowitz* vs. *Farrell,* C-9287-63 (New York State Commission for Human Rights, 1964).
22. New York *Times,* August 25, 1964, p. 1.
23. As reported in the daily press, similar demonstrations—aimed specifically at discrimination in the building trades—occurred in many cities across the country during the summer of 1963.
24. The laws of Massachusetts, Michigan, Ohio, Pennsylvania, Rhode Island, and Philadelphia.
25. Philadelphia Commission on Human Relations, *City Contract Compliance: Progress in 1963,* p. 6.
26. *Ibid.,* p. 7.
27. Norgren and Hill, *op. cit.,* p. 200.
28. James A. Moss, *The Negro and Employment Opportunities in the South,* 1962; *Civil Rights: Year-End Summary,* 1963; Benjamin Muse, *Special Report: Memphis,* 1964 (Atlanta: Southern Regional Council).

Conclusions

20 / Will the Negro Succeed?

Arthur M. Ross

Title VII of the Civil Rights Act of 1964 became effective July 2, 1965, consummating twenty years of sustained effort for a Federal fair employment law. It declares that the policy of the United States is to ensure equal employment opportunities without discrimination because of race, color, religion, sex, or national origin.

The object might be stated negatively as the elimination of unfairness in hiring, promoting, and compensating workers. A more significant interpretation is that the law is intended to facilitate the integration of disadvantaged groups throughout the economy.

Will the Negro achieve economic integration? Some writers hold that integration is impossible or undesirable. Others contend that Negroes are not essentially different from other disadvantaged groups who have coped with prejudice and discrimination in the past and have fought their way out of slum poverty. Oscar Handlin says, concerning Negroes and Puerto

Ricans, that "the experience of the past offers a solid basis for the belief that the newest immigrants to a great metropolis will play as useful a role as any of their predecessors; they themselves need only show the will and energy, and their neighbors the tolerance, to make it possible." [1]

□ The Culture of Slavery

But there is an important difference. Some of the previous immigrants, such as the Jews and the Japanese, have had long traditions of education, occupational achievement, and family solidarity in support of youthful ambition. If newly urbanized groups such as Negroes, Puerto Ricans, and Mexican-Americans lack these cultural reinforcements, the analogy cannot be carried very far.

The cultural situation of the Negro has been the subject of vehement debate in recent years. On the one hand, the Negro is often described as the purest type of American because he was brought to the New World in a condition of cultural nakedness, so to speak. He was forced to leave behind his history along with his language, his tribal and family customs, and his political and religious institutions. On the other hand, an elusive quality called "Negritude" is sometimes imputed to black men everywhere as the alleged nucleus of an exclusively Negro personality and culture.

Only a social anthropologist would be qualified to analyze this question authoritatively. But one point, fundamental to an understanding of the Negro's employment problem, is obvious even to a layman. Granted that the Negro was ripped out of his African environment and brought along nothing like German socialism, or Yiddish theatre, or Hungarian goulash. Granted also that the great majority of Negroes reject Black Nationalism and desire to become full participants in American society, with all its imperfections. Still it does not follow that the Negro has had no distinctive culture of his own since being brought to the New World.

The fact is that one hundred years after the emancipation, the culture of slavery still leaves a deep imprint on the Negro's personality and still colors his relations with the white community.

Slavery in the United States was particularly damaging because of the lack of a feudal tradition and the absence of any provision in the dominant ideology for hierarchical orders of society, each with different rights and obligations, but all regarded as human. In the Spanish and Portuguese colonies of Latin America, slaves were unequal but were still men. They had important legal rights. They could receive the sacraments. Families were kept together. Manumission was encouraged by religious and political authorities, and former slaves entered into the mainstream of society and intermarried with whites. But in the United States, formal and categorical inequalities could not be recognized. Protestantism assumed a direct and immediate confrontation between man and God, rather than a vicarious relationship mediated through a spiritual hierarchy. In the Declaration of Independence it was reaffirmed that all men are created equal; from this it followed that if one was not equal, one could not be a man.[2] Thus there was absolutely no choice but to define the slave as a chattel. He was bred like a farm animal, bought and sold, treated harshly or kindly, according to the whims of his master. Since he could not be equal, he was nothing. As I shall note presently, this all-or-nothing tradition still has a most important bearing on the Negro's problem in making his way in the American economy.

The deeply ingrained racial attitudes of white Americans—arrogance, condescension, physical aversion combined with a prurient absorption in Negro sexuality—were nurtured in the Protestant, Anglo-Saxon version of slavery that became established in the United States. Likewise, those aspects of Negro personality and behavior which most seriously impede his economic progress—improvidence, apathy, self-hatred, family disorganization—are equally the product of slavery and its aftermath. There is no evidence that these are intrinsic weaknesses of character. Formed by experience, they can be reshaped by a different experience. But they cannot be scolded out of existence.

□ The Negro and the White Community

The Negro's cultural history, which has endowed him with strengths as well as weaknesses, will not be the only factor affecting his progress as he settles down for the long pull. Relations with the white community will also be significant.

In his classic exposition of *An American Dilemma,* Gunnar Myrdal held that the conscience of the white community would be decisive. "It is a political axiom," he wrote, "that Negroes can never, in any period, hope to attain more in the short-term power bargain than the most benevolent white groups are prepared to give them." But Myrdal argued that the yawning gap between the principle of equality and the practice of discrimination was building up unavoidable tension in the white conscience. The resulting moral discomfort, Myrdal felt, would eventually close the gap and effect a reconciliation between ideology and behavior.

In retrospect, one is inclined to amend Myrdal's judgments. It can no longer be said that Negroes will attain only what the most benevolent white groups are prepared to give them. Techniques of protest can sharpen the moral consciousness and concern of the whites; techniques of pressure can force them to yield more than they ever intended. Moreover, the notion that a gap between ideology and practice inevitably closes up to produce a new equilibrium is more of a figure of speech than a demonstrable scientific truth. History at least seems to show that the process can be delayed almost indefinitely.

White sympathy has been of help to the Negro in recent years and certainly contributed to the enactment of the Civil Rights Law. One would normally expect that these compassionate sentiments would not persist very long except perhaps among emotionally sensitive groups such as religious leaders and intellectuals. Waves of sympathy have a fairly short cycle; most people find it difficult to concern themselves with the problems of others very long. Objects of humanitarian concern generally remain popular only so long as they remain relatively inert; quiet pathos is more appealing than unmannerly protest. A class of disadvantaged clientele does not constitute a threat, and charity is deeply satisfying because it fulfills the instinct of *noblesse oblige* without letting things get out of hand. The benefactor can feel that he has done good without having been forced into it, and considerable good may actually be done in this way.

At the same time, there are certain limitations from the standpoint of the beneficiary. The improvements are confined to what seems reasonable and proper to the benefactor. The charitable format must be preserved; if the clientele begins to demand as a matter of right what is being offered as a matter of grace, or to seek more than is given, the rules of the game are broken.

Agrarian protest did not become effective until the farmer began to exert economic and political pressures, although he had been the object of much sympathy and sentimentality in earlier decades. Prior to the 1930's, the industrial worker benefited somewhat from humanitarian measures, as well as from the gradual advance of national wealth and income; but decisive institutional changes in his favor were made only after he began to voice his own demands through his own leadership. And although the Negro made some gains during a century of remarkable patience following emancipation, he never broke out of the restricted sphere to which second-class citizens are relegated.

Generally speaking, humanitarian concern dries up when the clientele begins to act for itself. This is what happened, for example, when the sit-down strikes began to erupt in the 1930's. Yet it is not clear that the white community will turn against the Negro as rapidly as might be expected. It is true that many whites feel that they have already done the right thing, noting that the Civil Rights Act has been passed and seeing a Negro teller at the bank; and when they read of increased crime and delinquency among Negro youth, they wonder if their generosity should not have been received with more gratitude. On the other hand, it seems to be true at the present time that white sympathy has not dried up. It must be that the conscience of the white community has been touched very deeply this time. Poignant occasions such as the vast assemblage at the Lincoln Memorial in 1963 and the march from Selma to Montgomery have had a profound impact. Television has brought impressive Negro spokesmen—particularly Martin Luther King—into millions of white homes. Sheriff Clark, Governor Wallace, and others of their kind have helped raise sympathy for the Negroes who oppose them. Moreover, the national mood of concern for domestic social problems, which began to emerge in the late 1950's, has been deeper and more durable than might have been expected in the absence of a major economic depression.

Despite the perseverance of a generalized social conscience in the 1960's, the fact remains that specific resistance is encountered when specific Negroes come into competition with specific whites. Those who resist may or may not have effective veto power. But the locus and strength of resistance will fundamentally affect the Negro's progress toward economic integration.

□ Equality and the Achievement Ethic

Integration requires that the Negro make his own way, notwithstanding the crippling legacy of the slave system, in an achievement-oriented society. Equality, as an American ideal, has meant equal opportunity to pursue success, and success has increasingly come to mean occupational achievement. This is true not only in the United States, known since the time of DeToqueville as the country in which work is at the top of the agenda. In the older industrial societies of Europe also, occupational achievement is fast becoming the sole source of personal prestige. The time has passed when ownership of land, inherited wealth, and a distinguished family name were sufficient to guarantee a place in the top ranks of social structure. The vestigial leisure class, like the European nobility, serves as an object of attention for tabloid readers and to conduct experiments in exotic styles of life, but no longer stands at the center of the power structure. Professional or business success is the *sine qua non.* The communist nations continue to glorify and sentimentalize manual labor, and ascribe putative ownership of their economic systems to the workers and peasants. And the developing countries are sparing no effort to instill work commitment and discipline into large populations formerly occupied with casual, unrationalized agricultural activity in the villages.

Some writers contend that the achievement motive and the "Protestant ethic" are dying out in the United States, but there is more convincing evidence that instead of receding, work-oriented values are spreading throughout the whole population. We have now resolved that not only the slum-dwellers of Harlem, but also the isolated mountaineers of Appalachia, the impoverished Indians of the Southwest, and other stranded populations must all be pulled into the mainstream of economic life, inoculated with achievement motivation, and endowed with the requisite education and self-discipline. Poverty is no longer the predominant human condition but has become regarded as a form of moral turpitude. The percentage of women who participate in the labor force has risen from twenty percent in 1900 to almost thirty-seven percent in 1964; and whereas the majority of working women were under thirty years of age in 1900, today almost half of all women between thirty-five and fifty-five are in the labor market. One of the most widely discussed books in recent years contends that motherhood is no longer a satisfactory career for an intelligent woman.

Thus, the society the Negro wants to enter is one in which occupational achievement is virtually the only basis for self-respect and self-fulfillment. The tradition of honorable poverty —"poor but proud"—has faded. So has the tradition—and the fact—of a sturdy, self-sufficient yeomanry. The idea that one can maintain personal dignity in a degraded status—the idea symbolized by Uncle Tom as well as by Uncle Remus—is now discredited. Religion and the family are no longer strong enough to support self-esteem in a condition of poverty.

In the American economy there is one set of rules and values for all. If the Negro is to succeed, he will have to compete in accordance with these established rules, and he will have to make it all the way into "first-class" industries and occupations where competition is strong and pressures are severe. He will have to sacrifice certain privileges and immunities which have gone along with acceptance of a servile status—a monopoly over designated "Negro jobs"; a condescending tolerance, on the part of whites, of slack performance, petty thievery, and other symptoms of indiscipline; the cast-off garments of white employers, and so on.

Some of the practical problems of the transition are already evident. Should occupational aptitude tests be waived for Negroes on ground that such tests cannot truly measure the aptitudes of applicants with educational and cultural disabilities? Are white employers hiring underqualified Negroes in an effort to "improve their racial image" and then giving them nominal or trivial assignments? Is the loss of "Negro jobs" in some Southern plants outweighing the benefits of access to "white jobs"?

Kenneth Clark has aptly described what is involved in moving from a system of segregation:

> The transition from a system of injustice to a system of social justice cannot occur without personal and social trauma . . . When the cries of the segregationists have subsided, as they will eventually, then the Negro will be confronted with his own inner anxieties, conflicts and challenges if he dares to move into a society of open competition. It will then be clear that the problems of adjusting to change are not only difficult for whites but, in even more insidious ways, are quite painful for Negroes. The walls of a segregated society were not only damaging but protective in a debilitating way . . . Among the most important challenges fac-

ing the Negro today, as he prepares to take his place in a more democratic America, is that of preparing Negro youth to meet the single-standard competition of a non-segregated society.[3]

Thus it appears that Myrdal's classic exposition of *An American Dilemma* was essentially incomplete. Myrdal's "dilemma"—the gap between egalitarian values and discriminatory practices—was one which confronted the whites; and their case was hard. But the Negroes also have a dilemma: on the one hand, the legacy of slavery and segregation, and on the other hand, the dominance of the achievement ethic, the strength of individualism, and the severity of competition in the economic society he is demanding to enter.

□ Motivation

The Negro's dilemma lies at the heart of the much-discussed problem of motivation. The theory of an alienated Negro subculture has been overdone, in my opinion. The motivation problem is misconceived if one seriously doubts whether most Negroes really *want* to get off relief, hold good jobs, practice middle-class virtues, and join the mainstream of American society. The real question is whether they can afford to try. The persistence of passive docility among some Negroes, the voicing of erratic and unreasonable demands by others, the widespread irresolution, and the oscillation between romantic ambition and premature discouragement are not valid symptoms of indifference. On the contrary, they represent a vast yearning combined with a lack of self-confidence. What is missing is the internalized cultural support for participation in a highly disciplined, competitive economic order and for the requisite long-range career planning and preparation. The many Negroes who are currently making their way without this cultural support must be regarded as lonely pioneers making a hard journey with almost incredible fortitude.

The time horizon is the essence of the motivation problem. Young people who have sufficient confidence in themselves and faith in their chances can engage in long-term planning and preparation even though there will be no payoff for a good many years. "Undermotivated" people have no lack of desire, but they do have a lack of faith. They will respond to opportunity, but it must be immediate and visible.

We have had previous experience with "undermotivated" people. Many of the nine million unemployed workers at the beginning of World War II seemed completely demoralized. Yet they moved long distances under the stimulus of opportunity, somehow acquired the necessary training, and went back to work. Current experience with programs for "undermotivated" Negroes, under the Manpower Development and Training Act and the Economic Opportunity Act (the declaration of "War on Poverty") suggests that for people with short time horizons, job creation and skill creation must go together. Training and motivation cannot be successfully packaged like consumer goods and dispensed to all the unemployed, impoverished, and disadvantaged segments of the population. If high school drop-outs, for example, are brought into Job Corps training centers as a passive dependent class, their "second chance" will have no greater meaning for them than their first one did.

Those Negroes who have already assimilated the achievement ethic—and there are many of them—can plan ahead into a distant future. For those who have not, visible and palpable employment opportunity is necessary if a desire for training is to be stimulated.

□ Conclusion

Will the Negro succeed? There are several auspicious indications right now.

One is the general improvement in economic conditions. The unemployment rate for the labor force as a whole was down to 4.7 percent in March 1965; those seeking full-time jobs accounted for about 4 percent, and those desiring part-time jobs for the remainder. Further improvement is expected.

Second is the sustained attack on some of the underlying causes of the Negro's traditional economic handicaps. The Civil Rights Act, the Manpower Development and Training Act, the Economic Opportunity Act and the Aid-to-Education Act adds up to a massive investment in the mitigation of domestic social problems.

Third, and most important, is the continuing and growing determination in the Negro community that first-class citizenship must be achieved.

Notwithstanding these prospects, the path to economic integration will be steeply uphill. Currently fashionable metaphors of breakthrough, momentum, and contagion give rise to misleading expectations if taken too literally. Some aims of the civil rights movement, it is true, are subject to breakthrough and contagion. Rapid progress has been made in access to public accommodations, partly because hotel keepers, theater owners, and other proprietors are interested in obtaining their share of Negro purchasing power, and partly because no one is hurt very much. Despite dogged resistance in rural areas of the South, voting by Negroes does have the aspect of a contagion.

Why is it that segregation of neighborhoods, schools, and jobs is so much more tenacious than refusal of public accommodations or denial of voting rights? One reason is that the processes of change involved are naturally more sluggish. Another reason is that the interests of the whites (as perceived by the whites) are affected more directly and significantly. More dogged resistance sets in, frequently accompanied by effective veto power.

Housing and school segregation are outside the scope of this volume. But it is clear that even the best-founded crisis vocabulary cannot overcome the natural sluggishness of the labor market. Even if employment discrimination were wholly eliminated, the pace of improvement would be governed by the rates at which job vacancies opened up, Negroes gained access to formal and informal channels of recruitment, and the necessary skills could be acquired. And this says nothing of resistance on the part of whites whose interests are jeopardized.

If occupational progress comes no more rapidly than can be expected, impatience will surely mount within the Negro community. There is much writing about the Negro revolt and the Negro revolution, and there are incurable romantics on the left and the right who have pinned their hopes and fears on a rapid escalation of protest leading to some kind of apocalyptic resolution. The fact is, however, that the Negro is not in a position to initiate a revolution. He is not sufficiently numerous; he has no military power. He can revolt within the existing structure of society, but not against it.

Then what are the alternative expressions of heightened impatience? One is the strengthening of organized, rational forms of pressure. A second is a progressive alienation of the Negro, especially within the ghettos of large Northern cities: the spread of a criminal subculture; the rejection of teachers, social workers, and policemen, as agents of the power structure; departure from the labor force, addiction to narcotics, and other forms of individual withdrawal. A third is militant racism and retaliatory violence against whites, again concentrated in Northern cities where Negroes have more freedom of communication and greater possibilities of action.

In general, hostility and withdrawal will vary inversely with the success of rational pressure tactics and the degree of improvement in the Negro's economic position. But a precise relationship cannot be expected. As progress begins to be made, aspirations become more real, desires run ahead of achievements, and the impatience becomes more intense. As the goals come into sight, the harder it is to tolerate the remaining disabilities. For this reason an underprivileged group that is just beginning to satisfy its aspirations is always viewed as "unreasonable" and "ungrateful."

This chapter is not a counsel of permission, but of realism. It is not to say that the whites should be charitable, but that they must understand what is going on. It is not to say that the Negroes should be patient, but that they must be resolute. It is not to belittle short-term tactics but to emphasize the need for long-range strategy as well. For the journey will be long, and hard.

NOTES

1. Oscar Handlin, *The Newcomers* (Cambridge, Mass.: Harvard Univ. Press, 1959). Cited in Charles E. Silberman, *Crisis in Black and White* (New York: Random House, 1964), p. 39.
2. This point is emphasized in Frank Tannenbaum, *Slave and Citizen: The Negro in the Americas* (New York: Knopf, 1946); and in Stanley M. Elkins, *Slavery: A Problem in American Institutional and Intellectual Life* (Chicago: Univ. of Chicago Press, 1959).
3. *Youth In the Ghetto* (Harlem Youth Opportunities Report, 1964 [mimeographed]), pp. 5–6.

Index